Entrepreneurial Icebreakers

Entrepreneurial Icebreakers

Insights and Case Studies from Internationally Successful Central and Eastern European Entrepreneurs

Julia Prats
IESE Business School, Spain

Marc Sosna
IESE Business School, Spain
Technical University Berlin, Germany

and

Sylwia Sysko-Romańczuk
Warsaw University of Technology Business School, Warsaw

palgrave
macmillan

Softcover reprint of the hardcover 1st edition 2015 978-1-137-44630-5

First published 2015 by
PALGRAVE MACMILLAN

Palgrave Macmillan in the UK is an imprint of Macmillan Publishers Limited, registered in England, company number 785998, of Houndmills, Basingstoke, Hampshire RG21 6XS.

Palgrave Macmillan in the US is a division of St Martin's Press LLC, 175 Fifth Avenue, New York, NY 10010.

Palgrave Macmillan is the global academic imprint of the above companies and has companies and representatives throughout the world.

Palgrave® and Macmillan® are registered trademarks in the United States, the United Kingdom, Europe and other countries

ISBN 978-1-349-49597-9 ISBN 978-1-137-44632-9 (eBook)
DOI 10.1057/9781137446329

This book is printed on paper suitable for recycling and made from fully managed and sustained forest sources. Logging, pulping and manufacturing processes are expected to conform to the environmental regulations of the country of origin.

A catalogue record for this book is available from the British Library.

A catalog record for this book is available from the Library of Congress.

To all the entrepreneurs who positively impact economies and societies through their hard work

Contents

List of Figures

List of Tables

Prologue: Why "Entrepreneurial Icebreakers"?

ice·break·er ('aɪs,breɪkə)
nautical: a ship specially built for breaking navigable passages through ice.

In the transition from communism to capitalism, countries were in dire need of change on many levels, including moving from centrally planned state economies to market-based ones, from a rather internal and geographically limited view to looking more outward and global, from static structures to adaptive systems, from weak institutional environments to more reliable contexts, from company cultures that lacked experience with competitive forces to those that were able to compete in innovative, price-sensitive and customer-centric markets, and from a rather mechanistic conception of human behavior within organizations to creating contexts for creativity and innovation, and so forth.

Entrepreneurs are those who were and are able to start despite such weak and instable conditions, but who also helped to positively transform the very context by "breaking" inflexible and outdated structures, by making things more dynamic, by creating new ways of value creation, by changing mindsets, and by going beyond national borders and breaking pathways for themselves and for others into international markets around the globe, even becoming world-class players at the frontiers of their industries. They are small ventures, but with a huge positive impact in many ways.

Icebreakers are able to move in conditions where others cannot. They are explorers. They create pathways for themselves and simultaneously enable others to benefit from such established routes. They free those who are immobilized. They create value in many ways.

This is why we call the kind of companies that we introduce in this book *Entrepreneurial Icebreakers*. They create pathways of change and improvement internally and externally. They are change agents of transition economies and a driving force of transformation toward more competitive economies.

Foreword

Entrepreneurs are the driving force of economies around the globe. As many statistics and surveys have already proven, they are responsible for GDP growth and innovation in their countries, creating new jobs and social value.

But how can one become a successful entrepreneur? Is it just luck? Is it in your genes? Or can entrepreneurship be taught?

Based on our history and expertise in advising and guiding successful entrepreneurs for more than 100 years as a professional service firm and on what we have learned as a result of our Entrepreneur of the Year program, we believe that a combination of factors is involved.

It is personality and passion that make one person see opportunities where others see risks. It is their knowledge and professional expertise that leads them to invent competitive new products, services or business models, and of course also a bit of luck is needed to connect the dots at the right time, and to find the right people and investors to work with.

In Eastern Europe, the entrepreneurial ecosystem is relatively young. Nevertheless, some outstanding entrepreneurs have made their way and became successful in their local markets and beyond. Their insights will, it is hoped, inspire the next generation of entrepreneurs and make them better equipped for their own journey.

Don't try to copy, but be inspired and learn from the successes and failures of others!

Peter Englisch
Global Leader, Family Business Center of Excellence
Ernst & Young

Acknowledgments

"Alone we can do so little; together we can do so much." This quote by Helen Keller illustrates what is involved in the creation of a book. We would like to thank all those who generously shared their time and resources and provided us with the support we needed to write this book. This book could have never succeeded without their help and contributions.

Our sincere thanks go to: Marian Holienka (Comenius University in Bratislava) who worked with Alexander Cimbaľák on the case of ACE enterprise (Slovakia); Alexandru Ioan Mincu (ecole, Slovenia) and Vlasta Hudek (Rezultanta, Croatia) who worked with Emil Tedeschi on the case of Atlantic Grupa (Croatia); Juris Ulmanis (Visiting Professor, Latvia) and Adrian Tantau (Bucharest University of Economic Studies) who worked with Radu Georgescu on the case of Avangate (Romania); Galina Shirokova (St. Petersburg State University Graduate School of Management) who worked with Boris Beylin on the case of Big Filter (Russia); Makedonka Dimitrova and Ilijana Petrovska (UACS Institute for Entrepreneurship and Leadership Development, Macedonia and School of Business Economics and Management, University American College Skopje, Macedonia) who worked with Kristijan Danilovski on the case of Fx3x (Macedonia); Juris Ulmanis (Visiting Professor, Latvia) who worked with Gábor Bojár on the case of Graphisoft (Hungary); Tiit Elenurm (Estonian Business School) who worked with Sergey Babichenko on the case of Laser Diagnostic Instruments (Estonia) and with Tarmo Pihl on the case of Modesat (Estonia); Tomas Ricka, David Kula and Radovan Kacin (University of Economics, Prague) who worked with Zbyněk Frolík on the case of LINET (Czech Republic); János Vecsenyi, Péter Dietrich, and László Csepregi (all from Corvinus University of Budapest) who worked with Dávid Tibor on the case of Masterplast Group (Hungary); Frank la Pira (PhD) who worked with Ivo Boscarol on the case of Pipistrel (Slovenia); Anna Svirina (Chistopol Campus "Vostok", Kazan National Research Technical University, Russia) who worked with Renat Fardeev on the case of PKF Betar (Russia) and also wrote the case "Russian Cosmetics"; Sylwia Sysko-Romańczuk (Warsaw University of Technology Business School) who worked with Krzysztof Domarecki on the case of Selena (Poland); and Jolanta Mazur (Warsaw School of Economics) who worked with Krzysztof Olszewski and Solange Olszewska on the case of Solaris (Poland). The authors, and indeed the entire working group, are deeply indebted to all of them.

Furthermore, we would like to thank our partners and sponsors without whom this project and book would have remained nothing but an idea:

- Ernst & Young, specifically Peter Englisch (Partner, Global Leader Family Business Center of Excellence);
- The European Bank for Reconstruction and Development (EBRD), specifically Erik Berglof (Chief Economist and Special Adviser to EBRD's President), Anne Fossemalle (Director of Equity Funds), Peter Reiniger (former Business Group Chief in Central Europe) and Wojciech Ciszek (Banker, EBRD Warsaw);
- The European Commission (DG Enterprise and Industry), specifically Marko Curavić (Head of Unit Entrepreneurship);
- Leszek Borysiewicz, Vice Chancellor of the University of Cambridge;
- MCI Management S.A., specifically Tomasz Czechowicz (Managing Partner and Chief Investment Officer);
- Mikołaj Dowgielewicz, the current Polish Minister for European and Economic Affairs;
- The Polish National Capital Fund (KFK), specifically Piotr Gebala (CEO) and Marek Dietl (former Investment Manager);
- The Center for Entrepreneurship in Russia, specifically Victor Sedov (President) and Alla Danilova (Project Coordinator for Youth Entrepreneurship Initiatives);
- The Warsaw Stock Exchange.

We would like to express our deepest gratitude for their support during the entire process. We also want to thank individual collaborators who had significant participation during these years. First and foremost Piotr Zaborek (Warsaw School of Economics), for his generous and crucial involvement, work and commitment. He was with this research project from its inception, was a member of its nomination and selection committee, co-organized with us the first "New European Champions" event with all the entrepreneurs in June 2011 at the Warsaw School of Economics, and was deeply involved during the case review and development phase, among other activities.

A special recognition goes to Derek Abell, former Dean of IMD, Founding President of ESMT Berlin, and current Chairman of the Academic Board and member of the Governing Board at EFER, for his ongoing and insightful guidance and effective support in so many ways, including a case-writing workshop to the case authors. We also extend our deepest gratitude to Jordan Mitchell whose tremendous contributions have been absolutely vital to so many of our case authors.

We are also indebted to Ashley Metz. Thank you for allowing us to benefit from the wealth of your language in order to surmount the shortcomings of our own. Your contributions in the case writing, the work with the manuscript to which you have brought much clarity and focus, and your unwavering support meant a great deal to us and made a big difference to this book.

Moreover, we are extremely grateful to the European Forum for Entrepreneurship Research (EFER) for having been the source and enabler for this important project. At the apex of this pyramid of fantastic people and supporters stands Bert Twaalfhoven, Founder of EFER and tireless promoter of entrepreneurship. Without his vision, drive, intellectual contributions and financial support, this project would have never seen the light of day or made it to where it is now. Two other important people at the heart of this foundation are Karen Wilson, Founder of GV Partners, Advisor and Board Member at EFER and Senior Fellow at the Kauffman Foundation, and Antonia Sariyska (Operations Manager). During the project, we have also benefited from the insights of Tea Petrin, Professor at the University of Ljubljana, Former Minister of the Economy for Slovenia and EFER's Academic Advisor and Christine Volkmann, Entrepreneurship Professor in Wuppertal and Academic Advisor of EFER. All their involvement and backing has been vital to the success of each phase of this initiative and we thank them very much.

Much sympathy goes also to everyone who was involved in and contributed to the success which the "New European Champions" event in 2011 in Warsaw has been, specifically to Jolanta Mazur (Dean of World Economy Collegium, Warsaw School of Economics).

In addition, our gratitude goes to IESE Business School, Warsaw University of Technology Business School, and the Technical University Berlin, for inspiring us to work on projects that can contribute to the field of entrepreneurship. Without their effective support we would have not been able to complete this project and book.

We also owe special thanks to our publishing team at Palgrave Macmillan, especially to Aimee Dibbens and Kiran Bolla. Furthermore, we are very grateful to Josemaria Siota for his contribution during the editing process and communication with the many stakeholders of this project. Without their patience and professionalism during this long process it would have been impossible to publish this book.

The greatest amount of gratitude is due to our families, however. Indeed, this project and book would not have been possible without their constant support, understanding, and the time they have given us over the past few years to complete this initiative. We would therefore like to dedicate this book to them.

Notes on Contributors

Editors

Mª Julia Prats is an associate professor in the Department of Entrepreneurship at IESE Business School. She obtained her DBA from Harvard University, her MBA from IESE Business School, and her BSc in Industrial Engineering from Polytechnic University of Catalunya. Her research lies at the intersection of entrepreneurship and strategy. Articles have appeared in international journals, both for the academic community as well as for executives. She also has authored teaching materials and contributions to several books on entrepreneurship and strategy-related topics. She has been Visiting Professor for Graduate and Executive Education courses at several schools, among them the Wharton School of the University Pennsylvania, IPADE (México), and INALDE (Colombia), Fh Nordakademie (Germany), and University of Asia and the Pacific (Philippines).

Marc Sosna is a research fellow at the Entrepreneurship Department at IESE Business School (Spain) and a PhD candidate at the Department of Strategic Leadership & Global Management at the Technical University Berlin (Germany). He holds a Master in Business Administration. His research focuses on entrepreneurship and strategy and he has co-authored academic as well as practitioner articles in leading strategy journals, teaching cases, book chapters and course materials. Marc is involved in research, teaching, publishing, consulting, IESE's Learning Innovation Unit, and in various international executive education and in-company programs across four continents. Throughout those activities, he worked with several Fortune 500 companies and with 1,000+ top executives from all over the world and numerous industries. He has been a project manager and consultant for several international initiatives, including projects for and in partnership with the World Bank, the EBRD, the Batten Institute at Darden/University of Virginia, the CEO-Collaborative Forum, or EFER, among others. For the International Finance Corporation, he worked in entrepreneurship development projects in Nigeria, Kenya, Ghana, Tanzania and Rwanda. Marc has also worked for a listed technology company in Madras, India.

Sylwia Sysko-Romańczuk is a professor of Management and Entrepreneurship at the University of Technology Business School Warsaw. Her main areas of research are business models, entrepreneurial leadership and management, and new venture creation. She has participated in several international projects and courses in Manchester Metropolitan University, Harvard University, Hungarian Academy of Sciences, IESE Business School, among others. She is a former Deputy Minister in the Ministry of National Education of Poland, Director of Strategy and Development Department in Polish Public Television, TVP S.A. and scientific manager in the Institute of Organization and Management in Industry.

Contributors

László Csepregi (Corvinus University of Budapest, Hungary)

Péter Dietrich (Corvinus University of Budapest, Hungary)

Makedonka Dimitrova (UACS Institute for Entrepreneurship and Leadership Development, Macedonia)

Tiit Elenurm (Estonian Business School, Estonia)

Marian Holienka (Comenius University in Bratislava, Slovakia)

Vlasta Hudek (Rezultanta, Croatia)

Radovan Kacin (University of Economics, Prague, Czech Republic)

David Kula (University of Economics, Prague, Czech Republic)

Frank la Pira (PhD)

Jolanta Mazur (Warsaw School of Economics, Poland)

Alexandru Ioan Mincu (ecole, Slovenia)

Ilijana Petrovska (School of Business Economics and Management, University American College Skopje, Macedonia)

Mª Julia Prats (IESE Business School, Spain)

Tomas Ricka (University of Economics, Prague, Czech Republic)

Galina Shirokova (St. Petersburg State University Graduate School of Management, Russia)

Marc Sosna (IESE Business School, Spain and Technical University Berlin, Germany)

Anna Svirina (Chistopol Campus 'Vostok', Kazan National Research Technical University, Russia)

Sylwia Sysko-Romańczuk (Warsaw University of Technology Business School, Poland)

Adrian Tantau (Bucharest University of Economic Studies, Romania)

Juris Ulmanis (Visiting Professor, Latvia)

János Vecsenyi (Corvinus University of Budapest, Hungary)

About the European Forum for Entrepreneurship Research (EFER)

The European Forum for Entrepreneurship Research (EFER) fosters and promotes research and teaching in the field of entrepreneurship at institutions of higher education across Europe. EFER works with an extensive network of schools and professors from across Europe and around the world.

EFER's programs on entrepreneurship teaching have been developed to address the gaps and needs identified in Europe through the research work conducted by EFER over the years. As of 2013, 500 professors from 199 universities in 46 countries worldwide have been trained in teaching entrepreneurship through EFER's flagship training program – the European Entrepreneurship Colloquium (EEC).

After EEC many of the alumni professors have revamped their teaching approaches and are working on further building the entrepreneurship programs within their institutions.

EFER has also hosted numerous round tables, seminars and conferences. Through these programs and activities, EFER has focused on building links between academia, practitioners and students in Eastern and Western Europe.

More information about EFER can be found at www.efer.eu

About IESE Business School

For over fifty years, IESE, the graduate business school of the University of Navarra, has been at the forefront of management education, developing and inspiring business leaders who strive to make a deep, positive and lasting impact on the people, companies and society they serve.

IESE's success is built on a humanistic approach to business and leadership, complemented by a world-class faculty producing groundbreaking research; the global scope of its programs, faculty, students and campuses; a practical and relevant teaching methodology; and a growing alumni network of 40,000 professionals worldwide prepared to take on today's challenges and lead business into the future.

Inherent in everything IESE does is a focus on people – on the personal and professional development of every individual partaking in the IESE experience – as the primary driver of positive change and impact on business and society.

Over 100 full-time professors and around 70 external collaborators who represent almost 30 countries and hold PhDs from the top business schools in the world form IESE's faculty. Their dedication to teaching, the impact of their research and their experience working with companies around the world are central to IESE's continued success in providing excellence in management education.

For IESE, sustainable and long-term global prosperity can be achieved through a humanistic approach to business. This helps business leaders to influence companies and society positively, shaping the world for future generations. IESE strives to ensure that professionalism, integrity and a respect for others are at the core of everything it does.

IESE's alumni are an international community of more than 40,000 business and nonprofit professionals and entrepreneurs spanning over 100 countries. Every year the Alumni Association organizes hundreds of education sessions and reunions, creating links, enabling networking and making IESE an ongoing and valuable experience.

More information about IESE Business School at: www.iese.edu

About Warsaw School of Economics (SGH)

The Warsaw School of Economics (SGH) is the oldest university of economics in Poland. Its mission has continuously been educating economists and business leaders serving the nation, country and the region. SGH is famous for its tradition, flexible adjustments of programs to students' needs, unquestionable education level, and successful alumni.

Currently there are about fifteen thousand undergraduate, postgraduate, post-diploma and Ph.D. students enrolled. About eight hundred students from over 40 countries around the world take advantage of the SGH international offer. Warsaw School of Economics (SGH) has been developing its English-language programs on every academic level, including Bachelor, Master, Doctoral as well as MBA. Currently the SGH offer includes three English-language programs at Bachelor's level (Quantitative Methods in Economics and Information Systems, International Economics and Management), two at Master's level (International Business and ACCA-accredited Finance & Accounting in cooperation with EY), one at Doctoral level (Doctoral Program in Management and Economics) and the Canadian Executive Master of Business Administration.

About eight hundred highly qualified professors and Ph.D. researchers constitute the faculty of the Warsaw School of Economics. Our researchers take part in national and international projects in the areas of economics, finance, management, business administration and social policy that benefit society and business. They share their knowledge as expert advisors to the European Commission.

Warsaw School of Economics has created a unique way of cooperating with business environment. Several national and multinational companies with a status of the School's partners are involved in various projects. The companies have an influence on the programs offered by the School. Their representatives take part in a number of courses sharing their experience first-hand with students. Programs and specializations offered at the SGH facilitate obtaining renowned ACCA and CIMA certifications.

As the only university in Poland the Warsaw School of Economics is a member of CEMS Global Alliance in Management Education which includes 29 business schools from around the world along with their corporate partners. Together they provide a unique Master in International Management Program.

SGH alumni are among the most sought-after employees by companies operating in Poland and the region. We are proud to follow their evolving careers of consultants, managers, directors, advisors, business owners and individual entrepreneurs.

Find out more about Warsaw School of Economics at www.sgh.edu.pl

Introduction

One of the world's largest and most innovative hospital bed producers emerged from the post-communist Czech Republic. In Slovenia, a small aircraft manufacturer was founded while private flying was still prohibited, but went on to win three NASA Challenges – a feat which no aviation company had done before. In Estonia, a small start-up made waves with its unique technology and industry-leading capabilities, attracting acquisition bids from global companies. These are stories of growth – of job creation and of economic development in Central and Eastern Europe.

This book celebrates 15 internationally successful companies from Central and Eastern Europe (CEE) and Russia. Building from a series of case studies about those ***Entrepreneurial Icebreakers***, the book demonstrates different paths that companies founded in difficult geopolitical conditions took to international success. It illustrates the successes and failures of various approaches and identifies common characteristics and key dimensions for aspiring entrepreneurs to analyze as they begin their entrepreneurial journeys and seek to grow internationally.

For many years, we the authors, as well as the different organizations that supported this book, its underlying research and related activities, have been interested in developing frameworks, materials and pedagogical tools that could help entrepreneurs to succeed. Europe should continue growing its entrepreneurial culture and this especially applies to those countries that are newer to the market-based economy. In some instances, entrepreneurship is not yet a valid career choice and firms that do get started often stay within their national boundaries. As experience around the world has shown, entrepreneurship education is most successful when people learn from role models they can identify with. Much has been written about entrepreneurs in the Western world. They inspire the Mark Zuckerbergs to become the next Bill Gates or Richard Branson. But the conditions that made Western companies great and the lessons one can learn – inspiring as they are – are often not applicable to entrepreneurs in many of the countries in a transition context. The current entrepreneurship literature mainly focuses on businesses and entrepreneurs operating in Western regulatory and political environments and developed, sometimes homogenous, markets. However, in many places a lack of standards and rules, rapidly changing regulations and weak business ecosystems make operating environments and markets incomparable.

This was the trigger of our project: to identify entrepreneurs in CEE and in Russia who had started a firm and successfully expanded into international markets, and could serve as role models for many. The project was launched by EFER, the European Forum for Entrepreneurship Research, in collaboration with IESE Business School and Warsaw School of Economics. It consisted of identifying and exploring a selection of international (and some global) firms that were founded and grew in the transition period from communism to capitalism in that region. Resulting from a careful multistage nomination, eligibility check and selection process (for a description see Appendix 1: The Research Project), the common thread through the chosen cases is that they became relevant international players despite having started in challenging conditions. The benefits of identifying and learning from such firms are twofold: they provide the next generation of entrepreneurs with good role models to learn from, and provide universities with adequate teaching materials to provide a more suitable and customized entrepreneurship education. Also, people and organizations from other transition contexts will benefit from better understanding the dynamics in such companies and the challenges they face.

Through professors from top European universities, members of EFER's professors network, their research insights from years of working in the region, and through the words of the entrepreneurs themselves, readers will learn about growing businesses in unstructured environments. The book presents insights and features from founders and executive teams that, through outstanding execution, have been able to become leaders in their respective international market segments. It offers examples of decision-making, trade-offs and dimensions of success under various circumstances so readers can develop their own tools for thinking and ways of working in challenging environments. Developing an understanding of how they overcame the challenges of a difficult context to compete at the top of their industries has been a fascinating journey full of useful insights.

In the remainder of the book, whenever we refer to "CEE" this also includes Russia.

The content of the book

The book consists of two main parts. The first contains five chapters that, based on a deep analysis of 15 cases, highlight important issues that matter for growth and internationalization in emerging/unstructured markets. We will introduce a framework and shed light on topics that range from how firms overcame a negative country-of-origin effect to how locally grown companies scaled internationally. The second part features all those 15 case studies, where readers can learn about the companies and their development paths in detail. The cases are written and structured as teaching cases, so they can be readily applied in classrooms or any setting with a focus on learning about entrepreneurship and growth – especially in the context of transition economies.

The first chapter takes a look at the highly unfavorable context for entrepreneurial endeavors in Central and Eastern European countries at the beginning of the 1990s: the lack of a stable institutional framework, mismatched talent pools and the lack of start-up financing are just a few of the challenges that entrepreneurs faced. Observing their behavior while dealing with those realities has been enlightening. We soon realized that their beginnings were often similar to doing a sequence of *tacks* – a sailing maneuver that allows a boat to move upwind by a series of turns that create a zigzag shape. This realization crystallized a new term, ***tacking entrepreneurship***, defined and discussed in the ***second chapter***, which has helped us to conceptualize the entrepreneur's activities, especially at the start of their endeavors. In this same chapter, we also dive deep into the tactics that they followed to overcome key challenges presented by the institutional context. Here we also address how entrepreneurs have not only served as producers of goods and services, but also as creators of **market-supporting institutions** and "**quasi-institutions.**"

One common challenge for internationalizing these firms has been fighting against a **negative country-of-origin effect**. ***Chapter 3*** presents successful approaches to overcome this issue. Some of the most common tactics include: creating a strong product brand reputation, clearly creating and communicating value, and leveraging external stakeholders and media outreach.

Chapter 4 maps out the case companies' paths, analyzes their international expansion patterns and highlights insights from their specific approaches and tactics. It describes in a first step a high-level framework that clusters firms in three different types: ***Innovators, Price-Quality-Value Providers (PQVPs) and Climbers.*** This categorization takes a dynamic view and displays how companies have evolved along the mode of competition (relating to product/service characteristics) over time. In a second step, we analyze companies' geographic internationalization patterns and shed light on various successful approaches to international growth.

The last chapter identifies different actions – and their underlying logic – that stood out as important to many (even though to a different degree) with regard to international growth. Strong and adaptable leadership, having solid internal bases before jumping abroad, smart use of business intelligence, and adapting to cultures and clients were some of the most important foundations for success.

The chapters – and later, the individual cases – help practitioners, professors, students and everyone interested in the topic to get a good overview of the characteristics of such extremely difficult conditions, the featured companies and key insights about the firm's behavior that facilitated their move from lag markets to lead markets. By looking at the contributions from these entrepreneurs in many dimensions, one realizes that the impact of their work went beyond their firms; they were the protagonists of their countries' transition to the market economy.

The second part of the book includes a selection of 15 teaching cases that represent a broad level of diversity with regard to countries, industries, topics, growth phases, challenges and internationalization strategies. Firms are from ten different countries: Czech Republic (1), Croatia (1), Estonia (2), Hungary (2), Macedonia (1), Poland (2), Romania (1), Russia (3), Slovakia (1) and Slovenia (1). They cover nearly as many industries as we have cases, including science, software, movie animation, aviation, construction materials, cosmetics, manufacturing, and food, among others. The cases include amazing stories from entrepreneurs and their companies from a wide range of backgrounds: for example, one who was supported personally by Steve Jobs, one whose technology was so innovative that it was featured in an American TV crime series, and one that competed against giant competitors from Hollywood and even won an Oscar for its work.

These are the protagonists of the book:

Alexander Cimbaľák, CEO of **ACE enterprise Slovakia**. The company was founded in 2004 in Slovakia. Its product is an enterprise application integration solution based on unique technology, applied today in more than 40 countries worldwide.

Emil Tedeschi, CEO of **Atlantic Grupa**. The firm was founded in 1991 in Croatia and is active in a number of industries; it exports its products to more than 30 countries worldwide. Its primary activities include the production and distribution of food products such as sports nutrition and dietary supplements. Additionally, it is a manufacturer of personal hygiene products and distributor of general merchandise. Finally, the company also operates a chain of pharmacies.

Radu Georgescu, Founder of **Avangate (GECAD)**. The firm was established in Romania in 1992. In 2002, its RAV Antivirus Division, a software producer, achieved incredible global growth: 150 distributors in over 60 countries.

Boris Beylin, CEO of **Big Filter**. Founded in 1988 in Russia, it has, since 1997, supplied car filters to a wide range of countries covering markets all over the world.

Kristijan Danilovski and Milivoje Gjorgjevik set up **Fx3x** in 1997 in Macedonia. The company conducts 90% of its business on the global market, offering character animation and visual effects for feature films and commercials.

Gábor Bojár, CEO of **Graphisoft** in Hungary. The venture started in 1982 and has become a global leader and reference in the architectural software market. The company works with dedicated distributors in 80 countries and hundreds of Value-Added Resellers (VARs) and Systems Integrators.

"**Russian Cosmetics**"[1] was born in 2006. The company is a leading cosmetics–pharmaceutical holding with three production facilities and several distribution companies.

Laser Diagnostic Instruments (LDI) was founded in 1991 in Estonia by Sergey Babichenko. Its principal products and services are based on novel laser, electro-optical and photonics technologies aimed at real-time data assessment, and are used in more than 20 countries.

LINET, established in 1990 by Zbyněk Frolík, is from the Czech Republic. The company is a world-class manufacturer of hospital and nursing beds and sells in over 90 countries around the world.

Dávid Tibor, CEO of **Masterplast Group.** The firm was set up in 1997 in Hungary and is a leading producer and distributor of construction industry products, selling to 28 countries and employing workers in 13 countries.

Modesat was set up in Estonia in 2005 by Tarmo Pihl and his co-founders. The company designs high-performance wireless backhaul solutions that allow mobile networks to multiply the amount of data transmitted. It has opened offices in the United States and Israel. It was eventually acquired by a US firm.

Pipistrel was founded in Slovenia in 1989 by Ivo Boscarol. It manufactures light aircraft and sells to more than 50 countries.

Renat Fardeev, CEO of **PKF Betar**, started the firm in 1996 in Russia. Its main products are water- and gas-meter devices; the company has a dominant market share in Russia and several other markets and is expanding into the smart meter segment.

Selena, from Poland, and founded by Krzysztof Domarecki in 1992, is active in 15 countries and distributes its products, polyurethane foams, silicones and adhesives for construction, in more than 70 countries all over the world.

Finally, the Polish company **Solaris,** founded by Krzysztof Olszewski and Solange Olszewska in 1996, sells buses in more than 27 countries.

These firms' stories cover a large number of relevant issues reflecting the wide range of traditional and new strategic approaches, expansion modes and business models that have been deployed since the mid-1980s/early 1990s by entrepreneurs in Central and Eastern Europe. The cases illustrate entrepreneurship in different contexts with diverse venture types, internationalization patterns, governance models, founder teams, ages, international scope, as well as products and services. Each case discusses crucial challenges that the companies faced in becoming successful international firms.

The objective is to enable entrepreneurs, executive teams and business students to explore, analyze, and learn from the wide array of options available. This approach highlights nuanced topics, which students and executives in their respective countries can relate to.

Note

1. Name of company changed.

Part I

Conquering International Markets from Transition Economies

1

Entrepreneurship in Transition Economies

When Ivo Boscarol, CEO of Pipistrel – a light aircraft manufacturer from Slovenia – started his company, it was unimaginable for private persons in Yugoslavia to own their own aircraft, let alone their own aircraft manufacturing facility. If ultralight pilots wanted to fly, they had to do it covertly. They had to wait until the sports and army pilots finished flying for the day, then sneak in an hour or two of flying before darkness fell. As they flew late in the evening, using aircraft lights with triangular hang glider wings, the local people jokingly referred to them as "bats" – in Latin, Pipistrellus.

Ivo's first business was printing. He also had a passion for photography and even managed some rock bands. The photography helped him pay his way through college, though he got so busy with his businesses that he never graduated with the economics degree he had set out for.

At that time he had also developed an interest in flying. However, during the late 1980's, it was difficult to fly an aircraft freely in the totalitarian regime of Yugoslavia, as the military controlled the movement of all aircraft. Ivo had a desire to fly when and where he wanted. On a visit to Italy, he saw a motorized hang glider and decided then and there that he was going to own and fly his own aircraft. Ivo knew it was difficult, if not impossible, to bring the glider into the country in one piece, as it was not legal to own your own ultralight aircraft at the time. He purchased it anyway and imported it into Yugoslavia in bits and pieces, disguised as parts for something other than an aircraft. When he finally had it all and put it together, he wasn't satisfied with the construction. His conclusion was that it not only looked dangerous – it was made of aluminum and wire, with fabric wings and a small engine at the rear – but it was dangerous.

Ivo first modified his own glider to make it more robust and later those of other pilots who approached him. Eventually, the Italian company he had purchased the glider from contacted him and wanted Ivo to make the same modifications to their aircraft. Normally, modifications to an aircraft were not permitted without permits and drawings approved by federal aviation bodies which also require significant associated design drawings and so on, all of which must be carried out by a licensed aircraft maintenance engineer (LAME). As he spent more and more time modifying gliders he decided to build one of his own.

Ivo approached the country's aviation authority to get the required permits and approvals to build and sell ultralight aircraft, as they were technically not permitted in Yugoslavia. He was received with a great deal of laughter because no one believed that a private individual would try to build an aircraft in the Socialist Federal Republic of Yugoslavia. Furthermore, what kept the aviation department bewildered was that he wanted to build an ultralight aircraft – something nobody in the aviation department knew anything about as they were mostly managed by the military. The aviation department contacted a Slovenian state-owned aircraft manufacturer and asked if they knew anyone who could help them deal with the case, someone who was known as an expert in the field. They were given the name of Ivo Boscarol.

After many meetings, they gave Ivo approval. The problem, however, was that there were no systems, exams or regulations for those who wanted to manufacture their own ultralight aircraft. Ivo took this opportunity to write the exam – the same exam that he himself was required to pass to get approval to manufacture his aircraft. He subsequently wrote many of the regulations and requirements for manufacturing ultralight aircraft in his country. Ivo became the first totally private aircraft manufacturer in the former Yugoslavia – and went on to write additional chapters of aviation history.

Source: CASE 11: Pipistrel: The Freedom of Flight; p. 290

This book is about successful companies from Central and Eastern Europe (CEE) and Russia; about entrepreneurs, like Ivo, who not only defied the odds at home but also managed to build a global presence and reputation for their enterprises. We call them *Entrepreneurial Icebreakers*. We shed new light on how these entrepreneurs created value in less-friendly environments – for themselves as well as others. Our findings can enrich global and especially transitional entrepreneurship practice and research. We hope that prospective entrepreneurs will be encouraged to pursue and realize their ideas and are not stopped by the perception that it is an "impossible dream" when starting a company in a context that seems to put one on the downside of advantage. We also wish that professors and other players and organizations in the entrepreneurship-related ecosystem will benefit from the insights in this book and the materials we provide in order to improve business and entrepreneurship education.

When the context is not conducive to entrepreneurship

The rise of entrepreneurship throughout post-Soviet countries has fundamentally transformed their economies. Since the mid-1990s, the private sector share of GDP was constantly increasing, but did not have the same percentage of the national economy in all transition countries. It was, for example, approximately 80% in Hungary, 75% in the Slovak Republic and even 70% in the Russian Federation, but 20% in Belarus, 35% in Bosnia and Herzegovina, and 45% in Moldova (EBRD 1999). Private sector value added included income generated by the activity of privately registered companies as well as by private entities engaged in informal activity (EBRD 1999). A lot of research and reports were done to increase knowledge about the wealth-creation phenomena throughout post-Soviet transition economies. Such works explain how various countries adapted to the market economy and the political environments that enabled development. However, not much attention has been devoted to understanding how entrepreneurs from Central and Eastern Europe (CEE) have gone from lag to lead markets and have attained top positions in their respective industries.

In the first years of the 1990s, many CEE governments saw the transition to a market economy simply as a shift in the ratio of public to private businesses. Of the two routes to a private sector – ***privatizing existing firms*** and ***creating new ones*** – the policy debates focused almost exclusively on the first. Governments were concentrated on privatizing public enterprises which were struggling with new market rules, threatened with bankruptcy and at risk of creating social unrest among their thousands of employees. Everything worked against entrepreneurs at that time. Little attention was given to how reform policies could stimulate the creation and sustainability of new businesses. Indeed, the existing environment was hostile to new business creation. State-owned firms, fearing competition, harassed new entities and corrupt bureaucrats extorted bribes. Additionally, CEE markets lacked stable institutional frameworks. Entrepreneurs could not rely on courts to enforce their contracts. Bank loans were unobtainable by most and there was little legal or regulatory provision for shareholding. Issues like legal and employment restrictions made new business opportunities difficult to pursue and exploit (Johnson et al. 2002a). Still, about 5% of the adult working population of CEE countries attempted to start new firms or became self-employed.[1] They did this despite having little protection of private property rights and worse starting circumstances than state companies (Peng 2001).

The centrally planned economy was built around state orders, state ownership of production, administered prices and a monobank system. This infrastructure was created to serve large, state-owned firms that produced few consumer goods. Small- and medium-sized firms were almost nonexistent.

Trade and services were also a much smaller part of the communist economies than what was typical for a market economy. Privatization and liberalization reforms led to flexibility in prices, wages and production decisions, creating opportunities for potential entrepreneurs. Over the years, there was some evidence of an increasing clustering of countries within each geographical region according to their average scores on the transition indicators, as well as increasing similarities in the patterns of reform across the regions (see Figure I.1.1).

Considerable variation was seen in the macroeconomic indicators. The countries of Central Europe and the Baltic states registered moderate-to-strong growth (at an average annual rate of 4.5% since the mid-1990s). In Southeastern Europe (Bulgaria, Moldova and Romania), GDP contracted sharply. In the Central CIS, GDP continued to contract in Russia and Ukraine, but grew significantly in Belarus. Strong growth was recorded in Caucasus and Kyrgyzstan (see Appendix 2: Growth in Real GDP in Central and Eastern Europe, the Baltic States and the CIS).

Although there was a range of structural, political and geographical factors that distinguished the transition economies from one another, we focus on those that were of great importance to enhancing the entrepreneurial context: property rights' guarantees, efficiency of formal and informal institutions that support market economy development, access to external financing (capital markets), a cultural dimension related to entrepreneurs' perception in society, and human capital development.

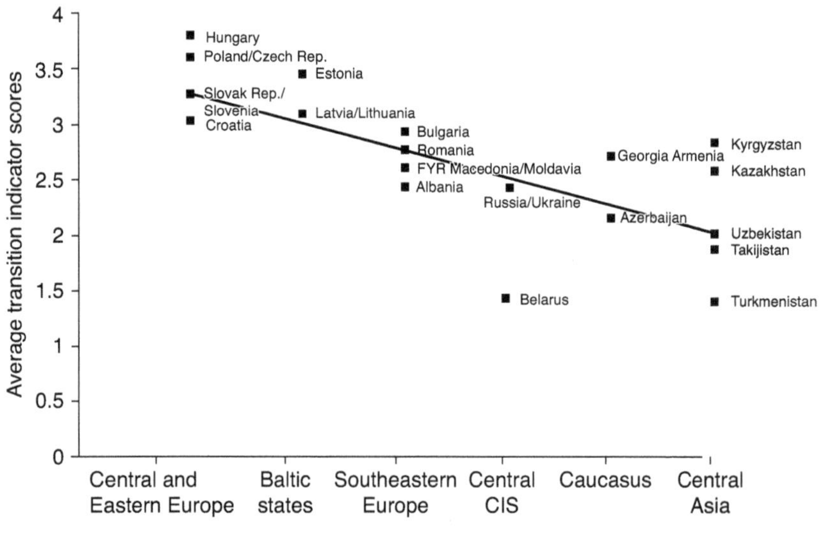

Figure I.1.1 Regional reform patterns

Source: "Transition Report 1999: Ten Years of Transition" (November 1999), EBRD, p. 27.

Weak property rights and institutional framework

The essential responsibilities of the state in a market economy are maintenance of macroeconomic stability and law and order, including basic property rights. Some transitional governments actively discouraged entrepreneurship by weakening property rights. The right to use an asset and transfer its ownership freely was and still is a "sine qua non condition" for developing entrepreneurial activity. Experience has shown that, where property rights are relatively strong, firms reinvest their profits; where they are relatively weak, entrepreneurs do not want to invest from retained earnings. Research confirms that less secure property rights are correlated with lower aggregate investment and slower economic growth (Johnson et al. 2002b). In the first decade of the transition period of post-Soviet countries, the European Bank for Reconstruction and Development (EBRD 1996), through a cross-country study, claimed that property rights were less secure in countries further to the east.

Similarly, the role of courts in reinforcing contracts varied across countries. Research shows that, in 1997, 73% of managers of Polish start-up firms would appeal to the courts to enforce a contract with a trading partner, but in Russia only 56% would. Interestingly, those who said the courts were effective offered more trade credit and were more willing to take on new trading partners (Johnson et al. 2002a).

Furthermore, financial and market-development-supporting institutions were essentially nonexistent under the old regime. The main constraints to develop an effective institutional infrastructure were: excessive and unpredictable taxation, policy uncertainty, arbitrary bureaucratic interventions and corruption. EBRD reported in 1999 that the frequency and size of bribe payments – or what might be referred to as the "bribe tax" on firms – varied at that time substantially among the transition economies (EBRD 1999). Firms in the region paid an average "bribe tax" that ranged from a low of 2% of annual revenues in Croatia to a high of 8% in Georgia. The average "bribe tax" in the CIS countries – 5.7% of revenues – was almost twice the level reported in Central and Eastern Europe – 3.3% of revenues. When added to what was already considered by firms to be an extremely high level of official taxation, the "bribe tax" imposed a severe burden on enterprises in the region (see Table I.1.1). Research confirmed that more than 90% of Russian managers of start-up manufacturing firms said they were asked for "extra-legal" payments in order to receive government services or a business license, compared with about 20% of Polish managers. Those firms in the sample that were the most concerned about corruption invested nearly 40% less than those least concerned. Asked whether payments to private agencies were necessary for "protection" of their activities, more than 90% of Russian managers and 8% of Polish managers said they were (Johnson et al. 2002b).

For the CEE region as a whole, it was important that liberalization and privatization processes moved swiftly. Consolidating and strengthening the

Table I.1.1 The frequency and extent of the bribe tax

Country	% of firms bribing frequently[a]	Average bribe tax as a % of annual firm revenues[b]
Armenia	40.3	6.8
Azerbaijan	59.3	6.6
Belarus	14.2	3.1
Bulgaria	23.9	3.5
Croatia	17.7	2.1
Czech Republic	26.3	4.5
Estonia	12.9	2.8
Georgia	36.8	8.1
Hungary	31.3	3.5
Kazakhstan	23.7	4.7
Kyrgyzstan	26.9	5.5
Lithuania	23.2	4.2
Moldova	33.3	6.1
Poland	32.7	2.5
Romania	50.9	4.0
Russia	29.2	4.1
Slovak Republic	34.6	3.7
Slovenia	7.7	3.4
Ukraine	35.3	6.5
Uzbekistan	46.6	5.7

Notes:
[a] Firms were asked to what extent the following statement is true: "It is common for firms in my line of business to pay some irregular 'unofficial payments' to get things done." Response categories comprised: Always, Mostly, Frequently, Sometimes, Seldom and Never. The standard error of the percentage of firms reporting frequent bribes is 0.045 (averaged across countries). Thus the statistical margin of error (with 95% confidence) is 8.8%.
[b] Firms were asked what percentage of annual revenues "firms like yours" make in irregular "'unofficial payments'" to public officials. The actual bribe tax as a share of annual revenue was computed on the basis of the midpoint (or the lower end in an open-ended category) of six possible categories listed in the survey: up to 1%; 1–1.99%; 2–9.99%; 10–12%; 13–25%; more than 25%. The standard error of the reported average bribe tax is 0.006 (averaged across countries). Thus the statistical margin of error (with 95% confidence) is 1.2%.

Source: "Transition Report 1999: Ten Years of Transition" (November 1999), EBRD, p. 125.

institutions, policies and practices that underpin a well-functioning market economy was of equal importance with establishing macroeconomic stability.

Limited access to financial capital

Secure property rights are necessary for entrepreneurial investments, but they are not sufficient. Free access to external financing also mattered for pushing growth. Research shows that if bank credit is not available it may be hard for entrepreneurs to take advantage of new opportunities. There is evidence that a well-shaped financial system contributes to investment and growth.

Without a well-functioning financial market infrastructure, CEE entrepreneurs had to start their businesses with limited access to capital. The main sources of financing were: (1) profit reinvestment, (2) trade credit and (3) bank loans. Retained earnings were usually the biggest single source of investable funds for growing on the domestic market.

When interfirm relationships were working well, firms received trade credit from their suppliers. Research shows that trade credit was almost nonexistent among Russian firms as of 1997, but in Poland it was as large a source of firms' capital as bank loans (Johnson et al. 2002b). New business starters had to find money with which to purchase equipment and raw materials. It was often difficult to identify reliable suppliers and customers when most firms were new and little information was available. Risks were inherent in any trading relationship and the prevailing unstable macroeconomic conditions also made it harder to predict trading partners' behavior.

As new companies entered the market and profits were driven down, credit became even more important. The banking sector in most countries was characterized by a lack of financial intermediation, strong ties to large state-owned enterprises and overburdened with underperforming loans and weak central bank supervision. With the exception of the Czech and Slovak Republics, the volume of credit to enterprises in Central and Eastern Europe was low by EU standards (where credit to enterprises was equivalent to more than half of GDP). In CIS countries, lending to enterprises was even lower (see Figure I.1.2).

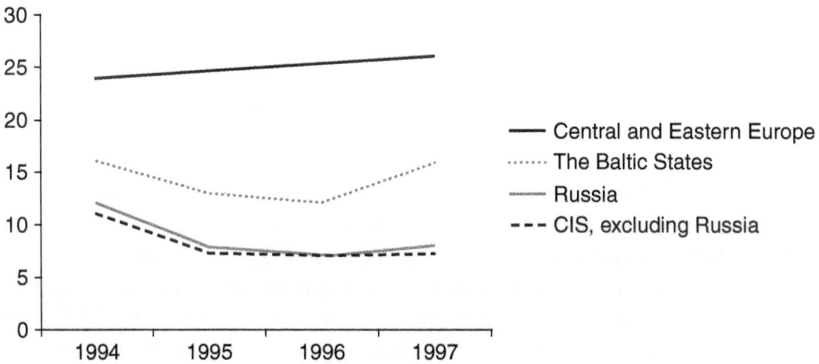

Figure I.1.2 Average bank credit to enterprise (in percentage of GDP)

Note: Outstanding bank loans to domestic nonfinancial enterprises, all types of ownership, end of period. Data shown are unweighted averages of regions. Included in the CEE countries are Albania, Croatia, the Czech Republic, Estonia, FYR Macedonia, Hungary, Poland, the Slovak Republic and Slovenia; the Baltic states comprise Estonia, Latvia and Lithuania; the CIS covers Armenia, Azerbaijan, Belarus, Georgia, Kyrgyzstan, Moldova, Tajikistan, Turkmenistan and Ukraine.

Source: "Transition Report 1998: Financial Sector in Transition" (1999), EBRD, p. 36.

Additionally, capital markets were at the beginning of their development, so market capitalization on stock exchanges was relatively low in most transition economies in 1997. Initial public offerings (IPOs) and capital increases through the stock market were very rare, except in the context of the privatization of large stated-owned companies. This also compounded the financial constraints new firms faced.

Ambiguous societal views

Another challenge facing CEE entrepreneurs at the time of transition was the rather ambiguous social attitudes toward the very idea of entrepreneurship. These attitudes have been aptly summarized by Wiesław Grudzewski, a noted Polish professor in management from the Polish Academy of Science. Speaking to young CEE entrepreneurs, Grudzewski advised:

> If you want to achieve success you have to work hard, very hard. If you achieve a small success, you still continue to work very hard in order to achieve a bigger success. Along the way, some so-called "friends" will cheat you....Do not give up! After more hard work, you may achieve a really huge success...But remember...The community will not accept your success, until it forgives you for it. And only when that happens you will be able to start enjoying your success.

Societies in transition were highly ambivalent toward entrepreneurship. After more than 40 years of state dominance, people were extremely risk-adverse and critical of failure. They also often considered success a source of envy rather than a cause for celebration. For an entrepreneur who aspires to be successful, but is constantly at risk of failure, this can be daunting. Such effects were magnified by how the press and newspapers wrote about entrepreneurs, creating perceptions that were all but favorable.

Well-educated employees without market competences

A well-functioning market economy requires and fosters the development of human capital in terms of business, management and accounting skills, as well as entrepreneurship. Given those needs, a serious limitation inherent in the CEE context was the lack of this type of skilled labor. At the time, the education system in CEE was not well suited to the requirements of a market economy. Problems included a lack of attention to social sciences, business law, economics and business administration. A strong academic emphasis was placed on mathematics and hard science, but not on problem solving. Though there was an excessive allocation of resources to fundamental research, product development was not emphasized (EBRD 1997).

Entrepreneurs in transition economies

Given all the challenges that we have just outlined, an obvious question is: How did anybody thrive under those circumstances? Our case studies are a first step toward addressing this question and facilitating a better understanding of those people who successfully entered the world of entrepreneurship and their actions.

Together with the Solidarity movement in Poland and as a result of the fall of the Berlin Wall in November 1989, most newly elected governments started to loosen restrictions on the private sector, which resulted in an initial wave of entrepreneurship.

The first entrepreneurs were mainly of four types: farmers, "gray economy" entrepreneurs, former communist functionaries and professionals (Peng 2001).

Farmers. When government regulations loosened, private farming became popular. Most farms remained small, though several attempted to grow beyond their family's holdings. Though a significant building block of the new market economy, representing a shift toward individual agency, most private farmers did not register their undertaking as a company. Farmer-entrepreneurs usually focused on food and vegetable production and low-tech manufacturing.

"Gray economy" entrepreneurs. Since the legal and regulatory frameworks to lawfully organize entrepreneurial ventures were underdeveloped, so-called "gray entrepreneurs" emerged to take advantage of these loopholes and serve as intermediaries, connecting individuals and organizations with economic exchanges that otherwise would not have taken place. While violating laws and regulations, these entrepreneurs did not necessarily belong to criminal organizations, although some of them certainly did. Most of these people were entrepreneurs in a classical sense, those who added value by brokering the connections among others. "Gray economy" entrepreneurs specialized in various intermediary services, both legal and illegal. Interestingly, despite its illegality, the gray economy was tolerated and partially accepted by the public.

Former communist functionaries or cadres. Former communist functionaries were a group of educated people who were in an advantageous position during the transition. Their potential, based on their know-how and their network of influential contacts called "a red net," made them well positioned to start successful businesses. However, not all of them were capable of doing it. During privatization, for example, strategically located cadres took advantage of their contact power in acquiring state property. Cadres also tapped into their personal networks to acquire valuable resources from their former colleagues still in the government. They maneuvered across different sectors as intermediaries. Cadres were known for their interest in relationship-intensive industries such as trading, media and entertainment, and property development.

Professionals. Professionals were entrepreneurs who previously held professional positions such as lawyers, managers, engineers or academics. In their particular area of interest, they were well skilled and well educated. Their expertise enhanced and improved the operation of new businesses, which traditionally concentrated on low-tech, labor-intensive sectors such as farming, restaurants, money-exchange points and retail shops. Professionals-turned-entrepreneurs tended to be more interested in knowledge- and technology-based ventures. Professionals were seen as better educated and having fewer connections with the state party or the gray economy. They were able to increase the legitimacy of private firms.

This book focuses mostly on the entrepreneurial careers of the fourth type of CEE entrepreneurs – professionals. Profiles of the entrepreneurs featured in this book are included in Appendix 3: Profiles: Firms and Entrepreneurs. All of them received a high-level education, with backgrounds mostly in engineering, law, medicine, economics and life sciences. Yet their education, acquired under communism, had not necessarily prepared them to pursue their entrepreneurial careers. So how did they do it?

Note

1. The figure was very similar to the percentage of nascent entrepreneurs in the United States and Western Europe.

2
Overcoming Start-Up Challenges in Transition Economies

Before the collapse of the Soviet Union, Boris Beylin, a mechanical engineer and CEO of Big Filter – a car filter manufacturer from Russia – worked at a large state-owned machine-building company in St. Petersburg. His engineer's salary was insufficient to support his two children and wife, so he looked for ways to make extra money on the side. It was the 1980s and blue jeans were fashionable and prestigious, but virtually impossible to buy. Boris and a few friends signed up to take men's tailoring classes and set out to sell blue jeans. It was his first venture.

He bought two sewing machines and fabric from foreign sailors. After a year and a half of working at the machine-factory during the day and sewing jeans at night, Boris decided it was time for a change. He left both jobs and established a car repair shop. The shop was the second of its kind in the city. As that form of business was sanctioned by the Soviet Union, it was set up as a cooperative with eight owners. However, it did not last long because the owners disagreed about how to manage their cash flow. Of its closure Boris said, "All of the members except me wanted to spend the profit instead of reinvesting it in the business. I knew it wouldn't work. The cooperative broke up and that's when I decided to go alone and start my own company in a new legal framework."

There was another problem with the repair shop that Boris had noticed: there was always a shortage of spare parts, with a clear need for fuel filters. Building on this observation, Boris decided to start a company that would produce fuel filters. He bought land and an old factory from a former state-owned transport company in an area that was abandoned and in ruins. After restoring the factory, the transport company, suddenly interested in its castaway assets, sued Boris and wanted everything back. Fortunately for him, he won the lawsuit. Again, he was in business.

Source: CASE 4: Big Filter: Russian Filters in the International Market; p. 155

Starting and growing a company is no easy task, but entrepreneurship in an extremely unpredictable context is exponentially more difficult. Like a long-distance runner who gets additional weights attached to his arms and legs while forced to run on uneven and slippery ground, Boris' first entrepreneurial steps were laden with issues and difficulties, compounding an already challenging context.

The previous chapter presented some of the key features of the context that the case protagonists found when they began their entrepreneurial journeys. In contrast, research on entrepreneurship has shown that knowledge of and access to opportunities, the possibility of capturing future benefits and of attracting and retaining the right resources, knowledge of organizing properly, and the overall stability of institutional settings are important conditions for making entrepreneurial activity flourish. By looking at those factors, one recognizes that they are at odds with the reality. This applies not only to entrepreneurs depicted in our case studies but also to a much larger group of businesses in other transition economies around the world that faced or will face unfavorable contexts. Such conditions add the liability of a weak setting to the liability of newness[1] for young start-ups.

Reality shows that despite the absence of these levers in transition economy contexts, entrepreneurs did not stop their undertakings. Actually, they started all kind of ventures. Yet they behaved differently compared to other entrepreneurs in more stable markets – especially at the beginning in order to survive, develop and grow. This section dives deeper into the behaviors of entrepreneurs when more favorable conditions were in short supply or even completely absent.

Tacking entrepreneurship

- An engineer sewing jeans at night to support his family, before starting a car repair shop, followed by starting an international fuel filter business.
- A person who made some money with small decorative owls created from sisal twine, prior to going into the flower business, before starting a company that first produced semi-finished iron products and eventually made him a global hospital bed industrialist.
- A computer equipment trader who morphs into a construction materials entrepreneur.
- A photographer who starts printing advertising buttons and other materials as a first venture and eventually turns into a light airplane manufacturer who writes aviation history with his achievements.

The entrepreneurship literature has described a number of approaches related to opportunities, opportunity-related processes and business venturing. Among others, those include opportunity entrepreneurship and necessity entrepreneurship[2] (Reynolds et al. 2002), causation and effectuation[3]

(Sarasvathy 2001) and heuristics-based logic. When we analyzed the cases of Central and Eastern European entrepreneurs and the contexts in which they had to operate, we felt that while some of those concepts can – individually or in combination – help to describe and explain part of what we have seen, there was also "something else" that was not captured by existing frameworks and theories. To more fully describe our observation of the behaviors of transition economy entrepreneurs, we therefore created a new complementary concept that we call: **Tacking Entrepreneurship**. We are convinced that it represents the development of many individuals' entrepreneurial journeys in transition economy contexts, particularly during the early phase.

The expression "tacking" comes from sailing. It is a method used to sail upwind, that is, when the wind is blowing from the direction in which the sailor wants to go, she must sail several degrees in an off-direction in order to capture the force of the wind on the sails. This requires the sailor to make a series of turns, or *tacks*, in order to get closer to the target, creating a zigzag path, where each tack is sharply divergent from the previous one. In our sailing analogy, we see such headwind as the institutional setting – it requires a unique, indirect approach. For our entrepreneurs, *tacking* was a way to advance. We apply the term "*tacking entrepreneurship*" to the behavior of individuals, not ventures.[4] It happens at the nexus of the individual and the transition economy context.[5] It is a discovery-driven approach that is embedded in a setting where founders had difficult conditions, feeble "entrepreneurship heritage," and – if at all – only a few specific "role models" to look up to. There are several characteristics that describe *tacking entrepreneurship* – certain behaviors which distinguish it from other entrepreneurship concepts.

Unlike many entrepreneurs in Western markets, they did not necessarily pick an idea or start a venture based on what they were passionate about. Rather, they set out to accomplish "something," taking advantage of whatever they found on their path. They went for "the next good-enough-opportunity" in close proximity with the aim to optimize its benefits. Picking such an opportunity did *not* necessarily include systematic search, specific selection criteria, or any deeper evaluation of different options or opportunities before making a choice. It can be described as taking advantage of an opportunity "in the heat of the moment" – not as a decision or pursuit based on an analysis and not with any future long-term specific purpose in mind. People started trading with what was tradable to make financial surpluses when real ventures were still forbidden.

As we described in the previous chapter, in the first years of the 1990s, the level of complexity and uncertainty in post-soviet countries was so high that people tended to try to control things around them as it was not possible to control the larger environment. Entrepreneurs acted with determination and full commitment to new ventures, only looking at their current activity and trying to evaluate how to best move it forward. In some regards, such behavior could even be compared with that of small children: psychologists claim that children are brave because they have no past-experience memory and they do not extrapolate the future based on past knowledge; instead, they commit to the "now" fully and go forward.

Many of our case entrepreneurs started their journeys without any compass. If one path came to a dead end they initiated the next "tack" to move to the next possibility of doing something and to pursue an opportunity in a very different field of activity. Due to a lack of experience, transparency and the high level of uncertainty, there was no conscious long-range strategizing applied to such opportunities. *Tacking* was not built on strategic foresight, but it represented the act of dealing with the difficult (entrepreneurial) reality in the best possible way.

The entrepreneurship literature often refers to the strong role of cognitive processes in opportunity-related aspects and talks about "means-ends frameworks." In tacking entrepreneurship, the cognitive part is "tamed" and plays a very different role compared to "action." Opportunities became means in themselves, but to rather undefined and unclear ends. Each "tack" of the journey was a transient piece, and the entrepreneur went through an ongoing state of evolution without knowing even the next destination of the journey, let alone the final destination. It was about the entrepreneurs' willingness to make and sustain the effort, to keep investing to capture the trends, and to continue fighting where one could win at that moment in time. They learn and gain market-relevant competences and skills experientially on each part of the way, through each tack, but it is an unplanned patchwork learning process that has no previous definition of a specific direction and purpose in light of a future plan.

However, such an approach works only until a point in a company's development. If one of the tacks turns out to hold true potential and business becomes more substantial, entrepreneurs start to become more cognitive in their opportunity-related processes. What we saw was that many entrepreneurs then applied effectuation principles[6] (Sarasvathy 2001) to their business dealings while being small ventures, and eventually shifted to more strategic approaches and toward opportunity-based entrepreneurship as their firms kept growing, maturing and were becoming more deeply embedded in their ecosystems and industries.

Like a boat tacking its way upwind, entrepreneurship in transition economies traces a peculiar shape. The final sum, then, is the trace of a life rather than simply the history of one company.

Substitutes for a conducive environment

Through the cases analyzed we identified how entrepreneurs have overcome challenging situations in which certain key resources were missing – or the context highly unfavorable – and not only survived, but managed to build successful national and finally, international businesses.

These entrepreneurs were savvy enough to not expect better circumstances for acting, and persistent enough to bear the burden of not finding the support. They made things happen in spite of everything. By displaying a selection of them, it becomes clear how manifold and especially how creatively the entrepreneurs reacted to instability. What stands out is that they applied a wide range of approaches from "official" (e.g., pursuing a lawsuit to fight for one's right) to "grass-root/guerrilla" methods and from "reactive" to "proactive" to help their companies overcome such challenges.

How? ... if you cannot choose

Previous research shows **that knowledge of and legitimate access to alternative options** is a very powerful factor in starting a company. The rationale behind this is simple: if potential entrepreneurs are exposed to diverse business opportunities, chances are that there will be a match between their interest/capabilities and the potential venture. Awareness and access to entrepreneurial options increases with market transparency, client preferences' knowledge, familiarity and willingness to search, among others. However, as it has been described above, many entrepreneurs in our sample did not necessarily pick opportunities through a systematic search or any deeper evaluation of different options. Reasons for that included a lack of market data and transparency for understanding real consumer needs, an absence of general business information and scarce business training which reduced their prospects and ability to optimize their choices. Thus, under such handicapped conditions, potential entrepreneurs had reduced visibility on and bandwidth of options and needed to react more ad hoc. Indeed, it could be said that alternatives arose and founders either picked or discarded them after a brief estimation of the opportunity – either tacking in a new direction or continuing the current activity. Furthermore, in some cases serendipity played a bigger role than rational analysis.

A good example is Krzysztof Domarecki, CEO of ***Selena***, a Polish construction products manufacturer. He started trading computers brought from outside Poland. An important customer was unable to pay and he agreed to a barter, choosing construction materials instead of computers. The barter helped Domarecki to learn more about construction materials and the existing market demand, eventually leading him to fully focus on this segment and scale up his business. Today, ***Selena*** is a multinational firm selling construction products in more than 70 countries all over the world.

Source: CASE 14: Selena Group: Internationalizing Through Multilocality; p. 347

This is just one example of the list of entrepreneurs that went through comparable beginnings. However, not having the chance for exposure to an array of market opportunities did not paralyze the entrepreneurs' activities. The entrepreneurs had the persistence to try again and again until there was real potential for development and growth. Factors that did potentially increase the amount of options and opportunities an entrepreneur could get exposure to was the size of one's personal network – and here, at the start, it was not necessarily the international network playing a dominant role, but often the local network as a starting point for one's venture that would later become international.

How?...if you cannot appropriate the value

Another relevant enabler of entrepreneurial activity is **the expectation of capturing future benefits**. Value creation is only the first step of an entrepreneurial undertaking; for building a sustainable venture there must also be internal and external mechanisms that support value capture. On the one hand, there are **internal** mechanisms – those dependent on an entrepreneur – that refer to designing and fine-tuning the right economic model (meaning, having the right price to capture the highest value). Scanning their models, the result is simple: often these entrepreneurs left money on the table for the clients. It does not mean that they did not make money, but the offerings were above expectations taking into account the price/quality ratio. We will further discuss this point in the next chapters.

On the other hand, **external mechanisms** – independent of an entrepreneur – refer to the right to use an asset and freely transfer its ownership. If property rights are relatively strong, firms reinvest their profits. If those rights exist and are trusted, they provide a motivational basis for entrepreneurs, but also represent the lifeblood for future growth and sustainability. However, entrepreneurs might find problems with exactly this: in a number of the cases featured in the book, there was a real threat for the appropriation of accrued benefits through some stakeholders or constituencies – meaning, political situations were not stable and a government body could simply seize assets or other factors could endanger such mechanisms, making investments less attractive. Such might appear in the form of profit privatizations, high taxation percentages, or other measures. Sometimes even based on wrong assessments, these potential threats were a real energy drain for the entrepreneurs as is shown in the following example of ***PKF Betar***, a (smart) meter producer from Russia:

In early 2007, Renat Fardeev, CEO of ***PKF Betar***, had received very disappointing news: the Russian Federal Anti-Monopoly Service had started an official investigation into Betar's practice of selling water meters. The basis for the investigation was the government's belief that Betar had reached 49% market share. Betar refuted such a high market share number since the figure included all of the fake Chinese manufactured meters that illegally used the "Betar" brand name. It calculated its own market share to be 31%.

Source: CASE 12: PKF Betar Company: 'Meters' Away From Further Growth; p. 312

In general, though, the entrepreneurs in the sample did not get discouraged by such dangers. Even if property rights were not secured, profits were usually reinvested in the firm to make it grow. They accepted the risk of losing much or possibly even everything. They remained focused and believed so strongly in their ventures that they did it nevertheless. Their mind-set and approaches allowed some entrepreneurs to surmount some barriers created by profit appropriation.

For instance, Mr. Frolík, who would become the founder of the hospital bed producer ***LINET***, showed determination and innovative thinking in his previous venture, which allowed him to build up a stock of financial resources for the "real" venture later on. He launched a business in the primary sector. Thanks to greenhouses and automation, he was the only one in the Czech Republic who was able to deliver flowers in winter. With his flower business he got around the prohibition of business by selling agricultural surpluses, which was allowed at that time.

Source: CASE 8: LINET: To Be an Object of Desire, Not of Choice; p. 235

How?...if you cannot find resources

Even if an opportunity has been crafted and a way to create and appropriate value has been defined and seems feasible, the **availability, access to, and mobility of resources** is a key determinant of a start-up's future success. Such resources include the team, investments, capabilities and infrastructure. Typical difficulties are well captured by the description of ***Laser Diagnostic Instruments***'s situation:

Laser Diagnostics Instruments (LDI), the Estonian firm producing laser instruments and software, had been presented with a number of key challenges in its attempt to grow internationally. First, ***LDI*** had experienced difficulty in finding the right managers and partners who could match technological knowledge with international management and marketing skills. Second, ***LDI*** was challenged to convert the start-ups to viable stand-alone businesses that were self-sustaining and non-reliant on external funding. Third, setting up new enterprises and traveling to disparate locations was usually a high investment in time and money in the early stages.

Source: CASE 7: Estonia's Laser Diagnostic Instruments (LDI) AS: Beaming Towards Growth; p. 210

One way to deal with such situations was to start with low-commitment models toward potential clients and partners and subsequently increase the mode of collaboration to higher commitment models which would allow access to more resources, the right people and higher growth potential. In that way, risk-averse stakeholders and prospective clients could be attracted more easily and then convinced through hard facts once they used the product. ***LDI***, for example, started by first licensing out their technology to a European client and once the licensee saw and experienced the full potential of their technology they went on to create a common joint venture. Building on such initial successes and an emerging market track record on top of an excellent scientific track record, the same model was applied in other parts of the world with ***LDI*** setting up further JVs in, for example, Canada, to serve the North American market.

In other cases, if a company had accumulated enough resources with its current business, an acquisition of a similar company was a way forward – one, for example, applied by ***Atlantic Grupa***, a Croatian producer and distributor of food products and supplements – to quickly get access to existing brands, people and established infrastructure, among other important factors.

The type of resources in shortage differed. In some countries it might have been easy to get good scientists or engineers, especially during certain periods, such as when large parts of highly qualified workforces were laid off during the transition period. ***LINET***, the hospital bed producer, illustrates these incidences:

> In Slany, close to the country's main economic center, Prague, he identified a large former state company, ČKD Slaný, a producer of truck crane superstructures that had just gone bankrupt and dismissed a lot of qualified and educated people who were now looking for employment. This was the opportunity he [Mr. Frolík, the entrepreneur] had been looking for. He was particularly interested in staff from the construction department, who would later play a key role in the history of ***LINET***.
>
> *Source*: CASE 8: LINET: To Be an Object of Desire, Not of Choice; p. 235

Likewise, ***Big Filter*** capitalized on the closure of a large Russian state company to hire a highly qualified workforce of engineers.

Even later in their growth path, ***Fx3x***, a Macedonian visual effects and movie animation company, provides a great example for building a strong talent pool to support the company's growth vision without spending too many resources. They created a macro-educational project that promoted and trained future prospective employees for the company as a mean to overcome the lack of qualified candidates:

> ***Fx3x*** developed the 3D @ E-Schools project in cooperation with a local USAID program. It developed a distance-learning platform for Alias's Maya®, software

for 3D computer animation and offered the possibility for students to develop animated characters. The outcome was successful. The first-level training was accomplished in 27 schools and provoked interest among 400 students for visual effects. The talent pool ensured strong base for future expansion plans.

Source: CASE 5: Fx3x: Star Performance without a Star Attitude; p. 179

However, in general managerial skills were the scarcest. Entrepreneurs are usually not experienced in building firms. A lack of basic market-knowledge-based skills is one of the key primary causes of failure that research has identified. Also, our case entrepreneurs had none or only a few role models to learn from, due to the regulations of a closed economy. The ways they learnt were diverse. Some of them acquired the capabilities by *tacking*: accumulating experiences and developing skills and business knowledge. Others traveled abroad to better understand the basics.

K. Domarecki from ***Selena*** visited the United States and came across the notion of core competence, which greatly impacted him. He used to say: "Management and marketing are applied sciences. I took a book, pored over it page by page and applied the knowledge."

Source: CASE 14: Selena Group: Internationalizing Through Multilocality; p. 347

Also Gabor from Graphisoft mentions ways that allowed learning "away from home":

Years went by at the Institute of Geophysics until Gabor learned of the possibility of Hungarian software programmers being "loaned out" to the "West," via another institution – a computer science institute called SzKI. SzKI had a manpower-leasing agreement with software companies in Vienna and Munich. Within the framework of this agreement, it was possible to travel outside of Hungary, with special permission, to visit partnering companies that were cooperating with SzKI. Not only would a talented programmer be able to work with Western companies, and with state-of-the-art computers, but a programmer would also receive the always sought-after hard currency in the form of a per-diem allowance. This was the most appealing attraction to any Hungarian software programmer.

Source: CASE 6: Graphisoft: The Architecture of International Growth; p. 193

Though financially often very difficult for small ventures, hiring experienced managers with decades of experience in foreign target markets could help accelerate a company's internationalization. They would benefit from the person's network, and leverage their ability and credibility to attract additional high-profile talent as well as investment from external shareholders. We have seen such approaches especially in high-technology firms that moved quickly toward global lead markets, especially the United States.

One example is ***Modesat Communications***, an Estonian technology provider of mobile backhaul solutions, which made two key hires: first, to expand globally and make inroads with major international original mobile equipment manufacturers (OEMs), the company recruited as new CEO the 44-year-old Peep Põldsamm, an executive with over 20 years of experience in mobile telephony including posts as the VP R&D of Levicom Group, Strategy Director of mobile operator Tele2 Estonia, CEO of Estonia's State Infocommunication Foundation (RIKS) and founder of Bravocom, the first mobile virtual network operator in Estonia.

Secondly, they hired former VP R&D of Samsung Electronics and Director of Broadcom, 63-year old Korean national Dr. Sanguoon Chung, as ***Modesat***'s VP R&D and Chief Technology Officer based in San Diego, California.

Source: CASE 10: Modesat Communications OÜ: Riding a Big Wave with a Small Boat; p. 269

If raising funds is a challenge for any entrepreneur, it was even more difficult for most of our protagonists, as no – or hardly any – investment community or ecosystem of investors and business angels existed and banks were usually not ready for such early investment stages.

As mentioned before, some entrepreneurs accumulated minimum initial starting capital before launching the "next venture" which might turn into the "real venture," as other sources of capital were in many cases not available. Without much planning, the founders of firms such as ***Solaris*** (a bus manufacturer from Poland) and ***Big Filter*** (car filters) started off with car repair shops, while ***LINET***'s (hospital bed producer) founder had, as described earlier, engaged in a small-scale flower business. Saving earnings was the key to launch or participate in the next opportunity. Some ventures financed themselves on the first contract they managed to obtain, and only a few were really able to obtain external funding – especially at the beginning (one such example is ***Modesat Communications*** which obtained business angel/Venture Capital and government funding).

Personnel and financing are critical assets to start, but new organizations must rely heavily on social relations among strangers, too: with clients, suppliers, employees, institutional regulations and others. One way to attract resources from stakeholders (especially foreign ones), and to build trust, was to demonstrate strong commitment to one's venture.

How far some of our entrepreneurs were willing to go in order to make their venture successful and how much they believed in their endeavors is shown in the example of Gábor Bojár in an earlier venture before he founded ***Graphisoft*** in Hungary, which became a world-leading reference in architectural software:

> One potential customer and project after another did not materialize. The ones that did materialize were small and far between. At one point, lacking cash for daily operations, Gabor and his wife even took their wedding rings and silverware to a pawn shop to continue financing the company.
>
> *Source*: CASE 6: Graphisoft: The Architecture of International Growth; p. 193

Considering the context, attracting foreign capital seemed to be an option only for a chosen few. Even if investors existed, they might not have fully understood certain technologies or the context and thus would decide not to invest.

In general, like many founders, the entrepreneurs in our cases spent the minimum to get started; both ***Big Filter*** and ***LINET*** were founded in run-down places: an abandoned factory ("The area was abandoned and in ruins. There wasn't any sewage, electricity or infrastructure of any type") and an old run-down farmhouse, respectively.

Another approach was to exhaust as fully as possible the local context and its available "perks" as well as national or international sources – for example, ***Fx3x*** got financial support from USAID, ***Big Filter*** took advantage of cheap government loans to buy foreign equipment, while some others focused on attracting capital from available European funding frameworks. However, in certain cases local governments were not effective in making national or international funds available to companies, which is a problem especially for small firms.

How? ... if you cannot enforce the law

As an overarching construct, the **degree of stability and reliability of a setting** – most strongly influenced by the existence of, trust in, and functioning of its institutions such as national and regional governments, courts, banks, trade unions, stock exchanges and so on – is usually presented in business literature as a crucial factor for entrepreneurial activity. As introduced in the previous chapter, the overall instability of institutional conditions invited individuals to "wait and see." In many Central and Eastern European countries, one can observe a surprising degree of entrepreneurial activity during the transition period despite unstable conditions. However, to attract foreign direct investment, as well as to prepare the ground for small companies to really grow big – as opposed to staying small or remaining in the "gray zone" of the informal economy – institutions need to play by clear rules, create transparency and enforce laws if players have not obeyed them. For some years, in many countries, this was not the case:

> The Berlin Wall had not yet fallen, and so-called Western CoCom (Coordinating Committee for Multilateral Export Controls) rules were in effect, placing an embargo to Central/Eastern Europe on certain technology goods believed to have arms and defense purposes not favorable to Western interests. The black market in Hungary thrived.
>
> *Source*: CASE 6: Graphisoft: The Architecture of International Growth; p. 193

In a number of our firms, intellectual property protection was critical, but possible infringements were difficult to enforce. Also, our introductory case in this chapter illustrates such problems of instability during transition periods when the former owner of a state-owned company claimed back a whole plant and land after it had been restored to full functionality by the entrepreneur. In Poland, for example, private businesses were hardly tolerated by the authorities; they were limited to ten employees. Another big challenge, for example, for ***Solaris*** (Poland), was "running the business with no local sources of supplies available" – building and spare parts for their buses were not readily available and difficult to obtain.

The following section outlines that instead of viewing themselves as victims of the circumstances, many of our case entrepreneurs took a very proactive role as change agents and stabilizers of their economies.

Building quasi-institutional frameworks

An important observation that we need to emphasize at the outset is that the creative potential of our CEE entrepreneurs can be analyzed at two levels. According to a classic definition of the well-known economist Joseph Schumpeter, an "entrepreneur" is someone coming up with new modes of production (Schumpeter 1934). But CEE entrepreneurs innovated not only with products and business models. They also very often successfully introduced new "soft" market institutions supporting a fast and robust growth of their ventures. **These entrepreneurs were not only producers of goods and services, but also producers of market-supporting institutions and quasi-institutions.** Reputational incentives substituted for court enforcement of contracts. Trade credit substituted for bank credit. Reinvestment of profits substituted for outside equity (McMillan and Woodruff 2002). Investments in developing business networks substituted for obtaining market information, interpreting regulations and enforcing contracts. In an environment in which formal institutional constraints such as laws and regulations are weak, informal institutional solutions help to at least partially overcome the infrastructure deficiencies by facilitating economic exchange among members, which could be seen in CEO of Technimex K. Domarecki's approach in accepting a barter as "a form of money surrogates and bank warranty":

> In 1987, together with his friends and colleagues from the Wrocław Technical University, he founded Technimex, the first company trading in computer equipment and software. He used his vast experience of the Eastern markets to import computer equipment. Unfortunately, from the end of the 1980s, computer margins began to drop in Poland, so the company started to look for development opportunities in the markets of the Soviet Republics. The Russians had nothing to pay with, so Domarecki agreed to a barter. The Ministry of Provisions of one of the Republics suggested that instead of computers, Technimex should pick some goods from their storehouses for the barter.
>
> *Source*: CASE 14: Selena Group: Internationalizing Through Multilocality; p. 347

Barter was a very popular instrument in business payment relationships. In 1999, EBRD reported that transactions in barters made up more than 10% of transactions for just under a third of firms in the survey, and over 25% of transactions for nearly one-fifth of firms (EBRD 1999).

Also, ***Pipistrel***, featured at the beginning of Chapter 1, is an example of how the entrepreneur Ivo Boscarol actually created the first regulatory framework for his industry in order to establish and develop his business.

The mental attitude that shines through with entrepreneurs in such unstable contexts is that they are simply psychologically aware and open to accept instability as a way of living; they took it as a personal challenge. There was a high probability for the worst-case scenario to happen – and such negative (or even "fatal") impacts could come from any direction. Thus, little energy was wasted on mourning the suboptimal conditions, but rather spent on acting in extremely resource-conscious ways (even if that meant starting with very limited – or even nonfunctioning – tools and equipment), while creating external sources of stability and step-wise improving the business.

This insight provides a promising perspective for all those who might doubt their potential for success while feeling captured in a difficult context. But there is no need for despair – the entrepreneurs featured in this book have clearly shown how far one can go from even the most basic and disadvantageous conditions and remote places.

Notes

1. The liability of newness phenomenon describes the different risks for a young organization to fail. It states that the risk is higher at inception and decreases over time (Stinchcombre 1965).

2. The GEM introduced the terms necessity and opportunity entrepreneurship in 2001 in its statement that a distinction should be made between entrepreneurship that reflects a voluntary pursuit of opportunity and entrepreneurship that reflects the necessity to engage in such activity in the absence of other employment opportunities (Reynolds et al. 2002).
3. Effectuation is a concept from Professor Saras Sarasvathy and defines a way of thinking that serves entrepreneurs in starting businesses in situations of uncertainty. Situations of uncertainty are situations in which the future is unpredictable, goals are not clearly known and there is no independent environment that serves as the ultimate selection mechanism. Causation is the opposite of effectuation. The most important difference between causal reasoning and effectuation is that an entrepreneur using causation has a given goal and searches for means to reach his goal; if the entrepreneur uses effectuation instead, he will start with the means he has and from this point he looks at possible goals.
4. This does not necessarily mean that it couldn't be applied to ventures as well. A part of the practitioner-oriented literature has described "pivots" as moves by companies to reinvent themselves if a previous business model and strategy has not been successful, but it is of a different nature to what we refer to as a tack.
5. This is in alignment with Scott Shane's approach who fixes his perspective not only on the individual and not only on external factors, but fully on the nexus of the individual and the opportunity, which avoids being either too phenomenon-centric or too discipline-centric.
6. Entrepreneurs do not start with a given goal, but with the tools he or she has. In many cases, they are concerned about minimizing losses more than optimizing profits. Surprises are not necessarily seen as something bad, but as opportunities to find new markets. And instead of predicting the future, they try to control some of the factors that determine the future.

3
Overcoming a Negative Country-of-Origin Effect

Laser Diagnostic Instruments' NarTest technology aimed to fill the gap between a manual drug search and laboratory analysis, answering the need for a rapid conclusive result with basic lab-based analysis of the substance. As of 2011, the NarTest NTX2000 device was the only photonic-based analyzer capable of testing for drugs outside of a traditional laboratory. The device had the ability to detect six types of illegal drugs (heroin, cocaine, marijuana, ecstasy, amphetamine and methamphetamine) with 99.6% accuracy. It was handheld and portable and able to produce results within 5 to 15 minutes in any environment. It could be powered from a car battery and only required a half day of training to be used. It was estimated that law enforcement agencies could save up to 90% by using the device versus conducting tests in a standard laboratory. LDI had introduced a novel drug analyzing technology to the law enforcement system in the United States in 2006 which had been used in thousands of cases. However, in 2010 came a severe drawback when in a court case in North Carolina, the Court of Appeals rejected the use of their NarTest NTX2000 on account of unreliability. The lawyer representing the drug dealer had reportedly challenged the technology, referring to the device as ***"voodoo sorcery" because it was invented in the "East" and "does not contain any science behind it."***

Source: CASE 7: Estonia's Laser Diagnostic Instruments (LDI) AS: Beaming toward Growth; p. 210

In 1887 the English government passed a law requiring products manufactured outside of England to be labeled with their country of origin in order to protect British products from foreign copycats of lower quality. And still today, the label "Made in ... " – despite its brevity – likely has one of the most significant impacts on people's perceptions, value attribution and purchasing behavior across a wide range of product categories. This is true from a positive as well as a negative point of view. As more manufacturing has moved to developing countries, even brands that are among the strongest in the world – such as Apple – fear the (negative) impact of this short label and prefer, as in this case, to print "Designed by Apple in California" on their products, before adding the "Assembled in China" label. Certain countries stand for excellence in specific product categories, such as Belgium for chocolate, or France for wine. Germany has built such a strong country image for engineering and car manufacturing – so much that French car maker Citroën created a parody TV ad campaign in 2008 claiming its C5 model was "unmistakably German." While this is a rather funny anecdote, it demonstrates how strong country images are known to influence consumers' perception of a company's products and services.

Thus, while companies from certain countries might benefit from a positive country image – especially in specific product categories – start-ups from emerging economies that have not yet built up a strong track record in any field, or countries that are rather known for unstable conditions, will actually have to deal with a negative country-of-origin (COO) effect on top of dealing with liabilities of newness and the challenges that internationalization brings by itself. Studies of the effects of country-of-origin on consumers' perceptions of products from developing countries tend to imply that stereotypical judgments rendered by respondents involved unfair biases against these countries (Reuber and Fisher 2011). These countries and their companies face unfair obstacles when selling products abroad (Gaedeke 1973).

One example illustrating such difficulties comes from ***Solaris***, which faced negative COO-effect problems despite the fact that they already had a signed contract from a client that "only" needed to be executed. Interestingly, this effect manifested itself not only among people in foreign countries, but also in their own country.

> The first contract was won in a competition for 72 modern low-floor buses for the city of Poznań. Finding a bank willing to finance the vehicles' production in a Polish factory with no earlier manufacturing history was a challenge. Some Polish banks refused just as all the German ones he had approached. So many times he asked himself, "How should I convince the bankers that my calculations are reliable? That I shall be able to pay the money back in time.... Why do they need a long sales history record instead of looking into the future? There must be a way to get the first deal financed!"
>
> *Source*: CASE 15: SOLARIS Bus and Coach: A Bus Tour to Global Markets; p. 372

Sensitivity to country of origin varies by product category. It is strongest for durable goods (Jain 2012) and luxury goods (Aiello et al. 2008) and weakest for "low involvement" product categories (e.g., toilet paper). Interestingly, we came across many cases where the entrepreneurs not only wanted to build a strong reputation for their own company, but they also wanted to improve the image of their country on the global economic playing field. Some entrepreneurs even took this aspect into their business model design, saying that one of the disadvantages of providing a white-label solution would be that nobody would know that the technology was developed in their country.

The negative country-of-origin effect was a severe challenge that many of the entrepreneurs featured in this book faced. Conscious of the barrier, they worked hard to surpass the hurdle and strengthened the firm's reputation through diverse mechanisms to overcome the challenge which we will describe below.

Brand and reputation building

We define an organization's reputation as its overall appeal to its external stakeholders. An organization's reputation is a combination of individual-level cognitive processes that create collective social cognition and attitudes. Moreover, emerging literature on reputation development has identified various reputation-building signals, such as signals of product/service quality and media rankings/reports (Deephouse and Carter 2005; Rindova et al. 2005).

Positive brand recognition is bound with credibility. Firms we studied worked to build credibility mainly in three ways:

1. by delivering and communicating strong value propositions;
2. by involving (reputable) stakeholders;
3. by using media and other outreach activities to work to their favor.

These are not independent actions. Focusing firm's capabilities, partnering with the right external stakeholders, and marketing the brand strategically helped these firms gain credibility and increase customers' willingness to pay.

However, just how difficult it is to escape a negative COO effect is illustrated by research findings that suggest that, *"the COO effect plays an equally important role in consumer product evaluation for both strong and weak brands."* The conclusion is that, *"even for a product with a strong brand image, the negative consequences of COO stemming from consumers' unfavorable attitudes towards the manufacturing country are not likely to be completely eliminated"* (Chu et al. 2010: 1055). This also means it is not a one-off task, but a company has to work continuously in order to reinforce its positive signaling and branding in order to counterbalance the stigma. Arguably, this task is most daunting at the beginning when one has a weak brand and not yet any, or only a limited, international track record.

Creating and communicating quality

From the very beginning quality was a high priority for the companies in our sample. This was true for companies' products at the differentiation end of our continuum as much as for those with products having a stronger emphasis on price. There are several ways that firms in our sample created an image of quality.

Internal quality culture

Quality culture started within the firm. Firms in our sample felt it was important to live a "quality philosophy" on a day-by-day level and continually improve business excellence in order to show they were reliable firms. In some cases such initiatives were institutionalized. For instance, Slovenian ***Pipistrel***, Polish ***Selena*** and Hungarian ***Graphisoft***, among others, had implemented significant quality initiatives. ***Solaris***, for example, strove to create reliable, long-lasting vehicles which became part of their brand promise.

> Other brand positioning measures implemented by ***Solaris*** were reliability and longevity of vehicles. The vehicles were technically almost 100% of the time at the disposal of the owner. For example, in the case of Tramino, the parameter reached 99.5%.
>
> *Source*: CASE 15: SOLARIS Bus and Coach: A Bus Tour to Global Markets; p. 372

Of course, to unfold its full effect, it is not enough to only have quality, but to also do marketing about it – however, perceptions take time to change, specifically on such a macro-level. Russian Cosmetics' CEO points at that, saying:

> "Of course, some great marketing campaigns would start to change the brand perception. I believe it is possible to prove we are producing high quality cosmetics in Russia. We just don't have 5 to 15 years to prove it!"
>
> *Source*: CASE 13: Russian Cosmetics: "Healing" Skin Care Products in Russia; p. 329

External quality verification

One way the companies in our sample dealt with their unfavorable default images was to seek external validations. Emerging literature on reputation development has also highlighted media rankings and reports (Deephouse and Carter 2005; Rindova et al. 2005). We saw a number of companies proactively strive to attain international quality[1] standards, even before such a request would come from clients or partners. ***Selena*** is an example of a company that did not only seek international quality certifications at a company level, but walked "the extra mile" and even attained country-specific certificates down to the product level in order to reinforce and benefit from this signaling effect.

> ***Selena*** was proving the quality of its products not only by fulfilling international standards, for example ISO 9001, but also by obtaining attestation certificates and product quality certificates issued by respective authorities in a given country.
>
> *Source*: CASE 14: Selena Group: Internationalizing Through Multilocality; p. 347

In addition to standards, filing patents and building up a patent portfolio was another way to not only protect one's intellectual property, but also to send hard-fact signals to customers and partners, and gain further external validation. Sergey Babichenko, the founder of ***Laser Diagnostic Instruments (LDI)***, holds a number of patents in their specific area that also allowed them to build very innovative products. Also ***Modesat Communications*** patented their highly innovative technology to secure IP and signal thought leadership within their specific markets.

Attentive customer service

Firms in our sample were also able to craft an image of high quality by providing attentive customer support, including more customizable solutions. This gave them unique and compelling positioning versus established and much larger competitors in lead markets and helped proactively to dispel doubts. In the case of bus manufacturer ***Solaris***:

> Responding quickly to customers' wants and building the vehicle individually adjusted to their requirements while the giant producers as a rule limited their offer to standard specifications and a certain number of optional equipment versions remained one of the major competitive instruments of the product strategy.
>
> *Source*: CASE 15: SOLARIS Bus and Coach: A Bus Tour to Global Markets; p. 372

With such measures, good international clients were won by breaking their negative expectations and surprising them positively through the mix of high quality, strong commitment to fulfill clients' needs, increased flexibility and competitive pricing.

Leveraging external partners

A powerful approach to overcoming a negative COO effect is to leverage external stakeholders. Benefits can be direct – for example by launching joint ventures, strategic alliances, or from working with a partner as a reseller – or indirect, from brand spillover. "Standing on someone's shoulders," can be a shortcut or even a necessary step to get started in highly competitive markets. However, companies also need to be aware of the costs that might possibly come along with such an approach.

Below we illustrate several examples of how companies have worked with partners to enhance their own profile and positioning.

Distribution partners

Working with established distributors – either international or reputable national ones – is an effective way to gain visibility and credibility and to lower negative perceptions with consumers.

Graphisoft, for example, got access to Apple's distribution network:

> By 1990, ***Graphisoft*** worked intensively with Apple and had built a close relationship with them. ***Graphisoft*** knew Apple products inside out, knew many people at Apple, understood the company's unique internal corporate culture, and distributed their own products through Apple's international distribution network. This, ***Graphisoft*** felt, was a real competitive advantage.
>
> *Source*: CASE 6: Graphisoft: The Architecture of International Growth; p. 193

Also, ***ACE enterprise***, a software company from Slovakia, decided to pursue a partnership in order to mitigate a possibly negative perception that there were no top-notch IT companies from their home country and to facilitate rapid internationalization and gain access to large players. In the United States, they secured distribution partnerships with leading firms such as Intergraph Corporation and in Germany, their second lead market, they created a partnership with Bentley Corporation. After that, they were able to deliver solutions for clients such as Siemens, Volkswagen and E.O.N.

Supply side

Also, relationships with suppliers can offer opportunities to introduce quality, credibility and brand-enhancing elements – either through partnerships with well-known suppliers or by acquiring foreign suppliers in countries that have a positive country-of-origin effect in a specific product category.

An example is ***Solaris***, which reliable suppliers to ensure product/service quality standards and boost their brand strength: as described in the case,

"The respected brand names of a manufacturer, together with brand names of the major components (engines) are a promise of meeting the buyers' expectations as to the product quality and reliability."

Source: CASE 15: SOLARIS Bus and Coach: A Bus Tour to Global Markets; p. 372

Another example comes from Russia:

Russian Cosmetics,[2] a Russian skin-care company, distributed its products through the retail sector and through the professional sector (cosmetologists, beauty salons and spas). They had to battle both channels' negative perception about the quality of domestic brands. In order to do so, they acquired two foreign cosmetics laboratories in France and Switzerland, which culminated in the placing of a three-city label, "Paris–Geneva–Moscow," on ***Russian Cosmetics***' products. The association with the well-known "capital of beauty," Paris, was essential in overcoming the negative perception of Russian-made cosmetics. In addition, the company and its founder also benefited from the skills and capabilities of the two foreign laboratories.

Source: CASE 13: Russian Cosmetics: "Healing" Skin Care Product in Russia; p. 329

Joint ventures

Joint Ventures are also a possible way to improve the probability of succeeding in a foreign market – especially in lead markets, where reputation and local contacts and knowledge are even more important in order to be competitive. As briefly mentioned above, for ***Laser Diagnostic Instruments (LDI)*** from Estonia, this was a favored approach; the company established joint ventures, among others, in Canada and the United States to enter the North American market. One of these ventures' research findings culminated in the development of a drug analyzer that used a patented technology based on ***LDI***'s Spectral Fluorescence Signature (SFS) to detect the most common narcotics within 5 to 15 minutes. The benefit of the device was its ability to provide drug analysis at 10% of the cost of a standard laboratory-based analysis. Within three years, ***LDI*** and their US partner sold the NarTest device to North Carolina police departments and it was even featured on the popular television crime series, *CSI*.

Investors

Companies, especially young ones, also benefited from having received funding from well-known and successful investors. Such investments signaled that the company made it through the due diligence process, a sort of indirect validation. Likewise, well-known investors sent the message that a company had the potential to play a significant role in their market segment or industry. ***Modesat Communications***, a technology company, received funding from the four founding Skype engineers (aside from an investment from an Estonian government program), which helped them build credibility and notoriety in their market despite their small size.

Existing brand power

One of our sample companies applied an approach that illustrates how, over time, a company can leverage existing foreign brand power for its own means. Their foreign partners allowed them to first gain a strong foothold and company brand in their home market, then expand to other regional markets and eventually internationally, while also increasing their business activities through backward and forward integrations. ***Atlantic Grupa*** from Croatia was founded in 1991 and established a first distribution center for selected FMCG products from international brands in Zagreb, Croatia. During that same year, the company initiated business dealings with Wrigley, the world's largest chewing-gum producer, followed a year later by an agreement with Mars, the world's largest producer of chocolate confectionery. Further distribution agreements were created with international heavyweights such as Sara Lee, Duracell, Mars Ice Cream, Durex, Ricola AG, Gillette and Johnson & Johnson. Having established themselves as the distributors of such branded products and benefiting from the international credibility that this had brought them, they also bought, revived and distributed products with strong local/national brands and later used this channel to sell their own products and brands after entering the manufacturing of products themselves across several categories (e.g., they bought a mineral water bottling operation).

Strategic partnerships that include changes of shareholdings and ownership

One of the most drastic ways to involve and "access" stakeholder credibility, but which also has the largest long-term implications, is that of providing shareholdings to such international partners. ***LINET***, the Czech hospital bed producer, offered a majority share (50.01%, though the founder retained certain veto rights) to a small but renowned German company in order to associate itself with the "Made in Germany" quality label that was the preferred standard in the market at that time and to disassociate itself from the problematic image of its home market. Even many years later, when a location-based decision for a new entity had to be taken, the negative COO effect hadn't weakened much, as illustrated in the case, "[The] Czech Republic's lack of prestige on the international business stage was an important detractor." This early move allowed ***LINET*** to tap into external know-how, which helped them build their own competencies and brand as well. Also, the foreign partner lent ***LINET*** an image of quality and reliability which brought greater business stability despite the turbulent times.

While the advantages of the above-mentioned approaches are obvious and at times possibly even the only option in order to access certain markets or market segments (or to accelerate the process), they all come at a price; it is important to be aware of the disadvantages and potential downsides stemming from different market- and partner-evolution dynamics.

Power asymmetry

One of the main problems originates from significant power asymmetries between two such partners: on the one side a small start-up in a difficult context, with no track record and lacking any ecosystem around it, and on the other side a well-established international partner with a strong brand and in a gatekeeper position. That means that it will be very difficult for start-ups in general and even more difficult for those from instable transition economies burdened by a negative country-of-origin effect to negotiate favorable terms. Pushed by their own ambitions, entrepreneurs need to be careful not to enter agreements with strong international partners that are likely to require significant work, but with a low potential payoff.

Another potential conflict occurs when partner companies' strategies evolve differently, resulting in one company getting locked out of attractive markets that are cultivated by the other partner. Also, the market and geopolitical environment might change, causing ripples that put tension on the partnership. ***LINET*** ran into this problem. Initially their partnership constellation was very advantageous, especially for ***LINET***; both companies had evolved independently for a long time. ***LINET*** focused on the Central and Eastern European market and their German partner on Western markets, which had been less available to ***LINET***. Issues started to arise when in 2004 the Czech Republic joined the European Union, which offered ***LINET*** access to markets in which their German shareholder already did business. Though their product portfolio was initially very different, they eventually started to compete in some product categories, though they did not have any real synergies in either material acquisition or in business development.

Similarly, the founders of ***Solaris*** experienced how a partnership with a foreign partner and shareholder could be a double-edged sword. After Krzysztof Olszewski had spent many years working in Germany for the company Neoplan Bus GmbH, he founded Neoplan Polska. By giving away a 30% stake of the company – retaining the remaining 70% – he received an investment from Neoplan Bus GmbH to produce buses in Poland under Neoplan's license and brand name. However, Solaris's market was restricted to Central and Eastern Europe in order to avoid competition between the Polish company and Neoplan Bus GmbH in the Western markets. The Neoplan partnership was an advantage and surprisingly quickly Neoplan Polska gained a visible position on the Polish bus market. The well-recognized

Neoplan brand was considered a marketing strength and the German partner supplied the bus designs. However, soon Mr. Olszewski discovered the disadvantages of the relations with Neoplan Germany, realizing the limitations in pursuing his own creative ideas, as he was bound by the rules and regulations of Neoplan's licensee agreement. Additionally, he was not able to react strategically to certain market developments – possibly to an extent that could endanger the survival of his firm. For example, at the end of 2000, due to major foreign investments in the bus and truck industries in Poland (Volvo, MAN, Scania) Poland started to turn into a major bus production center in Europe. Olszewski feared that the growing position of his company on the home market was about to be challenged by the global players who located their factories next door. Due to this development, he knew he had to find customers abroad. With Neoplan Bus GmbH as a shareholder, however, he could only look East to find new markets. Fortunately for ***Solaris***, though it was not easy, in the fall of 2000 Krzysztof Olszewski managed to buy out the Neoplan Polska shares and avoided having MAN as a new partner-competitor who had acquired Neoplan Bus GmbH. He also broke free from the market restrictions imposed by Neoplan Germany.

Those selected examples illustrate some of the potential problems that are inherent in partnership relationships and which need to be managed accordingly.

Media and outreach

Client endorsements

Being able to receive positive endorsements from well-known reference clients is a powerful way to gain credibility and drive further business development efforts – possibly also through direct connections to such clients. Among our sample companies, ***Graphisoft*** is a very good example of this. Steve Jobs, in his function as the CEO of Apple, made a surprise visit to CeBIT. A day earlier, Gabor was informed of this and was told by Apple's staff to prepare a five-minute presentation for him. Gabor and his team spent all night preparing the five-minute presentation. Gabor recalls:

> When Steve Jobs arrived to our demo, he had so many questions. Steve spent a whole half an hour learning about the technology behind ***Graphisoft***'s software. That was when Steve Jobs personally endorsed Graphisoft to receive complete marketing support from Apple.
>
> *Source*: CASE 6: Graphisoft: The Architecture of International Growth; p. 193

This marked a turning point for ***Graphisoft*** and opened further doors for them.

International fairs, conferences, research events

Another common way to not only learn, but to gain international visibility, traction and credibility was to participate in and contribute to international industry fairs, conferences or research events (for more science-driven products). For example, ***Laser Diagnostic Instruments (LDI)*** used such events to showcase their latest research, impress through knowledge and competence, and build contacts that could be followed up to pursue commercial activities.

Also ***Fx3x*** left a big impression on such an event with a guerrilla strategy combined with a widely distributed expert endorsement:

> In the summer of 2004 they were arranging the $9m^2$ expo space, a company being represented on the smallest company stand that year. So, armed with a guerrilla strategy consisting of branded uniforms under the logo of ***Fx3x*** with a copy line that said "Balkanization of animation," a selected team of six – the two owners, three artists, and the company PR person – went to LA in August 2004, in an environment where the majority in the industry were against outsourcing. They used creative marketing tools they could afford offering their services with a forward-thinking guerrilla promotional printed slogan that said "Practice safe effects, use a budget protector, work in Macedonia." On the first day of the exhibition, they were widely known by the present larger studios as "The Macedonians." In three days, after 60 meetings and exchanged contacts, ***Fx3x*** got their foot in the door.
>
> One of the elements that helped immensely was an article Brad DeGraf wrote for *The Computer Graphic World*, a trendsetting magazine in the industry which distributed 30,000 free copies at the exhibition. The article not only spoke in favor of outsourcing outside the United States but it presented ***Fx3x*** as the right company to work with. Among the promo tools was a barbecue party on the last day of the expo. At the party, the ***Fx3x*** team spoke about everything but business. Macedonia, famous for its hospitality, great food and parties, outdid the expectations for leaving a nice impression on the future potential clients.
>
> *Source*: CASE 5: Fx3x: Star Performance without a Star Attitude; p. 179

Awards (international business awards; country-level recognitions)

Marketing budgets were inherently small among our companies and not many, if any, would be able to win a "marketing spending war" in foreign markets. In addition, mere self-promotion was not as effective as receiving endorsements from other trusted sources and well-respected entities. Thus, an important and cheap way to build one's company and product brand and increase a firm's credibility in the eyes of external stakeholders was to try and win awards and subsequently be featured in industry-specific press. This was highly effective PR and marketing with no cost.

While some awards were focused on companies, others were on products, and some even on the entrepreneurs themselves – but no matter the category, all were deployed to enhance a firm's image. For instance, ***Modesat Communications*** took advantage of this inexpensive path to recognition; in 2009, they were selected as the most innovative company in Estonia due to their success in selling solutions to major telecommunications companies. Likewise, thanks to an Oscar nomination for *The Aviator* and an Emmy nomination for the TV miniseries *Path to 9/11*, ***Fx3x*** gained agency interest and additional contracts. Furthermore, by receiving a significant award from Apple, ***Graphisoft*** was well positioned for additional exposure:

> During this time, outside of Japan, ***Graphisoft*** was receiving awards and professional accolades for its software development and ArchiCAD. In 1995, ***Graphisoft*** received Apple's Eddy Prize, the equivalent of an Oscar in the software industry, at the MacWorld Expo in San Francisco. This award was followed by the Software Publishers' Association's (SPA) "Codie" Award, the Computer Graphics World Award and the Editor's Choice Awards of *Cadence* and *Cadalyst* magazines, which were traditionally supporters of ***Graphisoft***'s competitors. Gabor personally received an invitation and attended the Davos Global Economic Forum and the *Wall Street Journal*'s recognition as one of Eastern Europe's outstanding executives.
>
> *Source*: CASE 6: Graphisoft: The Architecture of International Growth; p. 193

Finally, ***ACE enterprise Slovakia***, though small, had received many awards both for the founders and for the company, which helped establish the firm as a thought leader in its industry. They won prizes at the International Business Award, European IT Excellence and the International Quality Summit Awards.

Winning prestigious global competitions

One step beyond winning awards was to win competitions – preferably on an international or even global level. These showcased a company's real strength and capabilities because in a competition, companies went head-to-head with others going for the same goal, despite resource and other constraints. One impressive example was ***Pipistrel***. Though they also earned a long list of awards, their truly outstanding achievement was to win three global NASA challenges. Beating international competitors was a significant boost to their credibility and went a long way to erase the COO stigma.

Membership in organizations, associations and consortia

One of the background checks that many times potential partners or clients would do on new firms going international was their local and/or international reputation, on both a firm's and a product's reputation as well as the entrepreneur's personal reputation. One further way to signal credibility and trustworthiness was to be a member or leader of industry-specific organizations, associations or consortia. An example is ***Solaris***:

Good business and personal relations were kept thanks to ***Solaris***'s membership in various organizations and programs such as the International Association of Public Transport (UITP), the Polish–German Chamber of Commerce and Railway Business Forum. Olszewski believed in personal contacts and they traveled a lot to meet their customers personally. When the president of Solaris visited the customers they felt appreciated and important. They could not count on establishing similar relations with the big corporations' top managers.

Source: CASE 15: SOLARIS Bus and Coach: A Bus Tour to Global Markets; p. 372

Similarly, the founder of ***Fx3x*** became the president of the newly formed Macedonian Association of Digital Entertainment (MADE), a civil society organization.

Source: CASE 5: Fx3x: Star Performance without a Star Attitude; p. 179

Also, activities in industry consortia can help to establish and enhance a company's credibility and brand by making significant contributions on a national and international level. In general, companies that were involved in setting industry standards would benefit not only in the sense of influencing the future of their industry, but by deriving reputational value from this.

Creating an international setup and image

A further attempt to shrug off or at least "dilute" one's national roots if they were burdened with a negative COO effect was to quickly develop an international company, establish real operations in foreign target markets, and cultivate an international image. ***Graphisoft***, after having failed several times to enter the United States, which was a key market for them, eventually made the decision to establish a subsidiary in the United States. The founder noted, "U.S. customers traditionally are wary of European high-tech products, and especially of ArchiCAD's remarkably high price of US$4,000." Nevertheless, by not relying on other distributors, focusing on projecting an "American," not European, image, and slowly developing its own reseller network, ***Graphisoft*** finally became a major American player.

Also, ***Modesat Communication***, while still being very small, opened a sales office in Israel and an R&D office in California, which was important considering that the United States was a global lead market in the technology space. This gave the company not only access to important knowledge, but also helped build the image of a strong global company.

Avangate, an e-commerce technology company from Romania, decided to hire a high-profile US management team and advisory board members with a strong track record in their industry in order to look "more American" and to gain credibility in the important US market, which was the largest and most important target market for them.

Also, companies that were not in the technology space set up global operations to help them counter negative stigma by benefiting from "credibility signals" created by, for example, doing business in important reference markets.

By having developed an international footprint and infrastructure, possible clients and partners might worry less about the company's home country and feel safer in that the firm also had operations in countries where potential troubles in the home country did not pose a threat to business continuity.

Atlantic Grupa, to cultivate an international image, contracted reputed package designers who had worked with the foreign brands Pepsi and Coke, to leverage their international expertise to create a physical image of quality. The designers created a special bottle that prepared the drink when the consumer twisted the cap and released a powder, which helped ***Atlantic Grupa*** project an innovative image.

In summary we can conclude that there are two different categories with regard to a negative stigma effect: the first one is relating to the country's overall image and the second one relating to a certain product category in relation to a specific country. Depending if one or the other or both detractors are at play, the degree of difficulty varies. In the worst case, a company is active in a product or service category with no credibility from the country's image as well as a negative image from that country itself. This forces the firm to fight both effects. For example, Macedonia poses a negative country-of-origin effect which is compounded by a lack of credibility in the product category of visual effects (in this case for ***Fx3x***). In another case, international partners or clients might acknowledge the outstanding scientists and engineers from Russia in, for example, metallurgy and rocket science, but the country itself and its business context is still negatively perceived by foreign clients and partners. No matter if those doubts and worries are grounded or not, if the context and general country image is perceived negatively, an entrepreneur has to deal with this. But at least in comparison with the first case, the company "only" needs to overcome the negative COO-effect, while actually benefiting from a positive country-of-origin effect with regard to the specific product category.

With that in mind, entrepreneurs and companies need to design which "tools" and approaches that might be most suitable in order to build international credibility and a strong, trusted brand. As can be seen from the sections above, there are multiple ways to tackle the challenge, though one has to be aware that the strength of those approaches differ and that for transition entrepreneurs the credibility building through leveraging stakeholders is the most effective and often also the fastest way to succeed in international markets. However, as discussed above, the potential disadvantages need to be considered, evaluated and mitigated as far as this is possible. There are no standard answers to this, but also in this sphere entrepreneurs need to experiment with the options and see their impact as they forge ahead.

Notes

1. The quality is defined as a set of features specified by institution and embodied in a product.
2. Name disguised.

4
Growth Strategies and Internationalization Patterns

It feels like we've been through a lot just to complete our first product. Now it is time to face the real challenge of seeing how we can sell it. My business partner prefers to go the safe route by trying to build some local customers before going international. My heart wants to chase international customers even though I'm aware of the difficulty in doing so.

Alex Cimbaľák, ACE's founder

Source: CASE 1: ACE enterprise Slovakia: "Drawing out" the Future; p. 115

One of the main objectives of the project behind this book was to understand how small start-ups from the transition economies of Central and Eastern Europe were able to overcome the challenges of a difficult context and grow into international players, competing at the top of their industries.

There are many firm- and market-specific factors that influence a company's decision to internationalize, such as the founder's willingness, available resources, competitive pressure, local market size, skills, international experience of the founders and employees, contacts, information and the exposure to international trends, among others. Clearly, not all firms are started on a leveled playing field. There is a significant difference if a company can benefit from a 200 million consumer market like the United States; or is started, for example, in a mid-size 40 million consumer market like Poland, or a small country like Macedonia with only two million inhabitants.

In addition to the size of the local market, another key factor that influences growth and internationalization strategies is the type of industry and the type of product or service offered. As we will see, some products will simply "demand" a company go international early on or that firms need to be "born global" if they want to become relevant industry players; this is specifically true for some very innovative technologies.

There are many possible ways to analyze firms' internationalization and growth strategies. We have chosen to apply a longitudinal perspective with regard to a companies' **mode of competition** (charted on a continuum of product differentiation versus price focus) as well as their **geographic internationalization pattern**. We mapped out our case companies' paths, analyzed their expansion patterns, and highlighted insights from their specific approaches and tactics.

Our *first analysis* – how, over time, companies positioned their products and services in the market – led to a high-level categorization of three different types: *Innovators, Price-Quality-Value Providers (PQVPs),* and *Climbers* (see Figure I.4.3).

Our *second analysis* illustrates – across those three categories – five main geographical expansion patters (see Figures I.4.4– I.4.7). We will describe their characteristics and draw out relevant insights and considerations.

Mode of competition over time

The first important dimension is *Mode of Competition* (regarding product/service characteristics). Here we differentiate between two characteristic features: **Cutting-Edge Products/Services** which are highly innovative offerings, differentiated, and technically/scientifically on a par with top international standards (or even beyond), as well as **Price-Quality-Value Offerings** which provide the same or better value/quality at a lower cost, relative to existing competitors. If applied on a continuum (see Figure I.4.3), we have on the top end a strong differentiation through innovative products and services at a global level; in the middle range the just described price-quality-value offerings; and at the bottom end, commodity products and services that mainly focus on price competitiveness. Our companies fall into the upper and middle segments of that continuum.

Our research results suggest three main types:

1. ***Innovators:***
   Innovators are companies that had cutting-edge products almost or right from the start with a high potential to shape industry frontiers. These types of innovative products and services usually relied on a strong scientific or technological foundation, were very knowledge-driven and -dependent, and had a strong propensity to be international as only the global market could offer adequate fit and demand.

2. ***Price-Quality-Value Providers (PQVPs):***
   PQVPs are companies that were able to provide higher quality products and services at a lower cost in comparison to competitors. It is important to mention that many of these companies also strove to innovate though they were not necessarily aiming at competing on the top level globally (i.e., the industry's global innovation frontier), rather, they wanted to build and maintain a strong position and stay competitive in their markets. Nevertheless, depending on their types of products and

related positioning, the companies had a certain degree of differentiation. On the lower end they might be faced with a trend toward commoditization, while on the higher end they could have a strong brand and even premium positioning. A significant number of companies in this category had a portfolio of products (and related services) that could be mapped across different positions of the product differentiation versus price continuum.

3. ***Climbers:***
   Climbers are companies that were able to transform themselves from Price-Quality-Value Providers into Innovators. Those companies started initially with less differentiated products and in less innovation-focused markets (though definitely not at the lower range of our continuum) and were able to eventually elevate themselves into the Innovators's sphere where they were capable of competing with the best in their field internationally. These companies started from modest beginnings, but displayed a strong determination and willingness to learn and improve.

Developing **Cutting-edge Products and Services** usually involved a high degree of technical and scientific knowledge, particularly if pushing the boundaries of innovation on a world-wide level. Most companies in our sample that fall into that category benefited from a large number of excellent scientists and engineers who could apply their knowledge, skills and

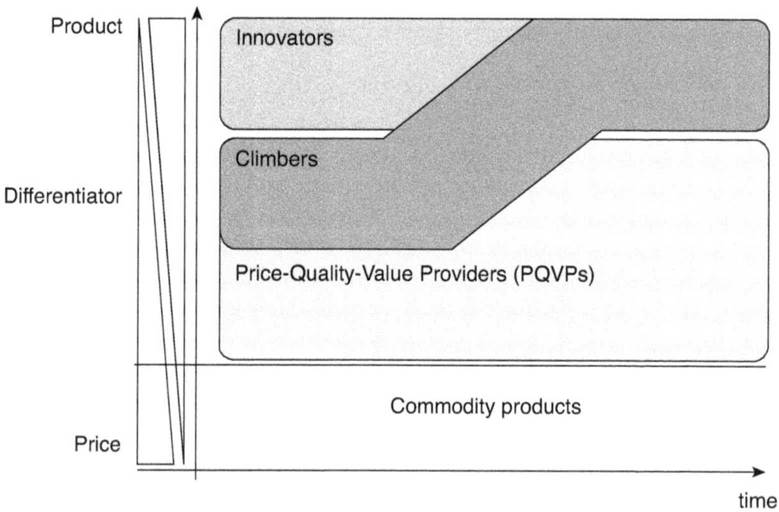

Figure I.4.1 Mode of competition over time
Source: Authors' own creation.

competencies to scientific and technical activities. However, "the business part" necessary to commercialize a product was more challenging (as described in the other chapters of this book).

An example of an ***Innovator*** with cutting-edge products is the Estonian ***Laser Diagnostic Instruments (LDI)***, a producer of laser instruments and software for a wide variety of applications. The company was founded by Dr. Sergey Babichenko, a physics PhD with nine patents and authorship of more than 100 scientific publications. Among other areas, they made a name for themselves by applying laser technology in two areas: detecting sea pollution and assessing the quality of foodstuffs.

Source: CASE 7: Estonia's Laser Diagnostic Instruments (LDI) AS: Beaming Towards Growth; p. 210

The **Price-Quality-Value Offering** approach was often enabled by the fact that extremely well-educated people became unemployed due to massive economic transformations. This allowed capable entrepreneurs easy access to such individuals and their skills and knowledge for relatively moderate compensations. This approach can work for one's home market, though we've seen it applied successfully when targeting higher-priced foreign markets.

Big Filter produced high-quality fuel filters in Russia and also offered 24-hour customer support, but could export both product and service profitably.

Source: CASE 4: Big Filter: Russian Filters in the International Market; p. 155

LINET also followed this approach and positioning in its early days, offering hospital beds constructed to Western standards, but for a lower price.

Source: CASE 8: LINET: To Be an Object of Desire, Not of Choice; p. 235

Selena, the Polish construction materials firm, focused on low price, high quality, eventually aiming to move up the price continuum to achieve higher margins.

Source: CASE 14: Selena Group: Internationalizing Through Multilocality; p. 347

International expansion patterns

The interesting question now is how companies in the three categories described above have really approached their internationalization and managed to become relevant players in foreign markets. To do so, we also looked at the sequence of geographical expansion (e.g., 1st Home

Market – 2nd Regional Markets – 3rd Multinational Markets – 4th Lead Markets), mapped their various international growth patterns, and aim to shed some light on the logic behind those approaches. For our purpose here we do not distinguish in which way the internationalization is accomplished (though we are aware of how different the implications are for companies): it may be through export, international partners, resellers, or through their own foreign production facilities and distribution channels.

The analysis of our companies' geographic internationalization patterns covers four different categories:

a. **Home Market**
   The *Home Market* is (usually) the starting point and – as mentioned earlier – an important variable to consider as its size (among other factors) often has a significant impact on the need or motivation of a company to internationalize as well as the time until internationalization.
b. **Regional Markets**
   Regional Markets refers to the expansion of companies in concentric circles into neighboring countries – often with a preference for the psychically and culturally close ones.
c. **Multinational Markets**
   With *Multinational Markets* we describe companies' business activities in a (large) number of different international markets (possibly geographically dispersed and not "regional" to companies' home markets).
d. **Lead Markets**
   Lead Markets is a term rooted in innovation theory and an important concept for evaluating a firm's internationalization decisions and patterns. Researchers Bartlett and Ghoshal describe lead markets as, "markets that provide the stimuli for most global products and processes of a multinational company. Local innovations in such markets become useful elsewhere as the environmental characteristics that stimulated such innovations diffuse to other locations" (Bartlett and Ghoshal 1990). For example, moviemakers outside of the Hollywood lead market are influenced by it both because of Hollywood's ability to export to "lag markets" and because they are tastemakers and innovators. Many auto-safety devices, such as the airbag and the antilock braking system (ABS), have become standard equipment in most countries, overcoming initial resistance after the German market took the lead (Beise 2005). Some countries are specifically strong in specific industries, for example Germany for cars, the United States in technology and so on, and competing there as a foreign company is challenging. For any given industry, several countries could simultaneously represent lead markets (or markets that appear very attractive, leading to a high degree of international competition – from a demand and supply side). The decision to

enter lead markets (or not) is a very significant one within a company's internationalization strategy and the answer usually has wide-ranging implications and needs a very diligent preparation. It has been established that, "innovations that have been successful with local users in lead markets have a higher potential of becoming adopted world-wide than any other design preferred in other countries" (Beise 2004). Thus, all companies that aspire to innovate will at some point need to make a decision if and when to internationalize. Even if they decide not to, but rather choose to remain in "lag markets," they will still likely be influenced by the trends and signals from lead markets.

For our analysis, we will take *Lead Markets* as a reference point to describe our companies' expansion behaviors, especially as our research objective was to better understand how small start-ups from transition economies could manage to grow and internationalize to eventually be able to compete in lead markets with other world-class companies. Nevertheless, we are aware that lead markets are not necessarily the most attractive markets or where the highest profits are possible.

International expansion approaches – a closer look

As Figure I.4.2 shows, the firms evolved in a number of permutations through this framework, which we will discuss in more detail in the next sections.

It is important to note that there is no "one best way" or "recipe" for successful internationalization. Rather, firms grew in their own ways, benefiting from unique, context-specific approaches. One should bear in mind that often entrepreneurs could not foresee the challenges that were about to hit them (or even opportunities that opened up), but their ability to react creatively allowed them to succeed, along with other factors like accepting personal risk and sacrifice. Consequently, we do not claim the entrepreneurs were purely strategizing behind those approaches and neither are we normative here, which means we are not prescribing certain sequences for specific company types or otherwise. We simply focus on describing what we have seen, share insights from those observations, as well as present some important aspects and dimensions to the interested reader or to entrepreneurs who might need to make decisions regarding a firm's international growth strategy.

The analysis among our case companies has identified five major international expansion patterns and, while some appear to be unique to a single category, we mainly see equifinality for each different type in expanding globally. Theoretically, any firm could apply any of the approaches (or adaptations thereof) that we describe below. Nevertheless, based on our sample, we found certain correlations between expansion approaches and categories and we will shed some light on the possible underlying logic and reasons for those. Thus, an interesting perspective is also how the same expansion path

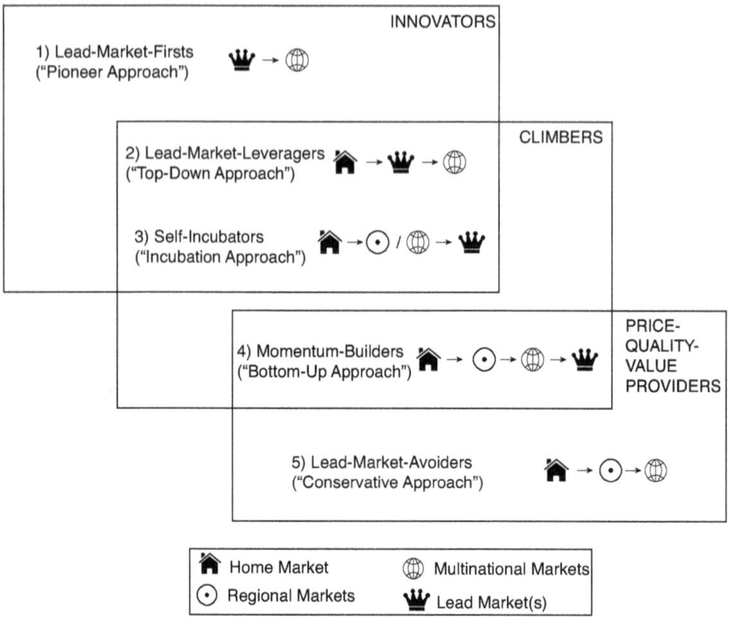

Figure I.4.2 Main international expansion patterns
Source: Authors' own creation.

can have very different implications depending on the type of company (*Innovator*, *Climber* or *PQVP*) – and pose different challenges.

1. Lead-Market-Firsts *("Pioneer Approach")*

Lead-Market-Firsts are companies that start their ventures' activities directly in a foreign lead market, that is, not developing any business in their home market first. We have found this approach solely in the *Innovator*'s category.

This approach is very rare as it is very risky and highly ambitious. It takes considerable confidence from a founder or founding team to make such a "stage entrance," especially as *liability of newness* will weigh even heavier in such highly competitive lead markets. Neither has the company any references to show, nor can they be sure that they are able to deliver at such standards without any prior experience in other markets. Despite those challenges, this approach also has its potential advantages: if a founder is designing and developing a product directly for a lead market and its specific requirements, it allows for an almost "pure" focus and customization, rather than requiring an upgrade to a value proposition that was originally developed for other (less competitive) markets. If the company is able to pull it

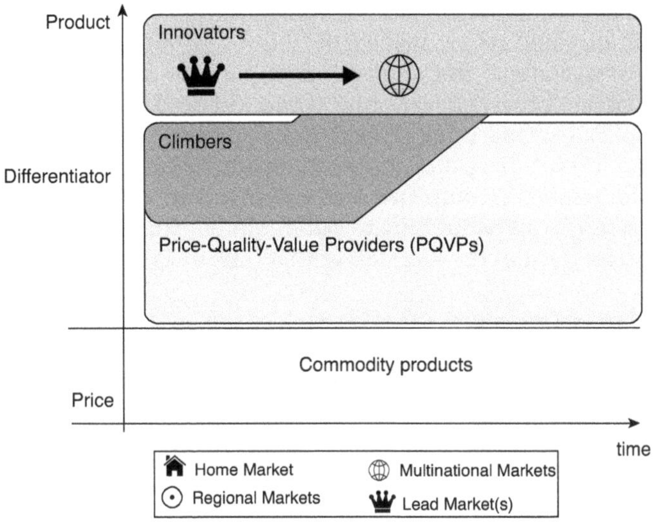

Figure I.4.3 International expansion pattern of lead-market-firsts
Source: Authors' own creation.

off, it can quickly gain traction. Usually, lead markets are of considerable size and allow firms to take advantage of that. Once they have proven themselves in such conditions, they can leverage their success and experience to drive business forward into other foreign markets by benefiting from increased levels of credibility.

One company among our cases who followed this "Pioneer Approach" was ***ACE enterprise*** from Slovakia. The founder, Alexander Cimbaľák, and his co-founder had eventually decided to directly target prospective clients in the German and US lead markets with their product and they used the input and requests from potential customers in their product development processes before starting to sell it. Despite a challenging start, they managed to eventually engage with influential partners who helped them to get into larger accounts and built a strong track record and customer reference list.

> The second option, and also the most risky and costly one, was to launch the product first abroad instead of starting in Slovakia. Alex felt Germany and the United States would be the most suitable foreign markets due to the high penetration of SAP enterprise software in use at major companies. Alex estimated that Germany and the United States made up about 15% and 25% of the US$5.6 billion SCM (supply-chain management) enterprise software market respectively.
>
> *Source*: CASE 1: ACE enterprise Slovakia: "Drawing out" the Future; p. 115

In order to be able to pursue such an approach, new ventures must have or aim to quickly build strong managerial and organizational capabilities. As this usually takes time, the importance of partners and other supporting sources from one's ecosystem are critical and will need to be leveraged to the fullest extent. A strong value proposition is a must-have requirement and prerequisite to even have a chance to compete. Considering the high risks and need for resources, companies attempting this approach would be likely to secure venture capital funding to pull it off, but this was not a very realistic option for most of the founders at that time in CEE markets.

2. Lead-Market-Leveragers *("Top-Down Approach")*

Lead-Market-Leveragers are companies that develop business first in their home markets but then jump directly into international lead markets before expanding into other multinational markets (possibly including further regional markets with reference to their companies' home markets). This strategy is shared by *Innovators* as well as by *Climbers*.

The general logic behind such an approach is to enter an international lead market as soon as a company has sufficiently "proven" its value proposition in its home market and feels equipped to compete for additional business "at the top." Once there, it executes a "top-down" international growth strategy – that is, using its positioning in the lead market to build credibility

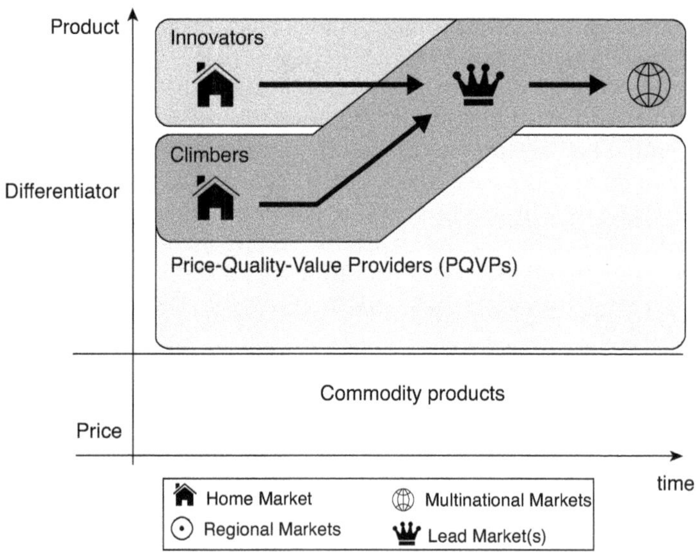

Figure I.4.4 International expansion patterns of lead-market-leveragers
Source: Authors' own creation.

to help enter (multiple) other foreign markets. As mentioned before, *"innovations that have been successful with local users in lead markets have a higher potential of becoming adopted world-wide"* (Beise 2004), thus, this "tailwind-effect" helps to drive a company's product and/or service offering into other international markets. The timing of launching the internationalization into other multinational markets depends on a variety of factors. If a company enjoys healthy enough margins and dynamics in a lead market, a focus might first be put on exploiting it before diverting attention by entering other, possibly less attractive, foreign markets. However, depending on the competitive situation, it might also be important to quickly internationalize into other markets.

The difference between *Innovators* and *Climbers* in the application of this strategy is that *Climbers* – aside from entering another geographic (lead) market – might very likely also need to "upgrade" their value propositions in order to be able to compete with a cutting-edge product (and/or service) at levels they have never served before. Opposite, *Innovators* already have a value proposition for their home market that will allow them to compete at the top-level internationally. Thus, while the timing for the same approach might be different between the two categories (*Innovators* are faster), they share a strong orientation toward international lead market(s) early on.

An example of an ***Innovator*** pursuing this path is ***Modesat Communications*** (Estonia) which developed cutting-edge software solutions for modems in the mobile backhaul market, which is part of telecommunication infrastructure. Their innovative product was technologically capable to compete with international players hundreds of times bigger than they were, allowing them to raise money not only from government funds, but also from an investment company that had been established by the four founding engineers of Skype. Soon after founding, they internationalized; aside from their headquarters in Tallin, Estonia they established offices in California, as well as Tel Aviv.

Source: CASE 10: Modesat Communications OÜ: Riding a Big Wave With a Small Boat; p. 269

An impressive example of a ***Climber*** who mastered this very difficult approach is ***LINET***. Based out of the Czech Republic, it was started as a manufacturer of semi-finished iron pieces before the founder started to focus on high-quality hospital beds and directly targeted the German market, which was the lead market in that industry at the time. The company built its footprint there (with the help of a partner), grew internationally and eventually became the fourth-largest hospital bed producer in the world, known for innovative designs.

Source: CASE 8: LINET: To Be an Object of Desire, Not of Choice; p. 235

For companies to be able to make this direct jump, they had to build significant credibility within a very short time. ***LINET*** did that through a strategic alliance (that included also providing LINET shares to the German partner), while ***Modesat Communications*** – as mentioned before – chose to hire two very high-profile industry veterans for the senior management team and further members for their advisory board, who would help the company to benefit from the reputational spillover and also to have access to important people and companies through their networks. At the same time, the company's founder and management team as well as employees could benefit and learn from the professional management style and systems brought on board by the experienced executives. Also, technology-related IP played an important role as it would allow for an exit through a strategic sale that was less dependent on the revenues the firm made, thus lowering the barriers for external firms to make investments.

3. Self-Incubators *("Incubator-Approach")*

Self-Incubators are firms that started in their home markets and then "incubated themselves" by either entering a regional foreign market or a few selected multinational markets first before jumping into lead markets. Many companies in the *Climber* category followed the *"Incubator-Approach."* However, it is not untypical for *Innovators* to take this path as well.

The *Incubator-Approach* has several interesting aspects and consists of two sub-patterns. The general logic for both of them is that a direct jump into a

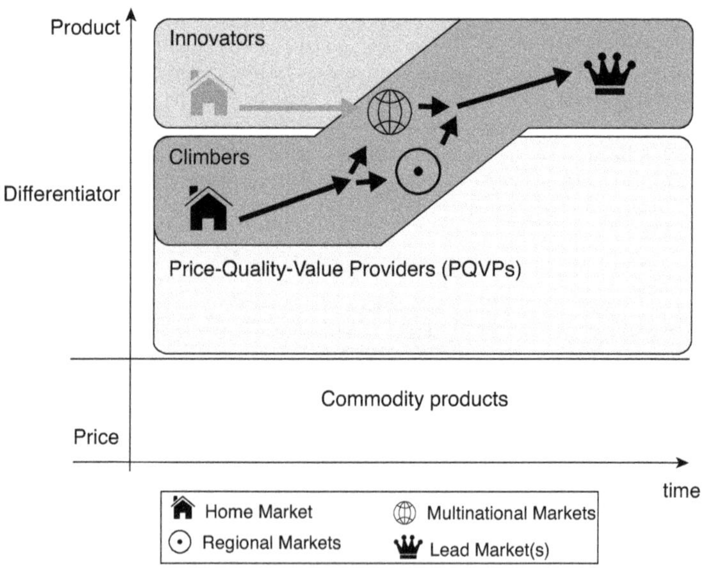

Figure I.4.5 International expansion patterns of self-incubators
Source: Authors' own creation.

lead market is too difficult (or for other reasons not feasible/attractive) and thus a company develops its business first in other (less competitive) international markets which can then be used as a "springboard" to a lead market at a later stage.

Such an approach allows a venture to first test itself in foreign contexts, prove the firm's internationalization potential and ability, and offer learning and improvement opportunities on the way to make the company more competitive. Aside from building managerial and organizational capabilities, a company also has the opportunity, and requirement, to build credibility and a strong brand – all success factors for competing "at the top."

The two sub-patterns differentiate in a way that one path leads through the use of regional markets as incubation grounds, and the other one through multinational markets that are beyond the regional cluster or physically close. While the choice could depend on the risk profile of the founder or management team (regional market path = more conservative), the decision of which markets to enter also depends on other factors such as new opportunities, customer presence, product fit and market potential, among others.

Some companies have only entered one or a few foreign markets before jumping into a lead market, while others have entered many and kept the lead market entry for a later phase. As mentioned above, several factors (organizational as well as market-related ones) play into this decision.

One example of a ***Climber*** who followed the regional-market-incubation path is ***Fx3x*** from Macedonia. While their entrepreneurial dream had always been to do visual effects and animations for Hollywood movies, which – without a doubt – is the global lead market in that industry, they first had to build up experience, resources, contacts and references in their home and regional markets before they eventually attempted (and succeeded) at getting a foot into the door of Hollywood studios.

Source: CASE 5: Fx3x: Star Performance without a Star Attitude; p. 179

An *Innovator* who followed the route through multinational markets is ***Laser Diagnostic Instruments (LDI)*** from Estonia. The company had expanded its technology to new industries such as law enforcement and health, creating three joint ventures with partners in the Netherlands, Sweden and Canada and then four spin-off companies in the United States, Canada and Russia.

Source: CASE 7: Estonia's Laser Diagnostic Instruments (LDI) AS: Beaming Towards Growth; p. 210

There is a very interesting behavior that we have seen among a number of firms that we call, "**second-layer incubation**." This term applies when firms not only "incubate" themselves from a geographical point of view, but also from a competitive point of view. While one might assume that "cutting-edge" products will always be applied to top-level segments (nationally or internationally), this is actually not true. We have seen companies that used highly innovative products in less demanding market segments or niches in order to add another "layer of incubation" before taking a step toward more competitive market segments or lead markets. However, there is a correlation between cutting-edge products and such a top-level focus as well as between products that emphasize a good price–quality ratio with less innovation-focused segments.

Let us first approach this logic from a country level: fragmented markets such as Western, Central or Eastern Europe provide new ventures in initial "natural protection" as every company needs to cross borders in order to compete in another country with different laws, regulations, approaches, languages and so on. This is very different in a single market like the United States where start-ups compete nearly immediately with everyone that has set foot in their market. While limited international competition can be an advantage for founding a company, it naturally becomes a disadvantage for rapid scaling. Nevertheless, such protective conditions are more forgiving and companies can more easily develop despite imperfect start-up conditions, whether related to the product, business model or available resources.

The same logic can be applied at the market-segment-level. If a company is initially and consciously targeting market segments that are less competitive and less demanding, or small niche markets that are not in the main focus of large competitors, it is easier and more affordable to be unique and top-of-mind.

Considering many of the difficult issues, such as that people had to learn new roles, that certain capabilities were missing (or only in short supply), that mental models were very different and difficult to change, that often a sound understanding of current or new competitive dynamics was missing or not easy to develop, and that there was a need for new relationships with customers and suppliers to be built, this approach allowed companies to "incubate themselves," giving them time to learn from mistakes and tackle challenges. For example, firms have overcome a lack of good people by hiring over time and by developing and training existing employees. A lack of resources could be overcome by reinvesting profits. Likewise, this available time could help companies learn to effectively organize their companies, refining routines over time, improving production output with quality standards, experimenting with the business model and building clients and credibility slowly.

In summary, entrepreneurs might decide to focus in less competitive markets and market segments first to protect themselves and develop their skills.

One company in our sample that applied such an approach was ***Avangate/GeCAD*** from Romania with their e-commerce technology. The company had developed an innovative software solution. The founding team was experienced and had even succeeded with a trade sale of their prior venture to a foreign acquirer. After establishing business in their Romanian home market, the company needed to decide on their geographic expansion as well as their competitive segments. Instead of directly targeting the US market, which was the lead market and most competitive globally for this business, they first went to Russia and India (geographical incubation) and focused on a less competitive niche that was paid little attention to by larger corporations (competitive incubation). Only later did they try to forge ahead into higher margin segments as well as into increasingly more international markets and also the US lead market after further improving their value proposition and strengthening their organizational capabilities and profile.

Source: CASE 3: Avangate: Preparing the Transatlantic Jump; p. 147

4. Momentum-Builders *("Bottom-Up Approach")*

Momentum-Builders are companies that follow a *Bottom-Up Approach*, focusing first on building business in their home market, then expanding into regional markets (often with a preference for physically close ones), from there into other multinational markets, and only then attempt to

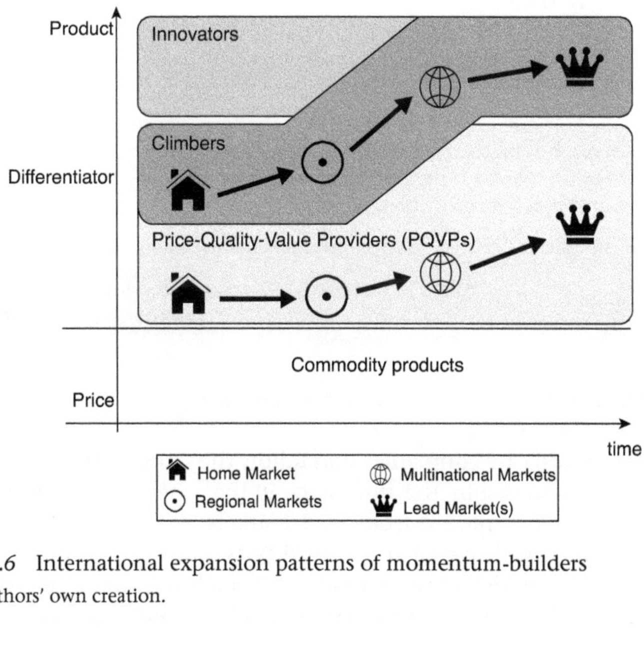

Figure I.4.6 International expansion patterns of momentum-builders
Source: Authors' own creation.

enter global lead markets. Thus, they are building up "momentum" before entering the most competitive markets. This strategy was mainly applied by *Climbers* and *Price-Quality-Value Providers (PQVPs)*, though with different underlying dynamics.

The *Bottom-Up Approach* – offering companies important "market stepping stones" in their ongoing development to build international competitiveness – is the most common one that we found among our sample companies.

The main difference between *Climbers* and *Price-Quality-Value Providers* is the speed at which those steps are accomplished as well as the extent of each phase with regard to the number of countries entered before the next stage is assumed. For *PQVPs*, this internationalization approach often resembled a pattern of expanding in concentric circles while some *Climbers*, on their way up, seemed to pick foreign markets not only in view of the market potential itself, but also from a perspective of how well this market could serve as a springboard to other important key markets. While the former appears to have been more opportunity-driven, the latter seems to have given stronger emphasis to strategic aspects of those markets for the company's further development and international growth. Many PQVPs – despite the significant importance of price as part of their value proposition – were innovation-focused and often aimed to move toward more differentiation in order to remain competitive. However, some retained emphasis on quality at affordable prices, from the beginning to today, in order to succeed in many international markets.

Exemplary for the latter case is the quote from Boris Beylin, CEO of ***Big Filter***:

"In my opinion, if one cannot manufacture products in accordance with international standards, it is better not to take up manufacturing such products at all. I did not see any reason for inventing anything radically new, so we decided to copy the models of filters that already existed abroad."

Today, the company is exporting their products to customers on all continents.

Source: CASE 4: Big Filter: Russian Filters in the International Market; p. 155

5. Lead-Market-Avoiders *("Conservative Approach")*

Lead-Market-Avoiders are companies that follow the same expansion approach as *Momentum-Builders*, but the difference is that they have either made a conscious decision to refrain from lead markets or they might have been there and decided to leave them. A third possibility is of course that they have simply not entered a lead market yet (something that might or might not happen in the future). We have seen this pattern only among *Price-Quality-Value Providers (PQVPs)*.

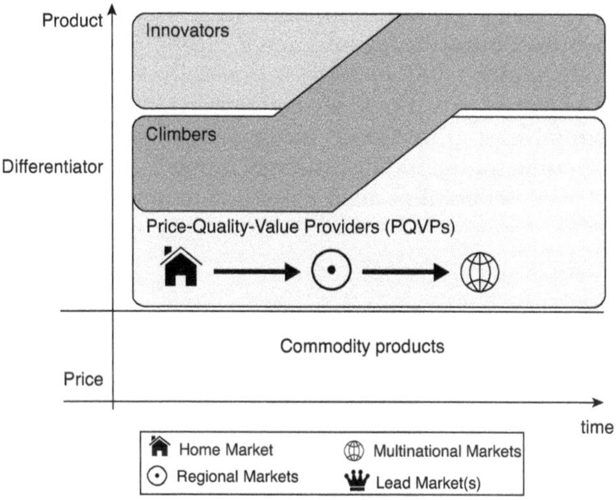

Figure I.4.7 International expansion pattern of lead-market-avoiders
Source: Authors' own creation.

Of course, *Innovators* and *Climbers* also have the option to avoid lead markets and rather build a "local/regional empire" in one or more markets, but at least the companies in our sample that fall into those categories have all entered international lead markets. In any case, even if one does not enter lead markets – by the very nature of the definition of this term – developments there will very likely affect also other foreign markets after a certain time lag. So, in a continuously globalizing world, the likelihood of escaping their influence is small and decreasing.

An example of a company that moved out of a lead market and decided to not compete there in the future – in that case Germany – is ***Masterplast*** from Hungary. The company's reasoning for that decision despite a great "theoretical fit" of their value proposition was:

> "The combination of the biggest economy and one of the most environmentally conscious nations of Europe had a lot of potential. It was very promising, but one thing was too different: it was not a developing country. In Germany, business was going on for 60 years, with decades of continuous business and personal connections. A Hungarian-based company could hardly get into this market where quality and safety (in a business continuation) were as important as good prices. These factors existed long before ***Masterplast*** tried to put their feet on the German market. Because the key elements of the business model were not present, the business model couldn't be successful no matter how big the potential market was."
>
> *Source*: CASE 9: The Masterplast Story: Constructing an Entrepreneurial Success Story; p. 253

If companies realize certain limitations with regard to business model transferability, managerial or organizational capabilities, lack of credibility, resources and partners, and so forth – especially with regard to highly competitive lead markets – it is surely better to avoid and not even attempt to enter them (at least at that point in time). Entrepreneurs can choose to extend the "momentum-building" through other markets and re-evaluate the situation at a later point or make a decision to not consider one or more lead markets.

Summary

First, firms tended to start by either differentiating themselves by product or by price, either offering **cutting-edge products and services** or **price-quality-value offerings.** Furthermore, companies' products and strategies evolved over time as they grew and entered new markets. Some started on the highly differentiated, innovative product side (**Innovators**), some focused on providing high-quality products and services at attractive price levels compared to international standards **(Price-Quality-Value Providers)** and some started as PQVPs and transformed into Innovators (**Climbers**).

Second, firms deployed different expansion patterns. We identified **five different internationalization approaches** of which some are unique to a category, while others are shared by two company types. To build our framework, we took *lead markets* as a reference point and looked at the approach and speed until reaching them. The approaches are: *Lead-Market-First* (Innovator); *Lead-Market-Leveragers* and *Self-Incubators* (both applied by Innovators as well as Climbers); *Momentum-Builders* (Climbers and PQVPs); and *Lead-Market Avoiders* (only PQVPs).

Third, a number of different factors influence the choice of such an approach. Some of the most influential ones are external market conditions (market potential versus competitive pressure), a founder's risk profile, and a company's product type, organizational resources and capabilities. *Innovators* tended to have a stronger lead-market focus, manifesting itself through higher speed until entering them in combination with a more direct approach. Aside from entering new markets, *Climbers* had to additionally improve their value proposition in order to be able to compete at industry frontiers, while *Price-Quality-Value Providers* took more time (longer "incubation phases") or – in some cases – refrained from those markets altogether (or have not yet attempted to enter them).

Aside from a geographic "incubation approach," companies also employed different **market-positioning** techniques. Some started first in **less competitive segments or niches**, which offered many benefits, such as the ability to test and improve products and the opportunity to develop skills before moving into **top-level segments**, while a few others aimed directly at them.

For *Innovators* with a quick and direct approach to international markets in general and lead markets specifically, the founder and his/her profile and credibility was of enormous importance to provide a reference to the market and ecosystem, as well as being a visionary entrepreneur and leader to their own employees. Also, external stakeholders and partners played an important role in providing credibility enhancement and international scaling opportunities.

5
From Lag Markets to Lead Markets

In late February 2013, Kristijan Danilovski, co-founder of Fx3x, a visual effects company, sat with its team watching the Academy Awards ceremony. Three of the movies they had worked on in the last year were nominated for Oscars. The night ended well, with Fx3x winning an Oscar for visual effects for their work on the movie The Aviator. *While the Fx3x team, especially the artists whose names appeared on the credits, celebrated their achievement, Kristijan already began thinking about what was next for Fx3x.*

Source: CASE 5: Fx3x: Star Performance without a Star Attitude; p. 179

In Slavic folklore, the Firebird is a highly coveted magical bird with feathers that glow brightly. The bird symbolizes both a blessing and an omen of doom. The Firebird stories – many versions of which exist in other cultures – follow a classic scheme: a lost, brightly glowing feather is the premonition of a hard journey. The story's hero sets out on a difficult quest to find and capture the live bird. Initially charmed by the wonder of the feather, eventually the hero blames it for his troubles. Along the way, he meets magical helpers and, hopefully, eventually returns from a faraway land with the prize.[1]

In some ways the Firebird tale seems a fitting and interesting analogy for entrepreneurship, maybe even more so in transition economy contexts and quite fitting to the realities of our founders in their early days. Entrepreneurship – after the fall of the Berlin Wall – came like a magical glowing bird from a faraway land into formerly communistic countries in which individual and private business activities were mainly prohibited. The glowing tail feather symbolizes an opportunity and the promise of a brighter future, which initiates a difficult quest to capture the live bird, or – in another sense – to capture and exploit an international opportunity in order to return from the faraway land with the prize. In the case of ***Fx3x***, this prize was not only the Oscar prize, but having become an international player in the top league of one's industry.

After exploring the trajectories of the firms featured in this book, it becomes clear that their achievements are truly remarkable. As individuals, many founders started *tacking* toward opportunity under very challenging circumstances and, once they were on to a viable opportunity, grew their firms creating diverse paths. Eventually they jumped from their disadvantaged positions into the international arena to finally enter the top category of international firms. At the same time, as in the Firebird tale, their stories were rife with trouble and sacrifice; the entrepreneurs went through significant personal and professional ups and downs, with some firms going out of business.

Chapter 4 has outlined the trajectories created by these successful entrepreneurs, but it is not always easy to trace the direct lineage between the early days and the successes seen today. As Alex Mincu, author of the ***Atlantic Grupa*** case noted,

> *"Yes, it looks like the entrepreneur built his business with a logic and an array of smart moves, but it is hard to say if this was a pure planned creation or a series of quick and correct gut decisions. It is most probably a mix of these and tons of talent and ambition doubled by a solid head start".*

We once again find strong traces of *tacking entrepreneurship* in such developments. Even in the absence of a long-range strategy – especially early on and during phases of high uncertainty – we can recognize certain tactics that have helped companies to move step by step from lag markets to international lead markets. However, companies were driven by different factors that were dominant to varying degrees in their successful international growth. There was no winning formula. Thus we adhere to the wise words of Aristotle who said: *"It is the mark of an instructed mind to rest satisfied with that degree of precision which the nature of the subject admits, and not to seek exactness where only an approximation of the truth is possible."* Consequently, in the subsequent sections we are not presenting "success recipes," but rather highlighting similar approaches, logics and tactics that were important to many young firms.

We analyze and provide many examples of how these firms benefited from strong and adaptable leadership and often built remarkable strength in their home bases before jumping abroad. We review how their international expansion was facilitated by competitive and industry analysis to better understand those markets and customer needs. We also show how, in many cases, the internationalization was done in good company through selected partnerships and alliances that put the firm on the right track from the beginning. We further illustrate tactics that made the firms adaptable to capture such international opportunities. Finally, we conclude by summarizing the firms' overall trajectories.

Strong at home – internally and in the home market

Understanding how to grow a firm is not obvious. Indeed, firm growth is a rich and difficult-to-grasp phenomenon. Entrepreneurs face multiple decision points in a relatively short period – and many times simultaneously – that may signify either the firm's turning point to achieve the next level, or the beginning of a decline that may kill the venture. Even more complex to achieve is a pan-European or global expansion.

In previous chapters, we have seen how the *tacking* period that many entrepreneurs went through, and the efforts to overcome the negative country-of-origin effect, made the firms portrayed in this book a special crop. Indeed, entrepreneurs had the strength to go several times through the loop of trial, learning and adaptation before they found the path that made them successful entrepreneurs.

Graphisoft provides two such examples, in their endeavors to (a) work with Apple and (b) to enter the US market:

> ***Graphisoft*** submitted a number of business proposals to Apple to become its exclusive distributor in Hungary, the third of which was accepted.
>
> Over the span of about ten years, a number of unsuccessful attempts were made to enter the US market. These included attempted entry via ***Graphisoft***'s contacts through its relationship with Apple Computers (for whom ***Graphisoft*** developed architectural software for the Macintosh computer), ***Graphisoft***'s existing Israeli distributor with a presence in the United States, Hungarian emigrants living in the United States, and by partnering with ***Graphisoft***'s distributor in France, Advent. Despite, and as a result of, these failures, Gabor was determined to develop and implement a strategy for ***Graphisoft*** to become a major player in the Architectural, Engineering and Construction (AEC) CAD market in the United States. In 1989, they finally established a subsidiary in the United States, Graphisoft USA.
>
> *Source*: CASE 6: Graphisoft: The Architecture of International Growth; p. 193

Academics and practitioners agree that internationalizing a firm is always a challenging task; doing so from a disadvantaged position forced the entrepreneurs to build even stronger firms and, in some instances, to also create a local ecosystem that could support their expansion.

Strong and adaptable leadership

Traditionally economists have concluded that the main purpose of business was to make money – the more the better – especially if it was possible to maximize short-term profits to deliver a fast return to shareholders. However, it takes an entrepreneur to start a venture and obtain shareholders before that venture has any financial or reporting obligations. Experience shows that entrepreneurs are inspired by something more than wealth accumulation; they are driven to create. Dr. Sergey Babichenko from ***Laser Diagnostic Instruments (LDI)*** reflected:

> *"People in applied research saw an opportunity to use private entrepreneurship as a way to finance and expand their research by offering commercially applicable research-based solutions. Some also hoped to increase their income, but research interests were often stronger and clearer than profit motives."*

Another example from our cases is ***Pipistrel***'s founder, Ivo Boscarol, who had, *"always seen himself as pushing the boundaries to do things better, cheaper, faster than anyone else."*

Though his firm was started in a less-than-encouraging context, Boscarol, and many of the entrepreneurs in our cases, seemed to be not only undeterred, but to draw energy from the extra challenges which their context imposed.

The backgrounds and profiles of the entrepreneurs in our sample were very heterogeneous, but, not surprisingly, there were some common characteristics underlying their behaviors.

First, and one of the most fundamental ones, was their **determination to be focused in the present**. However, this does not mean that entrepreneurs were narrowly focused. Simultaneously they remained alerted to the next best opportunity to "tack" or improve the status quo. They would either continuously enhance the course of their ship or jump ship if they stalled.

Secondly, they were relentlessly in action to **create solutions, maximize value with existing resources in the current context, and to move forward quickly.** Our entrepreneurs were tremendously hungry, and perceptively opportunistic; they didn't worry much about problems, but took risks and kept moving or *tacking* forward when they encountered challenges. *Grit* is the term psychologist Angela Duckworth uses for the ability to keep one's focus on long-term goals despite setbacks (Duckworth 2007). The interesting aspect is that for our entrepreneurs "the long-term goal" was very likely less defined as a strategic path of the current venture, but more as an overarching vision of entrepreneurial activity and value creation. And while they might not have been clear on the final destination, they were very aware that they would only be able to keep going if they delivered top-notch quality, continuously improved, and in many cases went the extra mile doing much more than what could normally be expected.

Thirdly, we observed that entrepreneurs were not shy about **making difficult and unpopular decisions quickly** if they felt that things were not going into the right direction or that the team was not the right fit. In ***Big Filter***, Boris – who had set up a cooperative with eight owners – broke it up quickly when he realized that the founders could not agree on how to use the profits that he wanted to reinvest and the others wanted to spend.

Another such example is ***Cortex/Graphisoft***:

Disagreements regarding the future of the company, as well as the lack of steady earnings, gave rise to tension among the founders and employees of Cortex. A turning point came at about the end of the year, when the Hungarian Ministry of Industry needed an advanced computer-aided design (CAD) model for the Paks Nuclear Power Plant, whose construction was experiencing a three-year delay. Gabor saw a tremendous business opportunity posed by the project's dilemma. The sheer size and reference value, if Cortex were to obtain this contract, was huge. Most colleagues at Cortex, however, saw too much risk and financial exposure in pursuing the project, as they perceived that Cortex did not have the resources or technological know-how to pull it off successfully. Gabor, and one of his partners, Gabor Tari (Tari), felt differently. Both Gabors left Cortex, with the aim of working solely on the Paks Atomic Reactor Project, and founded a new company that they named ***Graphisoft***.

Source: CASE 6: Graphisoft: The Architecture of International Growth; p. 193

Last but not least, **building trust and alignment** played a very important role in order to not lose any possibility for a next tack and to later create credibility and a stable foundation for a business.

Such was the situation of ***Avangate/GeCAD***:

Cristian, an original member of the RAV Antivirus team, approached Radu in 2004 with the idea of setting up an e-payment company to address the growing opportunity of this the segment in Romania. Cristian knew that e-commerce was growing by leaps and bounds globally and this trend would soon touch Romania. Radu and Cristian had a very trusting relationship and after a series of meetings and discussions, Cristian convinced Radu to make an equity investment and become an active participant in the new venture. The first product was to be an innovative e-payment system.

Source: CASE 3: Avangate: Preparing the Transatlantic Jump; p. 147

The above-mentioned characteristics could be seen among all founders, independent of the category of the internationalization paths presented in the previous chapter. However, along one dimension we found a vital difference: the importance of the reputation of the founding individual played a much stronger role among *Innovators* and *Climbers* as compared to *Price-Quality-Value Providers*. For the first two types that were focused more on developing cutting-edge products that could compete at an international level, the founder's knowledge and reputation became an important platform and enabler to position the company in innovative markets and lend it credibility, such as in ***LDI*** or ***Pipistrel***. If there was the feeling that the founder's profile didn't yet provide enough "gravitas," another person would fill this gap.

In the ***Modesat Communications*** case, the founder voluntarily moved into the second rank and brought an external high-profile candidate early on into the CEO position in order to leverage this person's credibility and high-level industry contacts.

Source: CASE 10: Modesat Communications OÜ: Riding a Big Wave with a Small Boat; p. 269

Among *Price-Quality-Value Providers*, the entrepreneurs were driving their ventures as strong as the others, but there was less of a need for them to stand out, take the spotlight, and transfer individual credibility to the company. Rather, they built their brands through high-quality, reliable products at attractive prices.

No matter if competing in the *Price-Quality-Value-Offerings*-category, if preparing firms to *"climb"* or if trying to position themselves in the *Innovator* segment (and – even more importantly – to remain there), founders had to find, recruit and train top talent. Additionally, they had to transform their own and their employees' mind-sets so they were ready to work in a highly competitive context. They also had to embed their own values into the firm's culture.

The same heritage process that happens with an artist and her sculpture or parents with their kids, happens with the entrepreneur and the company's culture. The core values of the founder would be the future DNA and "mental software" of the venture. Thus entrepreneurs tried to instill sound business principles and attitudes, including a commitment to excellence, a comprehensive view of the business world, a long-term approach to value creation, persistence and hard work, among others.

Strong internal base conditions

It is not surprising that all our firms, without exception, had outstanding products and services or a winning price/quality ratio proposition. This was an indirect condition to become selected for this project. A firm cannot successfully compete at a world-class level – one of the selection criteria in this project – and in many cases becoming a reference player in the sector, without having the right value proposition and being able to sustain that over time. Hence the tactics outlined below are not different from the ones followed by other industry leaders. However, this realization helps to strengthen the conviction that **managerial action is essential in spite of the context**, and even more important in transition contexts. Without an obsession for product and service quality, attracting the right partners and building the best equipment and infrastructure, these firms would not be where they are today.

In the previous chapter we already outlined the ability of the studied firms such as ***Big Filter***, ***LINET***, ***Selena***, ***Fx3x*** or ***Masterplast*** to become top quality producers.

> In the words of Boris, ***Big Filter***'s CEO: "I was quite confident that I could produce inexpensive, high-quality fuel filters in Russia that could be exported profitably. From the very beginning, the emphasis was placed on quality at affordable prices. Moreover, the system of customer support was built so that, for example, an export–import manager must answer all customer messages and inquiries within 24 hours. Customers are informed on the order status, all the necessary documents are sent on time with the necessary drawings, certificates, samples and test results. Openness and honesty are mandatory at all stages. Customers choose whether we deliver the products directly or through their distributors."
>
> *Source*: CASE 4: Big Filter: Russian Filters in the International Market; p. 155

Without a doubt, quality was a key variable and as such high on the agendas of our entrepreneurs.

> Also, ***LINET*** followed this approach and positioning in its early days: The aim of the hospital management was to gain the "Western quality," but its cost made it prohibitive for the hospital. ***LINET***'s founder, Mr. Frolík, took advantage of that and offered to the hospital a bed constructed according to the Western model, but at a lower price.
>
> *Source*: CASE 8: LINET: To Be an Object of Desire, Not of Choice; p. 235

Another example of this category is ***Selena*** (Poland, construction materials) which put their focus on product quality (with the aim to move up on this continuum) to achieve higher margins.

> Its mission was: "Advantage through product." It meant that the company was focused on achieving the highest quality in each of its product groups and solutions. This approach helped ***Selena*** to locate its products on premium and upper-premium shelves ensuring a high unit margin by local market standards.
>
> *Source*: CASE 14: Selena Group: Internationalization Through Multilocality; p. 347

The following quote of ***Selena***'s founder also provides a taste of related difficulties, in this case with regard to **ensuring consistency and quality**, and how they tried to solve it:

> The local suppliers very often could not guarantee the same quality of raw materials. It was not the case in Europe, but it was in Turkey and China. This resulted in the implementation of an audit system which helped to select suppliers from different countries and ensure a quality control system of raw materials that enter the plant.
>
> *Source*: CASE 14: Selena Group: Internationalization Through Multilocality; p. 347

Likewise, ***Fx3x* installed the latest infrastructure available**, despite the fact that there were no widely accepted standards for quality applied in the digital media industry:

> ***Fx3x*** introduced the latest digital network infrastructure accompanied with strict procedures for project monitoring as well as the security standards to back up safety of the data. Kristijan was happy to assure that their security was at the highest level during a facility audit by one Hollywood studio.
>
> *Source*: CASE 5: Fx3x: Star Performance without a Star Attitude; p. 179

Another good example was how ***Masterplast*** achieved highly efficient logistics by placing a manufacturing plant in Serbia, **improving their product quality, efficiency** and **gaining greater control**:

> In 2008, ***Masterplast*** launched its first EPS plant in Subotica, Republic of Serbia. As a result of a €2 million investment, the company began production in the new 6500 m^2 plant using a cost-efficient and modern production chain. The plant used 95% less water than previous generation facilities to produce EPS and had a much lower emission of greenhouse gases. EPS waste could be reused up to almost 100% which again contributed to sustainable production.
>
> *Source*: CASE 9: The Masterplast Story: Constructing an Entrepreneurial Success Story; p. 253

In addition to building a strong, innovation-driven culture, ***Pipistrel*** also incentivized their employees to contribute to **continuous improvement measures**:

> Each ***Pipistrel*** employee received €10 for contributing an idea, regardless of whether or not the idea improved some part of the product or process. At the end of each month the best idea received €500 and the best idea at the end of each year received €5,000. This approach resulted in an average of three or so good ideas a month from the 70 employees.
>
> *Source*: CASE 11: Pipistrel: The Freedom of Flight; p. 290

Also, equipment and infrastructure played an important part and we saw strong emphasis on purchasing and upgrading both whenever possible. Though a number of ventures really started out in less-than-optimal places (as described in previous chapters), the founders quickly restored facilities and tried to get high-quality equipment. ***Big Filter*** manufactured its products on imported **foreign production machinery** from Germany in order to achieve high-quality standards.

Local ecosystem

Supporting a local ecosystem is about **strengthening the firm's home-base conditions**. This creates positive externalities for one's own company, an emergent cluster, and even the home region/country, including the improvement of its reputation, job creation and other benefits.

As mentioned in Chapter 3, the activities of ***Fx3x*** had this effect. The firm developed the 3D@E-Schools project in cooperation with a Macedonian-focused USAID program, which provided first-level training in computer animation and visual effects' creation in 27 schools. More than 400 students benefit from the program. The firm built a local talent pool that could possibly help to accommodate future growth while also providing attractive opportunities for graduates of these schools to work on projects for some of the most internationally prestigious studios and movies.

Furthermore, as stated previously, the founder of ***Fx3x*** became the president of the newly formed Macedonian Association of Digital Entertainment (MADE), which was in line with the objectives to build a local cluster and thus improve the home-base context.

Business takes place in an increasingly specialized and interconnected world. Every company is more or less a part of one or more ecosystems and ecosystem-dynamics are important drivers that have the ability to support or detract from an individual company's opportunities, competitiveness and, consequently, chances to succeed. We have seen across the chapters that partners are important building blocks of successful international development. This makes partner ecosystems a critical dimension to be investigated by companies as they expand from home markets to international markets.

Opportunity abroad

Expanding and going abroad becomes a need as the opportunity evolves. An essential success factor in any market enlargement are activities related to one's industry, market segment and ecosystems, including those targeted at customers, suppliers, partners and others. Learning is a crucial element specifically with regard to: (a) the industry/ecosystem (on a national and international level), and (b) the specific target country a company is considering entering.

For all companies it was crucial to deeply understand the industry standards and the "rules of the game" to be able to compete.

Once ***Fx3x***'s founders had decided that it was time to make their original vision of doing visual arts work for the film industry a reality and they thus needed to compete internationally, they visited Los Angeles, the "Mecca" of the film industry, to learn firsthand which services and capabilities they needed to develop and which international standards existed:

In 2003, supported by DeGraf and Frey, ***Fx3x*** CEOs flew to Los Angeles to get more insights into the filmmaking industry. As Hollywood functioned on the basis of personal contacts and recommendations, the two ex-pats arranged for meetings with well-known visual effects studio executives. They got a chance to visit Universal Studios, 20th Century Fox, Pixar and Sony Pictures, all among the market trendsetters. Meeting potential clients was a great push forward for ***Fx3x***, but one meeting was not enough to get a trial job. There was no simple formula to win a contract. Kristijan's team concluded that the negotiations for potential partnering clients had to continue both from the home office and with direct marketing trips overseas.

Source: CASE 5: Fx3x: Star Performance without a Star Attitude; p. 179

Getting exposure to foreign countries, **understanding foreign (competing) products** and how business was done in those markets was a very important component of the learning and preparation experience. International trade shows played a crucial role for many of our entrepreneurs. ***Big Filter***, with its price-quality-value product, used such an approach to learn and to market their company:

The next step was to find clients abroad. One of the largest trade shows in the industry was called Automechanika and was held in Frankfurt, Germany. In 1997, ***Big Filter*** became the first Russian company to present at the trade show. Boris described the experience: "At first I was not very confident in presenting the products and communicating with potential customers and partners due to my low comfort level in English."

Source: CASE 4: Big Filter: Russian Filters in the International Market; p. 155

Another way to accelerate learning and increase the likelihood of success in a foreign market was to "learn from paradigms of interpretation" – for example, learn from and imitate specific companies that are perceived as best-practice companies in foreign markets (Aldrich 1999; Levitt and March 1988). Such a benchmarking and mimicking approach was followed by ***LINET*** with reference to the German partner as German companies were the worldwide reference for hospital beds at that moment in time.

When it came to internationalization itself, there was a pre-entry learning phase and a post-entry learning phase. While the former was typically more fact-based, the second phase allowed access to and the accumulation of more tacit knowledge. We have seen that our entrepreneurs tried to speed up this process of pre-entry learning and make it more relevant through learning from the experience of others, which meant accessing it through partners and network contacts that were established.

After initial exposure to and insights about the international competitive landscape and industry standards, the next step was defining which countries to actually enter. In general, many firms were opportunistic. Going abroad was necessary for developing the firm, and as soon as the team found a possibility, they acted upon it. Later in this process, our firms engaged in **deep analyses of potential target markets.** This usually included visiting some of those markets – sometimes extensively, as in the case of ***Solaris*** (the Polish bus manufacturer):

> Krzysztof Olszewski was aware that successfully entering the overseas markets needed direct investments. The two countries with the biggest population numbers, China and India, were the first choices to consider. China was in the process of building a modern bus industry, inviting partners from Japan and Western Europe (Germany) to support local companies in implementing the newest technologies. He decided to start investigations for India, planning to evaluate the country's demand potential and investment environment. After a number of trips to India and numerous analyses, he was convinced it was not the right place to establish a foreign subsidiary.
>
> *Source*: CASE 15: SOLARIS Bus and Coach: A Bus Tour to Global Markets; p. 372

Very often our case companies found themselves in conditions where there was no real local, regional or even national ecosystem around them and, in order to compete with leading players, they needed to access organizations in the international ecosystem of their industry.

Solaris **tapped into external knowledge and competencies** to strengthen their competitive positioning and stand out as innovative:

> ***Solaris*** employed the best European designer companies to work on the models of new buses. Its buses started to be recognized from the outside thanks to a unique front windscreen design.
>
> *Source*: CASE 15: SOLARIS Bus and Coach: A Bus Tour to Global Markets; p. 372

Also, ***Graphisoft*** found ways to **leverage existing partnerships**, most notably by having become such a close partner to Apple and knowing the company and their products so well that they could utilize Apple's international distribution network. This was a strong competitive advantage for them. However, working with international partners and linking to international ecosystems also brought significant challenges along. Alignment – especially when the partnership needs to be designed for the long-term – is difficult, as the following quote of Sergei Babichenko, ***LDI***'s founder, shows:

> It was important that industry partners could be trusted and would work with ***LDI*** to apply technological know-how. Typically these partners had to be focused on long-term development and not short-term business gains.
>
> *Source*: CASE 7: Estonia's Laser Diagnostic Instruments (LDI) AS: Beaming Towards Growth; p. 210

Adaptable

As illustrated, when our entrepreneurs evaluated international opportunities, many hard facts were taken into consideration. However, what made a difference to some entrepreneurs was not only understanding economic calculations, but also **learning and closely connecting with the local culture** before selling anything. In the words of ***Selena***'s founder K. Domarecki:

> Multilocality means understanding the distinctness of the local market, and drawing conclusions in business terms stemming from this distinctness. In China, the United States, Spain or Russia, a receptacle for drinking tea looks different. Why is the glass different? Because the culture of the country is different. The same happens with foam, silicone or adhesive. Each culture created a distinct construction technology; for example, in the United States, users require a long "open time of adhesive," as they have a technological process which makes it necessary for the adhesive to stay wet for 20 minutes, whereas a Chinese starts working immediately, and needs the adhesive to hold within 20 seconds; the task is the same: slat gluing. Therefore, we should offer a different product to everybody: the basic parameters should be the same, but their modifications should take into consideration regional building tradition, acceptable level of performance and climate conditions. Distinct culture refers also to distinct marketing communication addressed at the mentality of different nations. As a result, foreign companies have to learn that each market is governed by different requirements in terms of the product's parameters, technology, packaging, language or size of the can.
>
> *Source*: CASE 14: Selena Group: Internationalizing Through Multilocality; p. 347

This attitude allowed them to also get into markets that were not mainstream and not attractive for other firms given the level of effort that was necessary to compete there.

> When he decided to enter the Turkish market, he did not go to Istanbul, as commercial expeditions of multinationals usually did, but to a small town in the north of the country. What he found there was pure Islam with no trace of Western Europeans. He spent a few days with the local inhabitants in order to understand them, and not only for the purpose of doing business. On a Sunday afternoon, he

went to a mosque and spent four hours watching how Turkish Muslim families behaved. After a couple of days, a few men approached him and started a conversation about business.

Source: CASE 14: Selena Group: Internationalizing Through Multilocality; p. 347

Another approach that a number of companies applied to "bridge cultures" and to get in-depth insights into foreign markets while at the same time having a "working interface" to their own culture and company was to get in touch and **work with people from one's own country who have lived for many years in the foreign target market**.

Aside from the need to understand the target market's culture and to be up to date with one's industry developments, it became obvious how important deep local market knowledge was in order to adapt one's value proposition accordingly. To keep expanding successfully, often even the product needed to be adapted as part of a country-specific entry strategy. For instance, ***Graphisoft*** redesigned its country-entry strategy for Japan, increasing their product features – operating system compatibility – and even the size of the target companies:

Graphisoft's executives decided to enter Japan with ***Graphisoft*** veteran Imre Pakozdi, determined to make Japan a success. Japan was not only a large market, but also fit perfectly with ***Graphisoft***'s ability to adapt to the unique requirements of the local market. Strategically, ***Graphisoft*** did a number of things differently in Japan than they had done in other countries. The first was to offer both versions of ArchiCAD – Macintosh and Windows – simultaneously to distributors. The second was to address not only small and medium-sized firms, ***Graphisoft***'s traditional market, but also the big companies.

Source: CASE 6: Graphisoft: The Architecture of International Growth; p. 193

Similarly, ***Solaris*** accepted an invitation from Dubai to produce its product with an extremely high degree of necessary adaptation to new geographic conditions:

Due to the natural environment in Dubai (heat up to 60 degrees Celsius, dust, salty climate), poor quality gasoline used and cultural regimes (front family compartment for women with children and the rear one for the men is a must), buses are required to be designed and equipped differently from the ones for European markets.

Source: CASE 15: SOLARIS Bus and Coach; p. 372

This full contract from Dubai was split and awarded to three different producers by the authorities. However, after some time the two other producers from other countries eventually broke away from the contract, even willingly paying high fines in order to get out. ***Solaris,*** however, was able to deliver.

This way of doing business stemmed from the firm belief in having the client at the center of their business. For Domarecki, the CEO, it was important to **instill a strong culture of customer-centricity** within all of his employees as described by one:

> Domarecki was a very strong leader, personally involved in developing his multilocal company globally. He had an open approach to understanding human thinking, which helped create a culture of listening to the customers. It was common practice that product managers and sales representatives did not only analyze numbers from reports, but also went to construction sites to talk to the workers.
>
> *Source*: CASE 14: Selena Group: Internationalizing Through Multilocality; p. 347

Also, ***Masterplast*** offers a great example of where this culture of customer-centricity was extended to all levels of the company in order to gain a competitive advantage and to increase revenue while better serving existing and new customer segments:

> When it came to the company's success, one needed to understand the past characteristics of the Hungarian construction materials market. On the ruins of the former yard network there was a nonflexible logistic and supply system. Service was available only for large customers and the household market had to wait for the goods they needed. Dávid and Balázs realized this and eventually they found a solution that would give a real service to their future customers. The next step was their special delivery system: they employed qualified and reliable truck drivers who built very good relationships with the customers. They were two-in-one: sales personnel and truck driver as well. The drivers treated the owners of the yard in a way the owners were not used to: they always asked where to unload, asked for any other special needs and recommended products. This system worked really well as it was very new to the market and was based on trust; there was almost no shift in the workforce during these years. They were also willing to sell low quantities for small customers and offered next-day delivery. This way the yards didn't have to stock any goods – ***Masterplast*** provided everything for them when they needed it. This was a huge financial help to the yard owners, which was very much appreciated.
>
> *Source*: CASE 9: The Masterplast Story; p. 253

In certain cases, where the product category allowed for it, we saw entrepreneurs apply "**lean approaches**" including pitching unfinished products to potential partners and clients for testing their hypothesis. One example is the software company ***ACE enterprise Slovakia***. During their development stage, the founders Alex and Vlado traveled to a number of potential customers and partners in Germany to explain the idea behind the software:

> We literally went door to door, and got turned away quite a bit. However, we did manage to speak with a few potential customers and we received some positive responses and learned what people wanted and what they didn't. We not only gained some valuable information for fine-tuning the product, but also the first few preliminary contracts. We are probably one of the few companies that sold its product before it had been finished!
>
> *Source*: CASE 1: ACE enterprise Slovakia: "Drawing out" the Future; p. 115

Also, ***Graphisoft*** worked with pre-finished products quite successfully:

> Through a continuing series of programming trial and error, endless customer demonstrations, visiting trade shows, architect inputs and personnel changes, ArchiCAD was beginning to develop a customer following and loyalty. One of the very first customers, an architect in Bordeaux, France, Mr. M. Hulak, liked Version 3.1 so much that he refused to return the program, despite some minor bugs, because he was already using it to design real plans, and he was afraid that his work would stop.
>
> *Source*: CASE 6: Graphisoft: The Architecture of International Growth; p. 193

Price adaptations or **payment conditions** were also part of the necessary "tool kit" to conquer foreign markets.

> ***Graphisoft***'s US experience is a great example, even if this created new challenges:
>
> In the United States pricing was an issue for ***Graphisoft***. The average US$4,000 price of an ArchiCAD software package in Europe was 20 to 30% higher than in the United States. Customers in Europe accepted this price. The market in the United States demanded a lower price. This invited the potential problem of "grey imports," from the United States to Europe. To alleviate this pricing problem, ***Graphisoft*** offered what they perceived as a novel solution – "Pay per Use" (PPU). This was a method whereby a customer did not have to pay the full amount of the software package, but he only pays for the amount of time that he actually uses the program.
>
> *Source*: CASE 6: Graphisoft: The Architecture of International Growth; p. 193

Big Filter even took considerable risks in order to lower entry barriers and enable business to happen between them and international partners.

When shipping to new partners, ***Big Filter*** sometimes requested advance payment, but often took risks and made the delivery without it. Natalia commented, "We've never lost when we've decided to take a risk and send filters to a customer even without a sound formal contract and preliminary payment. If you want to conquer a market, you need to take some risks."

Source: CASE 4: Big Filter: Russian Filters in the International Market; p. 155

Looking across our cases, we have seen our entrepreneurs steadily working on a number of different levels – sometimes sequentially, sometimes simultaneously – and in different combinations in order to adapt to different cultures, clients and client conditions. This turns out to be a non-negotiable aspect for these firms that have developed their companies from humble beginnings into high performers or even innovators on an international stage.

Transitioning from tacking entrepreneurship to opportunity entrepreneurship

This book celebrates entrepreneurship in challenging contexts by shedding light on tactics and trajectories that have allowed firms to excel internationally. In previous chapters we described the realities of the early and challenging transition economy context, before introducing the concept of "tacking entrepreneurship" in response to dealing with high levels of uncertainty. The following quote of American writer Ray Bradbury nicely captures the mental attitude of our entrepreneurs when they started out:

> "The best scientist is open to experience and begins with romance – the idea that anything is possible". (Ray Bradbury, in the *Los Angeles Times*, 1976)

These companies went from "dusty-street-boys-pushing-boxes" status to supplying a whole region with some of the strongest international FMCG brands and being one of the largest regional food and food supplement producers and distributors, aside from running a leading private pharmacy chain; from flying self-improved motorized hang gliders secretly at night in prohibited areas to becoming an international light airplane producer who won three NASA Challenges; from producing semi-finished iron products in an old barn to one of the world's largest and most innovative hospital bed producers.

After what in some cases might look like a "random walk" in our entrepreneurs' early days and the subsequent struggle to master a race on a bumpy road, which meant competing with other international contenders on an unleveled playing field, we have seen a gradual shift away from *tacking entrepreneurship* to *effectuation approaches* and toward a stronger emphasis on *opportunity entrepreneurship* and strategy making. On the one hand, the entrepreneur becomes familiar with the macro environment, different industry drivers and the market's rules while transforming and maturing his start-up into a "real business." At the same time, the context for developing the entrepreneurial activity also changes and matures. Hence the entrepreneur starts crafting and pursuing opportunities for growth.

Although it may look like this transition is a logical one, and must be well documented for future entrepreneurs, nothing is further for the truth. Despite having results of many analyses conducted and the availability of a wealth of frameworks being presented in the business literature, a large share of uncertainty often remained, putting pressure on the founder's decisions as they would determine the future survival and success of the firm. The following quote from ***Modesat Communications'*** founder illustrates the frustration and difficulties of defining an international business model when competing as a young company with a cutting-edge product on a global level:

> "We've all read the business books about different business models, but a lot of the ideas seem too general and do not reflect the specific context of this business field, such as roles in the value chain, intellectual property issues, sector-specific cooperation partner options, length of development cycles and several other aspects."
>
> *Source*: CASE 10: Modesat Communications OÜ: Riding a Big Wave with a Small Boat; p. 269

As the case describes, Phil felt that academic frameworks such as Porter's positioning models, while good for discussing existing markets, were not suitable for understanding how value-chain options could be created within new global niche markets. Phil was certain that ***Modesat Communications*** had continuously innovated their software offerings but wondered whether their three main types of business activities were the best way to deliver solutions to global customers while generating positive cash flow and growth. ***Modesat Communications***'s challenge was figuring out where to focus in order to propel the company to dynamic growth or become a strategic player that would be potentially interesting for larger acquirers.

A final reflection

We have called our firms ***Entrepreneurial Icebreakers***. In nautical terms, for a ship to be considered an icebreaker it requires three traits most normal ships lack: a strengthened hull (i.e., body of a ship), an ice-clearing shape, and the power to push through sea ice. Transferring this analogy to companies, we can very well summarize that firms who start in difficult contexts and want to scale internationally and become world-class players need to: (a) strengthen their organizational body and value propositions; (b) shape the company's business model and clear itself as much as possible from a negative country-of-origin effect; and (c) be resilient and willing to work extremely hard to "push through" the difficulties and challenges that they will encounter along the way.

Also, looking across our cases, the following quote from Thomas W. Higginson can nearly stand as a conclusion that *"the most fertile soil does not necessarily produce the most abundant harvest. It is the use we make of our faculties which renders them valuable."* In fact, we do believe that especially those companies that managed to grow up and be successful in such conditions might be the best-skilled ones to take advantage of the major global growth opportunities in the future, which to the largest extent lie within other transition economy contexts and emerging markets, which constitute a context that they know how to navigate. Being experienced with such imperfect contexts, while also having managed to succeed in lead markets, gives them two critical sets of skills and competencies that provide them with all the abilities to become some of the strongest competitors on a global stage. Thus, what might have started as a "curse" could – after having mastered the challenging context – turn into a blessing for the future.

Note

1. Wikipedia: text of *Firebird* entry; accessed March 2014.

Appendices

Appendix 1: The Research Project

Overview

In 2011, the European Forum for Entrepreneurship Research (EFER) teamed up with IESE Business School and the Warsaw School of Economics to launch an ambitious project. We aimed to identify entrepreneurs in Central and Eastern Europe (including Ukraine, Russia and the former East Germany) who had built innovative growth companies in the transition period from communism to capitalism which had been able to expand successfully into foreign markets and compete there with other world-class companies. We looked for firms that were born and are still headquartered in those CEE countries.

Much has been written about entrepreneurs in the Western world but, as experience around the world has shown, entrepreneurship education is most successful when people learn from role models they can identify with. The current entrepreneurship literature focuses mainly on businesses and entrepreneurs operating in Western regulatory and political environments and developed, sometimes homogenous markets. However, in many places, a lack of standards and rules, rapidly changing regulations and weak business ecosystems make those environments and markets impossible to compare.

Our main objective was to identify founders and firms that, after being set up in very difficult und uncertain conditions, had been able to reach an international scale. Once identified, the research question was: HOW did they do it and WHAT can we learn from them? More specifically, are there general patterns that might help entrepreneurs in other parts of the world? Some years into this endeavor, the answer is that these entrepreneurs are going to serve as inspiring examples of entrepreneurial success to students, other entrepreneurs and executives from all over the world, but specifically from Central and Eastern Europe and other transition economies that share a number of contextual similarities.

The genesis

Europe is still far from the realities of a *single market*. Entrepreneurs from European countries face significant hurdles when it comes to growth and expansion as they have to overcome cultural, legal and language barriers – to mention just a few – in order to enter new countries. While US or Chinese entrepreneurs benefit from their large local markets, firms from most European countries very quickly need to cross borders to continue growing. These barriers, together with a reduced willingness to grow among European entrepreneurs, result in Europe being far behind the United States when, for example, it comes to the creation of *gazelles*, who generate the majority of new jobs. This lack of entrepreneurs who have set up high-growth companies that have successfully crossed borders and set up international operations is particularly strong in countries from Central and Eastern Europe, as well as Russia.

Another obstacle is that most European universities are owned by national governments and have – with only some exceptions – faculty mostly within the nation, while the student body is growing increasingly international.

For those reasons, we wanted to identify, research and present exceptional companies from these regions that have been able to grow internationally and can serve as role models for future generations of students and entrepreneurs.

Research methodology

Source of candidates

For sample selection we followed a multi-stage nomination, eligibility check and selection process. The first challenge that we faced was the lack of data that could help the research team get a good list of firms according to country. We decided to launch a snowball process. Sourcing of potential candidates and companies was done through the EFER alumni network (composed of more than 500 alumni from 46 European countries and 199 universities), private, governmental, and academic partners and networks in the entrepreneurship and business ecosystem – for example, professors outside the EFER networks, as well as venture capital or private equity funds or other investment firms that have made significant investment in the CEE region or are active there, such as MCI, the Polish Private Equity and Venture Capital Association (PSIK), the VC arm of the European Investment Fund, the Polish Science Foundation, the European Tech Tour (which started with activities in CEE and Russia) or the European Bank for Reconstruction and Development (EBRD). This process was followed by the exploration of other data sources to complete the information necessary for the selection process.

The selection process

The entrepreneurs' nomination and selection process consisted of several stages, with a rather wide "funnel" at the beginning and a much more narrow "funnel" in the subsequent selection stages.

The potential candidates were subjected to a multi-stage assessment procedure against two types of (quantitative and qualitative) criteria:

1. Eligibility criteria (First stage)
2. Selection criteria (First and subsequent stages)

In the first stage, we asked for a number of eligibility criteria and gathered some qualitative input with regard to the selection criteria, though on a more general level. While the eligibility criteria used a yes/no assessment and needed to be fulfilled in their entirety in order for the potential candidates to qualify for further consideration, the more qualitative information allowed us to understand those companies' characteristics and growth stories in greater depth.

1. Country of origin/location of the company – the company had to be established in one of the Central and Eastern European countries (including the GDR, Russia and Ukraine) and still have its headquarters located there.
2. Size of the company – the enterprise had to have experienced substantial growth in employees and/or revenues in the previous five years and provide a strong promise of significant growth in the future.
3. Age of the company – the company had to have been established during or after the political transitions took place (since the mid-1980s) and be at least five years old. Age variation, specifically to have some newer firms, was pursued to allow for some controls in the analysis.
4. Role of the entrepreneur – the founder still had to be in the top management team or on the board of the company. Preferably, the founder should still be the CEO.
5. Internationalization – international markets, either from a supply or market perspective, had to play a substantial role for the company and its growth.

During the second (and third) selection rounds, we did an in-depth quality assessment based on data obtained from them, in which we ensured a sufficient level of diversity with regard to countries, industries, topics, growth phases, challenges, internationalization strategies, and so forth. Some qualitative categories that were considered during the process were:

1. Personal/career (entrepreneur or start-up team; current CEO, if different)
   - Quick overview of previous career and educational background of the entrepreneurs or CEO
   - Age and nationality of the CEO
2. Basic company information
   - Where and when established?
   - Major financing events in the history of the company
   - Significant partnerships

- Industry or sector
- Product or service
- Main target customers
- Does the firm have a board of directors?
- Who are the company's auditors and bankers?

3. Internationalization
   - First year of internationalization and internationalization strategies
   - Sequence of foreign countries entered (plus years and internationalization strategy)
   - Revenue shares in foreign countries
   - How much did the company's main product or service need to be tailored to international markets (in %)?
4. Innovation and growth
   - What was the original market size when the company was founded?
   - How unique or innovative was the firm's main product or service in its market when the company was founded? (Scale 1 5)
   - How unique or innovative is the firm's main product or service (portfolio) today? (Scale 1 5)
   - Any past acquisitions? / Non-organic growth
   - Balance sheets and profit and loss

Figure A.1 Research planning

Although facing some restrictions related to censored and scarce information about certain companies, all researchers did their best to extract and analyze the company data.

On average, each researcher dedicated 20–60 hours of work per company throughout the whole process.

The results

Out of an initial pool of more than 100 highly qualified candidates nominated from countries across the CEE region and Russia, 24 entrepreneurs were selected by a prestigious selection committee to be "New European Champions." The selection committee comprised the following members:

Dr. Bert Twaalfhoven, founder and president of EFER; Karen Wilson, founder of GV Partners, advisor and board member at EFER and senior fellow at the Kauffman Foundation; Professor Derek Abell, former dean of IMD, founding president of ESMT Berlin and current Chairman of the Academic Board and member of the Governing Board at EFER; Professor Julia Prats, entrepreneurship professor at IESE Business School, academic advisor of EFER; Professor Tea Petrin, professor at the University of Ljubljana and former minister of the economy of Slovenia; Professor Christine Volkmann, entrepreneurship professor in Wuppertal and academic advisor of EFER; and Marc Sosna, research fellow at the IESE Business School's Entrepreneurship Department; and Piotr Zaborek (Warsaw School of Economics). In addition, those taking part in the nomination and selection process included Peter Englisch, partner and global leader of Ernst & Young's Family Business Center of Excellence; Erik Berglof, chief economist and special advisor to the EBRD president; Anne Fossemalle, director of EBRD Equity Funds; Peter Reiniger, former EBRD business group chief for Central Europe; Wojciech Ciszek, banker at EBRD Warsaw; Piotr Gebala, CEO of Poland's National Capital Fund (KFK); Marek Dietl, former investment manager of Poland's National Capital Fund (KFK); Victor Sedov, president of the US–Russia Center for Entrepreneurship (CFE); and Alla Danilova, project coordinator for youth entrepreneurship initiatives of the US–Russia Center for Entrepreneurship (CFE).

In June 2011 at the Warsaw School of Economics, we brought together companies, entrepreneurship professors, investors and players of the "entrepreneurship ecosystem" to honor the chosen entrepreneurs, and – even more importantly – to learn from one another during intense panels on various topics related to entrepreneurship and internationalization, such as international market entry and growth strategies, financing international growth, building strong brands in foreign markets, and building teams for international expansion.

For this book, out of those 24 companies, we have selected 15 and developed entrepreneurship teaching cases that represent a broad level of diversity with regard to countries, industries, topics, growth phases, challenges, internationalization strategies and so on. The book will enable educators in entrepreneurship, business administration, management, international business, innovation, firm growth and so on to work with relevant and realistic teaching materials for courses ranging from undergraduate to graduate courses, but also executive education or in seminars given by any kind of institutions that support start-ups and companies. For specific inquiries regarding the Teaching Notes, please contact EFER at info@efer.eu and check out EFER's website for any updated information on the book and related activities and materials.

Appendix 2: Growth in real GDP in Central and Eastern Europe, the Baltic states and the CIS

Table A.1 Growth in real GDP in Central and Eastern Europe, the Baltic States and the CIS[1]

	1989	1990	1991	1992	1993	1994	1995	1996	1997	1998	1999
Albania	9.8	−10.0	−27.7	−7.2	9.6	9.4	8.9	9.1	−7.0	8.0	8.0
Bulgaria	0.5	−9.1	−11.7	−7.3	−1.5	1.8	2.1	−10.1	−7.0	3.5	0.0
Croatia	−1.6	−7.1	−21.1	−11.7	−8.0	5.9	6.8	6.0	6.5	2.3	−0.5
Czech Republic	1.4	−1.2	−11.5	−3.3	0.6	3.2	6.4	3.8	0.3	−2.3	0.0
Estonia	−1.1	−8.1	−13.6	−14.2	−9.0	−2.0	4.3	3.9	10.6	4.0	0.0
FYR Macedonia	0.9	−9.9	−7.0	−8.0	−9.1	−1.8	−1.2	0.8	1.5	2.9	0.0
Hungary	0.7	−3.5	−11.9	−3.1	−0.6	2.9	1.5	1.3	4.6	5.1	3.0
Latvia	6.8	2.9	−10.4	−34.9	−14.9	0.6	−0.8	3.3	8.6	3.6	1.5
Lithuania	1.5	−5.0	−6.2	−21.3	−16.0	−9.5	3.5	4.9	7.4	5.2	0.0
Poland	0.2	−11.6	−7.0	2.6	3.8	5.2	7.0	6.1	6.9	4.8	3.5
Romania	−5.8	−5.6	−12.9	−8.8	1.5	3.9	7.1	4.1	−6.9	−7.3	−4.0
Slovak Republic	1.4	−2.5	−14.6	−6.5	−3.7	4.9	6.9	6.6	6.5	4.4	1.8
Slovenia	−1.8	−4.7	−8.9	−5.5	2.8	5.3	4.1	3.5	4.6	3.9	3.5
Central and Eastern Europe and the Baltic states[a]	**−0.2**	**−6.6**	**−10.7**	**−3.6**	**0.4**	**3.9**	**5.5**	**4.0**	**3.6**	**2.4**	**1.6**
Armenia	14.2	−7.4	−17.1	−52.6	−14.8	5.4	6.9	5.8	3.1	7.2	4.0
Azerbaijan	−4.4	−11.7	−0.7	−22.6	−23.1	−19.7	−11.8	1.3	5.8	10.1	3.7
Belarus	8.0	−3.0	−1.2	−9.6	−7.6	−12.6	−10.4	2.8	10.4	8.3	1.5
Georgia	−4.8	−12.4	−20.6	−44.8	−25.4	−11.4	2.4	10.5	11.0	2.9	3.0
Kazakhstan	−0.4	−0.4	−13.0	−2.9	−9.2	−12.6	−8.2	0.5	2.0	−2.5	−1.7
Kyrgyzstan	4.0	3.0	−5.0	−19.0	−16.0	−20.0	−5.4	7.1	9.9	1.8	0.0
Moldova	8.5	−2.4	−17.5	−29.1	−1.2	−31.2	−3.0	−8.0	1.3	−8.6	−5.0
Russia	n.a.	−4.0	−5.0	−14.5	−8.7	−12.7	−4.1	−3.5	0.8	−4.6	0.0

Continued

Table A.1 Continued

	1989	1990	1991	1992	1993	1994	1995	1996	1997	1998	1999
Tajikistan	–2.9	–1.6	–7.1	–29.0	–11.0	–18.9	–12.5	–4.4	1.7	5.3	5.0
Turkmenistan	–6.9	2.0	–4.7	–5.3	–10.0	–18.8	–8.2	–8.0	–26.1	4.2	17.0
Ukraine	4.0	–3.4	–11.6	–13.7	–14.2	–23.0	–12.2	–10.0	–3.2	–1.7	–2.5
Uzbekistan	3.7	1.6	–0.5	–11.1	–2.3	–4.2	–0.9	1.6	2.4	3.3	3.0
Commonwealth of Independent States	**0.6**	**–3.7**	**–6.0**	**–14.2**	**–9.3**	**–13.8**	**–5.2**	**–3.5**	**0.9**	**–3.5**	**0.0**
Central and Eastern Europe, the Baltic states and the CIS	**0.3**	**–5.0**	**–8.1**	**–9.5**	**–5.0**	**–6.0**	**–0.5**	**–0.2**	**2.0**	**–1.2**	**0.8**

Note: [a] Estimates for real GDP represent weighted averages for Albania, Bulgaria, Croatia, the Czech Republic, Estonia, FYR Macedonia, Hungary, Latvia, Lithuania, Poland, Romania, the Slovak Republic and Slovenia. The weights used for the growth rates were EBRD estimates of nominal dollar GDP lagged by one year; those used for the index in the last column were EBRD estimates of GDP converted at PPP US$ exchange rates in 1989.

Source: "Transition Report 1999: Ten Years of Transition" (November 1999), EBRD, p. 73.

Appendix 3: Profiles of Firms and Entrepreneurs

Table A.2 Overview firms and entrepreneurs profiles

	Founded	Origin	Ownership	Industry	Employees (2013)	Revenues € (2013)
ACE Enterprise	2004	Slovakia	Private	Software	30	1.00 m
Atlantic Grupa	1991	Croatia	IPO-2009	Food & beverages, distribution, pharma	4,228	661.83 m
Avangate	1992	Romania	Private	IT Solutions	170	n.a. [was acquired]
Big Filter	1988	Russia	Family b.	Car filters	245	14.65 m
Fx3x	1997	Macedonia	Private	Digital media, animations	116	n/a
Graphisoft	1982	Hungary	IPO-1998	Software	400	50.00 m
LDI	1991	Estonia	Private	R&D laser technology	17	0.12 m
LINET	1990	Czech Rep	Private	Healthcare	540	0.08 m
Masterplast	1997	Hungary	IPO-2012	Construction materials	628	81.30 m
Modesat	2005	Estonia	Private	Telecommunications	n/a	n/a
Pipistrel	1987	Slovenia	Private	Aircraft design & manufacturing	n/a	n/a
PKF Betar	1996	Russia	Private	Device building	510	41.94 m
Selena	1992	Poland	Private	Construction chemicals	1,700	260 m
Solaris	1996	Poland	Family b.	Automotive	2,284	360.00 m

ACE enterprise Slovakia

ALEXANDER CIMBAĽÁK graduated in hardware engineering at Slovak Technical University in 1995. He worked as a project manager implementing SAP projects in a private Slovak company from 1995 to 2003. In 2004, he decided to put his idea into reality, created unique visual integration technology and started ACE Enterprise with a business partner. Alexander Cimbaľák managed to convert a unique idea into an internationally recognized solution and build a dynamic, successful company. Besides his business success, he builds and promotes strong values of social responsibility. Moreover, he is one of the most award-winning Slovak entrepreneurs.

Description

www.ace-eprise.com

ACE ENTERPRISE SLOVAKIA is a young but internationally successful company providing comprehensive advice on the implementation of enterprise application integration solutions based on a unique technology it has developed, which allows interconnecting SWs effectively without a line of code. Thanks to this unique product and its strong international orientation with an unconventional approach from the very beginning, the company managed to create strong partnerships and address many multinational companies. Nowadays, its product is present in more than 80 countries worldwide. The company first saw its main opportunities on foreign markets but it started to orient itself to the home market after it managed to succeed abroad.

Internationalization

Internationalization has played a substantial role in the company's business and growth from the very beginning.

The company started to go international in 2005.

Current countries (2013): The company and its are present in more than 40 countries worldwide (on five continents), including the European Union countries, the United States, Mexico, China, South Africa and New Zealand.

Atlantic Grupa

ATLANTIC GRUPA

EMIL TEDESCHI is a member of the Parliamentary Committee overseeing Croatia's negotiating process with the EU, as well as of the Social and Economic Council. For the past two years, he was the president of the HUP (Croatian Employers' Association) and has been an active member since its founding. He is a member of the INSEAD Alumni Association and of the Program Council of the Zagreb School of Economics and Management. He is vice-president of the Supervisory Board of RTL Croatia and a member of the Management Council of MedILS. In 2002, he was named Manager of the Year by CROMA and, in 2005, he was selected as CEO of the Year by the Croatian business paper *Poslovni vjesnik*. In 2006, he was named Businessman of the Year by an expert jury of Kapital Network.

Description

www.atlantic.hr

ATLANTIC GRUPA D.D. is one of the largest regional food producers and distributors with well-known brands such as Argeta, Barcaffe, Cedevita, Cockta, Donat, Grand Kafa, Najlepše želje and Smokietc. It is the leading European producer of sports food with the Multipower brand, the largest regional producer of food supplements with the Dietpharm brand, a prominent producer of personal care products as well as the leading distributor of consumer goods in Southeastern Europe. The distribution portfolio of Atlantic Grupa includes global premium brands of distinguished producers such as Wrigley, Ferrero, Hipp and Johnson & Johnson. Atlantic Grupa is the owner of the leading private chain of pharmacies under the brand Farmacia.

Internationalization

The company started to go international in 2001.

Current countries (2013): It has firms and representative offices in 11 countries. It exports its products to more than 30 markets worldwide. After Croatia, the most important markets are Germany, Great Britain, Italy, Slovenia, Bosnia and Herzegovina, Serbia and Montenegro and Macedonia. Atlantic Grupa has developed partnerships with regional and national distributors.

Avangate (GECAD)

RADU GEORGESCU is one of the most prominent and successful technology entrepreneurs in Eastern Europe. He is the president and chairman of the board. He is a serial entrepreneur with a very deep knowledge of the software licensing market. His focus is on intellectual property, innovation and online. A huge believer of exponential growth and business models that support this, he has received many awards and recognitions (Order of the Star of Romania – rank of knight – awarded by Ion Iliescu, president of Romania, in 2003; Romanian Personality of the Year – awarded by Ion Iliescu, president of Romania, in 2003; Oscar Capital for the businessman of the year – awarded by *Capital Magazine*, 2003, among others).

Description

www.avangate.com (www.gecad.com)

AVANGATE is the leader in customer-centered commerce solutions, helping companies increase their online sales across touchpoints, manage subscription billing and grow their distribution channels to profitably scale and enter new markets.

Avangate's solutions include a fully featured, modular and secure commerce platform, which integrates online e-commerce, subscription billing, global payments, a partner order and revenue management solution, as well as a constantly expanding worldwide affiliate network.

GECAD Group's businesses are mainly software and services-related, employing innovation and professionalism to achieve performance in producing new software products and online payments technologies, in providing security services and online software sales and in supporting other high-tech companies to make the first steps in the world of first class business.

GECAD Software was established in 1992 by Radu Georgescu as a computer-aided design (CAD) software development company. Over time, GECAD's focus shifted from CAD software to security-related software, mainly antivirus software. Its most prominent product, Reliable Antivirus or RAV, was first developed in 1994.

Internationalization

RAV antivirus division matured and the software product reached the international market, gaining awards and recognition. In 2002, RAV saw incredible global growth: 150 distributors in more than 60 countries. GECAD ePayment International is based in Bucharest, Romania, with additional offices in Amsterdam and California.

Big Filter

BORIS BEYLIN is the president and founder of Big Filter. Previously he was awarded a degree in mechanical engineering in 1975, with a major in manufacturing.

Description

www.bigfilter.com

BIG FILTER is a powerful, modern and very fast-growing producer. The company produces all types of car filters for a large mass of vehicles for both foreign and Russian models. Big Filter Company and its products are widely known on almost every continent.

Internationalization

Since 1997, Big Filter has been supplying filters to a wide range of countries all over the world. Export operations play a great role in the company's activities as they account for about 40% in volume terms (about 10% of revenue). This direction is developing actively. Nowadays the company supplies to all continents.

Current countries (2013): About 35 – the United States, Canada, Costa Rica, Mexico, the United Kingdom, Belgium, Germany, Lithuania, Finland, Estonia, Poland, Romania, Italy, the Czech Republic, Greece, Cyprus, Israel, Egypt, Iran, the United Arab Emirates, Syria, Senegal, Turkey, India, Pakistan, Thailand and others (including all the CIS countries). A new and significant change is the delivery of car filters to the VW company in Mexico.

Fx3x

KRISTIJAN DANILOVSKI has been at the forefront of visual effects and CG animation in Southeastern Europe since the early 1990s, mainly in TV commercials and TV programs, first as a computer graphics animation artist, later moving to supervision and production roles. He co founded Fx3x in 1997 as a first-class visual effects and computer graphics animation company in the region. Following a string of successes in Europe, Danilovski was the leading figure in bringing part of the visual effects for *The Aviator* (2004) to Macedonia, in a first for the region. This was followed by several other feature films and TV shows. In 2007, he was nominated for an Emmy award for visual effects.

Description

www.fx3x.com

Fx3x is a Macedonian character animation and visual effects studio for feature films and commercials.

Internationalization

The prospects on the international market of digital media played a substantial role in the company's growth.

Currently Fx3x is completely focused on the global market, which provides more than 90% of the company's work.

Current countries (2013): Offices in Hungary, Germany, Japan, the United Kingdom, the United States, Russia, the Chinese mainland, Hong Kong, Singapore and Mexico.

Graphisoft

GRAPHISOFT.

GÁBOR BOJÁR, chairman and co-founder of Graphisoft in 1982. Under his management, the company became not just the most successful multinational software firm based in Eastern Europe but also one of the largest companies in the world in the field of computer-aided design for personal computers in the architectural, engineering and construction sector. Bojár and his company have received several industry awards, including being named one of The Wall Street Journal Europe's Top Ten Central European Executives for 1998 and the invitation to share Graphisoft's vision at the World Economic Forum's in Davos, Switzerland.

He was awarded a master's degree in physics from Eötvös Loránd University of Science in Budapest in 1973.

Description

www.grapghisoft.com

GRAPHISOFT is a pioneer and leader in developing Virtual Building solutions, empowering the broadest community of architects to deliver model-based projects that are better designed, more predictable to construct and less expensive to operate.

Internationalization

Graphisoft's global experience and presence carry an even deeper strategic value as the world's building and software markets transcend national boundaries.

The company works with dedicated distributors in 80 countries and hundreds of value-added resellers and systems integrators who ensure that customers receive support and personal attention wherever they are.

This multinational software corporation has offices in Hungary (headquarters), Germany, the United States, Japan, the United Kingdom and Spain.

Current countries (2013): More than 100.

Laser Diagnostic Instruments

SERGEY BABICHENKO is the vice-president of operations for LDI. His research and development experience includes lasers and non-linear optics, laser spectroscopy, laser remote sensing systems for ecological and industrial applications, analytical software and water ecology. Dr. Babichenko worked for 17 years in the Academy of Sciences as a senior scientist and as the head of the Laser Remote Sensing Group at the Institute of Ecology in Tallinn, Estonia. In 1999, he won the gold medal at the 48th World Exhibition of Inventions and Industrial Innovations in Brussels, Belgium. Dr. Babichenko is the author of 96 publications and holds five patents.

Description

www.ldi.ee

LASER DIAGNOSTIC INSTRUMENTS is an Estonian private corporation, operating in the area of research, development, manufacturing and the application of laser-based instrumentation. LDI offers online, in situ, airborne, contact and remote analytical sensors to address environmental, industrial and biomedical issues, together with a range of software products that control measurements and handle data. LDI's principal products and services are based on novel laser, electro-optical and photonics technologies aimed at real-time data assessment.

Internationalization

The company started to go international in 1992.

Current countries (2013): Export sales to South Korea, Indonesia, China, Finland, Japan, Australia, Ireland and the United Kingdom. Sales representatives in more than 30 countries.

Linet

ZBYNĚK FROLÍK is the founder and CEO of Linet. He worked as the director of the technical department in the largest Czech hospital, where he first noticed a gap in the hospital beds market as only a few uniform and unsophisticated products were on offer.

When the political conditions in Czechoslovakia eventually changed, he decided to fill this gap with his own solution. He was named Entrepreneur of the Year 2003 by Ernst & Young and Manager of the Year 2009 by the Czech Management Association, the Confederation of Industry and Trade and other partners.

Description

www.linet.com

LINET, founded in the Czech Republic in 1990, is a world-class manufacturer of hospital and nursing beds. With its continual drive to improve medical and nursing care, its products are now sold in more than 90 countries around the world. It focuses on development, innovation and the practical application of advanced technologies by working closely with medical professionals to design solutions based on their needs. In 2008, Linet was named best Company of the Region.

Internationalization

Linet is one of the five largest manufacturers of hospital beds in the world.

Current countries (2013): It has sold products in more than 100 countries and has six subsidiaries – in the United Kingdom, France, Spain, Italy, Sweden and the United States.

The main focus of the company is Europe but the company is also working in other markets such as Japan and Malaysia.

Masterplast Group

DÁVID TIBOR received his business degree from the College of Modern Business Studies in Hungary. Together with his partner Balázs Ács, he founded Masterplast in 1997. Due to its dynamic development and expansion, it became one of the leading producers and traders of building materials in the region. Masterplast grew from a five-employee company to an international company with more than 700 employees and revenues of 25 billion forint. It has 15 subsidiaries and has export contacts in a further 11 countries. Masterplast's philosophy focuses on a customer oriented approach, continuous development and well established partnerships.

Description

www.masterplast.hu

MASTERPLAST, founded in 1997 in Hungary, became one of the leading producers and distributors of construction industry products. Now the company group has more than 700 employees in 12 countries. Considering its business philosophy, Masterplast focuses on continuous product development, a consumer-oriented way of thinking and successful cooperation with its business partners. The company provides an all-inclusive solution with its products in the areas of heat, sound and water insulation, roofing and dry construction. The products of Masterplast have TÜV and ISO qualification. Through the company's subsidiaries and partners, its products are on the European market and outside of Europe as well.

Internationalization

Masterplast started to go international in 2000.

Its products can be found in Slovakia, Romania, Moldova, Serbia, Croatia, Austria, Germany, Poland, the Czech Republic, Ukraine, Russia, Bosnia, Albania (and Kosovo), Macedonia, Slovenia, Bulgaria, Lithuania, China, Belgium, Denmark, England, Estonia, France, Greece, Italy, Latvia, the Netherlands and Turkey.

Current countries (2013): Subsidiaries in Hungary, Austria, Bosnia and Herzegovina, Bulgaria, China, Croatia, the Czech Republic, Poland, Romania, Russia, Serbia, Slovakia and Ukraine.

Modesat

MODESAT communications

TARMO PIHL has a strong ICT background and in the past worked in the consulting industry, focusing on funding for ICT projects. After the success of his entrepreneurial ventures, he served on European Commission ICT program committees.

Description	**MODESAT COMMUNICATIONS** is a designer of point to point modem IP solutions for microwave, upper millimeter wave and satellite radios. The IPs help customers to design leading-edge products with the highest performance merits and to stand out from the mainstream. Modesat standard products are based on low-cost FPGAs, while more advanced products and features can be migrated to ASICs via several silicon partners.
Internationalization	The company started to go international in 2010. The company's product is present in seven countries: Sweden, the United States, China, Malaysia, Italy, India and France. The company has a direct presence in Estonia and two foreign countries – the United States and Israel.

Pipistrel

IVO BOSCAROL is a Slovenian flyer, businessman, entrepreneur and politician. He founded the aviation company Pipistrel in 1987 in Ajdovščina, the first of its kind in Yugoslavia. During his life he has been active in photography, offset printing and aircraft modeling. He graduated from the Faculty of Economics, University of Ljubljana. He started in aviation as a glider pilot and, in 1987, began flying motor hang gliders. He was six-time national champion in ultralight aviation. He has organized many aviation meetings.

Description

www.pipistrel.sl

Pipistrel is a Slovene light aircraft manufacturer established in 1987 by Ivo Boscarol and based in Ajdovščina. Due to legal restrictions imposed by the Yugoslav government during the 1980s, flying alternative and ultralight aircraft was illegal. This led to the first aircraft being flown secretly in the late evenings. The flying times and shape of the hang-glider- style wings earned the aircraft the nickname "bats." The company adopted the nickname, naming itself after *Pipistrellus*, the Latin name for a genus of bat. Its facilities are located in Ajdovščina and a new factory is being built near the town of Gorizia in Italy. The company was the first private aircraft company in Yugoslavia. By the 1990s, it had produced more than 500 hang gliders were produced and, by the year 2012, it had produced more than 1,000 aircraft. It employs 90 people.

Internationalization

The company started to go international in 1992.

The firm's product is present in more than 50 countries through its distribution network.

PKF Betar

RENAT FARDEEV graduated from Kazan Aeronautics Institute (which is now Kazan National Research Technical University). Later he started to work at the Chistopol plant of the watch manufacturer Vostok (famous for its Komandirskie brand) and his last position with the plant was head of a department. Then an idea arose to establish a company to build gas and water meters and, as one of those behind the idea, Mr. Fardeev was asked to become its CEO.

Description

www.betar.ru

PKF BETAR was established in the city of Chistopol (population 60,000) in the Republic of Tatarstan, Russia. Its headquarters are still located there. The company's main products are water and gas meter devices, and the company currently occupies 80% of the Russian market for those devices. The company was founded in 1996. Water and gas-meter design is done by the company's own R&D department, which allows the company to be highly competitive in a tough market. PKF Betar has been a leader in Russia in the production of devices used to measure the consumption of energy resources.

Internationalization

The company started to go international in 1997.

The company is establishing its own foreign subsidiaries.

Current countries (2013): Operating in Russia, Belarus, Kazakhstan, Mongolia and Turkmenistan. Uzbekistan, Azerbaijan and Tajikistan also purchase Betar products, but Betar operates via Kazakh partners in these countries.

Selena

KRZYSZTOF DOMARECKI is the founder and main shareholder of the Selena Group. He graduated in law from Wrocław University. He also studied philosophy. In 1992, he founded and led Selena S.A., the first company in the Selena Group, specializing in the sale of construction chemicals in Poland. In 2007, Domarecki became president of the Selena F.M. board of management. For his activities, he was named Entrepreneur of the Year by Ernst & Young. Since 2008, he has been a member of the Scientific Council of the Polish Building Research Institute.

Description

www.selena.pl

SELENA GROUP is a global manufacturer and distributor of a wide range of construction chemicals for professional contractors and home users. Selena Group's business activities involve all stages of product development: advanced research, production, distribution, sales and global marketing. The group applies the latest global solutions in all these fields to provide top world-quality assurance, which is confirmed by its numerous awards and international quality certifications. Approximately 1,650 people work for the company. Selena Group is the fourth largest manufacturer of polyurethane foam in the world and successfully competes with global corporations.

Internationalization

The company started to go international in 2000. Selena distributes its products in more than 50 countries.

Current countries (2013): Apart from the other markets to which it provides Selena products, the company is established in Poland, Spain, Italy, Germany, the Czech Republic, Romania, Hungary, Bulgaria, Slovakia, Finland, Russia, Kazakhstan, Ukraine, China, South Korea, Turkey, Brazil and the United States.

Solaris

KRZYSZTOF OLSZEWSKI is the founder of Solaris Bus & Coach and head of its supervisory board. He studied mechanical engineering at Warsaw Technical University and trained as an engineer in a car repair shop, earning a master's certificate. He has many awards and recognitions: Golden Cross of Merit of the President of the Republic of Poland, Manager of the Year 2004 of the Polish Association of Managers, and Manager of the Year 2006 and 2007 awarded by Ernst & Young, and Exporter of the Year 2008 awarded by the Polish Association of Exporters.

SOLANGE OLSZEWSKA is head of the Solaris Bus & Coach board. She studied dentistry at Warsaw Medical University. Her career changed direction in February 1995. Olszewska became actively involved in Neoplan Polska, the family-owned Neoplan sales agency for the Polish market that transformed into the independent manufacturer Solaris Bus & Coach in 2001. Her professional career in the bus industry was honored in 2005 when she was named Bus Builder of the Year.

Description

www.solarisbus.pl

SOLARIS BUS & COACH is a Polish bus manufacturer located just north of Poznań, exactly between two European capitals: Warsaw and Berlin. Solaris is well positioned among the leading players in the European bus industry and manufactures a wide range of modern city and suburban buses, trolleybuses and buses for special applications. In 2009, the company started production of railway vehicles. Since the start of production, more than 7,000 buses have been built and delivered to 300 cities in 23 countries.

Internationalization

The company started to go international in 2000.

Solaris is present in 23 countries: Austria, Bulgaria, the Czech Republic, Denmark, Estonia, France, Germany, Greece, Hungary, Italy, Latvia, Lithuania, Malta, Norway, Poland, Portugal, Romania, Serbia, Slovakia, Spain, Sweden, Switzerland and the United Arab Emirates.

Current countries (2013): It has its own foreign presence with subsidiaries abroad in Poland, Germany, Bulgaria, Finland, the Czech Republic, Turkey, Norway, Spain, Serbia and Austria.

Note

1. Data for 1989–1997 represent the most recent official estimates of outturns as reflected in publications from the national authorities, the IMF, the World Bank, the OECD, PlanEcon and the Institute of International Finance. Data for 1998 are preliminary actuals, mostly official government estimates. Data for 1999 represent EBRD projections. Estimates for Bosnia and Herzegovina are only available since 1995 and therefore are not included in this summary table. Data for Bosnia and Herzegovina are provided in the selected economic indicators at the back of this report. Estimates for real GDP represent weighted averages for Albania, Bulgaria, Croatia, the Czech Republic, Estonia, FYR Macedonia, Hungary, Latvia, Lithuania, Poland, Romania, the Slovak Republic and Slovenia. The weights used for the growth rates were EBRD estimates of nominal dollar GDP lagged by one year; those used for the index in the last column were EBRD estimates of GDP converted at PPP US$ exchange rates in 1989.

Part II

Case Studies of Internationally Successful CEE Companies

It is one thing to know and another to be able to teach.

– Marcus Tullius Cicero

Education consists of teaching men not what to think, but to think.

– Calvin Coolidge

This second part of the book includes a selection of 15 case studies that represent a broad level of diversity with regard to countries, industries, topics, growth phases, challenges and internationalization strategies. The cases were drawn from ten different countries: Czech Republic (1), Croatia (1), Estonia (2), Hungary (2), Macedonia (1), Poland (2), Romania (1), Russia (3), Slovakia (1), and Slovenia (1). They cover many industries, including science, software, movie animation, aviation, construction materials, cosmetics, manufacturing and food, among others.

The objective of the overall project and of this book is to contribute to entrepreneurship education; more specifically so by providing a pedagogical tool that supports the development of new and better entrepreneurs in Europe and all over the world.

We want to help students, professors, entrepreneurs and executives to reflect on the key challenges that firms born under very difficult circumstances have to overcome if they strive for growth and sustainability in the long term. Countries from Central and Eastern Europe have undergone a massive transformation which people have experienced on many levels way beyond economical factors. The change from communism to capitalism has presented everyone – but especially entrepreneurs – with unprecedented levels of uncertainty and a weak institutional context. At the same time it offered great opportunities for those who were capable of pursuing them (even if this was through unplanned discovery-driven approaches). While this transition is still in progress, we believe that the cases in our book provide great teaching materials for entrepreneurship in general and for transition economy contexts specifically.

We want to provide professors adequate tools and materials to teach these highly relevant subjects to students, entrepreneurs and managers. Given the fact that entrepreneurs and companies in many regions across the world face similar contextual conditions still today is another reason why the challenges presented in those cases – though possibly dating back a number of years – are actually highly up-to-date with regard to the issues they address and the discussion questions they pose.

A holistic education entails developing knowledge, skills, attitudes and values. And yet the training of a management professional clearly cannot be confined to the transmission, comprehension and practical application of concepts and tools. Where the claim to provide a rounded education is really put to the test is in the development of skills, attitudes and values. We expect our students "to reason in an orderly manner and with good judgment, based on common sense, about non-operational problems; to have fully assimilated the prudential criteria; to be both creative and realistic in their considerations; to not wander off the point; to decide and weigh the consequences of their decisions; to think operationally in their action plans and act decisively at the moment of truth; not to twist words and not to hide behind brilliant justifications; to articulate their ideas comprehensibly and persuasively, including overcoming their fear of public speaking. In this educational task we professors are the coaches, drivers and guides" (Segarra 2009: 2). This is the basis for teaching by the case method.

What is a case?

A business case imitates or simulates a real situation. Cases are verbal representations of reality that put the reader in the role of a participant in the situation (Ellet 2007).

Cases are first and foremost teaching vehicles. The main objective is not necessarily to make the right decision for the firm in the case in this specific situation based on a large amount of data, but to discuss and understand which dimensions are relevant to consider in such a situation and which consequences different decisions would have. It is about understanding the resource needs, implications and effects certain decisions would have in the illustrated context.

Based on real firms, each case challenges the reader's ability to confront complex problems by asking the right questions, and looking at the right proxies to navigate through the next unknown. The cases must be the base for fruitful discussion on the relevant issues presented in them.

By forcing the student to focus on a specific situation, the case is intended to serve as a general lesson on how to approach certain types of problems. The educational value of a case comes from having a significant issue to discuss. Each case aims to serve as a mind opener on specific elements in the development of a firm in this specific context that may affect its growth path (or even its survival).

The cases are not about "recipes" to successfully confront challenges. Long ago, we – as well as an ever-growing number of readers of business literature – have stopped believing in success recipes, one-size-fits-all solutions and normative advice. It is about developing heuristics to make better decisions. The professor must take an active part, stimulating the exchange of ideas, eliciting responses to each intervention, summing up at appropriate moments, asking direct questions and basically acting as a catalyst of thought. This obviously requires very thorough preparation, both in selecting cases and in preparing them.

Although all the cases included in this book were written with the objective of trying to shed light on the internationalization process of firms being born in difficult circumstances, every case touches upon different aspects of it. For instance, we may use the *Avangate* case to focus on critical decisions to take or enablers to put in place before entering the US market, the *Laser Diagnostic Instruments (LDI)* case to discuss business-model design issues to capture value in international markets, the *Selena* case to discuss the impact of organizational setups and CEO personalities on international scaling, or the *Fx3x* case to put students into the shoes of a CEO who stands at a fork in the road and needs to decide which growth strategy to go for considering the pros and cons of each possible path which all have different levels of resource commitments and risks.

The cases presented in this book are appropriate for training courses, seminars or even individual sessions on entrepreneurship and strategy. They can be used for MBA courses, executive education, in-company and undergraduate programs.

The cases at a glance

As outlined above, the cases include amazing stories from entrepreneurs and their companies from a wide range of backgrounds. Below is a brief overview of the companies and the challenges:

#1: ACE enterprise Slovakia	A young software entrepreneur had developed a new technology and needed to decide on market-entry and internationalization strategies. The case covers important growth aspects; business model decisions and how to use fast prototyping and customer feedback to quickly test market fit.	#2: Atlantic Grupa Croatia	Atlantic Grupa is one of the largest producers and distributors of food and personal care products and consumer goods in CEE. The company owned and/or distributed many well-known national and international brands. This case highlights a potentially pivotal decision: whether or not to acquire a company that would help them enter a new market. Emerging from a difficult context, the company held an initial Emerging from a difficult context, the company held an initial public offering in 2009 and in 2010, had more than 1700 employees and revenues over US$420 million.
#3: Avangate/ GECAD Romania	This case covers a typical and significant issue for this region: how can a young technology company overcome a negative country-of-origin effect – especially when operating in a highly security-conscious industry such as e-payment? Does a company need to disguise itself or appear American in order to be able to succeed in the US market and beyond? And what role could the current versus a potentially new international top management team play in those endeavors?	#4: Big Filter Russia	This case covers a family-run car filter business and the questions its founder/CEO faced about the company's growth strategy. Should they stay in a less competitive market, in which they served nearly all continents? Or should they move into much more competitive and attractive segments, directly supplying OEMs, and therefore competing with lead players such as Bosch, among others?
#5: Fx3x Macedonia	How far is it from Macedonia to the "Dream Factory"? In this case, a young entrepreneur creates an EMMY-award-winning, Hollywood supplier of movie animation with a workforce of more than 120 employees. In the process of attaining success – considering the fact that most mid-sized firms in that space died – the company faced a huge dilemma: whether they should (a) remain a smaller player with modest growth (which would also free them of trying to secure external capital), (b) try to raise significant VC money to push for rapid growth and become a large player; or (c) to try become a mid-sized player despite the fact that it seems to be a "death zone."	#6: Graphisoft Hungary	This case consists of two parts (A and B) and tells the evolution of one of the most successful companies from CEE, which has many interesting facets and sub-stories, such as the CEO's collaboration with Apple and direct support from Steve Jobs. While the first part centers on the company's development and selling or not selling Apple's distribution business, the second part focuses on whether doing an IPO is the right move at that time. Further sub-themes appear in the case, such as difficult market-entry decisions, building a brand abroad to overcome a negative country-of-origin effect, partnering with well know Western brands to improve their branding, as well as finance-related topics for international growth.

#7: Laser Diagnostic Instruments (LDI) Estonia	This story covers the challenges of a small scientific company with a cutting-edge technology, but with big question marks about the future. It's about finding the right market focus, a sustainable international growth strategy, and a business model to be able to appropriate the value they actually created with their technology – on both sides of the Atlantic. On top of that they need to deal with claims against a successful product application of theirs in the US market. A drug dealer's lawyer is calling their technology "voodoo sorcery from the East which has no science behind it."	#8: LINET Czech Republic	This is the story of a hugely successful Czech hospital bed producer, which rose to the top five in its industry worldwide. The main strategic issue is about the corporate restructuring that seems needed in order to keep growing as they plan to enter further countries. An evolving theme is that they start to compete more and more with a German partner company and shareholder who had helped them in the beginning to gain recognition in the market. Other challenging issues are not far, such as scalability, IPO alternatives and innovation advantages.
#9: Masterplast Hungary	This case describes the growth story of a construction material company and its young entrepreneur who founded the company directly after his university studies and grew it to more than 700 employees and US$100 million in revenue. The main challenge is where to build the next plant – a geographical expansion issue – and the background covers other issues such as HR and macroeconomic aspects.	#10: Modesat Communications Estonia	This case covers a small, but very innovative technology venture in the mobile backhaul market, which needs to decide on the best possible international business model and growth strategy in order to work with large technology giants, such as Ericsson and Nokia, and to find its most optimal positioning in the market.
#11: Pipistrel Slovenia	Inspirational, captivating, interesting.... All of them are adjectives that define the founder of this venture, a small start-up in the industry of ultra-light aircraft construction. The firm went on to break many aviation records and won three international NASA competitions. The discussion centers around an important strategic decision: should they remain in their current segment or try to take a large financial risk to build a completely new and innovative airplane model which would allow them to enter a new market segment?	#12: PKF Betar Russia	Inside a difficult institutional context, a medium-sized and mature family-run gas/water meter producer tries to determine the best strategic choices for the company; however, other macro-political forces affect their decision-journey.

Continued

#13: Russian Cosmetics* Russia	A strategic challenge regarding the marketing, sales and distribution strategies for their products is the focus of this case about a Russian family business that produces and sells cosmetics.	#14: Selena Group Poland	This case is about an entrepreneur who has built his company in a very different way and with a unique organizational setup and mindset. After nearly two decades, the founder moved to the board and hired a new CEO. Fundamental questions need to be answered to keep the company on its successful course: Is the current company structure still viable to grow effectively in the future? How should the founder and the new CEO collaborate, considering the different markets and growth contexts they encounter? What could such a change at the top – with two very different personalities – mean for the company?
#15: Solaris Bus and Coach Poland	This case is about a bus manufacturer founded in Poland in 1996 that, by 2009, had achieved national and international success, with more than US$400 million in revenues and 1,500 employees. However, the company's future strategy and next moves needed to be decided. Which role would "buses for the desert" play in those considerations? The case illustrates and poses questions for decisions on numerous challenging issues, such as market-entry strategy, market segment choices, country selection for further expansion, as well as branding.		

We are grateful beyond words to the entrepreneurs featured in this book who – despite their incredibly tight schedules – have shown great commitment to this project over a long period of time. In support of our vision and objective to provide better entrepreneurship teaching tools and materials, they provided their valuable time to openly share their stories from the early founding days until today, including the ups and downs, their doubts and even their mistakes along the way, as well as their successes. Without the deep insights they have provided to all of us authors, we could not have produced anything. Thank you once again!

CASE 1: ACE enterprise Slovakia: "Drawing Out" the Future

Marian Holienka

Slovakia. A young software entrepreneur had developed a new technology and needed to decide on market entry and internationalization strategies. The case covers important growth aspects, business-model decisions and how to use fast prototyping and customer feedback to quickly test market fit.

> Even the most sophisticated system is dysfunctional when it does not communicate with people and their environment.
>
> Technology is not important. What's important is the possibility of finding a solution to a problem.
>
> Integration software is sort of like making a good drink. (Alexander Cimbaľák, CEO of ACE enterprise Slovakia)

Introduction

In the summer of 2005, Alexander Cimbaľák, co-owner of the year-old ACE enterprise Slovakia (ACE), had reached a major milestone – he had completed the design of the company's first software product – the ACE enterprise Integrator. The product allowed companies to connect existing systems to enterprise software systems such as SAP[1] with a user-friendly interface, allowing users to work directly with information they needed rather than rely on an IT expert. Within the IT industry, the software product was classified as "middleware" under the broader category of "Enterprise Application Integration (EAI)."

For Alexander, running the company was a new experience.

> Every morning when I start the long walk up the stairs to the top floor of our small office, I feel excited. Sometimes I'm not used to seeing the first tangible symbols of actually getting this company up and running...for

> example, we already have corporate colors! [See Exhibit 1] Our office is just big enough to accommodate a few IT guys who have great enthusiasm and ideas.

Over the past six months, Alexander had considered the options for his young company to take its product to market. He considered three options: pursue local Slovak companies as customers, target international companies or sell and become the analytical arm of a big Slovak IT company. He noted:

> It feels like we've been through a lot just to complete our first product. Now it is time to face the real challenge of seeing how we can sell it. My business partner prefers to go the safe route by trying to build some local customers before going international. My heart wants to chase international customers even though I'm aware of the difficulty in doing so. Even though I know becoming part of the big IT company will give us all decent salaries, I'm worried that my entrepreneurial vision will be left behind.

Enterprise application integration (EAI) and the enterprise software industry

Enterprise software was defined as any collection of software used by companies to perform functions such as selling and order processing, customer information management, procurement, inventory, logistics, accounting and finance. Its main distinction from consumer software used by individuals was that it performed services for a large group of people (typically by using multiple servers connected by a network).

Although there were many different ways to divide up the market, enterprise software generally was broken down into:[2]

- Customer Relationship Management (CRM) systems estimated to be about US$9 billion globally in 2005 with growth projected at 6.7% annually over the following five years;
- Supply Chain Management (SCM) systems estimated to represent a total market size of US$5.6 billion with growth around 3%;
- Enterprise Resource Planning (ERP) estimated at US$25.4 billion with growth at about 10%; and
- Financial Management systems estimated at US$11.57 billion with growth at 6.4% until 2010.

SAP was the market leader in both SCM systems with 12% market share and ERP systems at 42% market share. The second company was Oracle with 10% and 20% market share respectively. Other major players included Sage (6% market share in ERP) and Microsoft (4% market share in ERP).[3]

The major players focused largely on solutions for large corporate clients. Enterprise software typically took many years of development and supported many projects. Since big software companies like SAP, Oracle and Sage were focused on providing a complete cross-enterprise solution, they were not always able to specialize in all areas, nor were they able to look after all integration needs. Typically major enterprise software companies frequently called upon smaller companies to help develop Enterprise Application Integration (EAI) solutions.

Enterprise Application Integration (EAI)

As enterprises used a number of diverse software systems to run their businesses, there was a growing need for application integrators – solutions providers who could help customers get all their systems to communicate with one another. For example, a company using SAP software as their ERP system would log its shipments by date and customer. This information was stored in the ERP system, but there was a clear need for shipment data to be readily available to sales people through the company's customer relationship management (CRM) system as well.

Application integrators also helped companies stay flexible since systems and internal processes often changed. Instead of having to do complete system overhauls, integration software helped by connecting new systems to old ones.

There were thousands of small software companies that served a particular niche in integrating enterprise software. In general the companies had either a particular technology or programming capacity as their main asset and partnered with larger firms to bring their software to market. Some major enterprise software companies permitted the smaller software companies to present themselves as a separate vendor, thereby allowing the small software integration company to build its own brand name. However, most of the major enterprise software companies attempted to offer a seamless solution to their customers and did not allow the small company to present itself as a separate entity.

SAP consultancy companies were certified by SAP. They ranged from large, widely known international companies to smaller local vendors that designed, implemented, maintained and upgraded SAP-based enterprise solutions. SAP consultants worked on projects with different degrees of difficulty, from less complex tasks such as user support, customization and account management to more complicated projects such as system analysis and integration solutions.

Alexander Cimbaľák

Born in Trencin, Slovakia in 1971, Alexander Cimbaľák grew up with a fascination for electronics and often experimented building amateur remote controls, disco lights and other gadgets. While his parents wanted him to become an actor, he quickly learned that electronics and computing were his calling. In the 1990s, with the burgeoning world of IT, Alexander started studying hardware engineering at the Slovak University of Technology, Faculty of Electrical Engineering and IT. After graduating in 1995, Alexander joined a small Slovak IT consultancy, eventually becoming a certified SAP project manager.

The idea behind ACE

Alexander first had the idea for a middleware application for enterprise software that used visual drawing to integrate systems while he was working as an SAP project manager. In his position he saw the company's inability to deliver integration solutions, as they were not recognized by the company as an important area. This caused customer dissatisfaction, project overcharges, employee frustration and poor motivation. He believed there was potential for a solution, but felt constrained by his employer:

> Where I worked, there was a clear definition of priorities and tasks in the company as well as a lot of internal regulations. I wasn't able to disrupt the established and defined boundaries to start solving the problems that so many projects experienced.

Alexander set out to work on his idea of creating a middleware application in the evenings and free time. He programmed the core functionality in Visual Basic and engaged two programming students to help round out the application. The first version took about three months to complete. He commented:

> We created an integrator between enterprise software and existing systems, which became a helpful tool for the team at my former company. However, the company did not support me, since it was not the work I was expected to do. Interestingly enough, my immediate team and also some customers thought the idea was great. Unfortunately, it did not lead to praise or even support. I felt discouraged. I realized that in order to pursue the idea, I would have to leave my job and do it myself.

Company creation

Alexander left the company to start ACE enterprise Slovakia with his partner Vladimir Drienovsky in 2004. Vladimir had lived in Germany for more than ten years working as an IT developer. When he returned to Slovakia, he started investing money, most notably in real estate. The two had met while Alexander was employed as an SAP project manager. Vladimir said:

"When I was working with Alexander, I recognized very quickly that he was unique."

Alexander commented on Vladimir:

> I was very happy to start a business with him since he understood the workings of the business world and had valuable contacts to generate sales. Although he didn't have contacts completely suitable to SAP integration in Germany, he believed that we would be able to sell to German companies. I was a bit afraid of starting my own business. Vladimir's support gave me a great deal of courage to do it. He calmed my fears when he said, "the worst thing that could happen is that the business could go bankrupt."

The pair started with €6,640, the minimum equity required to form an incorporated entity. Initially, to bring much needed funds into the company, Alexander and Vladimir did some consulting work for SAP to investigate the actual potential of SAP enterprise software implementation for small and medium businesses (SMBs) in Slovakia. At the time, the majority of SMBs perceived SAP implementations to be a massive undertaking and very expensive. The project's goal was to find out if there was an opportunity to make SAP-based solutions affordable and suitable for smaller firms. The team used the opportunity to learn more about the perceptions of SAP and save enough money to invest in ACE. Vladimir also contributed computers and volunteered the use of his car and property for the business. Vladimir assumed the role of CEO for the first year before handing the post to Alexander. Vladimir was still involved in the company, but continued to maintain his real-estate investment activities.

Product development

Alexander and Vladimir started with the technology that Alexander had created while working at his previous job. He said:

> I had developed software that was something like a prototype of the real product. I had used it for almost three years and was well acquainted with its weaknesses and limitations. I knew that in its current form, it would not be a full-value solution. I had a very clear vision for the new version – a major principle in the development of the product was not to be limited to what was possible and customary, but to create a product that would be simple to use.

Three of Alexander's former colleagues – Jaroslav (SAP consultant), Radovan (programmer) and Marek (programmer) – joined Alexander and Vladimir as ACE's first employees. Under Alexander's direction, the team built upon Alexander's first version of the software, making improvements in the usability and customer experience. The idea behind the software was to allow a user to digitally draw out a systems idea by using a mouse, touchpad or digital pen. Alexander explained:

> My vision was to be unique in the hardest area of IT business – enterprise integration. This is truly the area where you are in the middle of two professional systems: two systems, two worlds and, many times, two fighting sides. Because of this, it is very important to have a very different relationship with the customer and its partners. Therefore, we invented our own software technology based on visual drawing, not deep technical language or programming.[4]

During the development stage, Alexander and Vladimir traveled to a number of potential customers and partners in Germany to explain the idea behind the software. After being refused several meetings, they had the opportunity to present the idea to several potential customers and partners. Alexander recalled:

> We literally went door to door, and got turned away quite a bit. However, we did manage to speak with a few potential customers. We received some positive responses and learned what people wanted and what they didn't. We not only gained some valuable information for fine-tuning the product, but also the first few preliminary contracts. What's more is that our first customer was actually a potential partner with whom we wanted to develop a solution – the German operations of Integraph Corporation, a software company specializing in spatial information management (SIM).

In the context of typical Enterprise Application Integration (EAI) projects, many of the first customers believed ACE's product to be highly innovative. Some had even called it a breakthrough. The final product – the ACE enterprise Integrator – was essentially a technological software platform that allowed a user to integrate enterprise information systems with a simple drawing (Example Exhibit 2). For example, if a company had two systems that did not communicate with one another, such as an inventory system and an accounting system, ACE enterprise Integrator could analyze the structure and code of the systems and clearly identify data elements such as the inventory on hand and the accounts payable. Users could then drag-and-drop and design connections between the different data elements.

Initial feedback from users was positive since they did not need to invest a lot of time upfront in trying to define the business problem and business requirements in a detailed IT document. Despite the positive feedback from business users, IT support staff had reacted in two ways: half were pleased that there was a simple solution to solve tricky integration problems and the other half were nervous that the application would render their jobs redundant. Alexander commented:

> In a way, our software is not a new technology, but an unconventional approach. We solve the basic problem of IT in a big company where the person that creates a technological solution is completely different from the user. I feel that we have uncovered something that has been strictly a taboo before in that we give power to the users to integrate data instead of leaving it in the hands of highly skilled programmers.
>
> We put an instrument directly into the hands of the user, and they are amazed because suddenly with only a few movements, they can do something that could have only been done by involving the IT department, spending a lot of money and taking several weeks if not months!

At the crossroads of an important decision

In the summer of 2005, with a finished and ready-to-sell product, Alexander faced a serious decision, determining not only the future of his company, but also the future of his idea. It was time to enter the market and he had thought of three possible options: focus on the home market of Slovakia, attempt to sell the software internationally or continue building cash by joining a major firm. He was acutely aware of young companies that had minimal resources and had spread themselves too thin.

Alexander had thought about two potential revenue models. The first was to deploy their product as a "white label" solution to a large software company so the large company could in turn sell it to a corporate customer. Alexander likened this to the "OEM" (Original Equipment Manufacturer) model which was common in industries like automotive manufacturing where companies sold parts to the manufacturer. While this could open new doors to the company, Alexander was aware that he would probably need to sell his solution at a 60% discount to the customer.

The second revenue model involved appealing directly to the end customer by offering consulting and implementation. Under this model, Alexander could potentially sell licenses, offer training and certification, and charge yearly maintenance fees (or any combination of these according to particular customer needs). If the company could reach end customers directly, they wouldn't likely need to provide a discount. However, breaking through was difficult and they would most likely need to go through resellers, which required a 30% commission.

Option #1: focus on Slovak customers

The first option was to concentrate on the home market in Slovakia. This alternative represented relatively secure revenue inflow, but was limited to a small market; Slovakia had a population of 5.3 million people, GDP of approximately €45 billion, GDP per person of €14,500 and an IT industry valued at approximately €499 million with average 4% growth in last five years.[5] There were only a handful of successful IT consultancy companies operating in Slovakia and around 120 larger companies[6] that would likely be interested in an IT integration product. Although it provided opportunity to acquire various IT projects related to EAI and also to other types of IT solutions through established personal contacts, either alone or in cooperation with partners, Alexander was a little worried that it could become a constraint for his company's potential. He said:

> I believe we can do pretty good business concentrating mostly on the Slovak market. I can use my contacts and relations and that will help us to find some customers. It also has the added benefit of going direct and building a bit of a brand name.
>
> However, if we only stay in Slovakia, I am worried that we would limit ourselves a little bit. Would we just become one of many companies or freelancers operating here, open to the same problems and turbulences of a small country?

Vladimir saw this option as a good and safe way to lead the company. His appetite for risk was lower than Alexander's, and also his ambitions were more pragmatic, and could be fulfilled by simple business success, without the need to seek noble aspirations. Furthermore, Vladimir felt that the company would be able to pursue the second revenue model whereby ACE could approach customers directly and offer a combination of integration and consulting. Vladimir had estimated that ACE could likely achieve revenues between €100,000 and €200,000 in the first year, gradually growing to €500,000.

Option #2: go international

The second option was to launch the product abroad first. He felt Germany and the United States would be the most suitable foreign markets due to the high penetration of SAP enterprise software in use at major companies. Alexander estimated that Germany and the United States made up about 15% and 25% of the US$5.6 billion SCM (supply chain management) enterprise software market respectively.

Alexander commented on going international:

> We have created a tool that I think will completely change the world of EAI. I want to erase that border between those who produce IT tools and those who use them. Most of the people using enterprise software are in developed nations like Germany and the United States. Even though this

> option is the closest to my entrepreneurial vision, it is definitely the most risky because we may spend a bunch of money traveling and trying to appeal to international customers.
>
> If we do go international, I'm not sure if anyone will give us a chance if we try to go direct. The customers will want references from us and the partners will probably want us to do a lot of the work for free. Furthermore, if we do work for partners, we won't have our brand name attached to our work. I want to promote Slovakia with pride as the place of origin of our technology, and show everyone that we are equivalent technologists to anyone in the world. If we end up like an OEM, then it will take a long time to develop our brand name.

Alexander and Vladimir estimated that they would likely need to invest €100,000 in travel for the first year and that they might need to offer the software as a demo in order to eventually secure a reference customer. They were uncertain as to revenue projections but knew that they might not bring in any revenues for the first year.

Option #3: become part of a bigger IT company

Finally, the third option was to take up the offer to become the analytical arm of a large Slovak SAP partner IT company. Essentially Alexander and the company's employees would be absorbed into the other company and work on innovation projects. Alexander talked about how the offer came about:

> We got the offer to become part of the bigger firm thanks to analytical activities that we carried out in our first year of operations in order to earn a bit of money, and also thanks to our innovative product. The offer is certainly attractive and a great challenge because we have the opportunity to become a part of something big. By joining the big company, I wouldn't have any more worries about business development and strategic course. On the other hand, we would lose our identity, which is a big price.

The company was offering to buy 51% of ACE for €150,000.[7] Alexander's salary would be about double what he was getting paid through ACE, albeit his ownership would be diluted to 24.5%. The three other programmers would also be given jobs at the company for about 25% more than their wages at ACE.

Criteria

Alexander's decision was affected by several factors, both internal and external. One of the most important external factors was the nature of the industry and EAI sub-sector market. The IT services market was by nature an open market, with no barriers to prevent international competition. The only serious limitation was the willingness of partners to cooperate and the ability of ACE to convince international companies to purchase their product.

When considering internal factors, Alexander was focused on his personal goals, entrepreneurial vision, the strength of ACE's product and the ability to sell to demanding international companies. In addition to trying to erase the traditional border between IT users and creators while promoting Slovakia as a technological country, Alexander also wanted to create a company that would become a leader in spreading new technology. He said, "I don't want ACE just to become another employer, but rather become a community of fanatics dedicated to applying technologies in other ways and promoting our country."

Alexander believed that the strength of the ACE enterprise Integrator was in its ability to flexibly link information systems for people who were not programmers. This would provide companies with the added benefit of reduced IT costs and ultimately allow them to get more out of their Enterprise software. However, because EAI software was a sub-sector of the larger Enterprise Application industry, Alexander was uncertain about the effectiveness of targeting the end customer. He said:

> It's going to be hard to go to a major company who is using a big SAP or Oracle system and say, "Hey, we have this great integration tool." We don't have a recognized brand name or relevant references and are coming from a country that is not known as a technology leader. End customers are very much influenced by a strong brand name backed by a lot of experience.
>
> We can also appeal to some large SW vendors like Tibco, Intergraph or SAP and a bunch of their partners worldwide. These companies are offering their integration software to major companies. They will work with small companies but a lot of the time, they will usually not want the small company to be very visible to the end customer. In other words, it's not a place where one can easily develop a brand name.

From a financial perspective, ACE's fixed costs were mostly made up of salary and rent totaling €150,000 per year.

"Drawing" out the future

Alexander knew that all three of the options for the future of his software had their benefits and drawbacks. He had to decide where to focus. He said:

> Many people may say, "Try to do all three." The problem is time and resources. Where should I focus first? I can't do all three nor can I really

> even do the first two at the same time, since I'm only one person and have limited time and money.
>
> I am most interested in trying to build this business internationally since it is the best reflection of the EAI industry. However, the payoff may not be immediate.
>
> Even if we do try to go international right away, there are still some big questions to solve, such as: What's the best way to approach customers and other market players? How can I prove that even a young company from an unknown country can offer an innovative and reliable solution to complex enterprise integration industry? How can I first attract new customers and proceed with building up trust? Even if I give the software away for free to a couple of important reference customers, it doesn't mean that it will help me with future sales. And I have real expenses to pay such as salaries and rent.
>
> I'm at the crossroads of a really important decision. It feels that if I choose correctly and if I can execute, I will create a lot of jobs and a name for Slovakia in this space. I want to make sure that I don't waste my dreams and vision.

In its tenth year of existence ACE is respected for their professional experience. "Because our technology really draws business integration processes, we have a huge set of know-how in visual projects [see Exhibit 3]. In a vision of helping customers worldwide with their process modeling we create a visual Internet repository, where registered customers can 'touch and feel' our product and 'read and learn' from our experience. Knowing the background of our customers we create revolutionary 'walk across your city' web space where customers can find their solutions in a very intuitive 'city walk' way [see Exhibit 4]."

In general it means that currently ACE changed its mission from "Integration software vendor" to "Integration process consulting company."

Exhibits

Exhibit 1: ACE enterprise logo and offices

Figure II.1.1 ACE enterprise Slovakia: logo

Figure II.1.2 ACE enterprise Slovakia: offices (A)

Figure II.1.3 ACE enterprise Slovakia: offices (B)

Exhibit 2: ACE enterprise integrator software

Product Description

The ACE enterprise Integrator is a technological platform for creating and maintaining integration solutions. It is an SAP certified professional integration tool that allows users to visually integrate software without any programming. Users can integrate various heterogeneous systems without deep knowledge of the systems. The entire solution is based on the most up-to-date development platform, Microsoft.NET, making it possible to use technology features like multithreading, pipelining or load auto-balancing.

ACE enterprise Integrator consists of a robust server, where the execution of integration projects takes place, and a client application, **ACE enterprise Integrator Visual Designer**, which allows users to visually design their projects. By making use of "Drag&Drop" technology, it's easy not only to display, but also to find the required data from, for example, an SAP system and then transfer it into another system, or wherever required.

There is a growing need for integration solutions wherever companies use more enterprise information systems that need to exchange data in order to provide necessary information, but industries where the product had the greatest potential of deployment were: utilities, health care and hospital, offshore oil industry, production, automotive, logistics, retail, mobile maintenance, facility management, government defense, pharmaceuticals and city council solutions.

Source: Company files and authors' own creation/adaptation.

Exhibit 3: ACE enterprise platform (version 5.1)

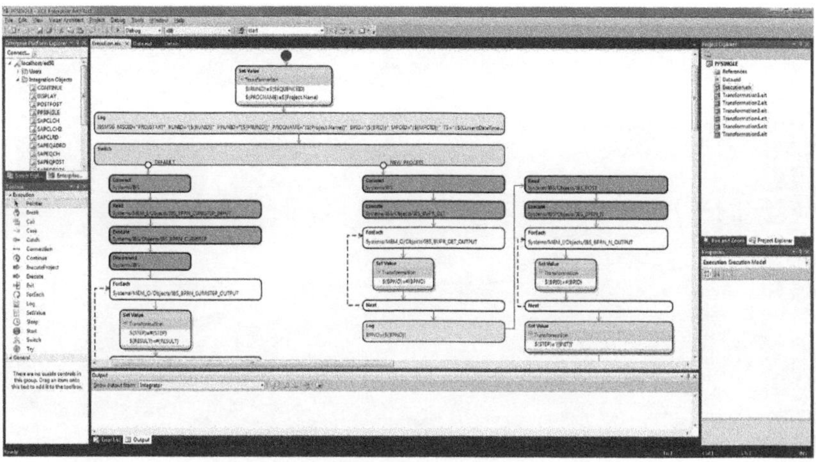

Figure II.1.4 ACE enterprise Slovakia: platform version 5.1

ACE enterprise Platform 5.1 is the next generation of the powerful ACE enterprise server: Integrator and Desktop. The new platform combines the power of both products into one environment, where application designers are able to integrate on both background and foreground levels.

ACE is currently running the fifth generation of ACE core technology (version 5.X of integration and presentation platform) in which are developed hundreds of solutions (ACE business templates) such as ACE Inspection Broker or ACE Mobility Manager Solution and many more. Thanks to more than 50 customers who are currently running solutions based on the ACE technology (more than 20 utilities), ACE has implemented many new features and visions into the next generation – 5.1. The better understanding of current customer needs in combination with latest technology standards means the highest level of improvements and ACE enterprise Platform represents the best technology so far.

ACE enterprise Platform presentation layer offers the possibility to build applications from blocks only by putting them into business process. Thanks to this process, development in ACE enterprise Platform is very fast. What makes the work in ACE enterprise Platform simple is the fact that the developer does not need specific knowledge about complicated programming languages and does not have to waste time with low-level details.

The user may change the process according to his company's specific needs, thereby achieving independence from a supplier in case of any later adjustments, in addition to a user-friendly working comfort.

Source: Company files and authors' own creation/adaptation.

Exhibit 4: ACE web repository solutions portal

Figure II.1.5 ACE enterprise Slovakia: web repository solutions portal

The ACE Web Repository Solutions Portal is a universal pre-sale and sale tool for utilities, production industries, retail and many other business areas. It allows the customers to browse through templates divided into different areas like Maintenance, Construction, Outage management, Metering and much more, thus covering the organization processes. The integration implementation phase can be speeded up by selecting a set of templates to implement, which brings the integration benefits in significantly shorter time.

Source: Company files and authors' own creation/adaptation.

Notes

1. SAP is a German software company that is the market leader in Enterprise Software.
2. "Marketing and Selling to Enterprise Customers, Market Research Report." Retrieved April 14, 2012, from http://www.msenterprisepartners.com/Pages/Default.aspx.
3. Ibid.
4. "International Business Awards." Retrieved April 4, 2012, from http://www.stevieawards.com/pubs/iba/awards/408_2651_21383.cfm.
5. Slovak Statistics Office, Štatistický úrad Slovenskej Republiky, Computer Programming, Consultancy and Related Services Industry (2004).
6. Larger companies are defined by companies that have over 1,000 employees.
7. Figures have been disguised to protect confidentiality.

CASE 2: Atlantic Grupa: Preparing for Leading in the New Europe

Alexandru Ioan Mincu and Vlasta Hudek

Croatia. Atlantic Grupa is one of the largest producers and distributors of food and personal care products and consumer goods in CEE. The company owned and/or distributed many well-known national and international brands. This case highlights a potentially pivotal decision: whether or not to acquire a company that would help them enter a new market.

Emil Tedeschi, the founder and CEO of Atlantic Grupa, had just finished a long management board meeting. On the way to his office, he weighed the pros and cons of the decision they had discussed. He had often expressed the desire to further expand internationally and become a true regional player. Now a new acquisition opportunity could accelerate reaching that goal. He and his team needed to decide if this was the right strategic move or not – and if they were prepared.

Acquisition discussions

It was June 2009 and Istrabenz Holding in Slovenia, facing dire straits, decided to sell Droga Kolinska, which owned and produced of a portfolio of food brands that were famous in the region. If Atlantic Grupa purchased the company, they would gain access to the products and brands of Droga Kolinska as well as better and stronger access to its markets. Droga Kolinska also presented the opportunity to fulfill another of Tedeschi's goals: to strengthen its manufacturing capability.

Emil knew that there would be other bidders. Thus, a decision of such importance must be taken in a very short time. The large amount of money involved as well as the risk of the spreading of the American financial crisis were factors heavily contributing to the complexity of the decision. Because of the recession, mobilizing cash for the purchase would be more difficult.

Not more than a year before Emil Tedeschi had considered acquiring Podravka (known for its internationally famous condiment, Vegeta), a Croatian state-run food and drug company plagued by corruption scandals and with a lower presence in international markets. The results of that analysis had been negative.

On the other hand, Atlantic Grupa had solid experience in such complex acquisitions and Emil remembered with pleasure the first big move he made in 2001 when acquiring Cedevita, a Coatian company established in the 1920s and since 1970 producer of the best-selling instant vitamin drink with the same name. Cedevita was a much larger and more complex business than Atlantic, which had no previous experience in manufacturing. Atlantic had acquired Cedevita from Pliva, the largest pharmaceutical company in Southeastern Europe. Pliva was a flagship of the Croatian economy with worldwide sales and business partners and high intellectual capital, including two Nobel Prize winners and hundreds of employees with PhDs. Besides nostalgia, Emil realized once more the tremendous impact this acquisition had contributed to the development of the Atlantic business and the learning they gained in the following years, which also led to an array of future acquisitions.

History of Atlantic Grupa

Atlantic was founded in 1991 when the first distribution center (DC) was established in Zagreb, Croatia. During that same year, the company initiated business with Wrigley, the world's largest chewing-gum producer. This was followed in 1992 by an agreement with Mars, the world's largest producer of chocolate confectionery. In 1993 the business expanded with the opening of the Split DC and further expansion saw the opening of the Rijeka DC in 1994. Additional assets were subsequently acquired: the Slavonski Brod DC in 1995; the Varaždin DC in 1996; and, in 1999, the Osijek DC which replaced the Slavonski Brod DC.

During that same period, distribution agreements were created with Sara Lee (1995), Duracell (1996), Mars Ice Cream (1997), Durex (1997), Ricola AG (1998), Gillette, which extended the Duracell agreement in 1999, Johnson & Johnson (1999) and Elite in 2000.

Atlantic entered the production business when it purchased a small producer of confectioned sandwiches (atmosphere-controlled packed sandwiches that had a longer shelf life) and created the Montana brand of sandwiches. Distribution of the Montana products started the following year. Consolidation of assets occurred in 2000 when Atlantic exited the distribution of frozen products and ceased business activity in that segment. In the same year, Atlantic purchased a large business complex/warehouse and

Figure II.2.1 Atlantic Grupa – the mountain
Source: Company files and authors' own creation/adaptation.

unified the Zagreb DC, central warehouse, Montana and the company's corporate headquarters.

A pivotal decision

In 2001, the acquisition of Cedevita was a milestone. Emil and his team, all in their early thirties, built with talent, competence and ambition and thus upgraded themselves from "moving-boxes-dusty-street-boys" to proven businessmen.[1] Both Pliva, Cedevita's parent company, and Covic, the CEO of Pliva, were well established in the European business world. Throughout the acquisition process, Emil and his team learned how to analyze, decide, finance and conduct a large-scale acquisition.

But even more important than the acquisition was the successful integration of such a large company. Atlantic Grupa managed to revive the once-famous Cedevita brand and develop it into an even stronger name by developing new packages, new flavors and new channels. The success was also secured by more efficient management, including Mladen Veber, Srećko Nakić and Zvonimir Brekalo (see Exhibit 8 for more details on the team).

Company background

As of 2009 Atlantic Grupa[2] was a Croatian multinational company which in its business operations combined the production, development, sales and distribution of fast-moving consumer goods with market presence in over 30 countries around the world. Atlantic Grupa developed into the leading European producer of sports food, the regional leader in the production of vitamin drinks and food supplements, a prominent regional producer of cosmetics and personal care products as well as the leading distributor of consumer goods in Southeast Europe. In addition to further development of the listed activities, a significant step forward in the current business operations was made through the acquisition of the chain Health Institutions, a process that started at the end of 2007 and continued throughout 2008 and 2009, thus making Atlantic Grupa the leading national private chain of pharmacies, united under the name Farmacia.

Atlantic Grupa's business operations could have been divided into two key components: Consumer Health Care and Distribution.

The Consumer Health Care Segment incorporated the following areas:

- *Health Food* – which was dominated by products under the brand Cedevita (instant vitamin drinks, tea, vitamin candies), Multivita (vitamin drinks) and Montana (sandwiches and ready-to-eat products);
- *Nutraceutics and VMS* (vitamins, minerals, supplements) – whose principal brands were Multipower (functional food for athletes), Multaben (assortment of weight-control products) and Dietpharm (vitamin products, food supplements containing herbal extracts and medicinal substances of natural origin);
- *Over-the-Counter Medicines (OTC)* – Purisan and Uvin H Forte; and
- *Personal Care* – in this segment the leading brands were Plidenta (dental care), Melem (universal cream), Rosal (lip, face and body care). In addition to the above, this segment also included the pharmacy chain Farmacia since 2008.

Distribution, as the second key component of Atlantic Grupa's business operations, worked in close correlation with the first and merged the distribution of brands from their own production with the distribution of well-known international brands. Atlantic was an authorized distributor for brands such as Wrigley, Johnson's Baby, Ferrero, Durex, Scholl and so on, which formed the company's strong distribution portfolio.

In 2009 Atlantic Grupa had 1,719 employees (3.12% increase of employees in comparison with the previous year). As a multinational company with

Figure II.2.2 Atlantic Grupa: the sun

Source: Company files and authors' own creation/adaptation.

firms and representative offices in ten countries, Atlantic Grupa exported its products to more than 30 markets worldwide. After Croatia, the most important markets were Germany, Great Britain, Italy, Slovenia, Bosnia and Herzegovina, Serbia, Montenegro and Macedonia. In those markets where it was not present with its own operating companies, Atlantic Grupa had developed partnerships with regional and national distributors.

Organizational structure

The organizational structure of Atlantic Grupa was set to change. In order to facilitate the system management, the entire business operations of all operating companies within the Group were to be restructured into four divisions:

- Consumer Health Care
- Sports and Functional Food
- Distribution
- Pharma

The principal feature of a divisional organization was the linking of business activities into special business units associated with specific types of products and services in Atlantic Grupa's business operations. Business operations, divided according to the listed divisions within Atlantic Grupa, were linked by the collective management of corporate support functions at the level of Atlantic Grupa, namely in the Finance and the Corporate Affairs areas. The Finance Area included Finances, Information Technologies and Investor Relations, while the Corporate Affairs area included Human Resources, Corporate Communications, Legal Affairs, Investment Maintenance and Corporate Security. Through those support functions, the procedures for performing the listed tasks contributed to the introduction of a single

Figure II.2.3 Atlantic Grupa: the wave

Source: Company files and authors' own creation/adaptation.

corporate standard and to more transparent and efficient business operations at the level of Atlantic Grupa.

In addition to the above, the dynamic development and growth of Atlantic Grupa created the need to organizationally integrate all activities related to the company's business development, primarily those related to the business strategy and new projects, which subsequently resulted in the decision of the President of the Management Board concerning the establishment of a new Office for Business Development. The Office for Business Development coordinated the development of strategic projects, identification of new potential targets in the expansion of business operations through acquisitions, mergers or strategic partnerships, communication with consulting firms and the investment community, as well as the preparation of the company's strategic documents. The functioning of this office was expected to be significant for the company's business development, as well as for the development of investor relations, presentation of Atlantic Grupa through communication with key financial and investment firms and for the participation in conferences that contribute to introducing the investment community to Atlantic's business activities and building the company's reputation.

Ownership and performance

The Management Board of Atlantic Grupa consisted of the President and all Vice Presidents of the Company which in 2009 held 15 Management Board meetings.

The majority share package of Atlantic Grupa was owned by Emil Tedeschi while the second largest shareholder was his sister, Lada Tedeschi Fiorio. With the recapitalization contract in 2006, a portion of the company's ownership capital was acquired by Deutsche Investitions – und Entwicklungsgesellschaft mbH – DEG, one of the largest European development financial institutions. For the purpose of additional stimulation and closer integration with the development of Atlantic Grupa, in 2006 members of the Management Board were allowed to purchase the company's shares. Following the recapitalization and public offer of Atlantic Grupa shares, about a third of the total number of shares was in circulation on the free market of the Zagreb Stock Exchange.

The year 2007 stays marked as the year in which the Atlantic Grupa shares were listed in the first quotation of the Zagreb Stock Exchange (ZSE) under the code ATGR-R-A, and already included in CROBEX index calculation due to its good liquidity.

In 2009 Atlantic Grupa shares realized a turnover of HRK 361.1 million (1€ = HRK 7.5). The average trading price per share was HRK 544.54, and the final price on December 31, 2009 was HRK 681.01. Atlantic Grupa's market capitalization on 1 January 2009 was HRK 1,185,597,600.

Despite the unfavorable macroeconomic environment, Atlantic Grupa in 2009 fulfilled the announced expectations.

Table II.2.1 Atlantic Grupa: profit and loss

	€ millions	**var 2008**
Revenues	304.8	10%
Sales	301.2	10%
EBITDA	27.0	16%
EBIT	21.1	19%
Profit before tax	17.4	26%
Net profit	13.3	24%
Net profit after minorities	11.6	24%

Source: Company files and authors' own creation/adaptation.

Emil Tedeschi

Emil Tedeschi, born in Split, Croatia in 1967, was the President of the Management Board. He was the founder and majority owner of Atlantic Grupa. In his business career before founding Atlantic Trade, on the grounds of which the company developed, he was, inter alia, the director of the Milan subsidiary of Meteor Holdings Ltd. London, one of the largest European paper and cellulose trading companies. In 2002 he was named Manager of the Year by CROMA (Croatian Managers Association); in 2005 he was selected the CEO of the Year by the Croatian business magazine Privredni Vjesnik; and in 2006 and 2008 he was named Businessman of the Year by the expert jury of Kapital Network. He was a member of the National Committee for Monitoring Negotiations for the Accession of the Republic of Croatia to the European Union and a member of the Social and Economic Council. He was the president of the Croatian Employers' Association (HUP), where he has been an active member from its establishment; his term ended in 2007. He was also a member of the INSEAD Alumni Association and a member of the Program Council of the Zagreb School of Economics and Management. Additionally, he was the Vice President of the Supervisory Board of RTL Croatia and an Honorary Consul of the Republic of Ireland in the Republic of Croatia.

Emil was also a member of the Young Global Leaders at the World Economic Forum and a member of the Business Advisory Council for Southeast Europe. He was appointed a member of the Economic Council of the President of the Republic of Croatia. Additionally, he received the award seal for regional business leader in 2009 given by Večernji List of Bosnia and Herzegovina.

Droga Kolinska

In May 2009 the Slovenian business daily newspaper Finance wrote:

> Within the sale of companies from its portfolio, Slovenian Holding Istrabenz is reconsidering the sale of Droga Kolinska. Analysts thought that Istrabenz will sell the company for warehousing of oil derivatives

Instalacija, by which they will decrease their debt for around €100 million, but, for the time being, what is certain is only that they will sell one part of their companies. The sale of Droga Kolinska was mentioned in November 2008, but official sale has never been announced. French bank BNP Paribas was selected for selling Droga, but with the approval of the

Figure II.2.4 Atlantic Grupa: other logos

Source: Company files and authors' own creation/adaptation.

> President of the Management of Istrabenz, Igor Bavcar, who allegedly gave the order for sale more than six months ago. So far, no potential strategic partner expressed the interest in buying Droga Kolinska, and private investment funds are most frequently mentioned as potential buyers. It was mentioned previously that it is possible that Droga Kolinska connects with Podravka or Centroproduct, but the estimates in Slovenia now are that such connecting is unreal.

The sale of the Ljubljana-based Droga Kolinska was supposed to be part of the debt restructuring program adopted by Istrabenz, which was fighting to clear nearly €500 million in debts after announcing insolvency at the end of April 2009. Istrabenz had considered selling Droga Kolinska, which it acquired in 2005 by buying Ljubljana-based food company Kolinska, which in turn bought rival food company Droga soon after, in 2008, but changed its mind several times. Droga Kolinska generated €326 million in revenues in 2009, reporting an operating profit of €23.3 million.

Exhibits 1 to 7 present more data on Droga Kolinska (2009)

Net revenues: In the first nine months of 2009, the Droga Kolinska Group generated €242.7 million of net revenues. Net revenues were not directly comparable with those generated in the same period the previous year due to the sale of non-core business. The first nine months of 2009 were characterized by difficult economic conditions, linked to the spread of the global financial crisis to the Group's strategic markets and its adverse effects on spending, particularly in the third quarter of 2009. Despite the difficult conditions on its most important markets, the Group performed better than expected. The Group's net revenues and profitability were particularly impacted by the 14% depreciation of the Serbian dinar, as the Group generated nearly half of its revenues in Serbia. Revenues on the Serbian market, expressed in the local currency, increased by 9% compared to the same period the previous year.

Table II.2.2 Atlantic Grupa: items from the unaudited balance sheet

	Items from the unaudited balance sheet of the Droga Kolinska group and number of group employees	**Sep 30, 2009**	**Dec 31, 2008**	**Index**
1	Net financial debt	155,126	190,214	82
2	Total equity	189,118	202,034	94
3	Total assets	430,408	481,568	89
4	Number of employees	2,619	2,953	89

Note: Value are given in € 000.

Source: Company files and authors' own creation/adaptation.

Sales of strategic businesses were in line with expectations: Despite the unfavorable market conditions, sales of strategic business were at nearly the same level as during the same period in 2008, and approximately in line with planned sales for 2009. If not for the drop in the value of the Serbian dinar and Russian ruble, which resulted in a loss of €11.7 million in revenues over the first nine months of the year, the Droga Kolinska Group would have exceeded planned sales by 1%.

Net revenues from strategic businesses expressed in euros were down 3% from the previous year, primarily due to the depreciation of the Serbian dinar. Revenues from non-core business were down 71% from the same period the previous year due to the disposal of those businesses. Sales of strategic business were in line with expectations with particularly good sales of Argeta spreads brand and the Smoki savoury snacks brand.

Debt and liquidity: In August 2009 the Group signed an agreement for a long-term loan facility in the amount of €118.6 million with a syndicate of seven banks. The Droga Kolinska Group used the funds from the loan to refinance its short-term financial liabilities to banks that would fall due for payment until the end of 2010, which meant that the indebtedness of the Droga Kolinska Group did not increase as a result of the new loan.

The Droga Kolinska Group fulfilled all of its obligations to creditors and suppliers in a timely manner and had enough cash to ensure financial stability, even in somewhat more difficult market conditions. Despite difficult market conditions, the Group reduced its net debt from €190.2 million at the end of 2008 to €155.1 million at the end of September 2009. The temporary increase of indebtedness of the Droga Kolinska Group in 2008 was the result of its decision to conclude the consolidation of the Group. In 2009 the Group began to reduce its net debt, in part through improved centralized cash flow management. In 2009 the Droga Kolinska Group had €30.3 million of cash on its accounts, thereby ensuring financial stability in the highly unpredictable operating conditions seen this year.

Operating result. From January to September 2009, the Droga Kolinska Group generated earnings before interest and taxes (EBIT) of €15.0 million. The fall in EBIT compared with the previous year was the result of accounting loss from the sale of non-core businesses in 2009 and the 14% depreciation of the Serbian dinar, as the Group generated around half of its sales revenue on the Serbian market. Excluding the one-off negative effect from the sale of non-core businesses on its operating result, the Group's EBIT would have exceeded €18.4 million, an increase of EBIT compared with the same period in 2008.

Net cash flow and net profit. Increased write-offs of receivables on the Serbian market owing to the temporary illiquidity of customers and exchange rate losses due to Serbian dinar`s depreciation contributed most to the Droga Kolinska Group's negative financial result and, consequently, its negative net result for the period. Despite the difficult conditions, the Droga Kolinska Group nearly halved its net loss, from €5.8 million at the end of June to €3.3 million at the end of September 2009.

Droga Kolinska and Atlantic Grupa

As Tedeschi drove home he realized that there were many reasons for and against the acquisition. Clearly Droga Kolinska would be the entrance to a number of international markets. Additionally, the acquisition of such a strong portfolio of brand markets and production capacities would allow Atlantic to raise operating efficiency and thus profitability. The acquisition could also provide the springboard for activity outside Central Europe. Another consideration was the strong potential for manufacturing, logistics and strategic sourcing optimization. Although Droga Kolinska was a good and solid company, the distress at the owner's level could irreversibly affect it, but also bring a better price for the buyer. If successful, an acquisition would position Atlantic well for competition once Croatia joined the EU (July 1, 2013).

In spite of these advantages, there were also some big concerns. Tedeschi had identified three. First there was the issue of the inherent tensions that could develop during an acquisition. Droga Kolinska had passed through several ownership changes starting from its inception as a group in 2005. It wasn't clear how the organization would react to yet another ownership change – this time coming from a foreign investor.

A second concern for Tedeschi was that Atlantic would not manage to mobilize the needed amount of money. The economic and financial conditions of Europe and the availability of funds from various sources could require a complicated financing scheme given the serious waves of trouble crossing the ocean from the United States. Could Atlantic gather the cash in time and also beat the other bidders? What would be a fair price to pay?

Lastly, there was the major concern regarding internal capabilities within the Atlantic management team to design and coordinate the whole thing: the acquisition, the transition and finally the much larger group. Emil remembered that after each successful acquisition he and his team underwent an intensive personal and organizational learning process. The miracle of change proved to be needed not only at the level of the acquired company but also – almost to the same extent – at the senior management level of the mother company. For each major project, Emil designated a member of his team to coordinate the efforts (to succeed and to grow with the emerged learning). Who could be the best champion for this new major endeavor?

All this and more ran through Tedeschi's mind as he made his way home.

Exhibits

Exhibit 1: organizational structure

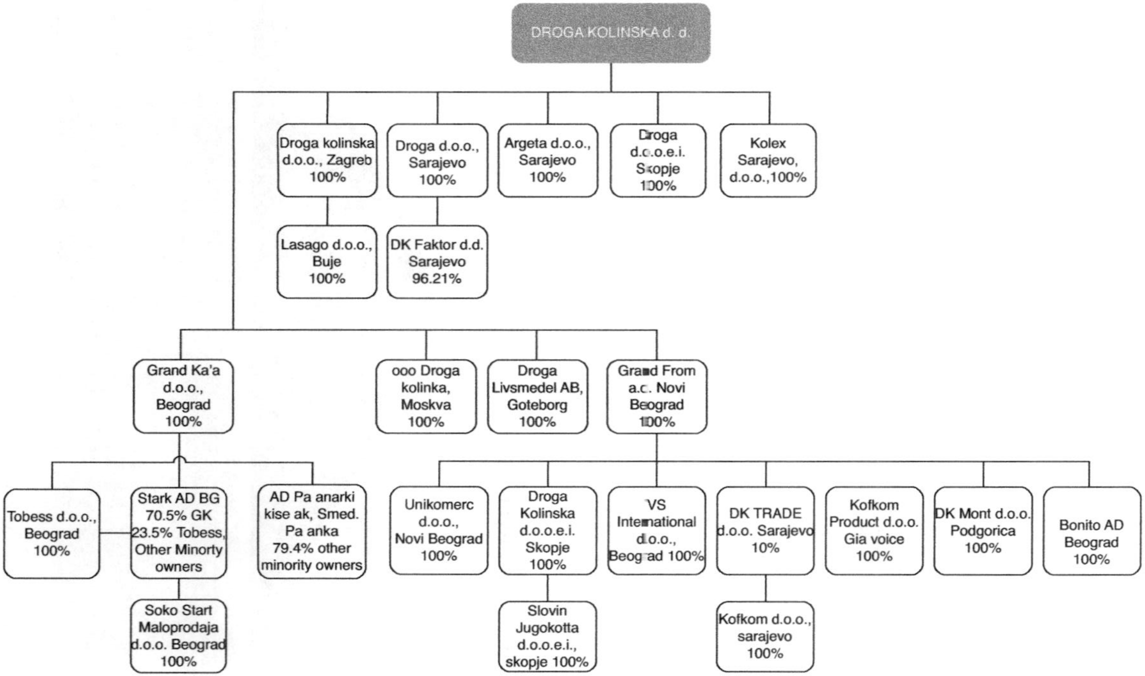

Figure II.2.5 Atlantic Grupa: organizational structure

Source: Company files and authors' own creation/adaptation.

Exhibit 2: 10 best-selling brands

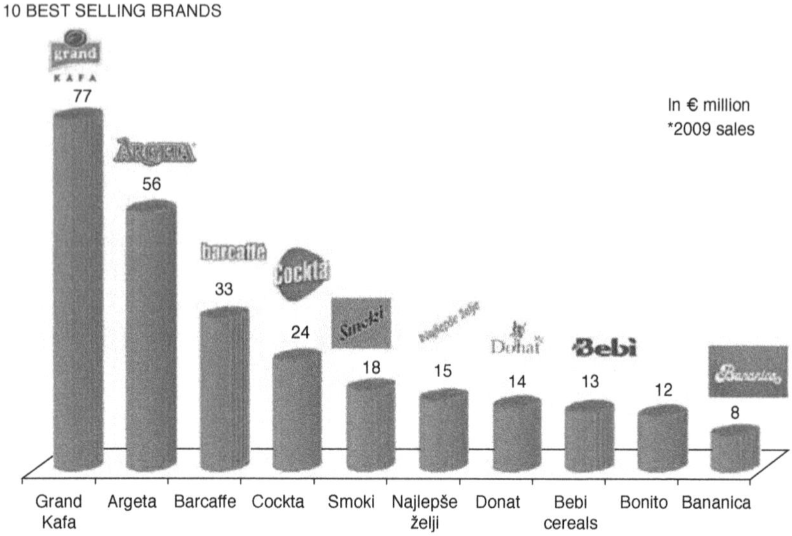

Figure II.2.6 Atlantic Grupa: 10 best-selling brands

Source: Company files and authors' own creation/adaptation.

Exhibit 3: business model

Figure II.2.7 Atlantic Grupa: business model

Note: The difference between the sum of the figures in the five main areas of sales (€309 million) and the total group sales figure (€325.8 million) represents the sales figures from the areas: warm drinks, other food and other areas, which are not included in the main categories.

Source: Company files and authors' own creation/adaptation.

Exhibit 4: sales profile

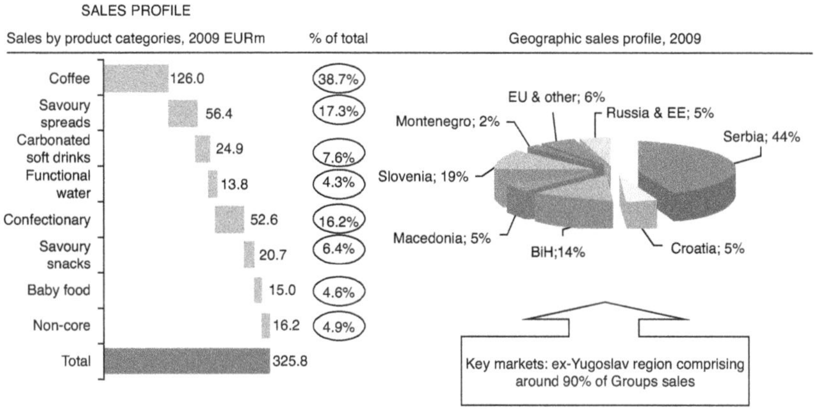

Figure II.2.8 Atlantic Grupa: sales profile
Source: Company files and authors' own creation/adaptation.

Exhibit 5: overview of the market position

OVERVIEW of MARKET POSITIONS

	Coffee	Snacks	Confectionery	Spreads	Carbonates	Baby food
Slovenia	#1 Turkish c. #3 Instant c.	#2 Extruded s.		#1 Savoury s.	#2 Cola carbonates	
Serbia	#1 Turkish c. #3 Instant c.	#1 Extruded s. #2 Baked s.	#2 Choco tablets #2 Bars	#2 Savoury s.	#3 Cola carbonates	
Croatia				#3 Savoury s.	#3 Cola carbonates	
BiH	#2 Turkish c.	#2 Extruded s.	#2 Choco tablets	#1 Savoury s.	#2 Cola carbonates	
Macedonia	#2 Turkish c.			#1 Savoury s.		
Russia						#2 Dried baby f.

5

Figure II.2.9 Atlantic Grupa: overview of market positions
Source: Company files and authors' own creation/adaptation.

Exhibit 6: production plants overview

PRODUCTION PLANTS OVERVIEW

Category	Location
COFFEE	Macedonia (skopje) Serbia (Beograd) BiH (Glavicice) Slovenia (Izola)
CONFECTIONARY & SNACKS	Serbia (Beograd, confectionary) Serbia (Ljubovija, snacks)
SPREADS	BiH (hadzici) Slovenia (Izola)
CARBONATED SOFT DRINKS	Serbia (Palanacki kiseljak) Sloveria (Rogaška)
MINERAL & FUNCTIONAL WATER	Serbia (Palanacki kiseljak, mineral w.) Slovenia (Rogaška, mineral water) Slovenia (Rogaška, functional water)
BABY FOOD	Slovenia (Mima)
OUTSOURCED	Croatia (Bob's Jastrebarsko) Croatia (Novak) BiH (Hencegovina vino)

Figure II.2.10 Atlantic Grupa: production plants overview
Source: Company files and authors' own creation/adaptation.

Exhibit 7: sales FY08

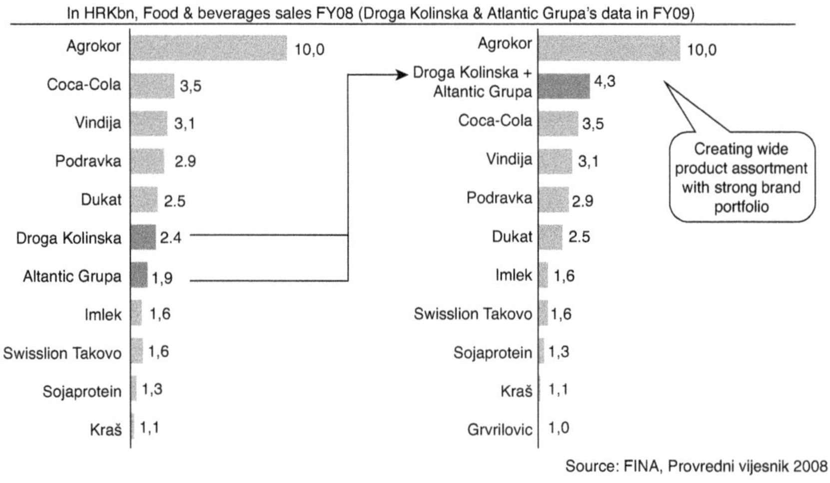

Figure II.2.11 Atlantic Grupa: sales FY08
Source: Company files and authors' own creation/adaptation.

Exhibit 8: people

Mladen Veber/Senior Vice President of business operations

Mladen Veber joined Atlantic in 1996 as the Director of the Rijeka Distribution Centre, while as the General Manager of Ataco (a partnership company in BiH) he made a key contribution to its development as one of the leading distributors in BiH. In July 2001 he was appointed Vice President of Atlantic Trade, responsible for brand management and international markets. In 2006 he was appointed Senior Vice President for Business Operations for all three divisions of Atlantic Grupa. Since 2001, he has been a board member of the Trade Association Council of the Croatian Chamber of Economy. A quite famous former professional basketball player, he is the President of the Management Board of the basketball club Cedevita. Mladen graduated from the Faculty of Mechanical Engineering and Naval Architecture at the University of Zagreb, and continued his education at the IEDC in Bled, Slovenia.

Srećko Nakić/Vice President of distribution division

Srećko Nakić has been building his career at Atlantic from 1994 and he participated in all phases of the company's development. He began as a sales representative in Atlantic Trade and in 1995 was appointed Director of the Distribution Centre in Split and, two years later, the Distribution Centre in Rijeka was also added to his list of responsibilities. In 2002 he became the company's Vice President responsible for overall sales and distribution in the Croatian market. In April 2005 he was appointed Atlantic Grupa's Vice President of the Distribution Division. He is responsible for managing the distribution system of Atlantic Grupa for the entire region of Southeast Europe. He attended the Faculty of Maritime Studies in Split and completed the General Management Program at the IEDC Bled School of Management.

Zvonimir Brekalo/Vice President of sports and functional food division

Zvonimir Brekalo started his career in Atlantic Grupa in 2000, where he was responsible for distribution development of the Johnson & Johnson brand selection in the Croatian market. In 2001 he became Director of Central Services of Ataco, and in 2003 a member of Neva's Management Board. After Neva's acquisition in 2003 and Haleko in 2005, his key contribution was integrating the new companies within Atlantic Grupa, with direct responsibilities for sales and marketing, as well as business development activities in export markets. In 2007 he was appointed Vice President of Atlantic Grupa responsible for the Sports and Functional Food Division. He graduated in Dental Medicine at the Medical Faculty at the University of Zagreb, and continued his education at the IEDC Management School of Business in Bled.

Source: Company files and authors' own creation/adaptation.

Notes

1. A 2004 MBA classroom case discussion excerpt – Atlantic Trade Becoming International (2001).
2. In 2002 Atlantic integrated its entire operations and became Atlantic Grupa, in 2006 became a joint stock company and at the end of 2007 successfully organized the largest IPO in the region. Asked once by a journalist about the name of the company Emil remembered: "Now, we can romanticize the story about the origin of our name: it connects America and Europe, the ocean offers opportunities.... The truth is prosaic. When I established Atlantic, I wanted to have a branch in Milan. I lived in Zagreb and in Milan. We were so small that I couldn't afford a secretary to answer the phone. I leased a space within a company called Atlantica. And then I thought if someone answered – 'Pronto Atlantica' that they wouldn't get the impression that we were so small that we didn't have anyone to answer the phone."

CASE 3: Avangate: Preparing the Trans-Atlantic Jump

Juris Ulmanis and Adrian Tantau

Romania. This case covers a typical and significant issue for this region: how can a young technology company overcome a negative country-of-origin effect – especially when operating in a highly security-conscious industry such as e-payment? Does a company need to disguise itself or appear American in order to be able to succeed in the US market and beyond?

And what role could the current versus a potentially new international top management team play in those endeavors?

In the spring of 2003, RAV Antivirus users received an "Important Announcement," via email, which proudly stated,

> As you are aware, we at RAV have always maintained that our computer antivirus technology is amongst the best available. Microsoft Corporation has recently acquired our technology, which we believe confirms this to the market.

Romanian entrepreneur/investor Radu Georgescu had only created the RAV Antivirus product a year earlier. As the champagne corks popped at the little-known company, GeCAD Software, Radu already felt the need to look for new opportunities. Over the next few months most of the RAV Antivirus development team moved to Microsoft in the United States. A few chose to stay behind. One of them was software engineer Cristian Badea.

Creating a market

Cristian, an original member of the RAV Antivirus team, had approached Radu in 2004 with the idea of setting up an e-payment company to address the growing opportunity in Romania. Cristian knew that e-commerce was growing by leaps and bounds globally and this trend would soon touch

Romania. E-commerce was then at a very early stage and most local companies had little or no knowledge of how to take their businesses online.

Radu and Cristian developed a very trusting relationship and after a series of meetings and discussions, Cristian convinced Radu to make an equity investment and become an active participant in the new venture that they named GeCAD e-payment. The first product was to be an innovative e-payment system.

GeCAD was originally established in 1992. The name combined the Ge from the first two letters of Radu Georgescu's surname and CAD from Computer Aided Design (CAD) because they thought that they would work in the CAD domain. Cristian became President of the new company.

As hoped, the new company with Cristian at its helm as CEO was immensely successful. The first transaction using the GeCAD e-payment system was made in March of 2004 and by the end of the year Romanian shoppers had initiated more than 19,400 transactions. A number of Romanian companies took this opportunity to open up a new channel of distribution for their products and services.

Strong initial growth

It was a pleasant surprise that the company was profitable almost from inception. However, in 2006, Radu and the Board of GeCAD e-payment decided that changes were needed and asked Cristian to step down as the CEO. Though removed as CEO, Cristians became CIO of GeCAD. The reins were handed over to the more commercially oriented Carmen Sebe who, like Cristian, was part of the former RAV team.

GeCAD e-payment continued to grow in Romania and had by now developed a sound and secure payment-processing platform with the capacity and scale to handle large volume. They had created an integrated platform that included the most popular payment options (credit and debit cards and PayPal). In addition, the system was modular (customers could choose parts), with state-of-the-art security and revenue management.

Founding Avangate

In trying to find Electronic Software Distribution (ESD) companies for RAV antivirus in 2006, the team at GeCAD e-payment decided to launch a new company they named Avangate. Avangate's main business objective was to enable new and small software companies in emerging markets to sell and deliver their products online. GeCAD e-payment became a division of Avangate. The company's initial focus was to create a new business opportunity leveraging the existing technology platform infrastructure and the key people who had driven the company's success. They aimed to create an ESD (electronic software distribution) product that was easy to use and would help small software vendors take their products to market quickly. First, they planned to focus on markets and market segments that were difficult for large companies lacking this experience to service. They would focus on high-growth markets like China and Russia as potential growth markets for online software vendors, starting with the low-end segment of each market, then working upward as they gained experience. They planned to create a revenue model through which the company would benefit from the revenue growth of its customers.

The strategy was a success. By 2010, Avangate was a profitable business with a 70% market share in the segments it had entered and was growing at 80% per annum. Meanwhile, GeCAD e-payment continued to maintain a 95% market share in Romania.

A way to grow?

In 2010, MIH Allegro, an active Central and Eastern Europe business-to-business (B2B) e-commerce player based in Poland, sought to acquire the Romanian e-payment operation. The management and shareholders of GeCAD e-payment were in a quandary. They perceived the fact that now they had two highly successful businesses – the domestic GeCAD e-payment e-commerce business and Avangate's online software-selling distribution business – as a dilemma. Management and employees at GeCAD e-payment enjoyed the stability of the Romanian market as well as the prestige of working for a "star" Romanian company. Shareholders were also proud; however, they felt that the growth of the Romanian e-payment business was largely dependent on the growth of the market itself. They anticipated international growth in the e-payment business, but there was also great potential international growth in Avangate's business segment. Radu believed that Avangate had excellent technology and back-office capabilities and that this distinguished them from emerging competitors.

A new positioning for Avangate

Before deciding to sell the e-payment operation of GeCAD e-payment, the management team decided to separate Avangate from GeCAD e-payment and position it as an independent entity purely focused on helping international software companies sell their products online.

Having had success in the emerging markets, mostly in Central/Eastern Europe, and with its self-service product, Avangate's management decided to look westward at the potentially lucrative and high-growth European and North American markets. Avangate had already conceived and developed a unique product called ARMS, a proprietary channel and order management system for the software industry, which had been successfully tested with a few large customers. It was felt that ARMS would provide Avangate the competitive edge that it would need to climb up the segment ladder of independent developers and software as service providers and to tap into the small and medium enterprises (SME) software market.

And, creating this new focus had been a success. At the same time IDC (International Data Corporation) said the Software as a Service (SaaS) market was on its way from growing from US$55 billion in 2011 to US$106 billion in 2014 (24% annual growth). Avangate was growing faster. Between 2006 and 2012 its transactions grew at a 73% annual rate. Starting with 150,000 on 2006, they had grown to four million by 2011. And its total customer count increased 97% annually – from 48 to 2,800.

An issue of reputation

One if the immediate issues faced by Avangate, when contacting potential customers in North America, was its pedigree as an Eastern European company. After all, what is, and where is, Romania? Was Romania the same as Transylvania, where Count Dracula came from? People from that part of the world are cheats and crooks. One could not trust them, especially when it came to money and software related to financial transactions.

Nevertheless, believing in Avangate's competitive advantage, at the end of 2010 the shareholders of Avangate made a firm decision to embark on a growth strategy for North America with the eventual objective of listing the company on NASDAQ.

Avangate's Board of Directors explored a number of options:

1. Find a strong distributor, such as Microsoft, to help them achieve their goals;
2. Hire an experienced international management team to lead the company from Romania;
3. Physically move and transfer the Avangate corporate office to the United States.

Which option should Avangate choose? What are the tangible and intangible challenges for each option? How can Avangate become North American?

Exhibits

Exhibit 1: senior management team at the end of 2010

Radu Georgescu/Co-founder and Board Chairman

Radu has over 20 years of experience in founding and developing companies – Software, Internet, e-Commerce, Security. In 1992 he set up GeCAD, and in 1994 he and his team began developing RAV antivirus, as well as three other software products. In 2003, he had more than 150 resellers in 60 countries with RAV and, that same year, this technology attracted Microsoft's attention, the company with which he eventually negotiated the sale of RAV. Instead of joining Microsoft, he decided to remain an entrepreneur and in 2004 incorporated another five technology companies with GeCAD.

In addition, he advises a number of start-ups and mature technology companies.

Diwaker Singh/Board Director

Diwaker Singh has over 35 years of international management experience, the last 25 of which have been as a Chairman/CEO of large multinational companies. Singh's business experience spans across business sectors including telecommunication, aviation, logistics, tourism, investment banking and real estate.

His career highlights include the establishment of the first private cargo airline in India, the first mobile network in India and the first 3G mobile telephony network in Europe. Singh has lived and worked in Europe for the last 15 years.

He received an award from the President of Romania in 2004 for his contribution to improving the investment climate of the country. Furthermore, he is actively involved in supporting start-up and early stage business ventures in Europe and has raised over US$300 million in the last ten years toward this end.

Cristian Badea/Co-founder and CTO

Cristian has extensive experience selling software over the Internet, payment methods, fraud detection techniques and broad experience in Web applications, both for internal and external use in an SMB.

He received a Bachelor in Computer Science at Universitatea Politechnica din Bucuresti.

Carmen Sebe/CEO for five years

She is a technology industry executive with significant operational, general management, P&L and international experience.

Previous to her current position as Avangate COO, she worked as Sales & Marketing Manager in RAV Antivirus (acquired by Microsoft in 2003). After that, she became the CEO of Cvantage, GeCAD e-payment and Avangate.

She has extensive experience with new products and markets, winning key accounts and business partnerships, in addition to expertise in transition planning/execution, organizational development and product development.

Source: Company files and authors' own creation/adaptation.

Case B: Avangate – what happened next?

Avangate decided to hire a new high-profile senior management team and advisory board members from the United States to provide the company with the best possible platform and chances to successfully enter into the US market (see profiles below).

In 2011 the 3TS Growth Fund invests in Avangate.

In 2012 Avangate wins the Red Herring Top 100 Europe Award for Most Innovative Companies.

In 2013 the company is the winner of the CODiE Awards – Best-Selling e-Commerce and Billing Platform.

In October of the same year, Francisco Partners – a leading global private equity firm focused exclusively on investments in technology and technology-enabled services businesses – acquires Avangate. Francisco Partners is a leading global private equity firm focused exclusively on investments in technology and technology-enabled services businesses.

The geographical setup at the beginning of 2014 is as follows:

- North America: Corporate: Redwood Shores, California
- Western Europe: HQ: Amsterdam, the Netherlands
- Eastern Europe: Development, Marketing and Support: Bucharest, Romania
- APAC: Sales Support

They continue to follow their vision to become the number one commerce (e-Commerce + billing + distribution) provider in the world for software and online services markets.

Profiles of the new senior management team members

Carl Theobald/President and CEO

Carl Theobald is a seasoned technology executive with a proven track record of building high-performance organizations and bringing world-class products and services to market.

Prior to joining Avangate in 2011, Carl served as SVP at Serena Software, one of the largest independent software companies in the Application Lifecycle Management market. Running more than half the company, Carl was responsible for all of Serena's products and services – including launching Serena's first-ever SaaS-based solutions.

Carl has also held multiple executive roles at Oracle including running Oracle's sales, marketing and e-commerce products division.

Throughout his career, Carl has also helped to build multiple venture-backed companies, including RubiconSoft, a company he co-founded to provide better visibility into demand for the manufacturing industry.

Carl received an MS in Engineering–Economic Systems from Stanford University and a BS in Electrical Engineering from Princeton University, where he graduated summa cum laude. Carl is passionate about playing the piano and music composition, receiving the "Most Outstanding Musician Award" from the New England Conservatory.

Michael Ni/CMO and Senior VP, marketing and products

Michael Ni brings over 20 years of experience as a marketing and product executive in bringing successful innovation-driven businesses to market – from start-up to Fortune 500 companies.

Michael's business experience spans across software, telecommunications, consumer packaged goods and digital media.

Prior to joining Avangate, Michael served as VP Products at Amdocs, where he drove the definition and development of next-generation customer management, retail and commerce applications. In addition, he has held executive positions at leading CRM/ERP vendors, technology start-ups, and in strategy consulting. These roles include GM/Managing Director at MyWire, a venture-backed new media company; VP of Product at Oracle/PeopleSoft, where he drove the definition and development of the "Fusion" next-generation applications platform; VP of Product and Operations at venture-funded OnePage, Inc. (acquired by Sybase, Inc.) as well as Marketing Strategy Consultant at PricewaterhouseCoopers.

Michael received an MBA from Harvard Business School, an MS from Stanford University and a BS in Mechanical Engineering/Robotics from Massachusetts Institute of Technology.

Joseph Brown/Senior VP of global sales

With over 30 years of general management experience in technology companies ranging from start-ups to Fortune 1000 companies, Joseph G. Brown has led sales and marketing organizations around the world – in Africa, Europe, the Americas and Asia.

Prior to joining Avangate in May 2011, Joseph served as the General Manager of RightNow's EMEA operation, where he directed RightNow's success in a number of vertical markets including the Telecommunication, Travel & Entertainment, Consumer Product Goods and Retail markets. He has also held executive positions at other leading technology vendors including President of Séance Software, President and CEO of Edify Corporation and Senior VP of Worldwide Field Operations at Auspex Systems, Inc.

Joseph received his MBL from the University of South Africa and his B.Comm from the University of Witwatersrand. He is passionate about golf and has played at many of the leading courses around the world. During the wintertime, Joseph and his wife Elizabeth can be seen at Stanford University's football and basketball programs.

Source: Company files and authors' own creation/adaptation.

Profiles of the new Advisory Board members

William J. Lansing/Member of the Advisory Board

William J. Lansing has extensive e-commerce experience, having served as CEO and Director of a number of public companies including Digital Diver, InfoSpace, ValueVision Media, NBC Internet and Fingerhut. Mr. Lansing was a partner at the private equity firm, General Atlantic Partners, and also served as Vice President of Corporate Business Development for General Electric in addition to being a member of General Electric's Corporate Executive Council. Mr. Lansing currently serves on the board of directors of RightNow Technologies (NASDAQ: RNOW), a SaaS CRM company, and FICO (NYSE: FICO), a decision analytics company.

Thomas Kendra/Member of the Advisory Board

Thomas Kendra is a veteran of the IT industry, with over 30 years of experience and numerous executive and board level roles, including his current role as a member of the Executive Board of Directors for ACG Silicon Valley, a leading organization for senior M&A and corporate development executives. Previously, he was the Executive Vice President of the enterprise products and solutions business line at CA Technologies, Inc. (formerly Computer Associates) and also served on the Board of Directors of Pareto Networks. Additionally, Mr. Kendra was the Group President of the security and compliance group at Symantec Corporation.

Source: Company files and authors' own creation/adaptation.

CASE 4: Big Filter: Russian Filters in the International Market[1]

Galina Shirokova

Russia. This case covers a family-run car filter business and the questions its founder/CEO faced about the company's growth strategy. Should they stay in a less competitive market, in which they served nearly all continents? Or should they move into much more competitive and attractive segments, directly supplying OEMs, and therefore competing with lead players such as Bosch, among others?

On the frosty winter morning of January 15, 2011, Boris Beylin, the founder of the Big Filter Company – a Russian producer of car filters – was driving to his Saint Petersburg office thinking about a problem that had started to weigh heavily on his mind: Should the company more aggressively go after the international original equipment manufacturers (OEMs) market or stay focused on their primary customers in the spare parts aftermarket? Boris would soon discuss this question with his management team in the first of many sessions to form the five-year strategic vision.

Big Filter had been highly successful since its establishment in 1988, growing to revenues of €14 million[2] (580 million Russian rubles [RUB]) and nearly 300 employees by 2011. The company supplied over 1,300 types of filters not only within Russia and CIS (Commonwealth of Independent States)[3] but also to over 30 countries as diverse as the United States, Canada, the United Kingdom, Israel, Egypt, Germany, Italy, Finland, Turkey, Taiwan, United Arab Emirates, Costa Rica, Syria and Iran. Though the company had achieved marketing and financial success, Beylin had set his sights higher. He believed that he could take the company to the next level and, in order to do so, he would likely need to build capabilities for foreign manufacturers producing cars in Russia such as General Motors (GM) and Volkswagen (VW).

After arriving at the office, he joined his management team for the first strategy session. The team had prepared a package outlining some of the key market trends. He knew the session would be filled with key questions: Should the company put a focus on selling filters to foreign OEMs manufacturing in Russia? If so, would the company be able to recoup the €1.1 million investment? How could the company's resources be divided between the spare parts business and the new foreign OEM business? Which strategy would position the company to reach even greater heights?

Boris Beylin

Boris Beylin received a degree in mechanical engineering in 1975, with a major in manufacturing. Until 1988, before the collapse of the Soviet Union in 1992, he worked as an engineer at a large state-owned machine-building company in Saint Petersburg (then Leningrad). His engineer's salary was insufficient to support his two children and wife, so Boris looked for ways to make extra money on the side. His first venture was sewing blue jeans. He explained:

> In the mid-1980s, it was very fashionable and prestigious to have jeans, but virtually impossible to buy them. Since they were in short supply, a few of my friends and I signed up to take men's tailoring classes. I bought two sewing machines and we bought fabric from foreign sailors – Saint Petersburg is a big seaport city. I worked at the machine-factory during the day, and then sewed the jeans at night.

Making customized jeans brought in much needed extra income. However, after a year and a half of moonlighting as a jeans maker, Boris decided to make a radical change: stop sewing, leave his day job at the factory and establish a car repair shop. The shop was the second of its kind in the city. Since new ventures were sanctioned by the Soviet Union, he set up the shop as a cooperative with eight owners. However, it did not last long. Of its closure Boris said, "All of the members except myself wanted to spend the profit instead of reinvesting it in the business. I knew it wouldn't work. The cooperative broke up and that's when I decided to go it alone and start my own company."

The birth of Big Filter

Rampant change in Russia – specifically, the dissolution of the Soviet Union under the restructuring efforts (known in Russian as Perestroika) – allowed for the establishment of new sole proprietorships. Boris took the opportunity to re-establish the car repair shop as a solely owned business in 1988. While he was pleased with the freedom of running his own business, Boris quickly realized one key problem: there was a shortage of spare parts to repair the cars that were coming into his shop. He recalled:

> I knew there was plenty of opportunity to produce car parts. So I used some of the money I had earned at the cooperative to buy land and an

> old factory that belonged to a state-owned transport company. The area was abandoned and in ruins. There wasn't any sewage, electricity or infrastructure of any type. Once I fixed up the building and restored it to working order, the transport company actually sued me so that they could get everything back! Luckily, I won the lawsuit.

On a trip to the United States, Boris saw plastic filters in an automotive store. As an engineer, he immediately saw the opportunity to produce plastic fuel filters back home at low cost and high quality. Upon returning to Saint Petersburg, he began analyzing the market for plastic fuel filters and discovered that the international fuel filter market was undergoing significant transformation. Fuel filters for old carburetted cars were being replaced by two alternative types: inexpensive, low-quality fuel filters produced in Southeast Asia and expensive, high quality fuel filters produced in the United States and Western Europe. He commented on the opportunity he saw:

> I was quite confident that I could produce inexpensive, high-quality fuel filters in Russia that could be exported profitably. The timing was right for Russian manufacturers to export since it was quite easy to get cheap loans from the government for acquiring foreign equipment. Also, the intellectual potential of Russia's labor force was very high; many qualified engineers had just lost their jobs in Soviet enterprises. Finally, the exchange rate of the ruble was negligible, inflation was enormously high and the price of electricity and oil had dropped dramatically.

In 1994, the company released its first fuel filter. Three years later it expanded its lineup to air filters. From the beginning, Boris believed that it was necessary to focus not only on domestic consumers, but also on export. He said, "In my opinion, if one cannot manufacture products in accordance with international standards, it is better not to take up manufacturing such products at all. I did not see any reason for inventing anything radically new, so we decided to copy the models of filters that already existed abroad."

Stages of internationalization

The company set up its production line with acquired machinery from Germany. The next step was to find clients abroad. One of the largest trade shows in the industry was called Automechanika and was held in Frankfurt, Germany. In 1997, Big Filter became the first Russian company to present at the trade show. Boris described the experience, "At first, I was not very confident in presenting the products and communicating with potential customers and partners due to my low comfort level in English. With each subsequent trade show, I boosted my confidence. To improve my English, I listened to language instruction cassettes and CDs while driving."

The first export shipment was made to Romania in 1997. Orders to Israel, Germany, Hong Kong, Finland and Egypt quickly followed. According to Boris:

> From the very beginning, the emphasis was placed on quality at affordable prices. Moreover, the system of customer support was built so that, for example, an export–import manager must answer all customer messages and inquiries within 24 hours. Customers are informed on the order status, all the necessary documents are sent on time with the necessary drawings, certificates, samples and test results. Openness and honesty are mandatory at all stages. Customers choose whether we deliver the products directly or through their distributors.

Following the Frankfurt experience, the company became a regular participant in international trade shows and conferences. At one such conference, AutoRussia, Boris met the director of the European division of the major automotive parts manufacturer, Magna Corporation. Boris recalled:

> When I met the director from Magna, we decided to carry on with our business conversation over dinner. At one point in the evening, he looked at me and said, "Sorry, but I'm finding you to be quite pushy." At that moment, I realized that I had come a long way with my English and that I was able to make my point heard. At least language would no longer be a barrier to international growth!

Despite his assertive methods, Boris understood the paramount importance of personal connections and relationships with partners. Joined by his wife, Esfir Beylina, Finance Director, and daughter, Natalia Beylina, Foreign Operations Director, the team strove to deepen international relationships. Natalia commented:

> In Russia, it is very common to do business at restaurants and saunas. During international trade fairs, we don't have enough time to entertain in this way because operating our own exhibition stand is very hard work. It's crucial to sort out the important visitors and keep detailed notes of people's questions and interests. Sometimes I'll even write physical descriptions like, "the man with the long moustache," on the back of people's business cards so I can remember who I was talking to. On most days at a trade show, I end up having over 50 different conversations and it's vital that I take notes so I can remember each customer.

After trade shows, Natalia made it a habit to convert her informal notes into a more structured database, often adding information about the potential customer's national or local markets by researching on the Internet (size of a potential market, types of cars, and so on). Then she composed a letter in which she recommended the most suitable filters for the local market. By capturing the relevant information about the potential customer's country, she was able to point out the most popular models of filters and recommend a specific order. All correspondence was entered into the database.

Natalia estimated that only seven to ten of the 250 contacts made during a typical trade show eventually placed an order. Despite this seemingly small share, these customers were usually quite loyal. Natalia believed that customers replenished orders based on their satisfaction with the quality and cost as well as timely deliveries and flexibility. When shipping to new partners, Big Filter sometimes requested advance payment, but often took risks and made the delivery without it. Natalia commented, "We've never lost when we've decided to take a risk and send filters to a customer even without a sound formal contract and preliminary payment. If you want to conquer a market, you need to take some risks."

Boris added:

> Sure, you always get some customers that don't want to play by the rules. However, we supply all the products to European partners without preliminary payments or formal contracts. The business might be over next day when you decide to make all transactions formal. So many regulations and legal requirements in Russia are aimed at hampering business operations instead of facilitating them. Besides, the majority of customers react negatively when you start talking about a contract right away. I learned this lesson early on when I was dealing with a US customer who became very nervous when I mentioned a contract; we ended up shipping to him directly and it worked out for the best.

As for foreign companies' opinion toward Russian suppliers, Boris believed that there was a good trend although some suspiciousness remained. Boris said, "It takes years to earn an international reputation as a good, reliable partner. In the automotive components industry, you can't really just focus on the domestic market. Car companies operate globally and it is important to develop your business according to international standards." In the initial stages of the company's development, sales were made directly to car repair shops and parts locations in Saint Petersburg. As the company grew, it established a large dealer network covering all territories of Russia and the majority of CIS countries.

Expanding the product line

The product range of the company grew significantly since its first year. The company introduced new models of filters, continuously enlarging the product range for foreign cars. In 2000, Big Filter started mass-producing plastic injection filters. In 2001, the company added oil filters as well as new plastic filters, specifically designed for Japanese automobile manufacturers. In 2003, Big Filter acquired a computerized automated line from Germany to produce air panel filters. The production equipment was the first of its kind in Russia. The company continued investing in increasing its lines and capacity; in 2009, it launched a line of cabin filters and, in 2010, it retooled many of its production lines. The company financed all new machinery purchases and line expansion organically through its own cash (see Exhibit 2 for the company's capacity by line).

Big Filter as of 2011

By 2011, Big Filter offered about 1,300 types of car filters (fuel, air, cabin and oil). The company had 48 distributors to cover Russia and CIS countries and supplied car filters to over 30 additional countries; the company had shipped products to all continents except Australia.

Annual unit sales were 15 million filters translating to total revenues of €14 million (approximately €1.00 per unit). Export sales accounted for 38% unit sales and about 12% of the total revenue. The reason for the lower value of export sales was because of the product mix. For the export market, the company sold inexpensive plastic fuel filters to developing countries. Although plastic fuel filters were becoming less common in newer automobiles, there was still a large aftermarket in developing countries. The product mix was substantially different for Big Filter's domestic market; the company sold a broad assortment of fuel and air filters within Russia and CIS countries. The difference between both markets was evident by the average selling price; €0.36 selling price per unit for export versus €1.43 selling price for the domestic market.

Employees

The company's employee base grew to keep up with demand. In 2010, it added 40 new people, taking the entire company to 300 employees (some of them had been working since establishment of the company). There were about 20 top managers (7% of the workforce with an average age of 40 years old), 70 engineers and middle managers (23% of the workforce and an average age of 35 years old) and the remainder were production and back-office employees (average age of 27 years old). In addition to the permanent workforce, the company employed temporary staff. The number of temporary staff fluctuated based on demand (throughout the year, there were about 60 temporary employees on average).

Manufacturing

Big Filter's site was made up of a 12,500 square meter manufacturing facility, a supplies storage area, four container freight storage areas, the finished product storage area and two administrative buildings. The manufacturing facility was divided into five workshops: a plastic molding shop and workshops for each product type: oil filters, fuel filters, injector filters and air filters. In addition, there was a pre-production department which consisted of a tool workshop and quality assurance equipment. During peak manufacturing periods – March to October – the factory required about 170 workers.

The production process was divided into the following five main steps:

1. Processing the filter element
2. Assembling the filter
3. Quality control
4. Labeling and packaging
5. Storage and shipment

Big Filter took great pride in its quality control. To avoid defects during manufacturing, they inspected and tested 100% of their products. The following operations were carried out and recorded in daily journals:

- Upon arrival, all purchased raw materials, as well as separate component parts for manufacturing, underwent an initial inspection;
- Every two hours supervisors monitored the parameters of technological process at workplaces: the adhesive weight, the temperature of the heating furnace, and the geometric dimensions;
- Teams of highly qualified specialists of the Quality Management Centre monitored the controlled parameters during shifts including steadfast compliance to the workflow, thereby eliminating the possibility of errors made by job operators; and
- Any malfunctioning equipment or deviations from the product's specified dimensions were followed by immediate adjustment and re-check

Big Filter was the only Russian company among other domestic car filter producers that had a quality certificate acknowledged by the international expert group IQNet. The company had also achieved the ISO TS 16 949 required by all global automotive manufacturers.

The strategy session

Big Filter's management team congregated to lay out the strategic plans for the next five years including the most crucial question: Should Big Filter attempt to enter the foreign OEM market? Among the participants were:

- Sergey Nesmeyanov, Director of Development
- Natalia Beylina, Director of Foreign Operations

- Nikolay Alexeev, Director of Production
- Vyacheslav Ivanov, Director of Sales
- Alexander Sterligov, Director of Marketing
- Boris Beylin, President

As the session got underway, a few of the company's top managers insisted on more aggressively competing in the foreign OEM market. Other managers were more cautious and wanted a more careful market assessment including major competitors and a thorough SWOT (strengths, weaknesses, opportunities and threats) analysis before choosing a new strategic direction. It quickly became clear that several managers were skeptical that Big Filter could effectively compete in the foreign OEM market.

In 2011, the market for car filters was very attractive and had posted high growth despite the global economic crisis. However, where there was growth, there was also intense competition. The market within Russia had changed dramatically in the previous two decades; originally, the majority of filters were for Russian cars such as Lada and Volga. With the import of several foreign brands, namely BMW, Kia, GM, Renault, VW and Ford, there were over 3,000 models of filters available for the aftermarket.

One manager said, "This business is not a cakewalk," referring to the difficulty of new Russian firms establishing themselves in the market. Generally the barriers to entry required capital investments over €5 million and the establishment of a sales network.

Competition could be divided into three major groups:

1. *Widely known international brands:* MANNFILTER, FRAM, Purolator, Bosch and Champion. Most of the major international brands of automotive filters were produced in China or partly produced in Europe and completed in China. Prices were typically 15 to 25% higher than the average price for filters in Russia.
2. *Russian brands known within the CIS region:* Avtoagregat, SCT, NevskyFiltr, NAC and Citron. This group differed in their focus on quality, but most were considered to have lower quality than the major European and US filters. The filters were manufactured either in Russia or China. The prices were typically at about the market average.
3. *Unknown Brands:* This group of producers made products in Russia and China but did not put any resources toward quality or brand development. They were typically 15 to 25% less than the market average and usually copied products from the first two groups. It was estimated that there were about ten smaller firms that produced no-name filters.

Big Filter considered itself to be part of the second group of producers, although it differentiated itself through higher quality. Exhibit 2 shows a competitive analysis and an evaluation of Big Filter's position.

While filters could not be substituted per se, many newer automobiles had embedded filters that did not require regular replacement. Furthermore, some domestic and foreign producers made low-quality filters which periodically affected the sale of high-quality filters.

The bargaining power of major automobile manufacturers was very high as they demanded high quality, low prices, fast replenishment and constant innovation. However, the aftermarket was very different as the buyers were heterogeneous: car service centers, corporate retail chains, markets and numerous other independent shops. While large retail chains required tough terms in their contracts, they were not major customers for car components or filters.

Market size

The Director of Marketing, Alexander Sterligov, had prepared some detailed studies of the market including an assessment of the current market (Exhibit 3), data on vehicle manufacturing in Russia (Exhibit 4) and preliminary growth estimates by market segment with Big Filter's estimated market share (Exhibit 5). He estimated growth in the following three segments of the market:

1. OEM – Growth from 4.3 million units (€5 million in revenues) in 2010 to 7.3 million units (€8.1 million in revenues) in 2011. He believed that the most dynamic growth would come from the foreign light motor vehicle market mostly because he expected foreign automakers would increase their production capacity. He estimated growth to stay strong for the next couple of years, reaching 9.6 million units and €11.2 million by 2013.
2. OES (service stations for vehicles under warranty) – Decline of –10% from 8.9 million units to eight million units in 2011 mostly because of warranty coverage ending on a certain portion of the vehicles and thus becoming part of the aftermarket.
3. Secondary Aftermarket – Increase of 7% from 213 million units to 227 million units in 2011.

Potential benefit to Big Filter

Vyacheslav Ivanov, Director of Sales, had projected two possible scenarios depending on whether the company decided to build additional capacity specifically for the foreign OEM market:

1. Do not build new OEM capacity – Under this scenario, Big Filter would continue with its focus on the aftermarket. The company would continue to opportunistically sell to the OEM market where it had capacity, but would not build any new capacity to serve the market. Ivanov estimated

that the company would see a slight lift in sales (albeit a market-share drop) even if it did not actively pursue foreign OEMs.
2. Build capacity – If Big Filter were to actively pursue the foreign OEM market, he believed that the company could increase OEM sales from 814,000 units (€950,000) to 1.3 million units (€1.5 million). By building capacity for the foreign OEM market, he believed that there would also be some upside for selling filters for foreign vehicles in the OES warranty market as well as the secondary aftermarket.

See Exhibit 5 for his sales estimates under both options.

Investment required

In order to increase capacity for the foreign OEM market, the company's management expected that Big Filter would need to invest €1 million to upgrade the production facility. Approximately €400,000 would go toward buying new, modern production lines for oil and air filters and €600,000 would be allocated to construct a new production area of 1,000 square meters to accommodate the equipment. There would be another €100,000 as a one-time expense for retraining company personnel. When calculating NPV on projects of this nature, the company had traditionally used a margin estimate of 25%, a tax rate of 30% and a discount rate of 15%. The estimated life of the equipment was ten years (depreciated using a straight-line methodology).

To finance the necessary inventory, Big Filter had traditionally upheld a policy of minimizing bank credits and maximizing suppliers' credits. The financial position of the company was quite stable; only about 17% of its capital structure was comprised of debt and the company had a current ratio (current assets/current liabilities) of 1.3. Because of the company's reputation, it was able to receive favorable payment terms from its suppliers of raw materials and equipment. Its three types of loans were:

1. Loans from suppliers of raw materials for a period of 30 days to 90 days
2. Loans from equipment suppliers for up to two years
3. Short-term bank loans of up to 1.5 years

Internal capabilities

Much of the discussion on competing in the foreign OEM market revolved around the internal capabilities and resources required. Sergey Nesmeyanov, Director of Development, summarized the main features of the primary market and the challenges that the company faced in entering the OEM market:

> It is necessary to prove that our manufacturing facility can produce high-quality products. We cannot manufacture low-quality products for foreign OEMs. We will need the capabilities to complete product drawings in accordance with each OEM. We will need to invest in IT systems, which could get costly, since our IT systems would need to link to the systems of each OEM. I think it could be an extra €200,000 above and beyond the amount needed for production and training.
>
> We need to be prepared to disclose all of our manufacturing processes as well. They will demand to see our raw material and equipment suppliers and they will have the right to veto any that do not meet their standards. Furthermore, they will want the right to conduct plenty of audits, looking at quality, technology, storage of raw materials, storage of finished products, personnel and the technical preparation of the product. The positive thing is that many of these requirements are fulfilled with the quality certificate ISO TS 16 949, which we have.
>
> Naturally, the prices for OEMs are going to be lower. Finally, we will need to look at our entire staff's level of competence when working with OEMs. It goes without saying that fluency in English is also very important.

Those in favor of staying focused on the filter aftermarket argued that there was still plenty of room to grow by expanding to new countries. Natalia Beylina, Director of Foreign Operations, noted that in addition to growing to new geographies, the company could also increase the value of its exports by adapting products for its partners:

> Our export motto is, "Export without borders." For instance, in September the company will again participate in the largest international exhibition of automotive components in Frankfurt, Automechanika 2011. At the exhibition we are planning to meet with the majority of our current customers, discuss plans for next year, solve vital problems, as well as try to find new customers. Our company is interested both in the world's largest companies, which get private label supplies, and small trading companies, which could become our regular customers. For example, in 2010 we added customers from the United States, Germany, Italy, India to the list of regular customers. The projected increase in exports is over 10%. I want to see us move in the direction of higher-value exports whereby we increase the average selling price of each unit. I think we can do this if we start adapting some of our higher-value products to our export partners.

Exhibit 6 shows a summary of the SWOT analysis done by Big Filter's management team.

How to move forward?

As the strategy session was in full swing, Boris turned aside and glanced through the window overlooking the factory yard. The yard, despite the cold weather, was bustling: auto loaders drove around, factory workers passed by and a supervisor angrily scolded a newcomer for smoking in the wrong place. Boris thought to himself, "an ordinary working day." The movement seemed purposeful, but he knew that the current strategy, developed in 2009 and embodied in the bustle below, was in need of revision (see Exhibit 7). Given the vigorous debates during the session, the team was unlikely to arrive at a consensus.

Was it time to make a bold move into the foreign OEM market? Were there enough company resources and competencies?

Or would the company be better off focusing on the secondary aftermarket parts business? After all, Boris was keen to spend more time with his family and young grandchildren. It had been an exciting adventure over the past two decades. Was Boris ready for another?

Exhibits

Exhibit 1: financial statements

Table II.4.1 Big Filter: balance sheet

		2008	2009	2010	Plan 2011
	Asset	**€ 000**	**€ 000**	**€ 000**	**€ 000**
I	**Fixed assets**	**388**	**1,236**	**1,139**	**1,674**
1	Capital assets	388	386	685	1,630
2	Construction in progress		850	454	44
II	**Current assets**	**1,302**	**2,227**	**2,058**	**2,543**
1	Supplies:	496	1,511	1,038	1,459
1.1	*Raw materials, materials*	*227*	*403*	*381*	*450*
1.2	*Finished products and goods for resale*	*261*	*1,093*	*646*	*957*
1.3	*Unexpired costs*	*8*	*15*	*11*	*52*
2	VAT	8	11	11	16
3	Receivables (up to 12 mths.)	755	700	1,003	1,055
3.1	*Purchasers and clients*	*740*	*613*	*934*	*992*
3.2	*Other debtors*	*15*	*87*	*69*	*63*
4	Immediately available funds	43	5	6	13
	Total assets	**1,690**	**3,463**	**3,197**	**4,217**

		2008	2009	2010	Plan 2011
	Liabilities	**€ 000**	**€ 000**	**€ 000**	**€ 000**
I	**Capital and Reserves**	**479**	**724**	**1,167**	**1,943.175**
1	Authorized Capital	0.5	168	196	196
2	Additional Paid-in Capital		85	84	0.025
3	Retained Profit (loss)	478.5	471	887	1,747.15
II	**Long-Term Liabilities**	**0**	**627**	**478**	**773**
1	Loans and Credits	0	302	304	0
2	Other Long Term Liabilities	0	325	174	773
III	**Short-Term Liabilities**	**1,210**	**2,113.6**	**1,551.05**	**1,501**
1	Loans and Credits	77	46	79	125
2	Other Short-Term Liabilities:	1,133	2,067	1,472	1,376
2.1	*Suppliers, Contractors*	*911*	*1,841*	*1,150*	*1,047*
2.2	*Payables to Employees*	*94*	*135*	*161*	*158*
2.3	*Payables to State non Budgetary Funds*	*20*	*25*	*30*	*37*
2.4	*Taxes Payable*	*92*	*45*	*54*	*66*
2.5	*Other Creditors*	*16*	*21*	*77*	*68*
3	Deferred Revenues		0.6	0.05	0
	Total Liabilities	**1,690**	**3,463**	**3,197**	**4,217**

Exhibit 1 financial statements (continued)

Table II.4.2 Big Filter: profit & loss statement 2009–2011

		2009	2010	plan 2011	2009 vs. 2010		2010 vs. 2011 plan		2009 vs. 2011 plan	
	Indicators	€ 000	€ 000	€ 000	€ 000	%	€ 000	%	€ 000	%
I	**Profit and loss**									
1.1	Sales net	8,366,125	10,954,887	13,949,514	2,588,762	30.94%	2,994,627	27.34%	5,583 389	66.74%
1.2	Cost of goods	–5,573,247	–6,755,689	–8,469,352	–1,182,442	21.22%	–1,713,663	25.37%	–2,896,104	51.96%
1.3	Gross profit	2,792,878	4,199,198	5,480,162	1,406,320	50.35%	1,280,964	30.50%	2,687,285	96.22%
1.4	Cost of sales	–129,256	–171,327	–287,939	–42,071	32.55%	–116,612	68.06%	–158,683	122.77%
1.5	Administration cost	–2,642,632	–3,415,785	–4,305,086	–773,153	29.26%	–889,301	–	–1,662,454	62.91%
1.6	**Sales margin (1.1–1.2–1.4–1.5)**	**20,990**	**612,086**	**887,138**	**591,096**	**2816.12%**	**275,052**	**44.94%**	**866,148**	**4126.52%**
II	**Other profit and loss**									
2.1	Interest receivable				0		0		0	
2.2	Interest payable				0		0		0	
2.3	Other incomes				0		0		0	
2.4	Other operational income	6,000	10,929	6,265	4,929	82.15%	–4,664	–42.67%	265	4.42%
2.5	Other operational cost		–1,462	–1,469	–1,462		–7	0.46%	–1,469	
2.8	**Profit before tax**	**26,990**	**621,553**	**891,934**	**594,563**	**2202.92%**	**270,381**	**43.50%**	**864,944**	**3204.71%**
2.9	Tax assets				–	–	0	–	0	–
2.10	Taxes payable		–9,272	–900	–9,272		8,372	–90.29%	–900	
2.11	Income tax	–20,365	–66,218	–203,608	–45,853	225.16%	–137,390	207.48%	–183,243	899.81%
2.13	**Net profit**	**6,625**	**546,063**	**687,426**	**539,438**	**8142.47%**	**141,363**	**25.89%**	**680,801**	**10276.25%**

Source: Company files and authors' own creation/adaptation.

Exhibit 2: competitor analysis and evaluation of Big Filter competitive position

Table II.4.3 Big Filter: competitor analysis and evaluation of Big Filter's competitive position

Market segments, companies / Characteristics	Premium	Middle class: Foreign vehicles	Middle class: Domestic vehicles	Niche players	Regional players	No name
	Mann & HumelMahle, Fleetguard, Bosch	**WIX–Filtron, Finwhale, SCT**	**Big Filter, Tsitron, Livny, Nevsky Filter**	**Difa, Mistral, Filtrserv, Sakura**	**Salut, Legion, Kolan, Trek, Tosol-sintez, Za rulem**	
Territorial scale	Global leaders, importers	Importers, big international players	Major national market players, competing within CIS	National market players or importers	Regional market players or small national players, STM	Small players
Product range	Wide (including premium class)	Mostly oriented for foreign vehicles	Oriented to domestic vehicles, mostly on light motor vehicles	Narrow specialized product range	Narrow product range or output of customized products	Narrow range
Quality	High, 100% manufacture quality control	Meets all the requirements of the secondary market	Meets the requirements of secondary market and has a claim on OEM-supplies	Quality adequate to its segment	Average or below average	Low
Price level	Relatively high	Average	Average	Prices oriented to segments	Below average or negotiated with customer	Low prices at the cost of low quality
Cooperation with automakers	Strong networks	Informal networks	No formal networks			

Source: Company files and authors' own creation/adaptation.

Exhibit 3: external environment of the company: major trends

Operating Environment: The business environment of car components producers in Russia was in flux as of 2011. First, there was no national state policy to support domestic manufacturers. The business community generally agreed that companies with good business perspectives could not attract financing at low interest rates and regular inspections of various governmental bodies usually turned out to be counterproductive. Also, getting a permit from a government department (registration of a new venture, various licenses, land issues and so on) was highly complicated.

Importing and Exporting: The Russian customs system did not create any incentives for domestic producers and caused producers to incur extra expenses and losses (long delays of cargo deliveries, never-ending additional requirements for transportation documents and so on). All of these factors led to artificially inflated expenses and delays in business development. Raw materials accounted for 50 to 70% of the costs of producing car filters. Generally the materials were imported and a Russian producer had to pay import custom taxes. Therefore Russian producers had a disadvantage to foreign producers who did not have the same heavy import taxes on raw materials. There was the possibility of getting reimbursements on the import custom taxes, but typically it wasn't worthwhile since the transaction costs of doing so were sometimes just as much as the reimbursement. Furthermore, if a foreign company supplied filters to a new foreign car assembly plant in Russia, it was exempted from the import custom tax, but a Russian producer who manufactured similar filters locally was not.

The Economic Crisis: The influence of the economic crisis on car filter production was relatively insignificant. The demand for car filters in the aftermarket was typically inelastic because filters were seen to be an important maintenance item for cars. The OEM market was usually more exposed to volume fluctuations since the sale of new cars was closely linked to economic conditions. The crisis caused a devaluation of the ruble, which reduced the price of Russian products for the international market and created additional advantages for Russian producers. Another positive outcome of the crisis was the decrease of workforce turnover.

Wages and Labor Workforce: The economic and social environment for businesses in Russia had seen several important trends since 2000. On the one hand, the wage level in large Russian cities (Saint Petersburg and Moscow) had been constantly rising. On the other hand, many enterprises experienced a deficit of human resources. There was not only a shortage of white-collar workers (engineers, designers, managers) but also of blue-collar laborers. Many Russians did not want to work at manufacturing enterprises and, to cover the labor deficit, many positions were taken by immigrant workers.

Customer Preferences: Over the last ten years, many Russians switched from buying national car brands such as Lada and Volga to foreign ones like BMW,

GM, Renault, VW and Ford, and correspondingly the structure of demand for car filters was also continuously changing from cheaper to more expensive models.

Technological Changes: Modern cars had substantially changed the requirements for modern filters. In the early 1990s, it was normal for some Russian producers to fill special molds using a medical syringe. Because of new requirements, this would be nearly impossible – high-tech equipment was required. For example, many of the new filter models were equipped with sensors which signaled the end of the filter's life. Furthermore, there were some filters that did not require replacement for the usable life of the automobile. Additionally, new technologies and communication devices had substantially changed the face of marketing and sales.

Market Review of the Russian Motor Industry in 2000–2010: The data on automobile manufacturing and sales, for both Russian and foreign automakers, are presented in Exhibit 4.

Source: Company files and authors' own creation/adaptation.

Exhibit 4: light motor vehicle manufacturing in Russia in 2000–2010, thousands of units (000s)

Table II.4.4 Big Filter: light motor vehicle manufacturing in Russia in 2000–2010 (thousand of units, 000s)

Indicator	2000	2001	2002	2003	2004	2005	2006	2007	2008	2009	2010
Manufacturing, total, including:	969.24	1021.98	980.68	1010.03	1110.08	1068.76	1176.34	1293.09	1469.90	595.81	800.00
Domestic	969.24	1015.34	969.55	956.36	977.28	911.03	897.44	834.71	877.09	316.87	450.00
Foreign, Total	0	6.66	11.15	53.64	132.8	157.73	278.90	458.38	592.81	278.94	350.00
Out of them Industrially Assembled	0					14.09	190.29	268.77	376.64	193.26	250.00

Source: Company files and authors' own creation/adaptation.

Table II.4.5 Big Filter: light motor vehicle sales in Russia in 2000–2010 (thousand of units, 000s)

Indicator	2001	2002	2003	2004	2005	2006	2007	2008	2009	2010
Total Sales, including:										
Domestic Models	932.60	930.11	969.35	980.00	789.20	783.50	715.30	692.1	392.2	430.00
Foreign Models, including:	482.90	625.60	653.10	630.80	925.20	1319.50	2030.70	2429.4	1012.6	1070.00
Manufactured in Russia	6.50	11.10	57.70	121.80	151.50	270.00	439.20	586.5	362.7	365.00
New Foreign	79.10	111.50	195.40	285.00	456.00	743.80	1206.40	1467.3	636.4	690.00
Used Foreign	397.30	503.00	400.00	224.00	317.70	305.70	385.10	375.6	13.5	15.00

Source: AEB, Federal State Statistics Service, State Transport Company, ASM-Holding, Autostat, PwC, i-Mash.ru, RBK Agency.

Exhibit 5: market estimates by segment

Table II.4.6 Big Filter: market estimates by segment

	ESTIMATES FOR 2011										
				DO NOT BUILD			BUILD CAPACITY			MARKET FORECAST	
	ACTUALS 2010			FORECAST 2011			FORECAST 2011			2012	2013
	Market Volume	Big Filter Volume		Market Volume	Big Filter Volume		Market Volume	Big Filter Volume		Market Volume	Market Volume
	000 units	000 units	Share %	000 units	000 units	Share %	000 units	000 units	Share %	000 units	1 units
OEM MARKET											
Domestic light motor vehicles	2,104	602	28.6.%	3,000	600	20.0.%	3,000	750	25.0.%	3,270	3,400
Foreign light motor vehicles	1,583	85	5.4.%	3,500	100	2.9.%	3,500	450	12.9.%	4,500	5,000
Motor trucks	589	127	21.6.%	750	100	13.3.%	750	100	13.3.%	1,022	1,200
Total OEM units (Automobile factories)	4,276	814	19.0.%	7,250	800	11.0.%	7,250	1,300	17.9.%	8,792	9,600
Inc/(Dec) % versus Prior Year				70%	–2%		70%	60%		21%	9%
Sales (€ 000)	5,000	950	19.0.%	8,100	920	11.4.%	8,100	1,500	18.5.%	10,600	11,200
Inc/(Dec) % versus Prior Year				62%	–3%		62%	58%		31%	6%
Sales/Unit (EUR)	1.17	1.17		1.12	1.15		1.12	1.15		1.21	1.17
OES WARRANTY MARKET											
Domestic light motor vehicles	4,230	256	6.1%	4,000	400	10.0%	4,000	400	10.0%	4,200	4,400
Foreign light motor vehicles	2,709	28	1.0%	2,500	25	1.0%	2,500	50	2.0%	2,700	2,900
Motor trucks	1,978	23	1.2%	1,500	50	3.3%	1,500	50	3.3%	1,500	1,500
Total OES units (warranty vehicle service stations)	8,917	307	3.4%	8,000	475	5.9%	8,000	500	6.3%	8,400	8,800
Inc/(Dec) % versus Prior Year				–10%	55%		–10%	63%		5%	5%
Sales (€ 000)	10,000	350	3.5%	7,000	500	7.1%	7,000	525	7.5%	8,000	8,600
Inc/(Dec) % versus Prior Year				–30%	43%		–30%	50%		14%	8%
Sales/Unit (EUR)	1.12	1.14		0.88	1.05		0.88	1.05		0.95	0.98

Continued

Table II.4.6 Continued

				ESTIMATES FOR 2011							
				DO NOT BUILD			BUILD CAPACITY			MARKET FORECAST	
	ACTUALS 2010			FORECAST 2011			FORECAST 2011			2012	2013
	Market Volume	Big Filter Volume		Market Volume	Big Filter Volume		Market Volume	Big Filter Volume		Market Volume	Market Volume
	000 units	**000 units**	**Share %**	**000 units**	**000 units**	**Share %**	**000 units**	**000 units**	**Share %**	**000 units**	**1 units**
SECONDARY (AFTER) MARKET											
Domestic light motor vehicles	65,742	6,681	10%	65,976	6,000	9.1%	65,976	6,000	9.1%	66,000	67,000
Foreign light motor vehicles	87,305	577	0.7%	99,043	800	0.8%	99,043	1,000	1.0.%	112,000	114,000
Motor trucks	60,331	954	1.6%	62,452	1,000	1.6%	62,452	1,000	1.6%	64,000	66,000
Secondary market units	213,379	8212	3.9%	227,471	7,870	3.5%	227,471	8,310	3.7%	242,000	247,000
Inc/(Dec) % versus Prior Year				7%	–4%		7%	1%		6%	2.0.%
Sales (€ 000)	285,000	12,000	4.2%	300,000	11,500	3.8%	300,000	11,750	3.9%	320,000	325,000
Inc/(Dec) % versus Prior Year				5%	–4%		5%	–2%		7%	2.0.%
Sales/Unit (EUR)	1.	1.		1.	1.		1.	1.		1.	1.32.
TOTAL	226,572	9,333	4.1%	242,721	9,145	3.8%	242,721	10,110	4.2%	259,192	265,400
Inc/(Dec) % versus Prior Year				7%	–2%		7%	8%		7%	2%
Sales (€ 000)	300,000	13,300		315,100	12,920		315,100	13,775		338,600	344,800
Inc/(Dec) % versus Prior Year				5%	–3%		5%	4%		7%	2%
Sales/Unit (EUR)	1.	1.		1.30	1.		1.30	1.		1.	1.30

Source: Company files and authors' own creation/adaptation.

Exhibit 6: primary SWOT analysis of Big Filter

Table II.4.7 Big Filter: primary SWOT analysis

	S Strengths	W Weaknesses
Internal environment	**S 1.** Experience of serial deliveries to car manufacturers. **S 2.** Long-term development plan, the system approach to development. **S 3.** The presence of functioning CPC and preparation to ISO/TS. **S 4.** Independence from external funding sources. **S 5.** A qualified team of top managers **S 6.** Stable quality of products.	**W 1.** Lack of adequate space to accommodate new equipment. **W 2.** Lack of skilled professionals in key areas (logistics). **W 3.** Low margin of filters in the case of supplies to the factories. **W 4.** Underutilization of equipment. **W 5.** The absence of a unified information system. **W 6.** Lack of special equipment for manufacturing of certain types of filters.
	O Opportunities	**T Threats**
External environment	**O 1.** The emergence of a new segment of the market by tightening requirements for the localization of the industrial assembly of foreign OEM according to Resolution No. 166 of the government. **O 2.** Stable dynamics of growth in the volume of car manufacturing and, consequently, the demand for filters. **O 3.** Financially stable position, the possibility of raising additional funds.	**T 1.** Further intensification of competition in the market with low product differentiation. **T 2.** Arrival of large international parts manufacturers to Russia. **T 3.** The instability of the global and Russian. economies and, as a consequence, the prediction of a drop in sales in the dealers' networks. **T 4.** Decline in working age population, labor shortages. **T 5.** Tendencies to the increasing demand for lifetime filters.

Source: Company files and authors' own creation/adaptation.

Exhibit 7: strategic plan of the Big Filter company 2009

1. **Goal** Take a leading position among the companies manufacturing car filters in Russian and CIS.
2. **Expected results**
   - 2.1. Increase in Return on Assets (RoA) up to 15%
   - 2.2. Provide the working capital ration not less than 1.25
3. **Time horizon** The above-mentioned indicator should be achieved in 2012 (in three years)
4. **Focus**
   - 4.1. Target segments
   - 4.2. Car factories
   - 4.3. Conveyer

4.4. Warranty vehicle service stations
4.5. Secondary market: Russian Federation and CIS countries
4.6. Distributors
4.7. Trade centers
4.8. Special clients
4.9. Dealers
4.10. Final wholesale buyer (КОП) and marketplaces (bazaars)
4.11. Branded stores
4.12. Individual customers and legal entities
4.13. Export. Secondary market
4.14. Positioning
4.15. Determine how to introduce the company and its products to the above-mentioned target segments
4.16. Offer several options of filter delivery by using the price/quality principle

5. **Means of achieving the goal**

5.1. Product
5.2. Make emphasis on the filters for foreign cars
5.3. Via network structures
5.4. Via the Internet
5.5. Truck filters is a new, promising direction
5.6. Types of products
5.7. Filters for foreign vehicles were sold for the first time via dealer structures – 2.35 million pieces a year
5.8. Filters of foreign vehicles on the territory of Russia and beyond – 5.6 million pieces a year
5.9. Filters for trucks – 0.75 million pieces a year
5.10. Filters for domestic vehicles – 17 million pieces a year
5.11. Pricing policy
5.12. Implement pricing policy at each level of product realization up to the end customer on the basis of the following factors:
5.13. Perception of prices on filters by end customers
5.14. Price elasticity of demand in the secondary market
5.15. Comparative analysis of costs, prices and offers of major competitors on the target segments of the market
5.16. Primary market
5.17. CIS secondary market
5.18. Export. Secondary market
5.19. Set prices for the secondary market considering strategic interests of the company in relation to the customer segments and groups of filters
5.20. Determine margins/discounts on different stages of distribution channels and conditions of providing them
5.21. Distribution

5.22. Via current and new centers (dealers in trade centers)
5.23. Via representative offices of warranty car factory networks
5.24. Via direct mail
5.25. Promotion
5.26. To develop a range of activities stimulating the retailers to sell actively Big Filter branded filters

6. **Resources**
   6.1. Production capacity
   6.2. Get ISO
   6.3. Ongoing company development notwithstanding the current state of the market
   6.4. To know and constantly study the filter business development on the global market (constructions, technologies, equipment, raw material)
   6.5. To determine which innovations should be implemented
   6.6. To implement new technologies and types of equipment
   6.7. Production lines for manufacturing filters for motor trucks
   6.8. Production lines of corrugated filters
   6.9. Semi-automatic lines for filter labeling
   6.10. Semi-automatic lines for filter packaging
   6.11. Establish a new structure of standard production procedure which would provide for better manufacturing conditions
   6.12. Logistics. Provide interactions with certain structures listed below
   6.13. Suppliers (one's own production, somebody else's)
   6.14. Storage
   6.15. Transportation
   6.16. Finance
   6.17. Personnel. Create a self-developing staff body which, depending on changing conditions, would be capable of self-regulation at each level
   6.18. Work groups
   6.19. To transform the existing teams of individual workers into groups with a leader, which could react independently and flexibly to changes occurring in the process of work
   6.20. Managers and engineers
   6.21. To work out a method of creating temporary teams comprising employees of different divisions on the flat level to solve immediately any occurring problems
   6.22. Incentives
   6.23. To create for the above-mentioned groups conditions under which team members would be interested in upgrading their skills and later use the acquired knowledge at work
   6.24. Finance

6.25. To provide optimal utilization of current funds
6.26. To determine sources of additional funding of all planned projects

Source: Company files and as' own creation/adaptation.

Notes

1. This case was written by Galina Shirokova – Professor at Saint Petersburg University Graduate School of Management, Russia. It was prepared solely to provide material for class discussion. The author does not intend to illustrate either effective or ineffective handling of managerial situation.
2. Several figures in this case study have been disguised to protect confidentiality.
3. The official members of CIS were: Armenia, Azerbaijan, Belarus, Kazakhstan, Kyrgyzstan, Moldova, Russia, Tajikistan and Uzbekistan. Although not official members, Turkmenistan and Ukraine were sometimes included within the definition of CIS.

CASE 5: Fx3x: Star Performance without a Star Attitude

Makedonka Dimitrova and Ilijana Petrovska

Macedonia. How far is it from Macedonia to the "Dream Factory"?

In this case, a young entrepreneur creates an EMMY-award-winning, Hollywood supplier of movie animation with a workforce of more than 120 employees.

In the process of attaining success – considering the fact that most mid-sized firms in that space died – the company faced a huge dilemma: whether they should (a) remain a smaller player with modest growth (which would also free them of trying to secure external capital); (b) try to raise significant VC money to push for rapid growth and become a large player; or (c) to try become a mid-sized player despite the fact that it seems to be a "death zone."

In late February 2013, Kristijan Danilovski, co-founder of Fx3x, a visual effects and animation company, was the guest of honor at the Macedonian National Television Studio One, which was covering the Oscar Awards[1] ceremony currently underway across the globe in Hollywood. Three of the movies that Fx3x had worked on in the last year were nominated for Oscars and Life of Pi had just won an Oscar in the visual effects category. While the Fx3x artists celebrated the achievement, Kristijan was already thinking about the company's next moves. Venture capital funding and potential mergers crossed his mind, among other considerations.

It was dawn in Macedonia when the Oscar ceremony ended. Kristijan called his partner and co-founder, Milivoje Gjorgevic–Misko, eager to discuss the future of their company. They met in their office, 3D Cinema, and started the day of big decisions with a cup of strong coffee.

Introduction

Established in 1997 in Macedonia, Fx3x was the only visual effects company in the wider region. Enjoying its first-mover advantage, the company also faced many challenges such as poor market conditions, limited Internet infrastructure and the lack of skilled artists. However, the biggest challenge was understanding their competitors and obtaining work in the US market. Guided by a strong passion for visual effects, continuous analysis of competitors and a clearly articulated business model, Fx3x's portfolio had internationalized in just a few years. By 2013, Fx3x employed more than 110 artists (Exhibit 3) who had worked on over 30 blockbuster films (Exhibit 4). Nonetheless, Kristijan and Misko believed they could perform even better and across the world, targeting Japan, the United Kingdom and Canada as well.

The visual effects industry[2]

In the 1990s, big US studios created 70% of the world's demand for visual effects. The film industry was a global and fragmented industry, experiencing significant international sales and representing many start-ups that tried to appeal to international rather than only domestic markets. The global market consisted of small studios of 20 to 50 employees and giants with over 600 staff that dominated the market (Exhibit 1). They pursued the same basic approach of offering the same movies to viewers around the world regardless of local tastes. This strategy paid off economically, as the same movie could be sold in markets around the world with voice-over or subtitles in the local language.

In 2009, demand for visual effects shifted to Chinese and Indian studios that provided low quality at lower prices. As the market became flooded with studios from Europe, India and China, mid-sized studios were forced to close or consolidate. The majority closed, with the exception of those operating in Germany, Canada and the United Kingdom where the government provided subsidies. Another strategy studios employed was to acquire similar studios located in different geographical areas, almost equal in size.

The film industry functioned on a project basis, where visual effects represented one phase of the project. The most common way of supplying visual effects was via big studios subcontracting smaller studios dispersed around the world. The studios had difficulty keeping skilled visual effects artists exclusively for themselves, despite investments in their personal training, because most artists preferred to be freelancers. The industry's upstream was characterized by highly mobile artists.

Apart from developing a base of skilled artists, visual effects studios had to keep up with the cutting-edge technologies and latest software developments for visual effects design. Technological advancement created issues of expenses and space management. Widespread Internet use and fast data exchange over the global net triggered the next outsourcing era for visual effects, thus rapidly increasing the number of competitors. As barriers to entry diminished, the market created incentives for new entrants. Lower capital requirements in equipment provided the opportunity for open Internet access to competitors' work, allowing easy follow-up on novelties and trends in the industry. The technology contributed to increased movie profits (Exhibits 3 and 4) by cutting costs for real-life scenes, costly sets and actions, unrealistic creatures or environment and so on.

The Academy Awards ceremony remained the most important and influential vehicle for identifying the cream of the global industry. The Academy's highest honors provided further opportunities for visual effects companies to expand their client base and win new projects.

The entrepreneurs

Kristijan Danilovski was born and raised in a Macedonian family in Skopje. At an early age he taught himself basic graphic design on a Commodore Amiga, one of the first computer brands scarcely available on the local market. The computer design turned into a hobby, but as no higher education in graphic design was offered in the country, he became a freshman at the Faculty of Mechanical Engineering. Kristijan's passion for video games triggered his interest in artistic work on visual effects. In 1994, during his studies, a friend's friend hired him to establish a graphic art studio for a local advertising and computer company. It was Kristijan's first career experience. His engineering precision, organizational skills and tactics were crucial for the visual effects company's start-up and growth.

Milivoje Gjorgjevik, curious by nature, was using AutoCAD for visualization of projects, a software application for 2D and 3D Computer Aided Design (CAD) and drafting[3] while studying to become an architect at the same university in Macedonia. The visualization of bringing life to inanimate objects got his interest. Being extremely creative, he started experimenting and committed to bigger challenges, so he and Kristijan ended up working at the same place. They had many things in common, one of which was the shared passion to work on movies. In less than a decade of pioneer work they created, as he defined it in a statement for the *New York Times*[4] magazine, "a clean industry from scratch. One that changes the mindset."

Establishing the business

Kristijan's dream of working on digital imaging was born with the release of the first George Lucas Star Wars movie in 1979, but only came to reality in 1997. He and Misko helped create an animation studio that had high-end Silicon Graphics equipment, but soon his ideas and the owner's went separate ways. The studio technology was appealing, but management did not understand the window of opportunity he saw in further developing the special effects side, so he quit that job.

Both Kristijan and Misko got in touch with visual effect studios in London and the United States. Kristijan bought a plane ticket to London to meet with a studio executive concerning a possible contract. With no great expectation except for full confidence in the quality of his work, he entered the studio with a show reel that he had prepared the night before the interview. The studio offered him a senior artist position and promised a salary as high as a CEO's compensation in his country. Kristijan went back to his hotel as happy as a kid. He could work on films!

A few days later, while waiting for an afternoon show at the Warner Brothers Theatre on Leicester Square, he visited another visual effects studio in the neighborhood. It was a rented office space with a couple of Silicon Graphics stations on large glass tables and several artists approximately his age. Realizing that his direct competitor offered identical or similar services to what he had in mind, he decided to enter the market himself. "Now I have no doubts! If they can do it, I can do it even better," concluded Kristijan. Having the similar technical setup at home, with all the financing they could muster from family and friends, Kristijan and Misko started the company XXX in 1997. A room in Kristijan's family's apartment was rearranged to become an office space.

Kristijan and Misko's professionalism and creativity in advertising production secured profitable projects right from the beginning. The entrepreneurs' skillful execution as well as their client orientation put them in high demand from the local advertising market, but this was far away from their vision. However, making commercials provided cash that was reinvested in new equipment and artists' training. Kristijan believed that they had to have the latest technology at their disposal in order to maintain a leading market position. For this purpose, in 1999 they committed to a three-year loan and purchased new equipment which enabled them to deliver complex solutions to clients, creating a competitive advantage in the local market. Their continuous investments initiated whole new services and expanded the visual effects market in Macedonia, creating new professions and a demand for skilled workers.

Despite the low economic performance of the country and the Western Balkans region, the company achieved high yearly growth of 150% and took up to 80% of the market share. In 2000, ever-increasing profits enabled moving the company to new premises that accommodated 15 creative minds in 400 m^2. The growth ceiling in Macedonia was fast approaching as Kristijan and Misko discussed the next strategic decision. They felt confident in their ability to provide high-level products and services. They usually wrapped up daily meetings by saying, "If our work is satisfactory for a few dozen top-performing local and international companies, it should be good enough for anyone."

Company products (as of 2013)

The company provided services in three industry sectors: film visual effects, film animation and visual effects in advertising, as well as post-production.

In particular, they offered a full sequence work service facility, from roto/paint to matchmove and CG (computer-generated) integration, as well as fluid dynamics simulations. The animation department was full service, delivering all stages from modeling, texturing, rigging, animation lighting and full integration with live action. Their service portfolio was improving as the demand for such production methods was increasing on the world market.

Going international

Upon deciding to expand in the region, Kristijan looked into his Turkish business links, while Misko screened the film industry in Serbia. Based on their own market research, Turkey seemed to be harder to break into. They also performed feasibility analyses through primary and secondary research of the industry's trends for the two markets. Kristijan and Misko thought there would be a demand for the service in Serbia, due to the fact that Belgrade was once the center of the Yugoslavian film industry. In 2001, they established a satellite office in Belgrade on their own, avoiding investors who were not interested in knowledge transfer. XXX was more interested in business angels than financiers at the time.

Table II.5.1 Fx3x: company growth timeline

Company founded	Expansion to Serbian market	Expansion to US market	Contract with Industrial Light & Magic	Challenge: keep growing or stay small and controllable
1997	2001	2004	2009	2013

Source: Company files and authors' own creation/adaptation.

The key figure in Serbia was Misko, who built a productive relationship with numerous studios and advertising agencies. From a management perspective, the Belgrade office was a successful experiment through which Kristijan and Misko gained confidence in entering a new market and reorganizing the company to meet the growing customer base. This growth stage led to the next dilemma. Misko said to Kristijan during a meeting, "This is not what we expected. We wanted to get closer to the film industry, didn't we?" The Belgrade office was not the desired stopover on the way to Hollywood.

The two devoted energy into industry analysis focusing on environmental trends such as the latest technological advancement and social trends, estimating that the demand for visual effects would grow especially given the customers' growing preferences for 3D movies (Exhibit 2). Worldwide outsourcing demand increased significantly, changing the conditions for gaining entry to the industry. Moreover, the big studios were conservative in selecting visual effects partners which hindered access to the distribution channels that remained a barrier to entry for XXX. On the other side, the wider region of ex-Yugoslavian republics[5] had just survived a turmoil and was trying to regain their political stability and safety, thus reflecting negatively on local outsourcing companies and their opportunities to provide services to the film industry. Given the circumstances, XXX focused on its professional development and reinvented its approach to clients from the US market. Despite all their efforts, they still needed the right business links and finances to make themselves more visible to the studios.

Strategies for growth

Luckily, Kristijan initiated long-term cooperation with an international donor, USAID. USAID's local projects supported the internationalization of the digital media industry in the country with training, advisory services, media trade shows and conferences.

In 2003, Brad DeGraf and Julia Frey, distinguished visual effects industry expats, joined XXX to advise them on internationalization prospects. DeGraf[6] was considered to be an innovator in computer animation in the entertainment industry or, as some called him, "The icon in the world of 3D animation." Ms. Frey[7] was a respected visual effects producer. DeGraf and Frey visited the company, scanned the local environment and prepared a market analysis. The picture they created for XXX was positive. The 15 artists from XXX had first-class capabilities in commercial production, film special effects, 3D animation and live action production. They believed that the most promising markets for visual effects were the United States and Western Europe.

XXX believed they could differentiate themselves from their competitors through distinctive partnerships and qualified staff. However, it was believed that studio size could be a major obstacle to getting Hollywood jobs because XXX was too small in human capacity to keep up with major film project dynamics and deadlines. This particular disadvantage was later transformed into a strategic resource despite a high unemployment rate, low income, limited access to technology and low computer literacy in Macedonia. They created a buzz for new talent among the young population that was more open to new trends. The existing network of primary school computer laboratories connected by broadband was a great starting point. Fx3x developed the 3D @ E-Schools project, deepening their partnership with USAID. They developed a distance-learning platform for 3D computer animation and offered the possibility for students to develop animated characters. The talent pool of 27 schools evoked interest among 400 students for visual effects, creating a strong base of artists for the future.

The experts' strategic proposal required deep changes in XXX's organizational structure, including closing the Belgrade office. There were several internal and external issues to be considered: studio rebranding, identifying and training more artists, developing internal quality control and internet infrastructure as well as creating a network of potential clients. First on the priority list was making the company known to clients. Following the expats' suggestion, the studio rebranded from XXX into Fx3x, since its first name was associated with another film genre in the industry which did not reflect the scope of activities they performed.

The firm's organizational structure was adjusted to suit emerging needs, including more delegation to junior artists. The firm was advised to get a public relations officer on board and to delegate media-related responsibilities to a professional. Both the administrative and the artistic staff reported back to Kristijan and Misko. They increased control over the company's computer stations to ensure a higher level of security. They were now ready to meet potential clients overseas.

The marketing trip to the United States

In 2003, supported by DeGraf and Frey, the Fx3x CEOs flew to Los Angeles to gain insight into the film industry. As Hollywood functioned on the basis of personal contacts and recommendations, the two expats arranged meetings with well-known visual effects studio executives. The group visited Universal Studios, 20th Century Fox, ILM, Dreamworks and Sony Pictures Imageworks. Meeting potential clients was a great push forward for Fx3x from a marketing prospective and even more so in understanding market demand, but it was not enough to enter the network of partners. Not considering failure an option, Kristijan and Misko continued with direct marketing trips overseas while, in the meantime, adjusting their working hours. They had to be av-ailable 24/7 just as their industry competition was.

To gain more information about their competitors, in 2004 the team participated in SIGGRAPH,[8] a major industry exhibition in Los Angeles. Furthermore, as magazines provided a good medium for raising brand awareness in the film industry, Brad DeGraf wrote an article for *The Computer Graphic World*[9] magazine, a trendsetter among visual effects industry professionals. In the 30,000 free copies, Fx3x was introduced as a trusted outsourcing partner from Southeastern Europe.

Despite the fact that the industry in the United States was still against outsourcing, DeGraf took advantage of the momentum that Fx3x had generated at SIGGRAPH and secured trial work on a Hollywood project. Finally, Kristijan and Misko concluded, "We made the right choice in spending all the money from the account to fly the team to the U.S., but without the money from our own pockets we would not have made it to SIGGRAPH. The risk paid off."

First tastes of Hollywood

The excellent piece of trial work got Fx3x a seat on the Digital Backlot team. In summer 2004, they were hired to do work for Sony Image Works on the Martin Scorcese film The Aviator[10] featuring Leonardo Di Caprio. Although it was a only approximately three minutes of the real-time movie, it gave them strength to continue. Back home, limitations in human resources and poor Internet infrastructure were working against the timely delivery of work for The Aviator. Kristijan was sometimes awake for 24 hours, solving logistical problems along the way, and encouraging the artists to persevere and meet their deadlines. Thanks to The Aviator's great success and Oscar nomination, agents became more interested in Fx3x for visual effects outsourcing. Kristijan and Misko used the recognition of their good work to attract additional contracts. An agent helped them to close several contracts in Canada. Their network broadened.

Following the first marketing trip and several additional short visits to the United States and Canada, Fx3x secured several more TV commercial projects for famous brands such as Fanta, American Express and AT&T. Some of those promotional spots were broadcast on big screens in Times Square in New York, which helped build morale and momentum. This was more inspiration than money.

Digital Media Park in Macedonia

Leveraging resources, Kristijan tried to explore new opportunities as the idea to create a Digital Park emerged among industry participants in Macedonia. A production and post-production facility with a stable broadband Internet connection could become a great strategic asset for winning more complex projects, thus creating a sustainable competitive advantage.

In 2006, again with assistance from the local USAID mission, Kristijan succeeded in acquiring the 15-year lease of a government-owned military warehouse. The space offered a unique environment for film sets, cameras and lights, but they were short of funds to turn it into a fully functional workplace. Kristijan and his team then prepared a grant application that later succeeded in winning a US$400,000 grant from the USAID Global Development Alliance. The project design envisioned office space and training facilities, dressing and makeup rooms, a small theater, a cafeteria, several studios accompanied with a few small apartments and even commercial store fronts. The modular design of the warehouse would have allowed more companies, when needed, to share space and resources. In the meantime, the TV miniseries *Path to 9/11* brought an EMMY nomination to Kristijan personally for visual effects, giving him an additional boost to pursuing his Hollywood dream.

In 2008, Misko and De Graf signed a short-term contract with the most preeminent company in the industry, guaranteeing high-level security and control at all stages of visual effects development. This was a growth opportunity, but also an organizational and network security challenge (Exhibit 5). They felt pressure to move into the new Digital Park premises, so they complemented the grant funding with over a million dollars of their savings and equipped the park with the latest digital network infrastructure and security standards. All staff were trained in accordance with new policies and procedures backed by detailed and strict business contracts and employee confidentiality agreements. Kristijan was happy to ensure that their security was at the highest level during a facility audit by one Hollywood studio, explaining to the auditor:

> We have no Internet access on the work network. Entry to the premises is controlled with keycard access points; all employees have their own level of authorization. We also provide 24-hour, on-site security. As for the power supply, we have an independent backup power system in place. The incremental backups are a routine already.

Growth and its challenges

In 2007, the number of artists at Fx3x rose to 30. The company took advantage of local employees' loyalty and their desire for a stable job. The renowned film awards gave the artists inspiration and the energy to work toward tight deadlines. Fx3x used their position to attract more loyal artists, resulting in a strong competitive advantage in the target market. Kristijan said, "We at Fx3x invest the last euro in cutting-edge technology and training. Artists are the most important links in the chain of Fx3x."

Fx3x's development was a major achievement for its owners; with stable organic growth over 15 years, they had created a company which competed impressively on the global market. It had brand recognition and won distinguished nominations and awards.[11]

Since 2011 the Fx3x investment trend in research and development had decreased down to 30–40%. They had 110 people on the payroll. As Fx3x became a mid-sized company, it became more difficult to sustain growth through internal activities. Should Fx3x further utilize internal growth strategies or was it time to look into external strategies for growth?

There were threats coming from competitors along the way. Chinese artists offered cheaper labor, but local artists could deliver work with excellent quality for a slightly higher price. The next question was whether they could recruit enough artists to support the super growth that was expected. Maybe they could open the doors to foreign artists from the nearby region or even wider. The internal growth strategy of developing new resources and new artists would require further innovation. Could Fx3x speed up its development? How could they decrease risk and expenses during the internal process of innovation?

Their competitors now also came from Canada and Germany, represented by medium-sized studios that provided another opportunity for acquisition or consolidation. An opportunity for a large number of firms in the fragmented industry would be to consolidate and establish industry leadership, while the common way to achieve this would be through a geographic roll-up strategy in which one studio would start acquiring similar studios that were located in different geographic areas.

They had a good negotiating position working for Industrial Lights & Magic (Exhibit 1), then with MPC Technicolor from London as well as London's Mill Film – all of them on films nominated for an Oscar in 2013. They managed to be among the first 15 companies in the world to adapt to the new stereoscopic way of working, and strove to be a company that would set trends.

They received offers for new film projects, TV serials and commercials. Clients were now looking for them. Fx3x considered opening a satellite office in Canada that would serve both the Canadian and US markets. However, L.A. was still far away from Vancouver, or Toronto, a place they'd already considered expanding to. Another option was to hire an agent for the US market, but that required leveraging the cost. They were still looking into figures trying to find out what would be the most cost-effective solution. In parallel, interested investors approached the company on several occasions to offer financing. However, Fx3x was more inclined toward a two-fold investment process that would bring know-how, secure further growth and maintain a "wanted" position on the global market. Should they consider an external advisor to help them make the right decision? Would it be difficult to sustain the passion of the management team and the employees if they grew further?

Exhibits

Exhibit 1: visual effects' studios in the film industry: world top six players

Table II.5.2 Fx3x: visual effects' studios in the film industry: world top six players

1. **Industrial Light & Magic – ILM**	San Francisco, US
2. **Weta Digital**	Wellington, New Zealand
3. **Digital Domain**	Los Angeles, US
4. **MPC Technicolor**	London, UK
5. **Double Negative**	London, UK
6. **Sony Imageworks**	Los Angeles, US

Source: Company files and authors' own creation/adaptation.

Exhibit 2: market share

Table II.5.3 Fx3x: market share for each production method 1995–2013 (US$)

Rank	Production method	Movies	Total box office	Tickets	Share
1	**Live action**	12,156	$185,611,449,804	40,304,846,122	80.47%
2	**Animation/Live action**	134	$15,775,874,831	2,539,745,739	6.84%
3	**Digital animation**	180	$13,778,781,156	1,980,698,181	5.97%
4	**Hand animation**	182	$5,213,025,859	3,649,586,351	2.26%
5	**Stop-Motion animation**	27	$540,147,342	87,429,898	0.23%
6	**Rotoscoping**	8	$38,857,454	13,136,163	0.02%
7	**Multiple production methods**	16	$16,828,075	2,104,938	0.01%

Source: "Production Methods." Accessed January 23, 2014: http://www.the-numbers.com/market/production-methods.

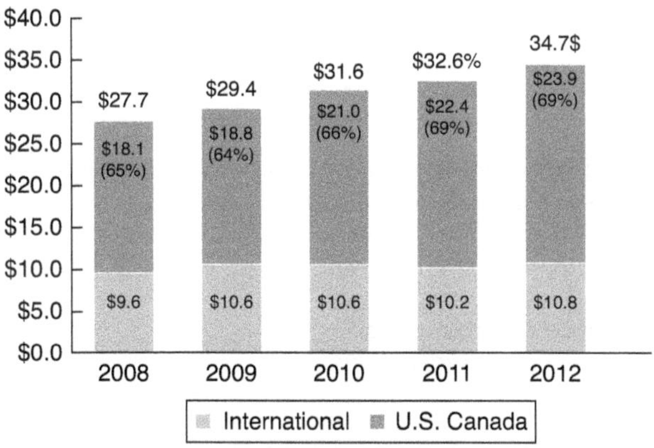

2008	2009	2010	2011	2012	% Change 12 vs. 11	% Change 12 vs. 08
$9.7	$9.9	$10.4	$10.8	$10.7	–1%	10%
$6.8	$7.2	$8.5	$9.0	$10.4	15%	53%
$1.6	$1.7	$2.1	$2.6	$2.8	6%	73%
$18.1	**$18.8**	**$21.0**	**$22.4**	**$23.9**	**6%**	**32%**

Figure II.5.1 Fx3x: global box office – all films (US$ billions)

Source: "Theatrical Statistics Summary 2012," American Motion Pictures. Accessed January 23, 2014: http://www.mpaa.org/Resources/3037b7a4-58a2-4109-8012-58fca3abdf1b.pdf

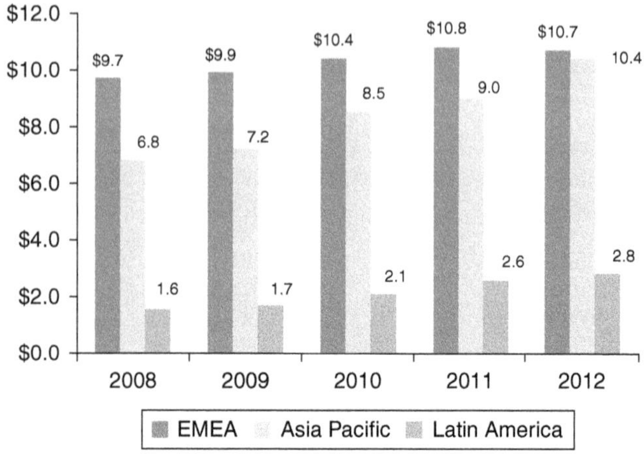

2008	2009	2010	2011	2012	% Change 12 vs. 11	% Change 12 vs. 08
$9.7	$9.9	$10.4	$10.8	$10.7	–1%	10%
$6.8	$7.2	$8.5	$9.0	$10.4	15%	53%
$1.6	$1.7	$2.1	$2.6	$2.8	6%	73%
$18.1	**$18.8**	**$21.0**	**$22.4**	**$23.9**	6%	32%

Figure II.5.2 Fx3x: international box office by region – all films (US$ billions)
Source: Company files and authors' own creation/adaptation.

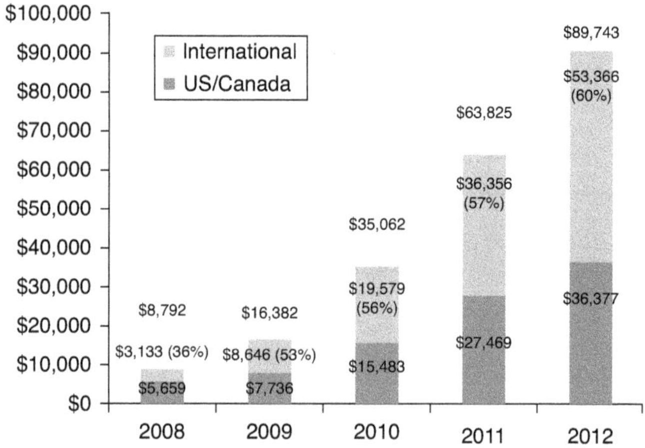

Figure II.5.3 Fx3x: digital screens, US/Canada and international (US$)
Note: [2012]: Total screens figures are forecasts as of March 2013.
Source: HIS Screen Digest.

Table II.5.4 Fx3x: worldwide digital 3D screens

	2008	2009	2010	2011	2012	2012 % of digital
US /Canada	1,514	3,548	8,505	13,490	14,734	**41%**
EMEA	594	3,510	8,143	11,570	13,963	**53%**
Asia-Pacific	344	1,584	4,659	8,590	14,219	**62%**
Latin America	84	362	1,104	2,142	2,629	**63%**
Total	2,536	9,004	22,411	35,792	45,545	**51%**
% change vs. previous year	**96%**	**255%**	**149%**	**60%**	**27%**	

Source: HIS Screen Digest.

Exhibit 3: fact and figures of Fx3x expansion

Table II.5.5 Fx3x: facts and figures of expansion

	Number of employees	*Revenue increase/ decrease (%)
1997	2	150%
2002	18	25
2004	15	45
2006	25	55
2008	40	38
2010	65	20
2012	110	35
2013	116	45

Source: Company files and authors' own creation/adaptation.

Exhibit 4: list of movies Fx3x worked on

Table II.5.6 Fx3x: list of movies worked on

Year	Movie/TV series
2012	• Life of Pi • Prometheus • Les Miserables • Wrath of the Titans • Avengers • Transformers: Dark of the Moon
2011	• Rango • Red Tails • Terminator: Salvation • Sherlock Holmes: A Game of Shadows • The Golden Compass • The Last Airbender • The Third Half • Resident Devil: Afterlife 3D • Dark Shadows • Punisher

Note: for full list of movies visit www.fx3x.com.

Source: Company files and authors' own creation/adaptation.

Exhibit 5: Fx3x organizational chart

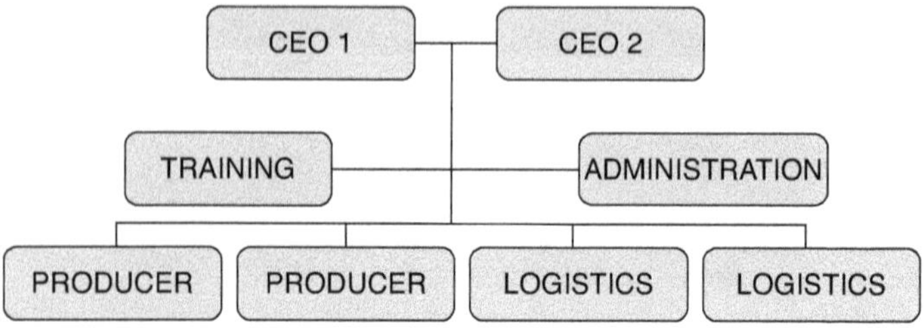

Figure II.5.4 Fx3x: organizational chart

Video Clip 1 – Fx3x selection of works http://www.youtube.com/watch?v=FFr_Jn2jtlQ

Video Clip 2 – CNN feature on Fx3x (from 6.56 to 9.50 minutes)

http://www.youtube.com/watch?v=AhWUTD8EUoQ&feature=endscreen&NR=1.

Source: Company files and authors' own creation/adaptation.

Notes

1. More information at www.oscars.org. Notice that his case is based on realistic events but not necessarily reflects the decisions and stands of the company.
2. Graf (2004).
3. Wikipedia – AutoCad. Available from: http://en.wikipedia.org/wiki/AutoCAD.
4. Wikipedia – AutoCad. Available from: http://en.wikipedia.org/wiki/AutoCAD.
5. Ex-Yugoslavian countries' crisis and armed conflicts, Kosovo conflict, Macedonian armed inter-ethnic conflict in 2001.
6. Graf (2004).
7. Julia Frey profile. Available from: http://www.imdb.com/name/nm0729079/.
8. The wider professional community involved in the visual effects, computer imaging and graphics is represented by ACM SIGGRAPH, the Association for Computing Machinery's Special Interest Group on Computer Graphics and Interactive Techniques since 1969. This association would lobby for industry recognition and would keep the industry participants informed about industry novelties. They organized conferences since 1974 that later got accompanied by formal commercial exhibits. If one wanted to be noticed and get familiar with the competition, SIGGRAPH participation was a must. Since 2008, as the computer imaging market expanded in Asia, exhibits were organized there too. See more at: http://www.siggraph.org/about/history#sthash.3oUky25T.dpuf.
9. Graf (2004).
10. Veteran executive takes helm of Modesat. July 22, 2008, February 11, 2012; available from: http://asi.ee/news/veteran_Executive_takes_helm_of_modesat.
11. Hollywood Reporter. Available from: http://www.hollywoodreporter.com/race/annie-awards-rango-jennifer-yuh-nelson-287137.

CASE 6: Graphisoft: The Architecture of International Growth

Juris Ulmanis

Hungary. This case consists of two parts (A and B) and tells the evolution of one of the most successful companies from CEE, which has many interesting facets and sub-stories, such as the CEO's collaboration with Apple and direct support from Steve Jobs.

While the first part centers on the company's development and selling or not Apple's distribution business, the second part focuses on whether doing an IPO was the right move at that time. Further sub-themes appear in the case, such as difficult market-entry decisions, building a brand abroad to overcome a negative country-of-origin effect, partnering with well-known Western brands to improve their branding, as well as finance-related topics for international growth.

CASE A

Introduction

It was late winter, 1997, and Mr. Gabor Bojar was making the five-hour drive from Solden, Austria to Monte Carlo to attend a banker's conference organized by the investment banking group Cowen & Co. Gabor decided to interrupt a previously planned, well-deserved ski vacation with family and friends to devote one day of presenting his software company, Graphisoft, its past, present and ambitious future plans, to potential investors in anticipation of possibly "going public." A possible IPO (Initial Public Offering), the dream of most entrepreneurs, had undoubtedly been on the mind of Gabor and many of Graphisoft's employees, many of whom owned a part of Graphisoft, as well as CSK, a Japanese holding company, and NIF (Nippon Investment Fund), a specialized fund managed by Daiwa Securities, that together had purchased a total of 16% of Graphisoft (11% and 5%, respectively) for US$7.5 million two years earlier. Gabor had convinced his wife to accompany him for the day to the place that 23 years earlier had been their honeymoon venue, to reminisce and to remember how they had arrived in Monte Carlo from Budapest in their "Zastava" or, as Gabor called it, a "heap" that he had bought secondhand, a small, ugly, Yugoslavian car, popular at that time in Eastern Europe. On this day, 23 years later, however, Gabor was navigating himself and his wife down the winding roads of the Austrian Alps, into Italy and finally into France and Monte Carlo, in his Jaguar.

As he made his way off at the Monte Carlo exit, Gabor thought about the labyrinth of roads surrounding the French highway system. "I could have just taken a right and been on my way," he said to his wife. Instead he had to cross the motorway twice instead of just taking a simple right turn. "The French, in contrast to the Americans, who are endlessly simplifying everything, like intellectual challenges. And to model while thinking in three dimensions is not easy – it is really an intellectual challenge, even with a program as elegant and as simple as ArchiCAD." Gabor knew the general differences in national thinking, and could make such conclusions, as he and his team had developed and adapted ArchiCAD, an architectural Computer Aided Design (CAD) program utilizing personal computers which had over the span of about 15 years enjoyed immense popularity amongst architects and building construction specialists in Europe, the United States, Hong Kong and Japan.

Hoping to get back to his family and friends in Solden by the evening, Gabor could not but help to wonder about his hesitation to continue the endless presentations and meetings in his Budapest Office, and elsewhere, with investment bankers, accountants and lawyers regarding preparing to "go public." He understood from his experience, especially in the United States, that the natural objective of every high-tech company was to list on a stock exchange. However, life was good. Graphisoft was enjoying tremendous success in major markets throughout the world. Some months earlier, Graphisoft had opened up an office in Hong Kong to take advantage of the great opportunity that China had to offer. Even prior to the Japanese investment in Graphisoft, the selling off of its Apple distribution business and the positive cash flow from its US and German offices had provided the necessary funds for Graphisoft to establish a Japanese subsidiary and to develop ArchiCad for Microsoft Windows-based PCs. From 1994 to 1997, parallel to the global IT market boom, and similar to many Silicon Valley companies, Graphisoft's revenues tripled and its profits quadrupled to reach 35% of revenues.

Hungarian software pioneers

As an aspiring scientist in the late 1970s at the Institute of Geophysics, a state-owned Hungarian company, Gabor Bojar wrote software code for calculators and for East European "computers." The mediocrity and bureaucracy of working at a state-owned company was not very motivating for the ambitious

Gabor. Gabor wanted something more, to be the "ruler of his own destiny," perhaps to even be his own boss someday, and to work and manage the most talented software programmers around. Years went by at the Institute of Geophysics before Gabor learned of the possibility of Hungarian software programmers being "loaned out" to the "West," via another institution – a computer science institute called SzKI. SzKI had a manpower-leasing agreement with software companies in Vienna and Munich. Within the framework of this agreement, it was possible to travel outside of Hungary, with special permission, to visit partnering companies that were cooperating with SzKI. Not only would a talented programmer be able to work with Western companies, and with state-of-the-art computers, but a programmer would also receive the always-sought-after hard currency in the form of a per diem allowance. This was the most appealing attraction to any Hungarian software programmer.

Gabor left the Institute of Geophysics and joined SzKI. This, the 1970s and 1980s, was still a time of extensive government control, both personal and commercial. The Berlin Wall had not yet fallen, and so-called Western CoCom (*Coordinating Committee for Multilateral Export Controls*) rules were in effect, placing an embargo on certain technology goods, believed to have arms and defense purposes not favorable to Western interests to Central/Eastern Europe. The black market in Hungary thrived, and if one had hard currency to purchase Western goods and to resell them in Hungary, one could make good business and earn good money. From time to time, with special permission, Gabor had the opportunity to travel to the West, most notably for three days at a time to Austria. There he would obtain small personal computers (PCs), to bring back home to resell and also to "play with" at SzKI. In a short period of time, Gabor was frequently in Austria, working with the Austrians, earning hard currency, and selling PCs in Hungary. However, the more he traveled, the more he realized that he was just a "servant" to someone else. Gabor was also mostly traveling by himself, and he missed his wife and family. Gabor dreamed of working at home, from his beloved Hungary, and bringing those well-paying contract jobs from abroad back to his homeland.

It was also during this time, in 1982, that certain forms of private enterprises, or partnerships, were allowed to be formed by private individuals in Hungary. Having a stable, government-guaranteed job, with access to the West, was considered a privilege and a luxury, for example, his job at SzKI, but in Gabor's eyes, the opportunity of doing something on one's own was an opportunity too good to be true. Gabor decided to leave SzKI and, together with a group of like-minded, software-programming associates, they founded the Cortex Partnership. The main business focus of this partnership was to contract out programming tasks. From the previous work experience of the partnership members, the group decided to specialize in modeling programs.

The beginnings of Cortex were not easy. One potential customer and project after another did not materialize. The ones that did materialize were small and far between. At one point, lacking cash for daily operations, Gabor and his wife even took their wedding rings and silverware to a pawn shop to continue financing the company. Disagreements regarding the future of the company, as well as the lack of steady earnings, gave rise to tensions among the founders and employees of Cortex.

A turning point came about at the end of the year when the Hungarian Ministry of Industry needed an advanced Computer Aided Design (CAD) model for the Paks Nuclear Power Plant whose construction was experiencing a three-year delay. The required software and computer hardware needed to help finish the project could only be acquired from the West, but was high on the CoCom list, hence, theoretically not possible to purchase.

The founding of Graphisoft

Gabor saw a tremendous business opportunity posed by the project's dilemma. The sheer size and reference value, if Cortex were to obtain this contract, was huge. Most colleagues at Cortex, however, saw too much risk and financial exposure in pursuing the project, as they perceived that Cortex did not have the resources and techological know-how to pull it off successfully. Gabor, and one of his partners, Gabor Tari (Tari), felt differently. Both Gabors left Cortex, with the aim of working solely on the Paks Atomic Reactor Project, and founded a new company that they named Graphisoft. (Since both founders were Gabors, both wanted the new company to have the letter "G" as the first letter in the new company name). A third person, a friend of Gabor's, Peter Hamor, came on board at Graphisoft, as an investor, or as what is termed today a "business angel." Peter trusted Gabor implicitly and, without a written contract, invested enough to carry Graphisoft through the first six months of operation, while Graphisoft was executing the Paks contract.

Again, without a written contract, but after a verbal commitment from a Ministry official, Graphisoft began months of modeling complex pipelines, based on hand-drawn, two-dimensional (2D) drawings to develop a program which could, in three dimensions (3D), model the pipeline system of the nuclear reactor and produce drawings to that effect. Six months later, and after a certain amount of doubt who the customer was – the power plant or the Ministry, with whom the initial contract would be signed, if at all – the Paks contract was finally signed with the Ministry of Industry.

During this modeling exercise, unbeknownst to Gabor at the time, Graphisoft had developed two important techologies which later became the basis for ArchiCad, Graphisoft's premiere product. The first was that Graphisoft developed what they deemed as GDL (Geometric Description Language), a programming language designed to easily import the many thousands of datastreams from 2D plans to script parametric objects.

(Parametric objects are digital representations of "real world" objects, such as chairs. The chair's parameters can be adjusted within the digital definition of the chair to change its qualities, such as its height, width, color and so on). The second technological advance was the ability to distinguish between visible and non-visible elements, a function that is critically important for displaying a 3D model. Current 3D technology allowed for this, for example, in computer games, using a high-speed solution on low-resolution monitors, but was not very accurate. The other solution required super, high-performance computers to which Graphisoft did not have access. Hence, Graphisoft had developed a solution that was relatively fast, sufficiently accurate, and worked on small computers, or PCs. The Ministry paid Graphisoft about 500,000 forints (about US$10,000 at that time) for the required drawings. Subsequent commissioned drawings from the Paks project, exceeding about one million forints, netted enough money for Gabor and Graphisoft, to pay off the debt of computer rental time that had been used, receive modest salaries, hire a secretary and begin marketing their new 3D modeling program, which they named RADAR.

From the initial success of RADAR, with Graphisoft's first large Hungarian customer, Gabor instinctively knew that the Hungarian market was too small to achieve consistent long-term growth and success. Gabor told his colleagues, "The true market is in the West." Everyone agreed and subsequently a decision was made that Graphisoft would "go global."

Entering new markets

According to the new "go global" strategy, Gabor decided that the next step would be to find Western business partners, ones that would consider Graphisoft an adjunct programming resource. The idea would be that Graphisoft would hire out its services on a high hourly rate, say 100 Deutschemarks/hour, to install RADAR. Graphisoft decided to target not the companies that offered large, expensive Computer Aided Design (CAD) workstations, but PC manufacturers, who were not threatened by the prospect of a 3D CAD program running on a small, inexpensive PC.

In the fall of 1983, Graphisoft displayed its 3D modeling program at a software exhibition in Munich, Germany. The 3D modeling program would be a kind of "teaser," demonstrating to customers Graphisoft's capabilities and prowess as an installer, or expert programmer. To Gabor's and the team's amazement, the interest in RADAR, in the product itself, was overwhelming. "There were much better programs out there, operating on bigger, 'state-of-the-art' computers. But they were very expensive," Gabor recalled. What he had not realized, at the time, was that a major paradigm shift was taking place in the computer industry, whereby the trend was that everything was going "small." Customers at the exhibition not only wanted to purchase the installation, but Graphisoft's whole program! Graphisoft was not prepared to offer RADAR for sale, but by the end of the exhibition had submitted proposals to various PC manufacturers totaling several million Deutschemarks. The Munich Systems Exhibition was the beginning of Graphisoft's global journey.

Getting a taste of Apple

Out of all of the proposals that were sent out to PC manufacturers, only one came to fruition, and not as originally anticipated. An Apple representative had seen Graphisoft's 3D modeling software at the Munich Systems Exhibition, and had expressed interest in RADAR. Gabor had envisioned that Graphisoft would just adapt the program to Apple's newest computer model, the "Lisa" computer (the immediate predecessor to Macintosh), and then Apple would act as RADAR's distributor. Apple offered an alternative option to Graphisoft – a commitment from Graphisoft that it would have RADAR ready to work on "Lisa" in time for the 1984 CeBIT, Hannover Exhibition, in April. For Graphisoft to achieve this, Apple would provide Graphisoft with four "Lisa" computers, 30,000 Deutschemarks for marketing-support expenses, free participation as vendors at Apple's Exhibit at CeBIT, and an introduction to Apple's distributors. In turn, Graphisoft would keep the ownership of the program, and its revenues, along with all of the responsibilities that went along with this: upgrades, dealing with customers' problems, complaints, and the like. As Apple computers were part of the CoCom embargo, Gabor and his team rented a flat in Munich, Germany, and spent the next 45 days doing their programming there.

Graphisoft kept its promise, met the deadline to Apple and had developed the very first 3D modeling software in a PC-category machine! As CeBIT was Apple's European launch of the Macintosh computer, swarms of people were crowding the Apple stand. As Gabor recalls "It is true that most visitors came out of curiosity about the Macintosh, but the Mac could only run a few simple applications. In contrast, our Lisa machine, displaying the revolving 3D image of the cardboard pipeline model sitting on top, was an eye-catcher. Graphisoft was the biggest draw within the Apple exhibit. If any of us wandered away from the stand for a little while, it was easy to find our way back – we just had to follow the crowd!"

Steve Jobs, the legendary founder of Apple, and at the time Chief Executive Officer, made a surprise visit to CeBIT. A day earlier, Gabor was informed of this and was told by Apple's staff to prepare a five-minute presentation for Steve Jobs. Gabor and his team spent all night preparing the five-minute presentation. "When Steve Jobs arrived to our demo, he had so many questions. Steve spent a whole half hour learning about the technology behind Graphisoft's software," Gabor remembers. That was when Steve Jobs personally endorsed Graphisoft to receive complete marketing support from Apple.

This was truly a turning point for Graphisoft, as, unbeknownst to them at the time, the generosity of Apple, with its free computers and distributor contacts, allowed Graphisoft eventually to build its own very strong distributor network. Also, Apple had proposed marketing the Lisa and Graphisoft concept as a 3D modeling application to architects, namely for the planning of family homes, small office buildings, hospitals, and the like. Gabor and his team understood the message. Graphisoft, as a small company, needed to develop a "usable product," one that is needed by a specific segment of the market. Gabor's team began to work on the product with a passion. At one point Gabor even risked prison by "smuggling" a Macintosh computer, an embargoed product, as carry-on luggage, on a flight to Budapest so that his team could develop a new version of the software for the Macintosh, a demo version, which was launched six months later. "A real entrepreneur is always willing to take a calculated risk," Gabor recalls. Graphisoft named this newly developed version "ArchiCAD 2.0."

An important strategic decision

By 1990, Graphisoft, as a software partner, was working closely with Apple; they had developed a great relationship. Graphisoft knew Apple products inside and out, knew many people inside Apple, understood the company's unique internal corporate culture, and was utilizing Apple's international distribution network. This, Graphisoft felt, was a real competitive advantage. Gabor now felt that it was only natural that Graphisoft enter the hardware distribution business and become Apple's exclusive distributor in Hungary.

Gabor's work colleagues agreed and Graphisoft submitted a number of business proposals to Apple to become its exclusive distributor in Hungary, a third of which was accepted. Graphisoft's signing of a distributor contract with the "great American company," Apple, made all the headlines in the Hungarian media. Having achieved this, truly becoming part of the Apple "world," writing software for them, selling its products, attending Apple conferences and meetings, provided a new sense of self-confidence and determination to Gabor and Graphisoft. At one point Gabor had even organized a high management delegation from Apple to visit Hungary to consider investment in a development center, a computer factory, or even its Central European office.

Important product decisions

Product-wise, Graphisoft was working hard to improve ArchiCAD but was still far from being able to bring a real architectural plan to full completion. Only a few distributors bought it, and it was not profitable for Graphisoft. To pay its bills, Graphisoft successfully continued to promote its profitable, customized RAPID software to the pipeline design market. Graphisoft also took on a number of "custom" projects. One of these was developing a 2D drawing program for a Hungarian company developing a UNIX-based computer that could run a CAD application. Another project was an updated version for UNIX (later MS-DOS) of the 2D CAD software program, called BIGRAPH, for an Italian architectural products company called Bieffe. Retaining the rights for the further development of BIGRAPH for the Macintosh, Graphisoft developed the most powerful 2D technical drawing program then available on the market called "topCAD." Graphisoft's strategy was to sell "topCAD" to its ArchiCAD distributors, hoping that the distributors would have a new product to promote to a large market. Graphisoft was developing a great competence in customization as well as valuable experience in sorting out the thousands of details that need to be resolved to develop a "final" product.

Graphisoft realized that serving pipeline design companies was a completely different business model than serving architects with ArchiCAD. Customers were very willing to pay big money for a RAPID-type product, but the pipeline design industry was small, and each customer required a certain level of customization of software and personal care. Many programmers were needed to meet the program customization demands and the growth prospects of the market seemed quite limited.

Regarding topCAD, most of Graphisoft's resellers were unable to break into the market for traditional 2D CAD systems. The main player in the market was AutoCAD, which operated on MS-DOS. Although inferior to Apple's Macintosh operating system, MS-DOS was, in fact, the "de facto" standard operating system in the computer world. The exception was a very strong distributor in Switzerland who was selling topCAD to engineers, not architects, and admitted that the only reason he sold topCAD was that selling ArchiCAD was too easy, and he preferred a challenge. For a while he was selling more copies of ArchiCAD in German-speaking Switzerland than all of Graphisoft's German resellers combined.

Gabor realized a couple of things from Graphisoft's experience regarding IT product development and customer requirements. The first was that compatibility was more important than being technically "the best." Apple's operating system was much better and more advanced than Microsoft's MS-DOS, but MS-DOS could run on IBM and all compatible platforms. Gabor recalled that his nine-year-old son taught him the importance of compatibility when he asked Gabor to buy him a new PC. To the loyal Apple devotee, Gabor, this almost seemed like heresy. His son already had an Apple computer, but explained to Gabor that he needed a PC to trade games with his friends. The ability to be "compatible" was more important than technical superiority.

The second thing that Gabor understood was that the number of software engineers required to develop a mass-market product is more or less the same as to develop a customized product. Manpower is not dependent on whether the software program is used by ten or thousands of users. Of course, if there are more users, there can be additional servicing tasks, but the opportunity for growth is greater for mass-market packaged software.

Given the above, Graphisoft decided to stop selling topCAD after fulfilling all of its warranty obligations. The biggest competitor, AutoCad, had emerged as the industry standard, and was "good enough" for the customer. After heavy debate at Graphisoft, going against the majority of opinion, Gabor also decided to drop the profitable RAPID program in favor of focusing and developing ArchiCAD. In addition, it was also decided to adapt ArchiCAD for Windows.

Building the ArchiCAD distribution network

Through a continuing series of programming trial and error, endless customer demonstrations, visiting trade shows, architect inputs and personnel changes, ArchiCAD was beginning to develop a customer following and loyalty. One of the very first customers, an architect in Bordeaux, France, M. Hulak, liked Version 3.1 so much that he refused to return the program, despite some minor bugs, because he was already using it to design real plans, and he was afraid that his work would stop.

Graphisoft's first distributor was in Italy – Istvan Toth, an architect of Hungarian descent. However, Graphisoft's very first big success came in France, when Gabor met Xavier Soul, the President of Abvent at Batimat, an International Building Exhibition. Abvent was mainly a software development firm, but became a Graphisoft distributor. A prior French distributor found at another trade show, a year before, had not worked out. Abvent had developed a general-purpose 3D modeling program for the Mac, called "SpaceEdit," which was later renamed "Focus" and then "Zoom." SpaceEdit was marketed to architects for schematic, simple, large-scale modeling tasks rather than for complex buildings, ArchiCAD's specialty. Abvent's main competitor was another French company, Gimeor, which had developed "Architrion," another 3D modeling program for the Mac, also used by architects, and priced somewhere between SpaceEdit and ArchiCad. As Mr. Gabor was soon to find out, Abvent's strategy was to squeeze Architrion out of the French market by using SpaceEdit as pressure from below and ArchiCad as pressure from above, which they eventually did.

Following Italy and France, other countries in Europe became strong markets for ArchiCad. The "smaller" markets of Portugal, Belgium, Austria, Greece, Turkey, Israel and the Middle East were also open to ArchiCAD's unique visual 3D style and ironically enough sold relatively more copies of ArchiCAD than the "larger" markets. Gabor attributed this to the fact that when American companies decided to go outside their home market, they immediately targeted the larger countries, not the smaller ones. The second reason was that Graphisoft found enthusiastic local representatives and guaranteed them exclusive distributor rights for ArchiCAD. In return the partners would take the responsibility for marketing and brand recognition, but would receive Graphisoft's technical support. For larger markets the marketing investment was very high and hence very risky for independent distributors, therefore Graphisoft ended up establishing subsidiaries in the larger markets such as the United Kingdom, Germany, the United States and

Japan. In one country in Africa Graphisoft achieved a 100% market share – in Namibia. All 30 architects in this country used ArchiCAD!

The US market

The United States, the world's largest software market and the center for the Information Technology (IT) industry, had been under consideration by Gabor Bojar and his team for many years. Gabor recalled, "For Graphisoft, the bigger the market, the harder it is to crack. The giants of our industry were American companies, and to take them on their home turf was even more difficult than on neutral territory such as France, or even Japan. However, if we want to be truly global we need to be in the United States. We need to be in Silicon Valley." Over the span of about ten years, a number of unsuccessful attempts were made to enter the US market. These included attempted entry via Graphisoft's contacts through its relationship with Apple Computers (for whom Graphisoft developed architectural software for the Macintosh Computer), Graphisoft's existing Israeli distributor with a presence in the United States, Hungarian emigres living in the United States and, by partnering with Graphisoft's distributor in France, Abvent. Despite, and as a result of, these failures, Gabor was determined to develop and implement a strategy for Graphisoft to become a major player in the Architectural, Engineering and Construction (AEC) CAD market in the United States. In 1989, Graphisoft finally established a subsidiary in the United States, Graphisoft USA.

"US customers traditionally are wary of European high-tech products, and especially of ArchiCAD's remarkably high price of US$4,000," Gabor recalled. Nevertheless, not relying on other distributors, focusing on projecting an "American," not European, image, and slowly developing its own reseller network, Graphisoft became a major American player, even defeating its main US competitor, which ironically enough was the French company, Gimeor. Gimeor subsequently left the market, having invested US$10 million in the United States, which had included financial support from the French government, but could not find the right strategy with its Architrion product. In contrast, Graphisoft was producing a positive cash flow in the United States.

Graphisoft developed a competence to adapt to local market needs very quickly, excelling in a number of things that larger competitors, especially American companies, were not willing, or able, to do. One of these was to adapt its products and marketing materials to meet local market needs and styles. Product packages included "localized" software, user manuals and technical documentation, all in local languages written by technically adept native speakers. Regarding product image, for example, in Italy emphasis was placed on the product's look, in France it was the artistic design, in Germany it was the technological precision and engineering standards, in Japan it was the local architectural dimensioning unique to Japan. Graphisoft developed a reputation as the software company with the best user manuals, technical documentation, and ability and willingness to serve the specialized requirements of the local market.

Another example of adapting to local market requirements was in pricing, namely in the US market. In the United States pricing was an issue for Graphisoft. The average US$4,000 price of an ArchiCAD software package in Europe was 20 to 30% higher than in the United States. Customers in Europe accepted this price. The market in the United States demanded a lower price. This invited the potential problem of "grey imports," from the United States to Europe. To alleviate this pricing problem, Graphisoft offered what they perceived as a novel solution – "Pay per Use" (PPU). This was a method whereby a customer did not have to pay the full amount of the software package, but only pay for the amount of time that he actually uses the program. Graphisoft installed a protection key – the protection device sold with each ArchiCAD package – which could be set to allow for "x" amount of hours of use and renewed after the time runs out. The idea being if an architect had more work, he would use ArchiCAD more, have more revenues, which would justify the use of ArchiCAD. The advantage for distributors would be that they would have a steady revenue stream; the client base was easily measurable and so, in essence, becomes an asset, which could potentially be sold.

Selling the Apple hardware business

In 1993, after an Apple delegation visit to Hungary, Michael Spindler, who was heading up the Apple delegation, indicated that he was not impressed with Apple's sales results in Hungary. He was especially bothered by the fact that Apple distribution was not Graphisoft's priority business. He insisted that Graphisoft clearly divide up its hardware and software business, even by having someone from Graphisoft reporting to Apple alone. After serious deliberation, Graphisoft decided to leave the hardware distribution business, not wanting to just be a passive investor for Apple hardware in Hungary. Gabor also understood that as Apple sales picked up in Hungary it would be even more difficult to reconcile Graphisoft's hardware and software businesses. The hardware business is capital-intensive and volume-driven. The relative profit earned is small compared to the sales volume. The opposite is true with software development sales. Relative profits on successful software development and sales are much larger, even if the absolute volume is less. Gabor concluded that he did not want Graphisoft's excellent software profits "subsidizing," the capital-intensive hardware wholesale business.

With Apple's help, Graphisoft sold its three-year-old Apple distribution business in Hungary to Nabil Bustros, a Lebanese Maronite Christian living in Paris who owned most of Apple's distributorships in the Middle East, and who was expanding into Eastern Europe. Gabor recalled that the negotiations with Nabil were not easy, attributing that to their respective

"Mediterranean temperaments" and the fact that the Lebanese are descendants of the Phoenecians, who invented the concept of money and acquired a knack for business at an early age.

Discussion questions

1. Evaluate the progress of Graphisoft and its situation in the winter of 1997.
2. What were the views and desires of the different stakeholders of Graphisoft in 1997?
3. Describe Graphisoft's relationship with Apple. What has been positive about the relationship? Has there been any downside?
4. Graphisoft's "Pay per Use" (PPU) program was a failure. What could be the reasons for this?
5. Discuss the strategic trade-offs between product technology leadership, branding (best versus "good enough"), standards, customization versus mass market.
6. Analyze the role of, and issues related to, having a large, multinational company as an initial "mentor," or "godfather."

CASE B: Graphisoft – IPO, OR NOT?

Japan

Selling off the Apple distribution business increased Graphisoft's capital reserves and made Graphisoft very strong financially. The US business was also generating positive cash flow and the German office was a continuous source of profits. The late 1990's was experiencing a global IT boom and during the period of 1994–1997 Graphisoft tripled its revenues, profits quintupled and reached 35% of revenues. Graphisoft's most significant investment during this period was the development of ArchiCad for Windows, and there were significant cash reserves left over for new investments. The question was where? Was it better to increase penetration in markets where Graphisoft was already present, or to enter new markets, such as the Far East?

Graphisoft's executives decided to enter Japan with Graphisoft veteran Imre Pakozdi determined to make Japan a success. Japan was not only a large market, but also fit perfectly with Graphisoft's ability to adapt to the unique requirements of the local market. Strategically, Graphisoft did a number of things differently in Japan than they had done in other countries. The first was to offer both versions of ArchiCAD – the Macintosh and Windows versions – simultaneously to distributors. The second was to address not only small and medium-sized firms, Graphisoft's traditional market, but also the big companies. In parallel, one large Japanese company especially took notice of Graphisoft. This was the world-renowned computer game maker,

Sega. The market for computer games was much larger than that for design software. Having a "game version" of ArchiCAD seemed a viable idea. Sega was searching for potential software partners to help them develop its games in 3D and had commissioned Daiwa Securities to represent them. Daiwa Securities held a number of meetings with Graphisoft in Budapest, London and Tokyo to discuss a potential partnership with Sega. Potential partnership discussions eventually did not materialize not because the financial due diligence was not acceptable, but because, according to Sega, Graphisoft's technology on its own was not suitable for developing computer games. This was again confirmed five years later when another computer game company in the United States, was also interested in partnering with Graphisoft and spent six months trying to unsuccessfully reconfigure Graphisoft's 3D software program for computer games.

Nevertheless, in addition, Daiwa Securities Tokyo Office knew that Sega's majority investor, CSK Corporation, had interests in another architectural design company, SuperSoftware Corporation (SSC). SSC's main market in Japan was manufacturers of traditional, prefabricated wooden houses. Daiwa organized a meeting between Graphisoft and SSC to explore possible ways to collaborate. After six months of discussion and negotiations, SSC purchased the 3D modeling core of ArchiCAD with the intention of incorporating the core into its own software for the specific prefabricated wooden home market. SSC also received distributor rights for the ArchiCAD program itself. This became Graphisoft's biggest deal to date.

Recognition for Graphisoft

During this time, outside of Japan, Graphisoft was receiving awards and professional accolades for its software development and ArchiCAD. In 1995 Graphisoft received Apple's Eddy Prize, the equivalent of an Oscar in the software industry, at the MacWorld Expo in San Francisco. This award was followed by Software Publishers' Association's (SPA) "Codie" Award, the Computer Graphics World Award and the Editor's Choice awards of Cadence and Cadalyst magazines, which were traditionally supporters of Graphisoft's competitors. Gabor personally received an invitation, and attended, the Davos Global Economic Forum and the Wall Street Journal's recognition as one of Eastern Europe's outstanding executives. In Gabor's view, the highest honor that he has received is the Hungarian government's outstanding scientific achievement, the Szechenyi Award, for "improving the international rank of Hungary's technical and scientific achievements." With the monetary acknowledgment of the Szechenyi Award, Gabor established a foundation to recognize outstanding high school science teachers.

What is Graphisoft worth?

With all of the years of hard work, software design, new product introductions, entering new markets, with all of the ups and downs, uncertainty, failures and successes, Gabor wanted to know how much Graphisoft was really worth. Graphisoft was owned by the company's employees and Gabor wanted the employees to know the value of their ownership status to motivate them to achieve greater results.

First, it was clear to everyone at Graphisoft that Istvan Gabor Tari, the Graphisoft co-founder, and Gabor himself, owned 51% of Graphisoft shares. Over the years, of the remaining 49%, "smaller portions" of Graphisoft shares had been distributed to Graphisoft employees, with a reserve for future employees and partners based on a formula of contribution and seniority.

Having sold the Apple distributorship, Graphisoft did not need additional capital. Their balance sheet looked excellent, but to assess the market value of Graphisoft, in 1993 Gabor decided to find a "professional investor" interested in injecting capital into Graphisoft. The ensuing process would put a real value on the firm.

Graphisoft chose CAIB, an investment company very much involved in Hungary's privatization efforts to find an investor for Graphisoft. An "Information Memorandum," an introduction and future plans for the company was created. Presentations and discussions ensued with a number of potential investors but no one wanted to invest in Graphisoft. Gabor felt that there were two major reasons for this. The first was that CAIB, together with Graphisoft, were targeting investors already active in Central/Eastern Europe. These were primarily investors who were targeting government privatizations whereby the investor would inject capital, Western know-how, technology, management and the like to make the privatized Hungarian company a viable "Western" company that would grow and potentially be resold. Graphisoft was not such a company – Graphisoft did not import Western technology; just the opposite, Graphisoft exported its own technology. Graphisoft's main markets were outside of Central/Eastern Europe, and Graphisoft did not need capital.

The second was that Graphisoft had not implemented Western-style financial reporting and did not have a trained staff in professional accounting and financial management. Graphisoft was not doing anything illegal or unethical. Graphisoft met all of the requirements of a Hungarian company, managing its money and filing completed tax returns to the local tax authorities on a timely basis. However, financial statements were not produced for managerial analysis, and therefore it was difficult for professional investors to easily understand and examine the complete, detailed financial picture of Graphisoft.

Another opportunity to receive a market valuation again came about in 1995, through Graphisoft's developed relationship with Daiwa Securities in Japan. Daiwa Securities, all along, had been trying to convince CSK to invest in Graphisoft. CSK's founder and President, 80-year-old Okawa-san, an extraordinarily wealthy businessman, one of the world's richest men, and deemed "Japan's Bill Gates," had bought and developed many companies and turned them around. Buying and developing the small American Sega company was, by far, CSK's greatest success story and Okawa-san was looking for the next great opportunity. Daiwa Securities believed in Graphisoft and was doing everything it could to convince Okawa-san and CSK to invest in Graphisoft. Daiwa even committed to also become an investor in Graphisoft. In Daiwa's proposed deal to both CSK and Graphisoft, a total of US$7.5 million would be invested in Graphisoft in return for 16% of the company. CSK would invest US$5.5 million and the remaining US$2 million would come from one of Daiwa's specialized investment funds, NIF (Nippon Investment Fund). According to this proposal Graphisoft was valued at US$47.5 million (which was more than three times the amount Graphisoft was valued at in the unsuccessful investor attempts with CAIB).

Graphisoft was pleased with this arrangement. Of course, this would make Gabor and other Graphisoft employees instant millionaires. It would be the first Japanese investment in the Hungarian software industry and one of the largest foreign investments in Hungary. However, Okawa-san did not approve of the deal right away. Before Okawa-san made any major decision, he had the habit of setting a day aside where he would concentrate on the decision just before falling asleep. Depending on his dreams, Okawa-san would know the right decision by morning. A few weeks later, at four in the morning Central European Time, Gabor received a phone call from Daiwa Securities. Okawa-san had woken up. Okawa-san requested slightly modifying the terms and conditions of the ensuing deal. The modification was not anything that important, but it was perceived by Gabor as a slight disadvantage for Graphisoft. Gabor felt that Okawa-san was testing his (Gabor's) character. Gabor responded very politely that if he (Gabor) had gained Okawa-san's trust, then the original terms and conditions of the deal that had been originally negotiated were acceptable to Okawa-san. If Gabor and Graphisoft had not gained Okawa-san's trust, then both parties had to work on this until he did. Okawa-san liked this response, left everything as originally agreed, and the deal was signed in February, 1996.

Although quite costly to initiate and maintain, Graphisoft became registered as a holding company in the Netherlands. At that time Hungarian corporate law was still in its infancy stages, and Dutch corporate law was one of the oldest, and most established in the world. The holding company became the owner of Graphisoft R&D Rt. Budapest, the global headquarters of Graphisoft, and its international subsidiaries. Together with the Japanese investors, Gabor and Graphisoft's owners/managers became owners of the Dutch holding company.

Per the newly signed investor agreement, part of the US$7.5 million Japanese investment was distributed to the owners of Graphisoft and the rest went into the holding company. The holding company used its portion of the investment to purchase a beautiful, large piece of real estate along the Danube river, in the northern part of Budapest, to build Graphisoft's new headquarters and to develop a scientific park, to be named Graphisoft Park. Inspired by the Nazca lines in Peru, the vision was to even have a large replica of Graphisoft's signature logo constructed of colored pebbles on the lawn, so that airplanes approaching Budapest Airport from the west could see Graphisoft Park.

One of the major points in the agreement, which took months to negotiate, was regarding the issue of going public. Gabor and the other managers/owners of Graphisoft were not completely convinced that they wanted to do this. After all, one of the major reasons that Graphisoft had courted potential investors was to know how much the company was worth. Now they knew. But Gabor also knew that going public was one of the primary motivations of Okawa-san and Daiwa Securities to invest in Graphisoft. Already Graphisoft was utilizing share options to motivate its employees, so in essence this was in a way a kind of guarantee that eventually Graphisoft would go public, since without an Initial Public Offering (IPO), the stock options would not be worth very much. The potential Japanese investors had wanted a stronger guarantee. Finally, Graphisoft agreed that if Graphisoft did not go public by 1999, then Graphisoft would have to spend half its current profits buying back the Japanese investor's shares at the original purchase price plus a fair rate of interest.

What to do?

As Gabor pulled into the same Monte Carlo hotel parking lot where he and his wife had stayed 23 years earlier on their honeymoon, he thought to himself: "The IPO process has already begun. It has gained tremendous momentum and perhaps could be difficult to reverse. Even worse, canceling the meetings would disappoint our investors and perhaps it would reduce the chances of a successful offering in the future." As he gave the keys of his Jaguar to the parking valet, among the parked Rolls Royces, Bentleys and Ferraris, Gabor was weighing the pros and cons and the strategic, legal and financial issues that an initial public offering raised in his head. Walking up the stairs and into the bankers' conference, Gabor remembered the honor of having the great Hungarian theoretical physicist, Dr. Edward Teller, the "father of the hydrogen bomb," at Graphisoft's US five-year anniversary and the words that Dr. Teller had once said: "When you get to the end of all the light you know and it's time to step into the darkness of the unknown, faith is knowing that one of two things shall happen: either you will be given something solid to stand on, or you will be taught how to fly."

Discussion questions:

1. Why do firms go public? Should Graphisoft go public? What are the advantages and disadvantages? Are there any other options?

2. Discuss the challenges of establishing a presence in "far away" huge markets (the United States and Japan) as opposed to many "closer" and "familiar" smaller-country markets.
3. How should Graphisoft expand its business in the future?

CASE 7: Estonia's Laser Diagnostic Instruments (LDI) AS: Beaming toward Growth

Tiit Elenurm

Estonia. This story covers the challenges of a small scientific company with a cutting-edge technology, but big question marks about the future. It's about finding the right market focus, a sustainable international growth strategy, and a business model able to appropriate the value they actually created with their technology – on both sides of the Atlantic.

On top of that, they need to deal with claims against a successful product application of theirs in the US market. A drug dealer's lawyer is calling their technology "voodoo sorcery from the East which has no science behind it."

Introduction

The term "laser" might conjure up notions of the popular films Star Wars or The Hyperboloid of Engineer Garin,[1] but over the last few decades lasers have moved from fiction to a viable business field. Lasers have become ubiquitous across a wide range of industries such as computing, electronics, medicine, science and the military.

One such business that explored the applied use of laser technology was Laser Diagnostic Instruments (LDI) AS.[2] Established in 1991 and based in Tallinn, Estonia, LDI produced laser instruments and software for a wide variety of applications. Led by Dr. Sergey Babichenko, a PhD in physics, the company had expanded internationally over the past 20 years and made a name for itself by applying laser technology in two areas: detecting sea pollution and assessing the quality of foodstuffs. The company had expanded to new industries such as law enforcement and health, creating three joint ventures with partners in the Netherlands, Sweden and Canada and four spin-off companies in the United States, Canada and Russia. By 2011 the company sold its numerous solutions to over 20 countries. Revenues had grown to €4.3 million in 2009 but fell back to €1.6 million in 2010 due to significant cuts in governmental spending and other customers during the global economic crises. As a result of the decline in revenues, the company's profit of €1.2 million in 2009 turned to a loss of – €130,000 in 2010 (see Exhibit 1 for financial results).

Babichenko and his management team wondered about the possibility of capturing more value in growing fields such as law enforcement and health. Did LDI need a laser-sharp focus in a key area or was it best to stick with its approach of participating in several industries across several geographies?

Lasers and photonics

Lasers are devices that generate a beam of light by stimulating photons from atoms. The word came to be in the 1950s from an acronym for its longer definition: "light amplification by stimulated emission of radiation."

Lasers are one of many technologies under the broader umbrella of photonics. Photonics deals with the generation, emission, transmission, modulation, signal processing, switching, amplification, detection and sensing of light. As of 2011, photonics had been widely applied in optical fiber communications in the telecommunications sector as well as many other application fields from holography and health monitoring to robotics and military technology.

The global photonic sensor market was approximately US$3.9 billion in 2011. The market research firm, Markets & Markets, projected a compound annual growth rate (CAGR) of 16% over the next five years, reaching US$8.17 billion by 2016.[3] The photonic sensor market was broken down by type (laser, biophotonic and fiber optic) and by application (oil and gas, military and aerospace, energy and infrastructure, industrial automation, medical and others). Markets & Markets summed up the burgeoning photonics field:

> The demand for products that use photonic sensors is on the rise. [An] increasing number of applications in the industrial segment such as smart structures, oil & gas, and border security are the major drivers for the photonic sensors market.... The restraining factor for the photonics sensor market is high cost and lack of standards; which ultimately results in lack of awareness and adaptability by the customers. Also, the market is quite segregated with long research and development (R&D) and Need Product Inhibition (NPI) cycles.
>
> The opportunities in the photonic sensors market are mostly application driven. A gamut of applications is expected to arise in the coming five years due to the increased usage of sensors. The use of fibre optic sensors would be gaining significance in the areas of oil & gas exploration, civil engineering majorly including border security and fencing. Bio-photonic sensors will emerge in the field of new medical applications and research laboratory.

The beginnings of Laser Diagnostic Instruments (LDI)

The Institute of Marine and Ecology of the Estonian Academy of Sciences (Eesti Teaduste Akadeemia) began using laser technologies during the Soviet period. When the Soviet Union collapsed and Estonia regained its independence in 1991, there were several teams in Estonia that started to work on applications of laser technologies as private ventures (previously all private entrepreneurship was deemed illegal by the state). Financing of academic research was not guaranteed in the turbulent transition to the market economy and people in applied research saw an opportunity to use private entrepreneurship as a way to finance and expand their research by offering commercially applicable research-based solutions. Some also hoped to increase their income, but research interests were often stronger and clearer than profit motives.

Dr. Sergey Babichenko and four other scientists with backgrounds in defense and space came together in 1991 to establish LDI to apply their knowledge of lasers and photonics to practical commercial solutions. They strove to develop technologies that would integrate lasers, optics, microelectronics and software in order to create complete systems for various business sectors. The integrated technology would provide a type of spectral "fingerprinting" since light could interact with all physical materials. As Babichenko put it, "Really, from the beginning, we were aiming for artificial intelligence. We knew how we wanted to use laser technology but were aware of the limitations of computer processing capacity in the early 1990s."

He added:

> Sometimes business people and consultants, when hearing about our applications in various business sectors, think that we are not focused. In fact we are quite focused: all our innovative solutions are based on integrating three technologies: lasers, spectral analysis and data processing. That integration is our core competence and it really works across borders of traditional business sectors.

One of the company's first products was the Fluorescent LiDAR (Light Detection and Ranging) System, which used lasers to monitor pollution in marine environments and detect leaks in oil and gas pipelines. The company's first international sale was equipping the Polish research ship, RV Oceania, with a LiDAR in 1992 for the vessel to conduct scientific experiments involving sea pollution.

Going international

It was clear from the time of establishing the company in 1991 that Estonia was too small a market for the majority of their advanced research applications. However, it was a challenge to establish international credibility before demonstrating research results internationally. Contacts for first international sales were mostly established during conferences and other international research events. Despite complicated political relations between Russia and Estonia in the early 1990s, LDI began selling to Russia. Academics who had worked within the Soviet system helped to find business partners in Russia. By participating in international conferences, Babichenko met more R&D contacts, helping to solidify sales to Germany and other countries.

In 1998, LDI licensed its technology to the Dutch analytical instrument manufacturer, Skalar, to create the Skalar Fluo-Imager. The instrument measured the concentration of different hydrocarbons in water, aimed at supplying vital information to oil refineries, pipelines and transportation facilities. Shortly thereafter the two companies created a joint venture, Skalar-LDI in Estonia.

LDI decided that Canada would be a next good next step as it could act as an incubator to eventually enter the demanding North American market. Babichenko and his team had made a number of Canadian contacts at scientific conferences and had learned that the Canadian government supported innovation in the field of environmental protection. Water pollution had especially become a hot topic in the country in the late 1990s. In 2001, LDI3 was established in Canada as a Canadian corporation with shareholding of LDI and Canadian private partners to bring the LiDAR technology to North America.

At the time of expanding into Canada, Babichenko met several academics who were keen on applying lasers in medicine. In 2001, LDI helped to establish Genestho Inc. in Canada's capital city of Ottawa and Genestho-Laser in Russia's capital, Moscow, in 2001. The idea behind Genestho was to use lasers to treat infections.

In order to help establish the new ventures in North America, LDI brought on a new business partner, Endel Siff, to provide angel investments for major developments in LDI and its related companies. Siff was often credited with being one of the most successful entrepreneurs in Estonia. He was well known in the oil transportation business as he had established two oil transit terminals in the Baltics as well as a port in Tallinn following the dissolution of the Soviet Union in 1989. He later invested in a number of businesses including one of the Baltic's largest banks, AS Hansabank, an IT consultancy called Aspit, air charter services as well as numerous real-estate holdings.

While supporting R&D offshoots in Canada, the LDI team discovered a new potential application of its core spectral analysis technology – the detection of illicit drugs. By 2004, LDI was ready to start commercializing the concept and worked with North American business partners to set up NarTest LLC in Morrisville, North Carolina. The company released a device – named the NarTest NTX2000 – a drug analyzer that used a patented technology based on LDI's Spectral Fluorescence Signature (SFS) to detect the most common narcotics within 5 to 15 minutes. The benefit of the device was its ability to provide drug analysis at 10% of the cost of a standard laboratory-based analysis. Within three years the NarTest device was sold to North Carolina police departments and was featured on the popular television series, *CSI*.

LDI continued creating joint ventures; in 2006, it worked with the Swedish company MetPro AB (Medical Technology Projects) to establish a new company, LDIAMON AS in Estonia, with the purpose of using photonics for adequacy monitoring of hemodialysis treatment. In 2008, it created another joint venture called Altomni Ltd. with Canadian-based PinPoint Environmental to expand the offering of worldwide environmental services with airborne LiDARs.

As of 2011, LDI's subsidiaries and joint ventures were at different stages. LDI maintained shareholdings and further business developments in NarTest, Genestho and Altomni. Profits from all enterprises were reinvested for further development and growth. Skalar-LDI and LDI3 had been hibernated due to reaching the accomplished mission of testing the technology and a lack of customers and funding.

Challenges in going international

LDI had been presented with a number of key challenges in its attempt to grow internationally. First, LDI had experienced difficulty in finding the right managers and partners who could match technological knowledge with international management and marketing skills. Explaining the nature of LDI products to potential customers was more complicated than selling vacuum cleaners to housewives. Second, LDI was challenged to convert the start-ups to viable stand-alone businesses that were self-sustaining and non-reliant on external funding. Third, setting up new enterprises and traveling to disparate locations was usually a high investment in time and money in the early stages.

To address the first challenge, LDI had attempted different approaches. LDI had initially made some of its contacts through scientific conferences; however, scientists were not always able to play the necessary management and sales role to commercialize the technology. LDI had also engaged head-hunters to find general managers for new projects. In a few situations, LDI had found Estonian, Finnish and Swedish managers who worked briefly with LDI management in Estonia before being sent to run a subsidiary or joint venture.

When seeking foreign partners, Babichenko had identified three main profiles:

1. Researchers who were prepared to share the research efforts with the LDI team.
2. Industry partners who had direct experience in a particular industry that LDI was targeting (e.g., health, law enforcement and so on). It was

important that industry partners could be trusted and would work with LDI to apply technological know-how. Typically these partners had to be focused on long-term development and not short-term business gains.
3. Distribution partners who understood the market and could help LDI quickly release a new product into the market.

Throughout the years, LDI had been recognized as being highly innovative, culminating in a number of awards such as the International Award for Technology and Quality in Italy in 1995, two awards from the World Exhibition of Inventions in Belgium in 2000 and 2002 and a nomination as one of the country's five most innovative Estonian companies in 2007. The company actively participated in many associations such as the European Association of Remote Sensing Laboratories (EARSeL), European Photonics Industry Consortium (EPIC) and European Integrated Mission Group for Security (IMG-S). LDI achieved its ISO 9001:2000 certification.

LDI as of 2011

As of 2011, Babichenko classified LDI as a "manufacturer of laser-based instrumentation and a development company concentrating on application-driven research." Together with a range of software products to control measurements and handle data, LDI offered online, in situ, airborne, contact and remote analytical laser and spectroscopy-based sensors that addressed various environmental, industrial, security, law enforcement and health issues.

In explaining the mission of the company, Babichenko said:

> "The main goal is to commercialize the research-based ideas that we develop. I am very interested in the commercialization of new technological solutions but not nearly as interested in owning mass production. I believe that profit and the positive social impact of LDI solutions can support one another. It's important for me to create sustainable businesses through partnerships, licensing the technology and through other operation modes that are not the same in different business sectors. For example, what will work in the environmental field will not work in law enforcement or health. In some sectors, joint ventures are good solutions. In other business fields, licensing could be considered."

Revenue streams

LDI's revenues were broken down into the following categories:

- Environmental surveillance services for sea pollution, mainly in the United States and Canada: 20% of revenue
- Industrial sensors for oil and gas: 35% of revenue

- Industrial sensors for food testing: 15% of revenue
- Law enforcement in Europe and the United States: 30% of revenue

LDI applications for the health sector were still at the early stage of commercialization and the company had not earned consistent revenues from its applied health technologies. Research financing was up to 20% of LDI's annual revenues, including about €1 million by European Union and Estonian institutions. The remainder of the revenues came from licensing, consulting and the sale of products and software.

Products and projects

LDI had six lines of products (see Exhibit 2 for photos):

1. Flourescent LiDAR System (FLS®) Series: The LiDAR (Light Detection and Ranging Systems) line of products provided real-time data from constantly changing natural environments for the purposes of environmental and resource surveys. LiDARs were used to monitor pollution in marine environments, oil and gas pipeline leak detection and oil exploration. The LiDARs were available to survey land and water from aircraft or marine vessels.
2. Remote Oil Watcher (ROW): The Remote Oil Watcher was a small cylindrical device about 50 centimeters tall and two kilograms in weight that could be mounted on important waterways in ports to monitor oil pollution.
3. SFS-Scanner®: The SFS (Spectral Fluorescence Signature) was a type of scanner that could be used to measure different physical substances in real-time or long-term continuous monitoring. The scanner was originally used for sampling different types of water such as wastewater at industrial sites, surface waters in areas with high nautical traffic and drinking water.
4. Instant Screener®: The instant screener also used the SFS technology but was intended to detect and measure non-water substances. The Instant Screener was the basis of the technology used in the NarTest drugs analyzer, however it could also be applied to control for waste, soil contamination, food processing, food freshness and control of bacteria in food. As such, it could be used in several fields such as pharmaceuticals, biotechnology, agriculture, medicine and law enforcement.
5. Multi-channel Optical Detector (MOD): This was a multi-purpose device, which measured spectral signals. It could be used with barcodes to provide rapid authentication of liquid products (beverages, fuels, hazardous liquids and so on) and allowed for keeping stock of products throughout the distribution chain.
6. Customized products, including Fluorescence Detector for Capillary Electrophoresis: This device was used to detect amino acids and other

harmful conditions within blood capillaries. The device was used in research laboratories.

In addition to the company's products, LDI had European Union and Estonian funding projects for the applied use of photonics in detecting bombs (the BONAS project), air turbulence (the DELICAT project) and oil spills (DEOSOM project). See Exhibit 3 for more information about the different projects.

Patents and unique technology

LDI owned nine patents:

- Three patents for remote sensing (water contamination detection)
- Three for law-enforcement applications (drug detection)
- One for product marking and authentication
- Two for rescue operations

Babichenko stressed that only 40% of the commercial value of LDI's technology consisted of the actual lasers, detectors and sensors. 60% of the value came from LDI's unique advanced software, which worked with all of the company's devices. The challenge was how to apply this software in applications that create such value for customers that can be captured through increasing revenue streams.

When talking about the areas where LDI was most recognized, Babichenko believed that the company had made a name for itself in the area of sea pollution and the quality control for foodstuffs. He explained:

> We are well recognized in the world in two specific photonics technology areas: systems for remote detecting of dangerous stuff in various environments, such as oil pollution in water and on land, and in using photonics technology for express analysis of various substances, including quality assessment of food products.

Because of LDI's reputation in detecting oil spills, the company was selected by the US government to participate in monitoring the BP oil spill in the Gulf of Mexico in 2010. Because of a lengthy selection process, LDI ended up being on the participants' reserve list and did not contribute their LiDARs to the project.

People

LDI 30 had 30 employees working in its central office in Tallinn. The company had three areas: research and development (R&D), engineering and production, and services. LDI's research and development group was headed by Dr. Larisa Poryvkina and made up of six PhDs and PhD students. Each person in the group was assigned to a specific project.

LDI's engineering department consisted of 11 engineers in mechanics, optics, electronics and software. The rest of the staff worked in production and services. There were only a few people focused on managerial jobs: Babichenko as the CEO, Poryvkina as R&D Director and the heads of the engineering and production departments. And all of them played an active role in research and technology development (see their profiles in Exhibit 3).

LDI worked with the Tallinn University of Technology in several areas to access talented students in areas as diverse as environmental science, food science and health studies. LDI tried to recruit students that could become competent sales people in the future. One LDI manager said:

> It's not easy to find the right mix of people since you need people that have the right business-to-business sales skills while being able to communicate with technology experts. Furthermore, the sales work is really about creating new markets. So it's not so much about convincing customers that LDI is better than its competitors because oftentimes there are no competitors! It's much more about convincing a technological expert that there's a better way to do it using photonics.

In addition to its office in Tallinn, the company had four employees at the NarTest office in Morrisville, North Carolina and approximately six other employees spread throughout its different international joint ventures.

There were a total of eight shareholders including Babichenko and Poryvkina. One of the company's major shareholders was Endel Siff through his investment holding company Primos OÜ. In addition to holding a stake in LDI, he also had invested in NarTest, Genestho and Altomni.

Potential opportunities for future growth

LDI had attempted to develop solutions that were tailored to a specific application and that would be customer-friendly, readymade systems where the hardware and software were integrated. LDI approached their products in multiple "layers":

1. Single sensor as a stand-alone unit or an element of a network
2. Complete system integrating different sensors for specific analysis solutions
3. Network of sensors and systems

Customers had the freedom of choosing which layer was most appropriate. For example, in detecting sea pollution, at the first level, a customer could use a single sensor in order to check if there was one type of pollution at one location. The second level allowed the customer to combine different sensors to detect different types of pollution. The third level permitted the customer to monitor various types of pollution within a larger area by using different sensors integrated within a network. Each level required more complex software.

LDI was able to serve clients that wanted to buy separate sensors. However, LDI managers felt that they could offer greater value to their customers by offering a tailored network of sensors and systems. Babichenko talked about the motivation of serving a number of different customer needs:

> High-level challenges like changing the world for better is a strong driver for our entrepreneurial team. It is, however, not easy to prove to state officials of developing countries that our innovative systems may create benefits for their countries.
>
> Our mission-oriented entrepreneurship focuses on solving several big problems such as drug trafficking and disease. We are confident in our ability to support law enforcement agencies in drug wars by providing them with cutting-edge technologies for drug detection. In the health sector, the treatment of multi-drug resistant tuberculosis (MDR-TB) has become a problem in both the developing and developed world.
>
> We have solutions that can help. The question is how to keep on growing in this area.

LDI's applications for law enforcement

Instant detection and identification of illicit drugs for fighting narcotics traffickers and terrorism was in high demand in many countries. The three most common methods for detecting drugs were through manual searches, dog "sniffing" and in-depth lab testing.

The disadvantage of manual human searches was the time and cost without guaranteed success since the volume of people at major border crossings and airports were too high to conduct comprehensive searches on everyone. While the traditional practice of using dogs was a good way to discover traces of narcotics when inspecting potential users at border crossings or in airports, the methodology did not work well when narcotics were hidden in some other substance. Furthermore, dogs were adversely affected after being exposed to large quantities of concentrated narcotics. Additionally, lab-based tests were costly and time-consuming.

LDI's NarTest technology aimed to fill the gap between a manual drug search and laboratory analysis, answering the need for a rapid conclusive result with basic lab-based analysis of the substance. As of 2011, the NarTest NTX2000 device was the only photonic-based analyzer capable of testing for drugs outside of a traditional laboratory. The device had the ability to detect six types of illegal drugs (heroin, cocaine, marijuana, ecstasy, amphetamine and methamphetamine) with 99.6% accuracy. It was hand-held and portable and able to produce results within 5 to 15 minutes in any environment. It could be powered from a car battery and only required a half-day of training to be used. It was estimated that law-enforcement agencies could save up to

90% by using the device versus conducting tests in a standard laboratory. Each device sold for around US$40,000, which included the software and training. The margin on the device was about 50%.[4] (See Exhibit 4 for a photo of the device.)

The NarTest unit was intended for purchase by police, customs, border guards and the US Department of Homeland Security. It was estimated that on a worldwide basis there were seven to eight million analyses completed within law enforcement on illicit drugs per year. Although it was difficult to size the market precisely, it was estimated that globally the amount spent on drug testing was over US$1 billion annually. NarTest was seen to have a strong advantage in its application niche, since its device could detect illicit drugs on site (out of the laboratory).

LDI had sold only a handful of units to law-enforcement agencies in North Carolina as well as Commonwealth of Independent States (CIS) countries. The first sales in Europe were planned for 2012. Since inception, the company had earned revenues of approximately US$1 million.[5] Poryvkina talked about the difficulty in introducing novel technologies within the law-enforcement system:

> Since the NarTest NTX2000 device was introduced in the United States in 2006, several of our analyzers have been used in thousands of cases. But it takes a lot of time, resources and effort to get the technology officially adopted for confirmatory evidence in the courts – we are still in this process.

In a court case in North Carolina in 2010, the Court of Appeals rejected the use of the NarTest NTX2000 on account of unreliability.[6] The lawyer representing the drug dealer had reportedly challenged the technology referring to the device as "voodoo sorcery" because it was invented in the "East" and "does not contain any science behind it."

Considering the setback to a more widespread roll-out, Babichenko wondered whether any changes to NarTest should be considered for future growth.

LDI's applications in health

In the health sector, lasers were used across several treatments since they helped destroy bacteria cells. Lasers had been used to treat endo-cavital infections (multi-drug resistant and destructive forms of tuberculosis and post-surgical intra-abdominal abscesses), open wounds, psoriasis, gynecological diseases, eye and other infections.

Overall, the international market for laser treatments in medicine was estimated to be about US$1 billion in 2011. The majority of the competitors using lasers in medicine were focused on treating the skin or eyes. There were about ten major players that manufactured laser devices to treat skin including Syneron/Candela, Cutera, Cynosure, Solta, Lumenis, Elen, Iridex, UltraShape,

Sciton and Alma Lasers. The top ten laser companies tended to be based in either the United States or Israel with revenues ranging from a few million dollars per year to around US$200 million. Most of the publicly traded companies had generated losses in the millions in 2010.[7] Industry observers believed that losses were generated due to the high cost of research and development, causing high selling prices and long purchase cycles. At the same time, many observers believed that photonics in health would be a dynamic growth area due to the wide gaps in treating diseases with existing drugs.

The customers of photonic health applications were hospitals, public and private clinics, physicians and health laboratories. Generally, all health practitioners were interested in "plug and play" solutions where producers offered the medical equipment along with integration to existing systems, a maintenance plan and clinical tests and certification. Babichenko commented:

> When looking at photonics in the health sector, it is very different from the law enforcement market, where LDI is able to offer their own full solution through NarTest. In the health sector, we really need different types of partners who are able to apply our devices in existing medical practice. One potential idea would be to license out our technology to medical equipment producers. The problem with this sector is that we might need to put in a lot of time and resources with a long payback time. Undoubtedly the sector will experience incredible growth, however!

Endel Siff talked about the emotional part of offering solutions in the health sector:

> In a company like LDI where the mission is not strictly profits, it is very emotional and very rewarding to see that our technologies can provide a cure to diseases. For example, in clinical trials of MDR-TB, the LDI laser system cured more than 60 patients who had previously been written off by standard medicine. Seeing such people recover from a disease has been a very exciting experience for us!

In addition to using LDI's technology for the treatment of diseases, the technology was also applicable to bacteria in water and food. When the mutant E. coli bacteria outbreak in Germany became a topical issue all over Europe, Babichenko sent a letter to the Directorate General Health & Consumers of the European Commission offering LDI's services to trace and detect the bacteria (see Exhibit 5). The Health & Consumers General Directorate (DG) directed Babichenko to send the proposal to another area within the government dealing with issues of water. Babichenko commented:

> The idea of offering LDI's services was to quickly detect the bacteria! It really had nothing to do with water. We exchanged a few more letters

> before I realized that it wasn't going to go anywhere and that I'd be better off focusing on areas where we could see real sales.

The future: beaming towards growth

Within the offices of LDI, several questions were constantly debated: How and where could the company create new markets? How should the company choose the strategic focus area(s)? Taking into consideration resource limitations, was it better to go for niche markets or to have a wider focus? What kind of partners would be needed in new markets? If a partner were to buy a license but did not cooperate in developing the technology, would it be a dead end? What were the market opportunities in photonics that supported short-term profit and long-term business gain? What kind of strategy would lead the company to long-term growth?

Babichenko shared some thoughts:

> Any business constantly has some recurring questions. The one question, which bothers me a bit is the idea of focusing only on one business sector or region. To me, it's the same as saying that a visitor to New York City should only go to Central Park or the Empire State Building. If you did that, how would you ever get to know New York?
>
> We're involved in some very important niche markets, including water pollution, law enforcement and health. I'm confident that we have good technologies in all sectors and I don't want to focus in one area and forgo business opportunities in the others.

Exhibits

Exhibit 1: financial information: LDI

Table II.7.1 LDI: financial information

Year	Revenue 000 € (Without revenues from projects sponsored by EU and Estonian authorities)	Profit k€	Number of employees
2007	1,700	105	27
2008	2,025	–70	29
2009	4,345	1,200	33
2010	1,550	–130	30

Source: Company files and authors' own creation/adaptation.

In addition to commercial revenues, about €1,000,000 project-based R&D financing has been annually available from EU-sponsored programs and from Estonian development agencies.

Exhibit 2: LDI products

LiDAR Device

Figure II.7.1 LDI: on a ship

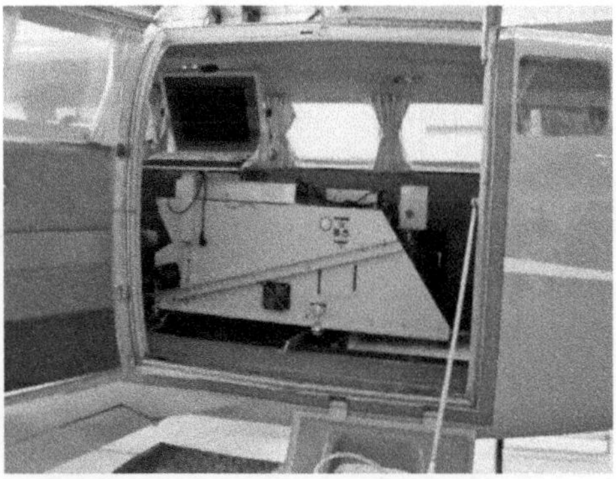

Figure II.7.2 LDI: mounted on a helicopter

Flexible Remote Sensing (FLS®) LiDARs

LDI laser-based remote sensing systems are designed to detect and quantify several types of organic matter in water and on land. Hyperspectral FLS LiDARs are an efficient means of conducting large-scale environmental assessment through the analysis of spatial distribution of organics ranging from oil pollution to phytoplankton. The FLS series of LiDARs can be mounted in aircraft, on surface vessels, in ground vehicles or on stationary installations.

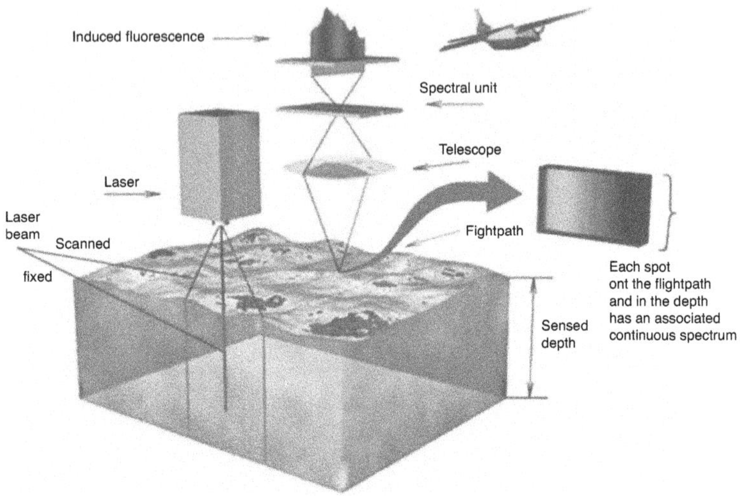

Figure II.7.3 LDI: Flexible Remote Sensing (FLS) LiDARs

The Remote Oil Watcher (ROW)

Figure II.7.4 LDI: the ROW mounted at ports (A)

Figure II.7.5 LDI: the ROW mounted at ports (B)

SFS-Scanners®

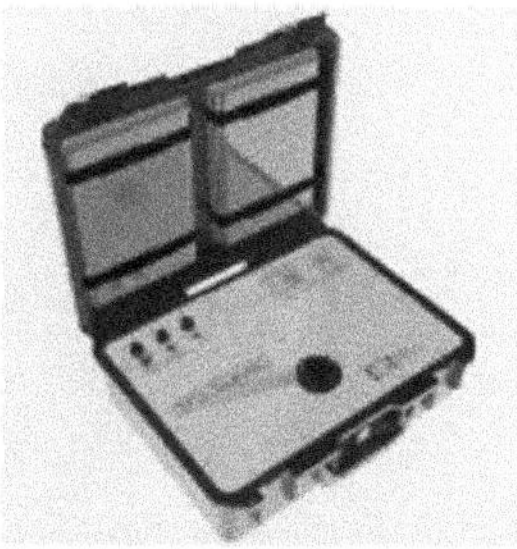

Figure II.7.6 LDI: SFS-Scanner field version

Figure II.7.7 LDI: scanner laboratory version

Instant Screener®

Figure II.7.8 LDI: instant screener in the field

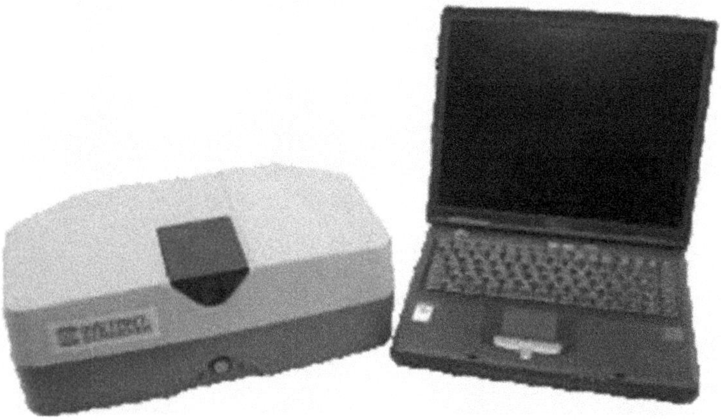

Figure II.7.9 LDI: instant screener with a PC

Source: Company files and authors' own creation/adaptation.

Exhibit 3: current LDI projects

European Union (EU) projects

Project BONAS: The BONAS – Bomb factory detection by Networks of Advanced Sensors – is supported by the European Commission within the frame of the 7th Framework Program (FP7). The aim of BONAS is to design, develop and test a novel wireless sensors network for increasing citizen protection and homeland security against terrorist attacks, in particular against the threat posed by IED devices. The sensor network will focus on the detection of traces of precursors used in IED production (particulates, gases and/or waterborne) present in the environment surrounding the vicinity of a "bomb factory." The project is planned for three years; the consortium consists of 13 partners and is coordinated by ENEA.

Project DELICAT: The project DELICAT stands for Demonstration of LiDAR-based Clear Air Turbulence detection. The objective of DELICAT is to validate the concept of LiDAR-based medium range turbulence detection, allowing efficient protection of the passengers and crew of the aircraft by taking the proper actions. The validation will be based on the comparison of the information on a turbulent atmospheric area, provided on one side by the remote LiDAR sensor and on the other side by the aircraft sensors (acceleration, air speed, temperature). The project is planned for three years; the consortium consists of 13 partners and is coordinated by THALES-Avionics.

BONUS+ Project Baltic Way: The core objective of Baltic Way is to establish key components of a reliable, robust and low-cost technology for the environmental management of shipping, offshore and coastal engineering activities, based on minimizing the probability of adverse effects hitting highly valuable areas. The three-year project is performed by eight partners from Estonia, Denmark, Finland, Germany and Sweden.

AMPERA Project DEOSOM: DEOSOM (Detection and Evaluation of Oil Spills by Optical Methods), an R&D project within the framework of the AMPERA (Accidental Marine Pollution ERA-NET) program, aimed at the development of such laser-based sensors for operation on board small boats or coastal platforms. The project team includes partners from Portugal, Spain and Estonia. INOV (project leader, Portugal) – an interface structure between knowledge-generation institutions and industrial entities specialized in LiDAR technique, telecommunications and data analysis. Partner groups from the University of Porto (CIIMAR, Portugal) and the University of Vigo (Spain) – consist of high-level specialists in geo-referencing and surveillance data fusion and analysis based on artificial intelligence methods. Three-year project is planned till August 2011.

Cooperative projects in Estonia[8]

Competence Center of Food and Fermentation Technologies (CCFFT): Since 2004 LDI is a stakeholder in the CCFFT and a partner in R&D projects. One of the strategic goals of the CCFFT is to apply and develop modern methods based on physics, chemistry and post-genomic processes design to improve product quality, production functionality and storage properties of the food products taking into account detailed molecular/physiological properties of raw materials, additives, starters and so on.

Source: Company files and authors' own creation/adaptation.

Exhibit 4: LDI management team

Figure II.7.10 LDI: Dr. Sergey Babichenko

Sergey Babichenko is currently the President and CEO of LDI. He is a PhD in physics, initiator and co-developer of LDI's key product concepts and designs. His professional career started in the Estonian Academy of Sciences, which led to the position of leading scientist. He has more than 25 years of experience in research, development and management of scientific groups, national and international projects. His list of professional credits includes two monographs, more than 120 scientific publications and nine patents in application of laser and spectroscopy technologies for environmental and industrial monitoring, law enforcement and search-and-rescue operations.

Babichenko is the Honorable recipient of the Belgian Royal Medal "Merite de l'Invention" for contribution to innovative high-tech. He is a member of the Board of Stakeholders of European Technology Platform "Photonics 21," Chairman of the Technology Area CBRNE at European Integrated Mission Group for Security (IMG-S), and Chairman of the Baltic Photonics cluster.

Larisa Poryvkina is currently LDI's R&D Director. She is a PhD in physics and is the principal developer of key LDI products and analytical techniques. She has extensive experience in research, development and engineering in applied spectroscopy, laser remote sensing and fluorescence technologies in industrial applications. She is a principal author of more than 90 scientific publications and six patents.

Larisa Poryvkina is the honorable recipient of OMPI–WIPO medal of World Intellectual Property Organization and diploma of "Best Female Inventor 1999," Geneva, Switzerland, 1999.

Source: Company files and authors' own creation/adaptation.

Figure II.7.11 LDI: Dr. Larisa Poryvkina

Exhibit 5: NarTest NTX2000 Device

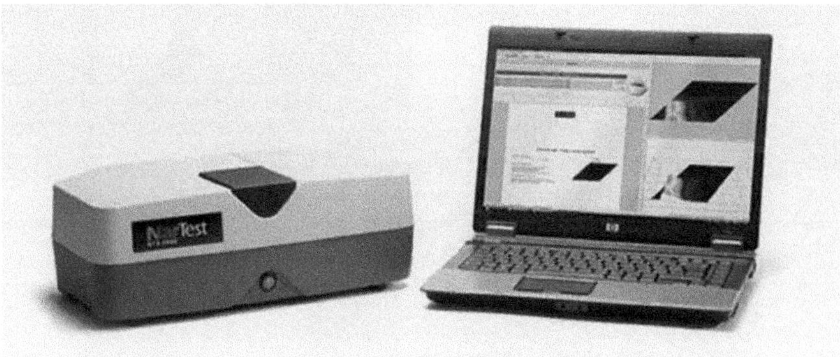

Figure II.7.12 LDI: NarTest NTX2000 Device

Source: Company files and authors' own creation/adaptation.

Exhibit 6: letter to European Health Commissioner

Tallinn, 15.06.2011

Directorate General Health & Consumers
B-1049 Brussels
Belgium

Dear Sir,
The recent events in Germany with bacterial contamination of food give a perspective on future actions to avoid such tragedies. Our company Laser Diagnostic Instruments would like to provide the techniques of express detection of bacterial contamination of water. This technique is effectively applied for monitoring of water intake, irrigation water, industrial and agricultural waste and so on. The analyzer SFS-Screener® is based on novel photonics technologies and can be easily used for on-site water analysis. Bacterial contamination is detected in a matter of a few minutes with no chemicals or consumables needed for the analysis.

LDI is able to provide the analyzers and operational training for the personnel of the responsive authorities and support any implementation of the technology in regular use. We are also ready to make a demonstration of the technology's capabilities on relatively short notice.

Looking forward to assisting in such matters to prevent incidents like this from happening.

Source: Company files and authors' own creation/adaptation.

Exhibit 7: LDI assembly workshop in Tallinn, Estonia

Figure II.7.13 LDI: assembly workshop in Tallinn, Estonia

Source: Company files and authors' own creation/adaptation.

Case B

Laser diagnostic instruments in 2014 – new focused strategy

The entire management team headed by Sergey Babichenko was recalled in 2013. The strategy to attack multiple markets without focus had failed and without a radical rethink in strategy the company faced bankruptcy. Instead of closing the company, LDI was reborn with Endel Siff taking an active management role alongside new CEO David Clark. They implemented a new refocused strategy to transform the company from a research lab into a market-driven enterprise focused on creating shareholder value. Endel Siff recapitalized LDI and retained the experience of the company's past, while David Clark, qualified in Natural Science and Manufacturing Engineering from Cambridge and experienced as a technology consultant, implemented the new strategy.

Referring back to Babichenko's final quote in New York City in the case, David said:

> By focusing on business opportunities in one area and executing fully we have a greater chance to succeed where others have failed by spreading themselves and resources too thin. We aim to be recognised for doing one thing well and delivering real value to customers before doing the next. The technology we have is only a means to an end; the focus always has to be on delivering value to the end-users in the best way we can.

The new management selected the market of oil-spill detection as their focus, streamlining the company with only one product line to take to market. Pending applications for new research grants not in line with the strategy were halted and involvement in future development projects would be pursued only if aligned with this strategy. The existing team was reviewed and under-utilized employees were made redundant to reduce costs for the company which had not made a profit in three years. At the same time, a new department for Sales & Marketing was created together with a new sales strategy, pricing system and commission policy, alongside fresh marketing materials, a new website and the establishment of a global distribution network. Even with four people recruited into this new function, at the end of 2013 the number of employees was only 17, half the size of the team in 2009.

The new team reviewed the product portfolio and halted development of Instant Screener, SFS Scanner and Fluo Imager. After many years of development (with the exception of Fluo Imager), none of these products had ever made a profit and they were still years from moving out of the perpetual prototype phase. None of the spin-out companies or partnerships previously established were bringing in any revenue for the company, so the majority were hibernated. LDI still retains an ownership stake in TFTAK and NarTest, linking it to the food technology and security markets for a return to these areas in the future.

In line with the decision to focus on one market, the Remote Optical Watcher (ROW) product was chosen to continue; it was the only product that had the potential to scale easily, and was ready for market. Unlike with other products, strong competition to ROW already existed confirming that a market existed. Unlike previous products developed by LDI, ROW does not require the user to have long training and it is easy to understand and demonstrate. It is the simplest and among the cheapest devices that LDI has ever created.

The ROW had already proven itself in local markets and the new management set about scaling and implementing quality control processes for serial production to take the product global. Non-core competencies such as machining and electronics fabrication were outsourced to improve quality, with research and development, final assembly and quality control retained in-house.

The focus for 2013 was to establish a global distribution network of resellers and distributors who had knowledge of their local markets and knew what real users really needed. LDI focused on demonstration units to prove the product and introduce the company, but despite this they achieved a sales turnover €119,000 in 2013 and established a pipeline of deals of around €2.5 million. With sales to South Korea, Indonesia, China, Finland, Japan, Australia, Ireland and the United Kingdom, LDI had now truly become the international company it had always sought to be.

Upgrading the ROW device (software, hardware and design) relies on good cooperation among developers, marketing and local partners. There is still potential to expand the product range to capture a larger market share in these countries and to enter new verticals within the oil-spill detection sector. Sales representatives of LDI in over 30 countries now report to the company and assist in the development of new versions to match different customer needs, which in the end the local resellers wish to sell and profit from themselves.

One can say that in some way LDI has returned to its roots – early detection of oil on water. This business opportunity is now exploited on the new technological level and with a laser focus not seen before in the company. Will the new strategy generate higher profit and sustainable value growth than the diversified portfolio strategy would have? We should ask it again after some years.

Figure II.7.14 LDI: Remote Optical Watcher (ROW) – new model
Source: Company files and authors' own creation/adaptation.

Figure II.7.15 LDI: David Clark (new CEO)
Source: Company files and authors' own creation/adaptation.

Notes

1. *Hyberboloid of Engineer Garin* is a 1965 Soviet science fiction film based on Aleksey Tolstoy's novel *The Garin Death Ray*, whereby an engineer builds a powerful laser on an island in order to become ruler of the world.
2. "AS" is the Estonian abbreviation for a limited company that can be listed on the stock exchange.
3. Global Photonics Sensor Market worth US$8.17 Billion by 2016. December 1, 2011, March 10, 2012; available from: http://www.marketsandmarketsblog.com/global-photonics-sensor-market-worth-8–17-billion-by-2016.php.
4. Certain financial figures have been disguised to protect confidentiality.
5. Certain financial figures have been disguised to protect confidentiality.
6. Vinluan, F. NarTest on losing end of NC Court of Appeals ruling. *Triangle Business Journal*, January 8, 2010, March 11, 2012; available from: http://www.bizjournals.com/triangle/stories/2010/01/04/daily62.html.
7. Syneron Medical Ltd. Annual Report. December 31, 2010; available from: http://www.sec.gov.
8. LDI website. March 8, 2012; available from: http://www.ldi.ee/index.php?main=379.

CASE 8: LINET: To Be an Object of Desire, Not of Choice

Tomas Ricka, David Kula and Radovan Kacin

Czech Republic. This is the story of a hugely successful Czech hospital bed producer which rose to the top 5 in its industry worldwide.

The main strategic issue is about the corporate restructuring that seems needed in order to keep growing as they plan to enter further countries. An evolving theme is that they start to compete more and more with a German partner company and shareholder who had helped them in the beginning to gain recognition in the market. Other challenging issues are not far, such as scalability, IPO alternatives and innovation advantages.

On a sunny May morning in 2011, Zbyněk Frolík, CEO of the LINET Company, looked over the LINET Company premises in the small village of Slaný, near Prague, and wondered about his company's future strategy.

LINET (an acronym for laboratory and hospital equipment – Laboratorní i nemocniční technika) was one of the most successful Czech companies, the European market leader and one of the top four hospital bed producers in the world. They were also a leading innovator in medical and nursing care. In 2011 LINET employed over 600 employees and had 11 operational subsidiaries around the world. It was Czech-owned, funded in part by foreign investment.

LINET hospital beds had enjoyed success in popular culture as well as favor from various celebrities. They were used in the Tom Cruise movie *Mission Impossible*, in the Turkish soap opera, *Scheherazade* and in Czech soap operas. The beds were also used by the Dutch queen, and various former heads of state: the Czech president Vaclav Havel, Italian Prime Minister Silvio Berlusconi, Cuban president Fidel Castro and Venezuelan president Hugo Chávez, among others.

The development of the company had been a huge personal success for Zbyněk Frolík, who had built it to an internationally competitive and leading business from humble beginnings in the post-communist country. Though it had achieved significant success, there were many important considerations for future development. Frolík wondered: What should the next steps for expansion be? How could they maintain the pace of innovation? What would LINET need to do to become the world leader? How could the company organize relations with its German co-owners more effectively?

Zbyněk Frolík's story

Zbyněk Frolík's first business activities dated back to the Communist Party rule, when running a business legally in the Czech Republic was not possible. He started his entrepreneurial journey when, during his compulsory military service, he made small owls out of sisal twine, which became a popular home decoration. Frolík taught soldiers to make the owls and allowed their officers to keep one in every ten they sold. The owls sold for a price of 150 Czech crowns per piece, the average daily wage at that time. This earned Frolík a monthly salary of 6,000 crowns, three times the average monthly civilian salary and much more than one would earn in the military service, where soldiers did not receive a salary. Having earned unprecedented income, Frolík was able to buy himself a car – a crashed Western Fiat Marafiori, at that time an almost inaccessible item.

After the military service Frolík worked as a full-time employee in the Academy of Sciences managing computers. Again his problem-solving spirit showed. When he could not repair a Russian-made mainframe computer, which broke frequently, he invited experts from Russia to Prague to help him. They helped to fix the oft-broken computer and Frolík allowed them to use a ramp at the Academy to repair Russian cars in their spare time, which they sold back in Russia.

After outsourcing his computer repair problem, Frolík had more free time during the workday. A father of two small children, he looked for an opportunity to earn more money. He decided to sell flowers. He got around the Socialist prohibition of independent business by selling agricultural surpluses,[1] which was allowed at that time. Thanks to greenhouses, automation and the advanced technology of hydroponics, he was the only one at that time in the Czech Republic who was able to supply cut roses, even in winter. He also delivered them, for example, to filmmakers (in a Czech popular movie "S tebou mě baví svět").

At that time Czechoslovakia was a closed, underdeveloped country with no direct access to Western markets. It was hard to buy up-to-date products and technologies. Nobody could satisfy customers' needs as there was no free market. Nowadays it is hard to imagine, but at that time Mr. Frolík was the first to specialize in this area. He ran this activity up to the revolution in 1989, when the market was flooded with cheap flowers from Holland.

In 1986 he was hired as technical director of the new University Hospital in Motol, Prague, the largest one in the country. There he learned to lead people; he had 260 subordinates. As technical director of the newly built hospital, he was also responsible for selecting and purchasing technical equipment for the whole hospital. For this, he got to go behind the Iron Curtain to the West, where he saw a functioning health system. Among other differences, he noticed a significant quality gap between hospital equipment in Czechoslovakia and in Western Europe, and became particularly interested in Scandinavian hospital beds.

Immediately after the revolution, Frolík resigned to start his own company, which was, to him, much more than a new job – it was a realization of newly won freedom. He approached his new initiative with a strong optimism that any risks could be overcome and a clear vision which he formed as the slogan for his beds, "to be an object of desire, not of choice."

The velvet revolution

During the early 1990s, then-Czechoslovakia went through fundamental change on all levels: political, economic and societal. With the disintegration of Czechoslovakia and the birth of the Czech Republic in 1993, change brought the transition from a socialist, central planning system with collective ownership to a free market economy based on private property ownership.

The change was quite radical as Czechoslovakia, as was East Germany, had been based exclusively on the state and state-owned companies, which represented almost 100% of GDP (about 4,000 companies). In comparison, Poland and Hungary had maintained a certain part of the economy in private hands, a sector which further expanded, even while still under socialist rule in the 1980s.

The transition was radical in the Czech Republic. Then Finance Minister Vaclav Klaus (who later served as Prime Minister, Chairman of the Chamber of Deputies and two terms as President) was the most prominent proponent of the move to a pro-market economy. His reform concept was swift execution accompanied by stabilization measures to prevent high inflation and adverse balance of payments. The first impact of this drastic approach was the unavoidable economic decline, which was short-termed. This went along with social hardship, immediately felt, while economic growth took time. In the beginning, there was a window of opportunity for these drastic changes, but soon social and political support for the transition was needed. Thus, these changes had to be done very quickly, before opposition would start to form. This led to radical change in the business climate and legal possibilities, which opened opportunities for capable people.

Starting a company during the transition came with many opportunities as well as risks. The Czech transition had a series of very favorable elements: geographic location in the center of Europe, educated workforce and rapidly gaining macroeconomic stability (low inflation, consolidated public finances and relatively high employment rate). However, the economy was slow on the uptake, many assets were technically obsolete, and company cultures lacked a view for value creation, holding on to "old ways" instead. There was also an overreliance on neighboring inefficient socialist economies and a weak institutional environment, with low legal standards and low enforceability. Tranformation and restructuring of the economy also brought a lot of skilled and experienced people to the labor market.

The Czech transition was characterized by ambivalence. On the one hand, it was a time of positive expectations, when people were convinced that in a few years the country would get to the level of developed countries like Austria or the Federal Republic of Germany. On the other hand, there was evident fear of a step into the unknown. The transformation process had not been verified in any country at that time and negative aspects of transformation, like fraud during privatization, led to collective concerns.

The transformation stabilized the democratic system and market environment. To a certain extent the CR became one of the most developed countries from the former socialist block. However, even 20 years later, this process was not completed. In particular, a functional institutional environment with a stable legal system, quality legal standards, compliance and enforcement, remained incomplete.

The birth of LINET

For Frolík, despite the challenges it was the perfect moment to create a company, be it for the sole reason that it was finally possible to do so! Putting himself to the task, he quickly realized how he could take advantage of the transition. In Slaný, close to the country's main economic center, Prague, he identified a large former state company, ČKD Slaný, a producer of truck crane superstructures that had just gone bankrupt and dismissed a lot of qualified and educated people. This was the opportunity he had been looking for. He was particularly interested in staff from the department of construction, who would later play a key role in the history of LINET. LINET Ltd. was established in 1990 in a rundown state farmhouse as a new start-up company. There was an idea, skilled people and a ready facility; he could start to realize his dream. To get the company going, Frolík and his partners needed the equivalent of €14,000, a large amount, but the only money the founding partners ever invested into the business directly, because the next development was funded by reinvesting profits. The intention was to produce hospital beds from the establishment of the company, but this required know-how, equipment and contracts. At that time, companies in Czechoslovakia competed mostly with cheap inputs (materials and labor). Products were less sophisticated, but cheaper. This was also the case with LINET. Its other production was based on semi-finished iron products for other industrial fields (shelves for stores or laboratory cages). The idea of keeping these other products was to help overcome the initial period of lower demand for LINET's hospital beds, generate enough cash, know-how and reputation to help reorient the strategy toward hospital beds as the main product.

Strategically, it was a good choice of location for a number of reasons. The factory was located near Prague, the capital of the country, and there was an industrial tradition, infrastructure and an educated workforce. Also, the international airport was nearby (about 30 minutes by car), which was important because of potential client visits. There was also sufficient land nearby for future expansion.

Focus on health care and hospital beds

Thanks to his former job as technical director of Prague's large hospital, Frolík had identified health care as a growing area for business. He had realized that in comparison with countries in Western Europe, hospitals in Czechoslovakia had deficient infrastructure. While sophisticated, modern hospital beds had to be imported and were expensive, the beds then produced in Czechoslovakia were technologically outdated. Therefore the area of hospital bed production was an obvious choice. However, it was already clear that the Czechslovakian market had limited absorptive capacity; Frolík already saw the future of the company on the international market.

While slowly orienting the company's strategy to hospital beds, Frolík reorganized the company. He hired new people and improved administration and management capacity. The aim was to maintain existing operations and cash flow and work in parallel on the new hospital bed business. They set up an R&D department and hired new staff. By maintaining the existing business, the company could relatively safely try many manufacturing processes, such as stainless steel welding and varnishing, which easily applied to bed production.

In the beginning, building on a not-so-differentiated workforce was an advantage, as everyone did everything, but as the company entered a critical growth stage, staff moved toward greater specialization. Care was taken to set up and improve different processes step-by-step. Frolík was then able to distance himself from daily operational activities and instead focus on the strategic development of the company.

LINET developed its first products and applied for its first tenders in Czechoslovakia in 1990. The aim was to offer Western quality, but at a realistic cost, to Czech hospitals. Their first contract was for the Motol Hospital, where Frolík had worked before. The contract played a key role: at that time, it was usual to pay suppliers relatively large advances. This early cash flow allowed LINET to produce its first hospital bed order without much pre-financing.

Building credibility

Frolík had realized that to increase company visibility and improve perception, it would be helpful to gain know-how from abroad and develop the image of a "Western company." At that time the label "Made in Germany" was preferred. Thus in 1991 he offered a majority share to WIBO, a small German company which produced beds and equipment for senior homes and nursing homes. The companies had evolved independently for a long time – LINET focused on the Central and Eastern European market and WIBO on Western markets which had been less available to LINET. The Wissner company (later WIBO), acquired a 50.01% share, while guaranteeing veto rights to the LINET founder.

This constellation was initially advantageous, especially for LINET, because the foreign partner gave LINET an image of quality and reliability which brought greater business stability despite the turbulent times. The German partner was to play a key role for LINET when expanding into Western markets.

LINET's expansion into new markets

By joining the EU in 2004, the Czech Republic gained access to the markets of EU member states. In addition to the option for faster expansion, this meant bigger competition between LINET and WIBO, though their product portfolios differed substantially. LINET offered medical equipment. In this area there were more sophisticated products, higher margins and a larger share of research and development than in non-medical equipment (rehabilitation and aftercare). WIBO made simpler products for aftercare and focused more on design than on technical and clinical parameters. They offered beds, furniture and equipment for homes for the elderly. Eventually, LINET offered less sophisticated equipment and accessories as well, and the companies began to compete in some markets. As they still operated separately in some countries, both companies had their own business representation and there were only small synergies in materials acquisition and other fields (research, expansion and tenders). It became an unpleasant situation for both companies and it was clear that something should be done in order to be more competitive and efficient.

When, in 2008, Europe grappled with crisis and stagnation, non-European markets offered more growth potential. Penetration into new markets required much greater consolidation of power and long-term development strategy between the two companies. Entrepreneurship in the health sector, even within the EU, was not easy. However, in developing countries or even in the United States, it was even more complicated, particularly for European companies which had to deal with larger distances, different cultural practices and public sector specifics. The US market was very sophisticated, highly regulated and dominated by two very strong companies. These companies were prepared to use all means, including long legal battles on intellectual property rights, to keep their market position. LINET tried to prepare very carefully for entrance to the US market. This included precise patent research to avoid legal actions from competitors, a well-built story (Mr. Frolík as a successful self-made man), step-by-step tactics (including small deals as references) and a long-term strategy (to demonstrate quality, competitive prices and gain a reputation for next bids).

Political and geopolitical issues could also play a major role in market expansion opportunities. For example, the Czech Republic was on the blacklist in China due to its support of Tibetan independence. However, such situations could be solved thanks to the German partner.

Technology and design

The key to LINET's success was its early capitalization on the trend toward electrical beds from mechanical ones. LINET also realized the importance of technical process and product innovation. The company looked to future customers and competitors' mistakes for innovations. They identified that beds could have a variety of clinical features that helped prevent patient and nurse accidents, made medical treatment more effective and reduced the risk of pressure bedsores and other problems.

In this area the turning point came in 1994 when LINET established its own development department. The company developed two high-quality beds: one was high-tech quality for critical care and special demands (Multicare). As it demonstrated LINET's technical excellence and design, it also served as a door opener, helping to sell the less technically advanced beds, which also were of high quality and excellent design. The second bed (Eleganza) was aimed at mass production.

During the second half of the 1990s, LINET developed a technical breakthrough: a motorized, telescoping electromotoric pole. Previously, beds had been positioned by lifting a lever. With the new pole, the bed could be more easily adjusted and cleaned. Innovations like this were particularly valued by nurses, who were an important consultative voice during the selection process of new beds. Equally, it was important that they like the bed as well. This technical innovation would later become a standard for hospital beds and, despite the strong patent protection, be copied by manufacturers worldwide. For hospitals, this innovation meant a significant qualitative improvement.

These two types of beds with the telescopic pole gave LINET a technological advantage versus the competition worldwide. They covered a wide range of hospitals' needs. LINET was therefore able to offer top-class products at a competitive price. The great success of the Multicare bed allowed the company an intensive cycle of innovations even though the Multicare bed was originally meant to attract customers to the LINET brand and not be sold at high volumes. LINET's management understood that permanent investment in innovation, design and the company story would be the key that would allow further market expansion.

LINET's quest for innovation brought about other revolutionary solutions: incorporating sensors for measuring heart rate, breathing, physical activity, patient safety and movement, and for performing other functions like weighing patients, X rays and automatic communication between the bed and hospital information systems.

In addition to the technical side, the company put strong emphasis on the design and aesthetics of their beds as well as their functionality, ergonomics, serviceability and likability. LINET involved nurses in the design and development, as they spent the most time with patients and their beds and were also increasingly involved in decision-making. LINET also worked with top designers to create new designs. Crucially, they also placed high importance on the opinions of the end-users: patients. They developed the motto "To be an object of desire," to highlight their interest in appealing to the stakeholders´ emotions. These new approaches began to differentiate LINET from competitors and attract attention from copycats – both from China and from Western European competitors.

The most successful products

ELEGANZA

Eleganza was an adjustable bed for acute care. This bed pioneered several new innovations including adjustable mattresses, bedside rails and simple, cleanable construction. These facilitated nursing work and enabled several key advantages including improved fall protection and infection prevention.

Multicare

Multicare was a bed for critical care. It had many key advantages. The bed was equipped with automatic side-positioning equipment which aided in the prevention of respiratory complications. It also had X-ray equipment on the bed and integrated controls, foot controls, automatic brakes and other controls which improved patient comfort and convenience. It also had improved safety features such as higher sides, smaller gaps and a bed exit alarm. Multicare became a classic design which also demonstrated the technological maturity of the company. It had been planned for limited production, serving mostly as an exhibition magnet, but the bed was eventually produced on a larger scale, with thousands produced yearly until 2010.

A key differentiator for LINET was design. To build this compentency, the company cooperated with highly qualified designers from the beginning.

The Czech example was Jiří Španihel, a leading industrial designer in Bohemia whose work had won numerous awards (e.g., Good Design Award 1999 and Japan and Hanover IF Design 1999 for a gynecological-urological examination chair and the Excellent Design Prize 2000, CR, for the hospital bed Eleganza). His work emphasized functional design focused on user comfort. Another designer was Ivan Dlabač from DIVAN studio who designed the Multicare bed and earned the National Design Award for it. Both the designers and their human-centric products played key roles in the LINET company development. Other designers, such as Christian and Michael Sieger (Sieger Design) and Carlos Bernal, contributed to the company's design-focused culture.

Innovation in employee education

LINET invested about 5% of its turnover in innovation (higher than the 3% average for industrial companies).

To continue its focus on technical innovation and design, LINET hired technical specialists to help found their own educational institution – the Academy of Productivity and Innovation (API). At first, the Academy trained LINET employees and eventually offered its services commercially to other companies as well. By engaging in external consulting projects, the Academy built a knowledge base it had not had access to previously. The API was unique in its narrow focus on productivity and industrial engineering. This service was in demand. For many companies in the Czech Republic, increasing productivity was one of the few ways to increase their competitiveness.

The company developed quickly, and the need for technical employees and quality managers grew. The company believed it took around a year to develop an employee, so they emphasized their own educational system and long-term employee support. They also tried to attract capable people with internships and projects for bachelor and diploma theses. The long-term investments paid off. In one example, Tomáš Kolář, who joined the company in 1994 as a master student, later became the director of the company.

More learning was brought back to the company via the founder, Zbyněk Frolík, who also contributed to the Czech government advisory body of research, development and innovation, where he represented the business sector. In addition, he passed on his experience in lectures at universities and, in general, he tried to influence the improvement of the quality of science, research and education in the Czech Republic.

Characteristics of the market

The market for medical equipment was highly regulated and characterized by long development life cycles and low stock rotation. For beds, development was around 10 to 15 years in developed countries and 20 to 30 in emerging markets.

However, in major markets, the situation was different. The US market had a big technological lead and was consolidated by two strong players. The Western European market was developed too, but fragmented. The developing world, especially the BRIC countries, were increasingly working to improve their healthcare systems, demonstrating attractive market potential. The whole sector of hospital bed manufacturing was dependent on innovation. A hospital bed was no longer just a simple frame and mattress. Present era hospital beds were able to carry out functions like patient monitoring and event detection, for example, of heart attacks. Requirements for beds steadily increased, and only those manufacturers who were innovative were able to keep their market position. In the first decade of the 21st century there were five major world players: LINET, WIBO, Hill-Rom Inc., Stryker Corporation, Stiegelmeyer Group and Paramount Bed Company. The largest company by turnover was Hill-Rom, with US$1.66 billion in 2011, approximately 20 times LINET's. (For more market data see Exhibit 2).

Hospital bed production had been proven a very resilient sector during the economic crisis. Even during the years 2008 to 2011, it showed overall growth, which was expected to continue. According to the agency IBIS World, sales[2] in the sector increased in the US during the years 2007 to 2012 by an average of 4.2% per year. In 2012 they were expected to reach an amount of US$2.5 billion. Worldwide sales were estimated at US$4.4 billion in 2010. The agency estimated the sector's growth for the following five years as well as an increase of its share of GDP of the United States. Growth was driven by increasing demand for hospital beds and beds intended for home care.

Demand had grown as a result of increased public and private health expenditures with the aging population in the US driving industry growth. This trend was expected to continue, fueling revenue growth across the sector. Although many health facilities had reduced bed capacity as they were forced to minimize costs and as safer and less invasive methods shortened required post-operative care, overall demand exceeded supply.

The biggest market for hospital beds was the United States with a share of more than 40%. Asia-Pacific represented the fastest growing market with annual average growth of 4.9% in recent years. In Europe the major markets were in Germany, France, Italy and the United Kingdom; together they represented a share of more than 65%.

The industry was relatively concentrated; the largest market share in the United States, which amounted to 65%, was held by Hill-Rom, also a worldwide leader. A major player in the US market was also Stryker with a share of about 30%. The leader of the European market was LINET Group SE, currently also trying to penetrate the US market. In turn the company Paramount Bed focused primarily on the Japanese market, where it reached 70% of the market share.

Many healthcare facilities rented hospital beds from suppliers rather than buying them directly. Beds with excellent design, allowing for the integration of high-tech solutions, were high in demand. Thus manufacturers were constantly forced to come up with innovations. Manufacturers were also keen to reduce bed costs because they reduced the total cost to healthcare facilities.

LINET in the period 2005–2010

The period between 2005 and 2010 was a period of growth for the company. LINET built new production facilities to fuel further expansion. In these five years, the turnover nearly doubled to €66 million and net income tripled to nearly €20 million. Return on sales amounted to 30%, which was a first-class result during the economic crisis. The number of employees increased by one-third during this period to almost 600 (see Exhibit 1). From the beginning, the business strategy had to respect the specifics of the sector: high regulation, hospital care as a public property and heavy political influence on the sector. Therefore, while penetrating foreign markets the electoral cycle in the country played an important role. Also, fast-growing markets were crucial, since completely new infrastructure, including hospitals, were built there. The company tried to influence the direction of the hospital bed sector through a systematic effort to determine standards and by filling an increasing number of patents (see the exhibits).

The majority of LINET's production was exported. In 2010 LINET exported into more than 100 countries on five continents.

The management of LINET had the idea that for penetration into the Western European markets, it would help to support cooperation with local companies in those countries. The company managed to convince some managers at local companies, however, that their owners did not like the intention. LINET used this tension to its advantage to recruit some of these managers and sales representatives for its expansion into foreign markets. These managers knew the local market very well, had relevant contacts, were proven managers and sometimes had an interest in demonstrating that their original employers had made a mistake. These new local managers helped LINET to penetrate the English and French markets. In Spain (2004), LINET acquired a local healthcare equipment producer, the company Desan Flex (25% share). LINET made an effort to build its own sales offices, which provided a good base for expansion into the local market. This happened, for example, in Italy, Sweden, Great Britain and in the United States. In problematic markets (e.g., due to isolation or corruption), the company tried to work with a reputable local distribution company.

From the company foundation, LINET's owners had high ambitions. They aimed to become the largest European manufacturer of hospital beds. In 2010, LINET became the fourth largest company in its segment of the world and number one in Europe. The next logical step was to become a world leader. Mr. Frolík saw the opportunity for his company. By 2015, LINET aimed to double turnover to €250 million and increase earnings (EBITDA) 2.5 times.

Further development, corporate structuring and relocation

After successful product development and expansion into foreign markets, the company faced new problems: how to organize its corporate structure and how to ensure further growth. Its lack of structure and the increasingly overlapping German partner were becoming complicating factors for future expansion.

One option was to remain in the country; however, the CR's lack of prestige on the international business stage was an important detractor. Additionally, the uncertain political environment, comparatively high corruption, and inefficient judicial and bureaucratic systems made the option less attractive. In addition, the German partners did not favor this option.

Germany was also not favored because of several public company regulations including the mandatory inclusion of employees in the supervisory board and a high tax burden. Therefore, third countries came into consideration. However, there were many factors to evaluate.

There were many open questions about corporate restructuring between the partners. It was necessary to convert shares in the existing companies to an eventual new entity. Czech LINET owners were not interested in buying the whole group, because they would have been in significant debt due to the high market value of both entities (about €300 million).

Consolidation would help cut costs. Before the consolidation, for example, goods had been exported from LINET to a third country through the German partner, who had added additional fees, then sold via merchants to the end customer. Therefore, simplifying the trade and distribution system had the subsequent effect of simplifying internal administrative processes, reducing the number of warehouses and unifying purchasing systems. Ultimately the supply accelerated, and goods were delivered to the customer under more competitive conditions.

The problem was how to effectively set up subsidiaries and utilize human potential for the expansion of the company. The management of subsidiaries had been very individual before that time. A consolidated company would necessarily introduce more rigid rules. Instead of relatively informal or familial relationships, formal structure with standard corporate rules would be necessary (business management guidebook, assessment of management performance and so on).

As a future option, LINET also considered floating on the stock exchange. If they were to do so, the company would need to be appraised. Therefore it was especially important for the owners that the company consolidate in order to create a valuation with maximum future cash flow.

What were the next steps for the company to expand from the largest European producer to serve other markets? They had increased annual production and financial indicators (between 2000 and 2010 the company multiplied its revenues 7x, EBITDA 15x and Equity 26x, achieved average ROS 18% and ROE 35%).

The management of both companies and their owners began to seriously consider what to do. They knew that LINET and WIBO were competitive companies, experiencing successful expansion, with high innovation potential, but in the future there were several threats, and also opportunities, which needed to be addressed.

Exhibits

Exhibit 1: economic performance

Table II.8.1 LINET: the economic performance

Financial year	2005/2006	2006/2007	2007/2008	2008/2009	2009/2010
Revenues	39,139,000 €	55,741,000 €	65,440,000 €	64,963,000 €	66,228,000 €
Value added	14,095,000 €	21,535,000 €	22,654,000 €	24,123,000 €	26,763,000 €
EBITDA	10,934,000 €	17,013,000 €	18,178,000 €	3,903,000 €	27,491,000 €
Net profit	7,358,000 €	11,583,000 €	12,908,000 €	1,482,000 €	19,876,000 €
Employees (Average)	334	371	496	538	528
% of revenues from foreign markets	Not found	86%	80.5%	78%	81%
Exchange rate	28.6 CZK/€	28.0 CZK/€	25.3 CZK/€	27.4 CZK/€	25.4 CZK/€

Note: [1] Financial year 1. 4. – 31. 3; [2] foreign markets does not include Slovakia; [3] exchange rate of the Czech National Bank (31.3.).

Source: Company's annual reports.

Exhibit 2: the market and competition

Supplement: characteristics of Competition Hill-Rom, Inc.

Hill-Rom, Inc. is a subsidiary of Hill-Rom Holdings, Inc. and, above all, a global player in hospital bed manufacturing. The company was founded in October 1929, when it started to manufacture wooden furniture for hospitals. The company's headquarters is in Batesville, Indiana. Currently the company employs over 6,200 people all over the world. It also has a very broad portfolio of products, from hospital beds and stretchers to communication systems between a patient and hospital staff. In 2011 the company achieved sales of nearly US$1.6 billion, which was 8% annual growth.

Stryker Corporation

Although Stryker is primarily a producer of medical orthopedic implants, surgical instruments and other medical facilities, it also manufactures hospital beds. The company was founded in 1941 and is currently divided into several separate operating units. In 2010, the total revenues reached US$7.3 billion, which was an 8.9% increase compared to the previous year.

The company achieves such high values mainly by its very broad portfolio of products. Revenues from the production of hospital beds contribute only about 5% to the company's total revenues. Despite this fact, the company is a major player in the production of beds, especially in the US market.

Stiegelmeyer Group

Stiegelmeyer is medium-sized German company with its headquarters in Herford, where it was founded in 1900. The company, however, started the production of hospital beds around 1950. It has its production facilities mainly in Europe and also focuses primarily on the European market.

Paramount Bed Co., Ltd

Paramount Bed was founded in 1947. It focuses mainly on manufacturing hospital beds, mattresses, hospital furniture and other small hospital equipment, especially for the Japanese market. In 2010 the company achieved sales of 45.6 million yen (about half a million dollars). The actual production of hospital beds reached almost 50% of the revenue. The company is a leader in the Japanese market with a share of almost 70%.

Source: Company files and authors' own creation/adaptation.

Exhibit 3: supplement: structure of products

Healthcare program:

- Hospital beds;
- Intensive-care beds;
- Mattresses and anti-decubitus systems;
- Stretchers;
- Birth and baby beds;
- Patient tables;
- Furniture and other equipment.

The Nursing program:

- Care beds;
- Mattresses and anti-decubitus systems;
- Patient tables;
- Furniture and chairs.

Other equipment:

- Special beds for home care;
- Mattresses and anti-decubitus systems;
- Stainless steel program;
- Medical furniture;
- Equipment rental.

Source: Company files and authors' own creation/adaptation.

Exhibit 4: basic types of mergers

A merger is an act of friendly agreement. In principle, a merger involves companies with approximately the same size, according to various economic measures and indicators.

A merger can be done by:

- Incorporation
- Blend

When incorporating and blending, the property structure of the continuing company is changed in relation to valuation of the original companies. Financial experts determine the value of net assets of all companies and calculate exchange ratios between shares of the acquired company or companies and those of the acquiring company.

Incorporation

An incorporation results in such a combination of companies where the incorporated company is discontinued without liquidation and simultaneously all assets and liabilities are transferred to the company into which it has been incorporated. An incorporation does not create a new entity as happens with a blend; the legal successor is the existing company.

Blend

A blend is a way of joining companies in which the blending companies are discontinued and a new company is created.

We can divide mergers into the following groups:

Horizontal Merger

A horizontal merger a merger of companies with identical production programs which operate on the same economic field and at the same level. In principle, the merging companies are competitors in a sub-segment of a market. This combination usually leads to the strengthening of market position, synergy effects and so on.

Vertical Merger

A vertical merger is a merger where merged companies come from different segments of the economic chain that results in a certain product. A company is merged with its customer or supplier.

Conglomerate Merger

A conglomerate merger is a merger of companies from various unrelated economic sectors. These mergers are divided into two types: pure and mixed. Within the mixed conglomerate merger a company wants to expand its product portfolio or to gain a larger market share by including the products unrelated to its primary activity.

Congeneric Merger

A congeneric merger is a merger of companies doing business in the same field, each of them offering a different product, but their products can complement each other. This merger helps to achieve product range completion.

Exhibit 5: company headquarters

choosing the location of company headquarters

When choosing the location of company headquarters, many aspects need to be considered. Overall taxation is still very important for companies – not only the basic rate, but the whole tax system of the country. Other important aspects are: adequate legislative protection, excellent business environment with minimal administrative requirements, and regulations and protection for financial information. At the same time, company headquarters must be respectful and of sufficient weight. A renowned address is crucial for worldwide business.

Germany

According to World Bank (Doing Business 2012) the business environment in Germany was in nineteenth place in the world. Germany had excellent ratings, especially in the enforcement of contracts, business freedom, maturity of the financial environment and legal protection of investors. However, it was necessary to allow for high mandatory administrative and legal obligations and entrepreneurs. German companies had been a symbol of precision and accuracy in the long term.

A tax rate on corporate income had been gradually reduced in previous years. First, in 2001, it had been reduced to 25% and then in 2008 to 15%. This rate was still valid in 2012. Moreover, there was a mandatory trade tax (its amount is determined by local authorities) and a solidarity contribution. The overall effective tax rate was approximately 29%.

In Germany, employees elected one-third of their representatives to the Supervisory Board, and in large companies with more than 2,000 employees and in coal and steel industries up to one-half. It was a duty required by law. However, the number of members could not be greater than 21.

The Netherlands

According to World Bank evaluation in collaboration with Pricewaterhouse Coopers (Paying Taxes 2011), the Netherlands offered domestic companies and foreign investors the fifth simplest tax system of the EU countries. Only Ireland, Luxembourg, Great Britain and Denmark had better rankings in 2010. Extensive tax benefits and deductions also increased business attractiveness in the Netherlands. For example, dividends and profits received from sale of shares were exempted from taxation.

Foreign investments were welcomed in the Netherlands. Foreign investors could count on high economic freedom and low corruption. Entrepreneurship in the Netherlands was accompanied by a minimum of corruption; the corruption index in the Netherlands (*Transparency International Corruption Perceptions Index 2011*) was the seventh lowest in the world. Foreign investors could also count on qualified personnel. However, labor costs were very high. Any additional services increased costs to foreign entrepreneurs.

corporate income tax

The tax rate on corporate income had dropped significantly in the previous ten years from 35% (in 2000) to 25.5% (in 2010). However, lower taxes could be paid. The Netherlands was a country where small companies paid less income tax. Firms with profit up to €275,000 paid income tax at 20% of their profits.

In the Netherlands, many major international companies are registered.

Switzerland

Switzerland was a country with a stable long-term political and legal environment, stable currency, functioning infrastructure, permanently growing economy, transparent tax system and liberal fiscal policy that was focused primarily on the efficiency of the state. The effectively functioning state was able to maintain a balanced budget together with an acceptable tax burden on individuals and legal persons. In addition, there was a range of incentives that motivated some international corporations and many smaller companies to base their headquarters and pay their taxes there. Linked to this was the fact that Swiss companies were very well perceived in the world as superiors in their fields. Switzerland had been a member of the business community EFTA (European Free Trade Association) together with Norway, Liechtenstein and Iceland), thanks to which it had a very close relationship to EU members, but was not an EU member.

The central tax rate on corporate income was 8.5%. However, individual cantons (autonomous member states of the confederacy) set their local tax rates on corporate income tax. The average combined tax rate for companies was about 21%. Switzerland was not a tax haven. Taxes were payed there and taxpayer morality ranked among the highest in the world. This was also connected with how the municipalities and employees of tax authorities treated the taxpayers. This could be compared to bank employees, who were trying to get new clients and to keep them for a long term by providing good services. Furthermore, Switzerland implemented a withholding tax of 35% when dividends were paid to a natural person permanently living outside the country. Business in Switzerland was accompanied by minimal corruption – the country had the eighth lowest in the world (*Transparency International Corruption Perceptions Index 2011*). However, there were very high administrative costs (minimum wage, rents, lawyer services, tax consultant fees and so on). Moreover, German tax authorities were very wary about moving the German capital to Switzerland.

The Czech Republic

The tax system in the CR was similar to the systems of most developed countries, especially European ones, but for entrepreneurs it was complicated and not transparent. Moreover, it had been changed frequently and that deteriorated its clarity. The tax rate on corporate income in 2012 was 19% (excluding investment fund, mutual fund, and foreign collective investment fund and pension fund, which pay 5%). In recent years the rate declined from 35% to 19%.

The administration associated with tax payment was far worse than in other countries. In the long term the Czech Republic had belonged to countries with the most complicated system of tax administration. According to World Bank research, the CR had the fifth most complicated tax payment system in Europe. The administrative burden on entrepreneurs hindered the development of companies.

Property rights were respected in the CR. The Czech Republic was also a signatory to international agreements on copyrights. Existing legislation guaranteed protection to all forms of property including patents, copyrights and trademarks.

Source: Company files and authors' own creation/adaptation.

Notes

1. Selling agricultural surpluses was defined by law as an activity that you could do besides your regular job. The intention of the authorities was to enable people not to engage in regular business, but to sell fruit and vegetables from their gardens.
2. Hospital Bed Manufacturing in the US Industry Market Research Report. Available from: http://www.prweb.com/releases/2012/1/prweb9136127.htm.

CASE 9: The Masterplast Story: Constructing an Entrepreneurial Success Story

Péter Dietrich, László Csepregi and János Vecsenyi

Hungary. This case describes the growth story of a construction material company and its young entrepreneur who founded the company directly after his university studies and grew it to more than 700 employees and US$100 million in revenues.

The main challenge is where to build the next plant – a geographical expansion issue – and the background covers other issues such as HR and macroeconomic aspects.

Introduction

In the late evening the night before their board meeting, Dávid Tibor, CEO of Masterplast, and his friend, co-founder and CFO, Balázs Ács, sat together in their office pondering the big question: What was the best next step in order to keep growing and internationalizing their company? So far they had built Masterplast from scratch to an €80 million revenue construction material wholesaler and producer with operations in 12 countries. In fact, Masterplast Group, with their headquarters in Hungary, had become one of the leading producers and distributors of construction industry products.

The company provided an all-inclusive solution with products in the areas of heat, sound and water insulation, roofing and dry construction. All of their products had TÜV and ISO qualification and through the company's subsidiaries and partners they were made available on the European market as well as outside of Europe. Based on strong logistics and joint services with partners, Masterplast offered a unique service element for their Hungarian clients: home delivery within 24 hours. This had been a win–win situation for both Masterplast and the construction yards. The yards were not cut out of these deals, as the clients ordered through them, while they had been able to provide this extra service for the products that were supplied by Masterplast. The company simply had more orders.

Thanks to their high-quality products and unique value proposition, the company had grown in the last 13 years and even got through the global crisis with only a relatively small decrease in revenues compared to many of their competitors in the construction material and real-estate business.

The founders believed that the consolidation phase would soon come to an end and that it was time to decide together with the Board which strategic moves the company should do now in order to position Masterplast for national and international growth. Growth had once again become their first priority, but they knew that it would not be as easy as it was in the past. A number of different growth strategies and options seemed feasible – each one with its inherent advantages and disadvantages. A wrong choice could have severe negative impact on the company's current operations and future ability to grow – a right choice could help Masterplast to propel itself into a position that would allow the firm to take full advantage of the market potential they saw in various countries.

It would be easy to say: "Let's grow!" But how, when, where, with which range of products? These were the questions that the Board would have to decide on, and the two owners had only two votes out of five, (also a strategic decision which had been decided earlier and proved to be right) so strong arguments and reasoning would be needed at the meeting.

The beginning

Dávid and Balázs were high school friends. Dávid's father owned a plastic packaging material production company where, during the high school summer breaks, the boys worked as sales assistants. Dávid's father had invented a technique to make heat-mirroring roof foil and patented it in Hungary. At that time in Hungary no one used roof foil to protect houses from wetness and heat. The only thing available for use at that time was foil from the agricultural industry, but it didn't resist the conditions a roof faced for years. It was very hard to convince people and customers about the need and value of using such a product.

The boys' job was to sell roof foil to privately owned building material yards that sold all kinds of goods for construction. The two 17-year-old guys in an old Ford Sierra station wagon were truly not the ones with the best sales practices, but they tried to do their best. After high school their lives went in two different directions: Dávid started studying at a business college and Balázs chose engineering studies.

They still had two years of college left when Dávid's father decided to give up the business. The two friends thought this was a good opportunity to found their own company on the base of the old one. Dávid's father provided a lot of professional help for them, as the main goal was to speed up the roof-foil business while keeping the packaging foil production as well. The three of them formed a company and they employed two salespeople in the summer of 1997. They started to purchase buckets and construction foils and cut the roof foil into shorter sizes (e.g., a 25m roll instead of a 100m roll) so they could sell to private customers as well. Two years later, Dávid's father sold his shares and the sales employees received a future option of shares (5% each) if they reached the sales goals in 1999, which they eventually did.

A few years later, in 2002 they closed the packaging foil part of the company and the main focus turned to the wholesale and retail trade of roof foil and other construction materials.

Masterplast's target customers were privately owned construction material selling yards, built from the former state-owned yards network (many state-owned businesses went bankrupt when competition came into the country after 1989, which they were not used to). In 1999 the first Do-It-Yourself (DYI) store was established in Hungary and Masterplast became one of their suppliers. First, they started to supply the stores with 2–3 different products. They gained another big buyer when the Austrian Raab-Karcher bought the former state yard network in northern-Hungary. The company decided to stay in business as a wholesaler and never had the intention to go into the retail business.

When it came to the company's success, one needed to understand the past characteristics of the Hungarian construction materials market. As mentioned, on the ruins of the former yard network there was a non-flexible logistic and supply system. Service was available only for large customers and the household market had to wait for the goods they needed. Dávid and Balázs realized this and eventually they found a solution that would give a real service to their future customers.

The next step was their special delivery system: they employed qualified and reliable truck drivers who built very good relationships with the customers. They were two-in-one: sales personnel and truck drivers as well. The drivers treated the owners of the yard in a way the owners were not used to: they always asked where to unload, asked for any other special needs and recommended products. This system worked really well as it was very new to the market and was based on trust; there was almost no shift in the workforce during those years.

They were also willing to sell low quantities for small customers and offered next-day delivery. This way the yards didn't have to stock any goods, Masterplast provided everything for them when they needed it. This was a huge financial help to the yard owners, which was very much appreciated.

When the two founders first started working in the company, they chose the name Masterplast as a vision for future international success. As the product line widened it was changed to Masterplast Group International to show that the company worked in many areas dealing with trade, production, delivery and product R&D.

Back in 1997 the two young men thought that a monthly wage of €200 was enough for college students and they kept their wages low during the growth phase. They believed that hard, good and professional work would pay off. They reinvested their money back into the company.

Going international

The company's international expansion started in 1999 in Slovakia, where they had a really good relationship with the local distributor of their products and established a company in 2000. Romania followed the next year when their former sales partner became the head of the Romanian company. In 2003, they expanded to Serbia and Croatia, building from their experiences in Slovakia and Romania. Serbia was a challenge because there was an embargo on the country after the war.

The owners of Masterplast had always believed in step-by-step learning; they wanted the local executives to experience what it was like to start the business in new regions. The local executives had to find and meet the local customers, choose contacts to deal with and agree on prices. This way all the executives would know how business is done in their market and in the company. For Masterplast it seemed to be more successful if the company headquarters was close to the main warehouse and logistics center and the company could continuously expand into the central regions of the country as it grew.

Of course those early managers had help from the Hungarian headquarters, and as the operations developed they could employ more people and start managing their affiliates.

In 2011 Masterplast had its own subsidiaries in the following countries besides Hungary:

- Slovakia
- Romania
- Serbia
- Croatia
- Austria
- Poland
- Czech Republic
- Ukraine
- Bosnia
- Macedonia
- Bulgaria
- China

Other countries were being served also, but not with a dedicated subsidiary. The country share of revenue for the group can be seen in the graph below.

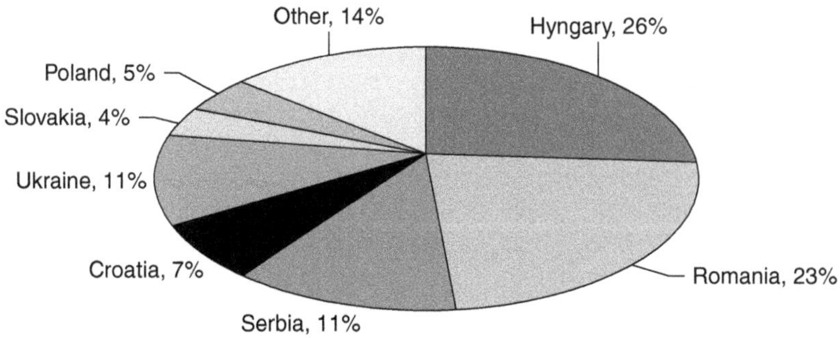

Figure II.9.1 Masterplast: share of the total revenue
Source: Company files and authors' own creation/adaptation.

Hungary and Romania were the biggest, followed by Serbia, where the EPS plant was located, while Poland had the lowest revenue contribution. Ukraine had 11% of all revenues in spite of the fact that the EPS family was not sold there.

Customized, high-quality products

Becoming a leading building material wholesaler brought new challenges for the company. Masterplast had been involved in production since the beginning as a joint venture partner. One of its main partners was Asbo Roof Industries in Belgium. The high-quality bituminous corrugated sheets for roofing made in Belgium had earned success in the EU markets and even outside Europe. To improve product quality and gain greater control over

Figure II.9.2 Masterplast: product
Source: Company files and authors' own creation/adaptation.

the market, Masterplast decided to build its own production plants. The company launched its first plant in Kál, Hungary in 2004 to produce metal profiles and PE foams.

In addition, Masterplast started the EPS production in its new plant in Subotica, Serbia in 2008.

EPS (Expanded Polystyrene) panel is used for heat-proofing buildings. It's usually white and made of pre-expanded polystyrene beads. This is a very similar material to the one that can be found in every electronic device's box to protect them from breaking.

Logistics

As the general strategy was next-day delivery with high-quality service, the company mainly bought smaller trucks. They bought secondhand trucks that were 3 to 4 years old, which was considered old in Western Europe. As the company grew, the fleet had to be renewed and they started buying new small trucks which looked better for marketing and had lower maintenance. However, they continued to buy half-priced used larger trucks for inland use. For international deliveries they worked together with larger shipping companies such as Waberer.

Manufacturing

The company had its roots in manufacturing roof foils, so manufacturing had always been in the minds of the founders. When they had achieved market leadership in Hungary and all was going well internationally, it was tempting to consider controlling the whole production chain for more and more products.

The first had been the safe choice: the company opened its first manufacturing facility in Kál, Hungary. Masterplast Group had built up a site that had several production and depot halls and started to produce PE underlays (heat-mirroring and other roof foils). By 2011 the company had invested more than €4 million in the region and they employed a staff of nearly one hundred people in the area, where the roofing foil printing, perforating and rewinding machine had been set up. During the years, the company also started producing corner bead – an element of the facade thermal insulation system. The next step was the production of drywall profiles and plaster profiles. Altogether, there were 10,000 m^2 of production- and warehouse capacity in Kál.

Decision to build an EPS plant

Environmental consciousness in the CEE region (and around the world) had led to a great increase in demand for heat insulation products. As a big and relatively cheap product, only local factories could be competitive in price, if the quality was sufficient. As the technology was known it was "only" a matter of money and the ability to find a market for building an EPS plant.

In 2008, Masterplast launched its first EPS plant in Subotica, Republic of Serbia that was only 25 kilometers from the Hungarian border. The new plant had an annual production capacity of 500,000 million.[3] After taking a deep look at the local opportunities, property prices, accessibility, public utilities and governmental support, Serbia seemed to be the most competitive place for setting up the company's new facility. As a result of a €2 million investment, the company began production in the new 6,500 million^2 plant using a cost efficient and modern production chain. The plant used 95% less water than previous generation facilities to produce EPS and had much a lower emission of greenhouse gases. EPS waste could be reused up to almost 100% which again contributed to sustainable production.

By the fall of 2008, Masterplast had been trading more than 1,000 products, among them everything that was needed to execute thermal insulation projects. Offering their own EPS product had a big advantage over their competitors. In addition, the company never sold any competitor products of the EPS system to their clients even though wholesale had been the most important department of the company. The level of service that Masterplast provided was a very important purchasing reason; sometimes it mattered almost as much as price.

Reasons for building the factory in Serbia were the following:

- Local markets
- Logistics
- Cost

The Serbian market demand for such products was huge, and the local Masterplast trading company did a great job. The two other countries in that area were Romania and Hungary. Romania had the biggest revenue of all of the Masterplast affiliates, and Hungary, the home country, had always been very important. The increasing demand due to higher energy costs and stricter environmental regulations had made the investment worthy, as the plant had been working at full capacity within two years and all stock was sold.

Logistics was crucial in trading and manufacturing companies and this was no exception. With a motorway from Budapest to the factory and the building of the motorway toward Romania, the region seemed to be a very good location. EPS was a low-value product compared to its size, so transportation costs were a main factor in the final price. Because of this it was not profitable to transfer the product beyond a 300 kilometer range.

Logistically, the factory could serve the largest part of Serbia, Hungary, Croatia and the Transylvanian part of Romania. At that time it was decided that the "Szeged region" (around the border in Southeast Hungary) was to be chosen. Because of the lack of motorway at that time to Romania, only Hungary and Serbia were competing for the factory.

The third reason was cost. This obviously had a deep impact on every investment. Labor and land costs were much lower in Serbia, as they were not part of the EU and this status was likely to remain for many more years. Also the regulations were less strict. This part of the country was inhabited by a large number of Hungarians, a fact that once again fit with the basic strategy of the company to put Hungarian employees into key positions. They even found a Hungarian-Chinese person to manage the Chinese subsidiary. After comparing all three factors, Masterplast had chosen the Serbian location.

The map on the next page shows which area was covered by the plant.

After the crisis

As mentioned, the company's focus had always been on growth and continuous development. During the expansion phase, it was important that the most possible countries would be served with a minimum risk. When the crisis hit the economy and the construction business in particular, action needed to be taken by all actors of the market.

Masterplast had used those years for consolidation and analyzed in which countries was it worth maintaining operations. The main focus in these analyses was the growth potential for the future and whether their business model would be viable in that business environment. The main aspects were:

- Size of the market
- Logistics (Are they reachable, or are they on a trade route for a big market?)
- Is the environment friendly for the main business model?

As a result they had decided to close their offices in some countries, while they found other markets where there were still possibilities. Among the closed offices were some Balkan countries (Macedonia, Albania) and Germany as well. Those Balkan countries were simply too small. Even a big market share would not have been enough to impact the overall performance of the Masterplast group. On the other hand, the potential issues that could arise required as much attention as a big-revenue country.

Germany was the contrary: the combination of the biggest economy and one of the most environmentally conscious nations of Europe had a lot of potential. It was very promising, but one thing was too different: it was not a developing country. In Germany, business had been going on for 60 years, with decades of continuous business and personal connections. A Hungarian-based company could hardly get into this market where quality and safety (in a business continuation) were as important as good prices.

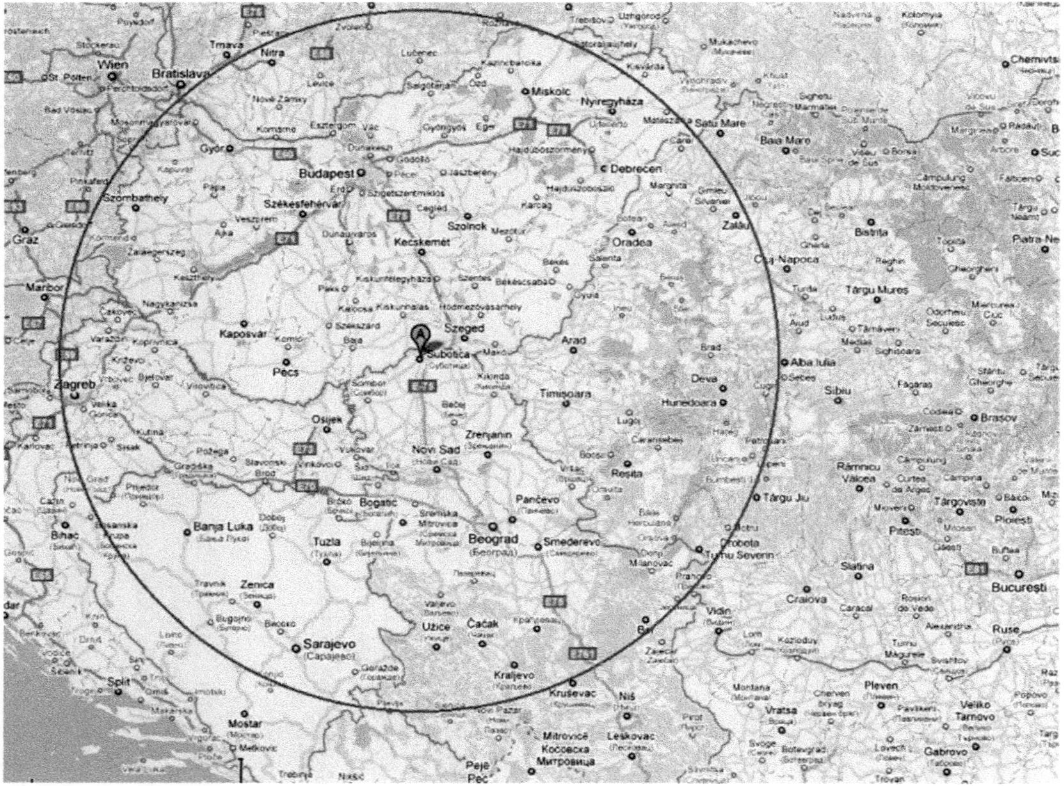

Figure II.9.3 Masterplast: areas covered by the plant

Source: Google Maps® 2012.02.25.

These factors existed long before Masterplast tried to put their feet in the German market. Because the key elements of the business model were not present, the business model couldn't be successful no matter how big the potential market was.

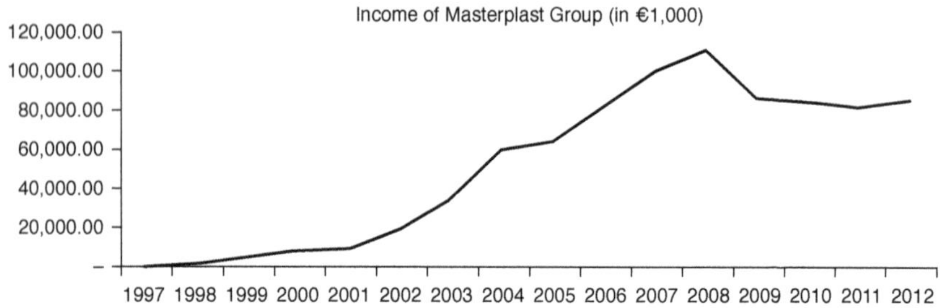

Figure II.9.4 Masterplast: group income (in €1,000)
Source: Company files and authors' own creation/adaptation.

The new growth phase

Entering new markets had always been a requirement; the remaining questions were: how, when, where and with which range of products. To answer these questions, a deeper knowledge of Masterplast's sales would be needed.

The company had been operating in Central Eastern Europe mainly, but with a differentiated product range. The construction material market was actually two markets for Masterplast: the EPS family and the rest. As mentioned before, the EPS (and the whole heat-insulating range) was available around 250 to 300 kilometers of Subotica (Serbia, Hungary, Southwestern Romania and Croatia). The rest of the products (foil products, metal accessories and others) were sold in the other countries as well. This led to two main choices:

- Find another country to start with the general product range
- Enter a current country with the EPS family
  - There were both branded and non-branded versions of EPS. The non-branded version was not as thick and therefore not as efficient so it was not Masterplast-branded. However, it was significantly cheaper.

To choose the second main option, a factory had to be built within a 300 kilometer range of the market otherwise it would not be feasible. Masterplast had already started producing its non-branded product for the Hungarian and Romanian market with huge success. As the numbers showed, price mattered over quality in these markets. In 2011, the insulation products by themselves contributed 45% of the group's revenue.

How could Masterplast expand better?

After some background search on the global and local markets, they found that a main trend in their field of interest was energy issues in Europe, especially energy efficiency and energy savings. Also, energy efficiency in Eastern Europe had been worse than in the West. With regard to the product range of the company, this could easily have been connected to heat insulation, and especially to the production of EPS. As there had already been a modern factory in operation in Serbia, exact estimations and knowledge were given to aid calculations.

Previously in 2011 it had been decided in the company's development strategy that in the following five years, an approximate investment of €5 million was to be made in the region. This was to be funded by the profits of previous years and an IPO in 2012.

There was only one country that had not been served by any products before: Russia, the biggest country in the world (almost four times bigger than the EU, with approximately 142 million inhabitants in 2010, 30% of the inhabitants of the EU). But to reach Russia one had to go through Ukraine.

Regarding the EPS family: in 2011 Serbia, Croatia, Hungary and Transylvania (West Romania) had EPS, while all the other countries were yet to be served.

Masterplast took the following major factors into account:

- The EPS plant in Serbia was running at full capacity already.
- The EU gave larger amounts of money for energy-saving projects for the regional member states, which indicated a big boom in the heat insulation products market.
- The building industry in Ukraine in 2011 had started to look like it was in Hungary in the late 1990s. Energy prices started growing, and people realized how much heating energy they were wasting while there were relatively easy and affordable solutions to avoid it. In Hungary, Masterplast had grown big because of knowing how to deal with that type of market.
- As the transportation limit of the EPS table was about 300 kilometers, the whole Ukrainian market needed about four plants, while Romania would need one for itself as well.

The building and machinery would cost about €1.5 million, the land could be bought or rented as well, and in some locations the land was already in the possession of the company. The factory could be built within less than a year.

The board meeting

"Good morning everybody! We have a very pleasant but hard task today. We have secured enough money for growing; now we have to find a smart way to spend it." These were the opening sentences from the CEO at the board meeting.

Exhibits

Exhibit 1: financial figures

Table II.9.1 Masterplast: revenue of the group

Year	Total Income (€1,000)
1997	551.72
1998	1,517.24
1999	5,517.24
2000	8,293.10
2001	9,800.00
2002	19,384.73
2003	34,672.41
2004	60,102.58
2005	64,685.77
2006	83,392.87
2007	100,570.84
2008	111,441.22
2009	86,529.00
2010	84,713.00
2011	82,173.00
2012	85,234.00

Table II.9.2 Masterplast: division of the main product families in 2011 and 2012

	2011	2012	Change
Main product families	**Thousand €**	**Thousand €**	**(%)**
Heat insulation system	35,075	38,041	8%
Roof foils and roof accessories	12,207	12,751	4%
Bituminous corrugated sheets	6,226	4,626	-26%
Metal profiles and accessories	7,444	7,716	4%
Other noise, heat and water insulation products	14,930	15,879	6%
Construction accessories	4,013	4,209	5%
Packaging materials	2,278	2,011	-12%
Total net income	**82,173**	**85,234**	**4%**

Source: Company files and authors' own creation/adaptation.

Exhibit 2: possibilities for a new factory

As mentioned above, a new factory would have the same characteristics (no matter which location was chosen), so a lot of designing and planning could be saved.

After the calculations, these main locations were taken into further consideration:

- Subotica (Serbia, bottom mark on the map)
- Kál (Hungary, light gray mark in the middle)
- Ivano-Frankivs'k (Ukraine, dark gray mark)
- Sfântu Gheorghe (Central Romania, dark gray mark)

Subotica – Serbia

The first solution would be to build the plant next to the first, as there was enough free land for the new building as well. The logistics had already been made; this would be the easiest from his point of view. All documentation was done, the local government and the people had accepted that a chemical factory was in the town.

On the other hand, from this location the Ukrainian and Slovakian market couldn't be reached at all, while most of the important Hungarian locations were in the farther part of the feasible delivery range.

Kál – Hungary

This was the home country, so negotiations with authorities would be easier. In Kál the building had already been there, only the machines needed to be set up. Because of the foil factory the logistics were also ready. This was the only EU site that the company had been thinking of. All of Hungary and most of Slovakia could be reached from this plant. Because of the border crossing issues, Ukraine, the biggest country in the region, could not be reached from there safely.

In the village Masterplast was already the biggest employer with over 100 workers, but almost no local tax discount was given so far. This was an underdeveloped region within the country and there weren't many possibilities for the locals to access new jobs, so this decision was crucial for the smaller region. If the board decided to use this location, the municipality would have to change its attitude toward the taxation policy of the biggest employer of the village.

Sfântu Gheorghe – Romania

Romania made the biggest revenues for Masterplast between 2008 and 2010, even bigger than those of Hungary. Transylvania was reachable from Subotica, but the more developed eastern regions (near the capital) are too far because of the distance limit. There were quite a number of native Hungarian speakers in the country and in the chosen closer region as well, which meant that language problems wouldn't be a problem in this place either. Highways from Hungary through the country would be built by the end of 2015. This plant could mainly serve Romania due to the infrastructure of the country.

Figure II.9.5 Masterplast: headquarters in Sárszentmihály (Hungary)

Note: The red mark on the left shows the Masterplast headquarters in Sárszentmihály [Hungary].

Source: Google Maps.

Ivano-Frankivs'k – Ukraine

Masterplast had been active in the country for six years with a big range of products, but not the EPS family, and there was a huge potential in the construction business. Their local logistics system evolved countrywide in five years; in the last few years the largest market growth took place in Ukraine. By 2010 Masterplast was the leader in the roof-foil market with 25–30% of market share. The country had the biggest potential both in future development and in size. Heating and oil problems were everyday problems, so efficiency had and would be a major issue for years. It was evident that the very low price of gas for citizens would not be sustainable, so energy efficiency was a task for the country in the mid-term at the latest. And energy efficiency could and should mean an increase in heat insulation systems in a country with very cold winters.

Ukraine was, however, not an EU state and was not planning to become one in the foreseeable future. This could be a problem for the ease of doing business, but a local factory could decrease a lot of administrative burdens. From the previous six years' experience it was clear that the bureaucracy and corruption was so difficult that it sometimes made business harder even for a company with experience, like Masterplast.

Source: Company files and authors' own creation/adaptation.

Exhibit 3: management

Dávid Tibor – CEO

Tibor is the Chief Executive Officer of the Masterplast Group Inc. After finishing his business college studies in 1999, he attended an intermediate level bank consultant course and is still a believer in lifelong learning. He speaks both English and German fluently and continuously attends business trainings and improves his managerial skills with international literature on management. He's married, the father of three children and lives in a nearby city close to the company HQ. He likes various sports: soccer, snowboarding and he was a former horse show jumper, which he still loves to do on his father's farm. He was a winner of Ernst & Young's "Entrepreneur of the Year" award in 2007 in the category of "Promise of the future." He was chosen as one of the three for the Most Creative Entrepreneur of the World award by the Junior Chamber International in 2008 in New Delhi. He also won a Hungarian prize from the National Association of Managers in the category of "Young Manager of the Year." In 2011 he earned the European Champion Award from EFER in recognition for the 14 years of the company's success. Tibor is personally committed to supporting start-up ventures and is the co-founder of a company for small investments, mediation and consulting.

Balázs Ács – Vice President and CFO

Acs is Vice President and co-founder of Masterplast Group Inc. He holds a civil engineering degree from 1999, is married, and a father of three. He does various sports in his free time; one of his favorite is ice hockey. Additionally, he likes traveling and is interested in old-time cars and lives in the nearby city next to the Masterplast HQ.

Source: Company files and authors' own creation/adaptation.

Exhibit 4: members of the board

Gábor Bojár

Bojar is co-founder of the world-famous Hungarian company Graphisoft and a member of Masterplast's Board of Directors. He has a university degree in physics and founded Graphisoft in 1982. Under his control the company was the largest exporter of software from Hungary and Central Europe. Graphisoft was among the top three architectural design software (CAD) development companies in the world by market share. Gábor Bojár was named one of Central Europe's top ten most successful entrepreneurs in 1998 by the Wall Street Journal and was invited many times to the World Economic Forum in Davos. Additionally, he won the Entrepreneur of the Year prize in 2006 from Ernst & Young. He has been a member of Masterplast's Board of Directors since 2008 and lives in Budapest with his wife.

Dr. Iván Gara

Gara was a member of the Masterplast Board of Directors, and an illustrious member of the Hungarian banking society. During his 30 years of experience, he spent ten years with the Hungarian State Development Bank, later he spent 20 years with Raiffeisen Bank Hungary and since 2005 he has been the owner of Ridge Road Financial Advisor LLC, which has customers like OTP, Commerzbank and KDB Hungary. He was first a strategic advisor to Masterplast and then became a member of the Board of Directors.

András Szőnyi

András Szőnyi studied at the Hungarian Polytechnic University and received a doctorate from Toronto University in chemical technology and also holds an MBA. He was the industry development officer at Ethyl Corporation Ltd. in Canada, has organized and operated a number of entrepreneurial ventures and was the main advisor to the Ontario Development Corporation (between 1970 and 1980). As a professor at Toronto University, he gave courses in corporate management and technologies and was the founder and first director of the Technology and Corporate Management Centre (between 1980 and 1990). Later, he was the professional development director of the Canadian Venture Capital Alliance. He has authored many books and his name can be found in a number of professional publications, even in the *Successful People* issued in Cambridge, England. He has a wide range of experience and knowledge in financial advice, business management, mergers and fusions, venture capital and strategic planning.

Source: Company files and authors' own creation/adaptation.

CASE 10: Modesat Communications OÜ: Riding a Big Wave with a Small Boat

Tiit Elenurm

Estonia. This case covers a small but very innovative technology venture in the mobile backhaul market, which needs to decide on the best possible international business model and growth strategy in order to work with large technology giants, such as Ericsson and Nokia, and to find its most optimal positioning in the market.

Introduction

In early 2012, Tarmo Pihl – CEO and co-founder of Modesat Communications OÜ[1] – was minutes away from touching down at the international airport in Tallinn, Estonia. Returning from a business trip to Modesat's subsidiary in San Diego, California, Pihl was thinking about the company's business model. Established in 2005, Modesat had grown to a 20-person enterprise focused on the development of software for mobile network equipment manufacturers. With its head office in Tallinn, it had research and development offices in San Diego, as well as a field sales office in Tel Aviv, Israel. The company made the majority of its money from the production of software for modems[2] in a segment of the communications market known as "mobile backhaul." (Mobile backhaul is part of the telecom infrastructure which carries information from base stations of the mobile communication network to base station collector and aggregation points, and then to mobile switching centers. See Exhibit 1 for a glossary of mobile telephony technical terms and Exhibit 2 for a diagram of mobile backhaul.)

Pihl was thinking of where he should focus his company to ensure future growth. His mind turned to the four main steps of the value chain in the development of mobile backhaul: component level vendor, system level vendor, integrator and service provider. Thus far Modesat's management was proud of having become a component level vendor. However, as the market for component level operations was around 1 to 2% of the network equipment market, they wondered if it would make sense to move downstream in the value chain. Having the best modem could enable advancing to the next step of becoming a system level vendor; however, the investment needed as well as the marketing power of big original equipment manufacturers (OEMs) were expected to be serious obstacles.

The company's main competitor, Provigent, had become successful with a System-on-Chip (SoC) solution. To compete head-to-head, would it make sense for Modesat to produce its own physical chips, thereby increasing the addressable market? Or should Modesat stick to offering its software for modems? For any change to their business model, what would be the financial and structural implications?

Tarmo Pihl

Tarmo Pihl graduated from the University of Tartu in 2000 with a degree in finance and international economics. He worked for five years at The Archimedes Foundation, where he provided consulting services for companies seeking research and development funding from the European Union. Through The Archimedes Foundation's international projects, he met a group of engineers based in Gomel, Belarus – Dr. Leonid Letunov, Aleksandr Grigoriev and Aleksandr Hrebtov – who had patented a novel technology for wireless communication (see Exhibit 3 for more information on the engineers' background.) The three engineers participated in The Archimedes Foundation's workshops and concluded that Estonia offered a good business climate for commercializing their ideas. Two other points helped to solidify their view of Estonia as a nimble and technologically advanced place: the fact that Skype had been programmed there and that Enterprise Estonia had helped other entrepreneurial companies reach international markets.

In 2005, the four individuals set up Modesat and in 2006, Pihl left The Archimedes Foundation to work full time at Modesat as well as his own consultancy, Invent Baltics. Pihl had acquired consulting experience in business and technology development and was motivated to become an entrepreneur. He also believed that the company's technology could become a change enabler for increasing communication speed, quality and energy efficiency in rapidly expanding mobile networks all over the world.

The history of Modesat Communications

In 2005, Pihl, Letunov, Grigoriev and Hrebtov established Modesat as a research and development (R&D) company in Tallinn, Estonia with the development office in Gomel, Belarus. Hrebtov's shares were subsequently bought out by the other partners and development work was concentrated in Tallinn.

Pihl took on the role of CEO and President, Letunov as Chief Researcher and Grigoriev as Senior Researcher. The company's original mission was:

> to simplify working principles of modern communication systems and release additional economic gains to our customers from more efficient communication equipment.[3]

The aim of the company's research was to reduce the energy requirements needed to operate wireless applications. Specifically, Modesat's technology helped to boost the signal coverage area and reduce sensitivity to noise interference for wireless applications. One of the company's key patents was its PilotSyncTM synchronization technology.

In May 2006, the Estonian investment group, ASI (Ambient Sound Investments), established by the four founding Skype engineers, invested €500,000 into Modesat. A month later, Modesat received €300,000 in grant money from Enterprise Estonia to develop a DVB-S satellite modem using its patented PilotSyncTM technology. Ambient Sound Investments CEO, Toivo Annus, said:

> We're thrilled to participate in a project that will benefit numerous technology platforms, from satellite modems to WiFi and WiMAX. Modesat develops technology that is clearly targeted at the global market and, even before the product-development phase, device manufacturers are paying attention.[4]

At the time of the investment, Pihl said:

> As is the case with data cables, wireless technologies, too, have bandwidth limitations. With expensive satellite links, for example, squeezing more data into an existing channel will lead to considerable savings. This is an area where Modesat's R&D work and intellectual property has solid international market potential.[5]

To expand globally and make inroads with major international original mobile equipment manufacturers (OEMs), the company recruited 44-year-old Peep Põldsamm, an executive with over 20 years of experience in mobile telephony including posts as the VP R&D of Levicom Group, Strategy Director of mobile operator Tele2 Estonia, CEO of Estonia's State Infocommunication Foundation (RIKS) and founder of Bravocom, the first mobile virtual network operator in Estonia. Põldsamm took over the CEO post and Pihl became VP of International Sales & Strategy. At the time of his appointment, the head of Modesat's primary investor, ASI, stated:

> Modesat has successfully embarked on the first stage of development, and to enter the international market we needed a top executive boasting both years of business experience and a knowledge of the technology.[6]

Upon joining, Põldsamm said:

> This is a time of big changes in the global communications business. A changing of the guard is taking place in terms of technologies. As a result, I see Modesat technologies as having great potential in terrestrial wireless as well as the space industry, which we are making preparations to enter.[7]

In 2009, Modesat was selected as the most innovative company in Estonia due to its success in breaking through and selling solutions to major telecommunications giants.

During autumn 2010, the company made two major steps. First, it received €1.85 million in funding from the Estonian Development Fund and a privately owned investment company called Bellus. The funding was to help the company finance the costs of integrating its technology into the two market leaders of total wireless radio link equipment.[8]

Second, Modesat hired former VP R&D of Samsung Electronics and Director of Broadcom – 63-year-old Korean national Dr. Sanguoon Chung – as Modesat's VP R&D and Chief Technology Officer based in San Diego, California. Põldsamm explained the rationale for hiring Dr. Chung:

> The requirements for bandwidth efficiency rise fast – Modesat is expanding its products' functionality in terms of capacity, application layer functionalities and interfaces to comply with the requirements the next generation mobile backhaul will pose. Dr. Chung will support the company to cope with the increasing customers' demand and growing engineering organization.[9]

At the Barcelona Mobile World Congress 2011, the company unveiled the industry's first modem (1024QAM adaptive modem) supporting up to 820 Mbps in a single FPGA (field-programmable gate array) chip. As an integrated chip, the FPGA was designed to be programmed after manufacturing. The chip allowed about 2.5 times more capacity in information flowing from the base station collector points to the mobile network.

In August 2011, Põldsamm left the company and Pihl resumed the CEO and President posts. By the end of the year the company had about 20 people of which 11 were based in Estonia. The company's main research office had become San Diego and the company maintained a sales office in Tel Aviv. The company's main customers were spread throughout a number of countries including Sweden, the United States, China, Malaysia, Italy, India and France. Sales revenues in 2011 were about €250,000 and the company had yet to turn a profit.

Modesat's products

As of 2012 the company offered a number of different types of modem IP (Intellectual Property) software for point-to-point radio communication devices. Modesat's current business was highly flexible and allowed the company to develop custom solutions for different types of networking technologies such as TDM (time division multiple access), Ethernet, SDH/SONET (Synchronous Digital Hierarchy and Synchronous Optical Networking).[10] Modesat presented its products in the following chart with the networking technology along the left and the segment of the backhaul market (in terms of speed or type) along the top (Table II.10.1).

Table II.10.1 Modesat: products at backhaul market segments

	All indoor trunk	Low–Medium capacity 2–50 Mbps	High capacity 50–900 Mbps	Ultra-high capacity 1 Gbps
TDM		+	+	
Optical SDH/SONET	+		+	
Hybrid		+	+	+
Ethernet	+	+	+	+

Source: Company files and authors' own creation/adaptation.

Modesat's core product was its software, Modesat IP Core. Their solution offered flexibility since it could be tailored to individual clients' needs. Modesat's software was intended for reprogramable chips, which were more expensive than traditional non-programmable chips. The direct cost of a traditional chip for mobile backhaul was US$5–8 and a reprogramable chip was between US$10 and US$15. Many industry observers pointed out that despite the higher initial cost of reprogramable chips, the maintenance was lower since software updates could be pushed out to the network instead of changing physical chips.

When we take an example of renovating 1,000 kilometer of mobile backhaul, the cost of one radio link and installation of such link is roughly US$4,000–US$5,000 and 50 links were needed for such distance, so the total investment into wireless links was around US$250,000. Installation, licensing and frequency planning cost should be added to this simplified calculation. When using reprogramable chips in mobile backhaul links instead of changing physical modems, the renovation cost of one radio link for the client was marginal, depending on the software upgrade license price, as no new physical installation of equipment is needed. Therefore, reprogramable chips in field would save operator cost on later software upgrades, whereas this was not the case with non-programmable, hardwired chips.

The one risk with reprogramable chips was that they opened up a greater possibility of intellectual property infringement since companies could deploy software without licensing it from the software developer. For this reason, mobile backhaul competitors were very careful when they disclosed detailed data about technical features of their software. Even price quotations were given only after signing a non-disclosure agreement (NDA). In giving quotes, Modesat considered the present and future state of their customer in order to develop a tailored solution. See Exhibit 4 for more information about technical features, advantages and disadvantages that Modesat representatives explained when introducing Modesat's core product to potential customers.

The mobile backhaul market

The mobile backhaul market was worth approximately US$6.84 billion globally in 2011, representing growth of 10.3% over the previous year.[11] The market was forecast to grow between US$7.9 billion[12] and US$10.4 billion by 2014.[13] Ericsson was the leader in the entire mobile backhaul equipment segment with about 20% market share.[14] There were approximately 30 companies manufacturing equipment for the segment including technology giants like Alcatel-Lucent, BridgeWave, Broadcom, Cisco, Huawei, NEC, Nokia Siemens and Tellabs. It was estimated that the top eight competitors accounted for approximately 80% of the entire mobile backhaul equipment market.

The OEMs of mobile backhaul equipment sold their products to mobile operators such as Vodafone, China Mobile, Telefonica, Orange, Verizon and AT&T. Mobile operators were constantly trying to determine which technologies were the most suitable for their mobile backhaul when trying to reduce costs while the traffic of mobile data increased. One analyst described the challenge as:

> We have seen a wholesale shift in backhaul strategies as operators try to reduce the costs associated with skyrocketing mobile data traffic. Six months ago when we surveyed operators around the world, most were taking a dual/hybrid backhaul approach (TDM plus IP/Ethernet). Just last month when we repeated the survey, most operators told us they plan to use a single IP/Ethernet backhaul, whether over microwave, fiber or copper. Mobile operators and transport providers now trust IP/Ethernet to do the whole job, including the tricky timing and synchronization required for most of the world's mobile networks.[15]

For the most part, analysts agreed that with greater demands on data, mobile operators would be strained to keep the costs of mobile backhaul under control. Juniper Research estimated that costs related to operating backhaul networks would quadruple from US$60 billion in 2011 to US$257 billion by 2016.[16]

Mobile operators could choose to run data in mobile backhaul through four types of connections: microwave, satellite, fiber optics and copper wires. It was estimated that approximately 50% of all data in mobile backhaul was run through microwave connections. Europe made use of microwave whereas the majority of backhaul in North America was via copper. Each type of connection had advantages and disadvantages; for example, fiber and copper boasted high speed and scalable capacity but took longer to deploy and were more expensive than microwave. While microwave was cheaper, some observers felt that there were challenges with the synchronization of data. Satellite had the advantage of reaching the most geographic locations, but was usually quite expensive to operate.

Across all types of connections, TDM and Ethernet networking technologies dominated the mobile backhaul market, making up about 89% of all revenues. However, the technologies were changing quickly and many analysts indicated that the current market leaders could be radically different in just a few years.

Revenues for mobile backhaul equipment were predicated on the growth of mobile subscribers. Although several analysts had varying predictions, one analyst projected about 1.5 billion new mobile subscribers by 2015. The growth in subscribers would mean more demand on the mobile network and, in turn, greater need for base stations and connections. The largest markets for growth were predicted to be China, India and Brazil. Some Modesat managers believed that based on market growth the company could realistically capitalize on revenues between US$30 and US$40 million during the next three years if they applied a smart business model and sound strategy. See Exhibit 5 for more information on the mobile backhaul market.

The major OEMs were classed as "Service Providers" although many played within various aspects of the other three upstream activities. OEMs accessed thousands of component suppliers when developing and manufacturing equipment. Modesat was one of the component level vendors that developed modem software specifically for microwave and satellite mobile backhaul.

There were four main groups in the value chain for mobile backhaul (Exhibit 1).

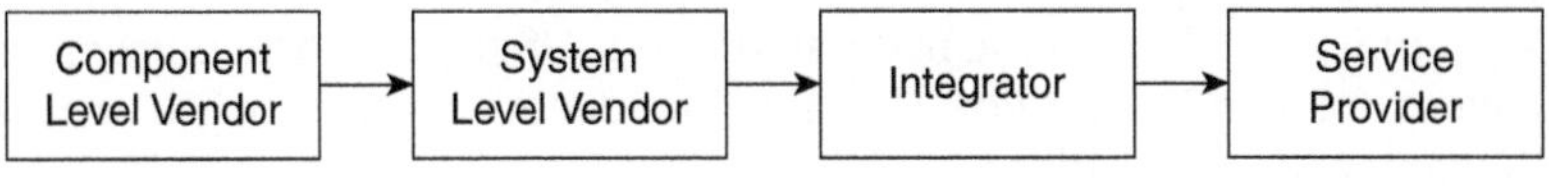

Figure II.10.1 Modesat – Value Chain for Mobile Backhaul

Source: Company files and authors' own creation/adaptation.

Modesat's customers

Modesat had a potential pool of around 100 customers that produced mobile network radio equipment. Radio equipment needed to be fail-safe as it provided a vital radio link within the mobile network, making it possible for the network to function all the time. Therefore it was common that producers of mobile network radio equipment asked suppliers to conduct rigorous tests in order to minimize the probability of any fault.

Mobile radio equipment companies such as Ericsson, Nokia Siemens, Huawei and Lucent-Alcatel were considered to be "Tier 1." There were eight "Tier 1" companies, which represented about 80% of the global market. The remaining market was made up of smaller equipment manufacturers.

About 80% of Modesat's revenues came from supplying its core product, Modesat IP Core, and related consulting support services to radio equipment manufacturers. 20% of the revenues came from supplying other services, mainly additional software and support services to meet further customization needs of generic equipment manufacturers.

One of Modesat's challenges was making its potential customer base understand all the benefits of the reprogramable backhaul modem. Apart from the benefit of lower maintenance cost by being able to push out software updates to a reprogramable modem (versus installing new non-reprogramable modems), the other advantage was deployment speed. On average it took between 8 to 12 months to bring a new non-reprogramable modem to market. Modesat was able to apply new program logic within one to two months. The flexibility and speed of customizing new mobile network configurations via a reprogramable modem was helpful to network operators for three main reasons: it allowed the network to support growth in the number of users; the reprogramable modems could be adjusted to different standards (e.g., 3G to 4G communication standard); and the operator could deploy changes by pushing out a software change versus physically installing new mobiles where distance and weather conditions needed to be considered.

Modesat's competition

Modesat's central competitor was an Israeli company called Provigent. Provigent focused specifically on supplying chips for the microwave segment of the mobile backhaul market. With offices in Tel Aviv and Santa Clara, California, the company posted revenues of US$25 million in 2010 and about US$40 million in 2011. In the first half of 2011, US-based Broadcom acquired Provigent for US$340 million.[17] A top Broadcom executive explained the rationale for the acquisition:

> Provigent is a unique asset with world-class microwave backhaul technology and strong engineering talent developing innovative and highly integrated semiconductor solutions for the microwave segment.

> Combining their microwave backhaul solutions with our industry leading network infrastructure and wireless solutions allows us to better serve our customers and expand our addressable market.[18]

At the time of the acquisition, the CEO of Provigent said:

> Provigent's System-on-Chip (SoC) solutions are used to solve a crucial problem in the infrastructure of cellular networks, which is the backhaul bottleneck. The many synergies with Broadcom's broad portfolio of wire-line and wireless SoC technologies and capabilities will accelerate product development and provide our customers with a compelling offering.[19]

Provigent's products were significantly different from Modesat's in that Provigent offered Systems-on-Chip (SoC) solutions, which were not repro-gramable. Provigent had an advantage as an early mover – they started commercializing their product in 2000 and managed to approach many large mobile operators before Modesat.

Modesat's revenue streams

Modesat was engaged in three main types of activities based on the software solutions that they had developed:

1. Network development evaluations with customers in order to explain how Modesat software could lead to faster speed or less energy consumption.
2. Integration of modems with Modesat software into customer's equipment.
3. Licensing Modesat's modem software as well as developing and consulting for OEM equipment providers.

While continuously developing their software solutions was necessary in order to stay relevant as a modem software provider for the mobile backhaul segment, it did not guarantee any revenues. Modesat made money through licensing its technology or consulting. Throughout 2011, the company generated one-third of its revenues from license fees for its Modesat Core IP software and two-thirds from consulting for its customers.

Licensing agreements worked whereby a system level vendor, integrator or service provider licensed Modesat's technology and programmed their modems at their own facilities. Consulting meant many work hours and travel cost and required communication skills for advising customers.

Modesat's management team had plenty of thoughts on Modesat's different revenue streams. Pihl commented:

> So far, the fastest way to get to the market and find clients has been doing custom work for OEMs. Such cooperation is flexible for clients and they

> can commit themselves step-by-step to Modesat solutions. Solutions can be tailored to the needs of each customer. But from a business point of view, they are not really generating high profits. These activities mean lot of traveling and related costs for a small development team. Is it the best way to get innovative solutions to customers?

Another team member said:

> We've all read the business books about different business models, but a lot of the ideas seem too general and do not reflect specific context of this business field such as roles in the value chain, intellectual property issues, sector-specific cooperation partner options, length of development cycles and several other aspects.

Pihl felt that academic frameworks such as Porter's positioning models, while good for discussing existing markets, were not suitable for understanding how value chain options could be created within new global niche markets. Pihl was certain that Modesat had continuously innovated their software offerings but wondered whether their three main types of business activities were the best way to deliver solutions to global customers while generating positive cash flow and growth. What should they do themselves and what should they outsource?

Modesat managers were looking for a solution whereby they could collect license fees for an extended period of time. As one manager said:

> Securing recurring revenues from Tier 1 clients would allow us the opportunity to develop the right business model. Our unique technology could allow us to overcome typical pressure on component producers to decrease their prices. However, getting Tier 1 customers to pay licensing fees to us is always a challenge.

Growth prospects moving forward

Modesat's challenge was deciding where to focus in order to propel the company to dynamic growth. Pihl and his managers were confident in the company's technological know-how and ability to apply its unique software to modems.

Modesat team had discussed the benefits and drawbacks of offering a Systems-on-Chip (SoC) solution like their main competitor. By pursuing SoC development, Modesat would need to change the nature of their business and invest at least US$50 million for industrial production facilities.

When talking about growth prospects, the company found itself explaining its business to investors who were not intimately involved in the mobile backhaul segment. A Modesat team member painted a picture of the industry:

> Exponential growth in data transmission is a key challenge for developing mobile communication networks. Chip markets for transmission stations serving new G3 and G4 networks are a huge growth area but it is not easy to predict which technological platform will win in order to install mobile backhaul modem chips which will maximize capacity of mobile networks and support further innovations in network management.
>
> In order to take advantage of this growth, we need funds for development and integration into our OEMs equipment. We cannot fund this through our present revenues. So, when it comes to talking with investors, it is easy to compare the end-user product in the mobile communication business, for instance Samsung smartphones, to the iPhone. But they are really confused about technologies that operate "behind the scenes." How can we explain our focus on mobile backhaul? They do not think in terms of bits per second per hertz. But at the end of the day, a new smartphone without a high capacity network does not make much sense. And our solutions are a key factor for increasing network capacity globally. One of our challenges has been how to explain the potential and markets of our technology to people that are used to counting money and are not technology experts.

Another team member added his view:

> It is even more tricky if you come from Eastern Europe and you're presenting to technology companies in Western Europe or the United States and say, "We have created a really unique solution for global networks!"

Due to the company's geographic base in Estonia, Modesat's managers often talked about matching internal human resources with areas of geographic growth. Attractive markets were recognized to be the United States, China, India and the Middle East. Was Estonia a good place for the headquarters? What about moving to California or Asia? One manager commented:

> Should we hire staff with similar or different competencies for these regions? It is clear that our sales staff are different from salespeople that sell vacuum cleaners. Our sales staff have to communicate with technical experts of business clients and test our software at client locations. Even more, they have to advise developers how to modify our software. Our competitive advantage is that clients can reprogram chips that have been configured by using our software but they need our competent assistance. I think that Modesat core competence and staff profiles after five years will depend on the business models that we choose. We have to be very clear on the link between business model and our core competence.

Finally, some Modesat employees were concerned about the lack of formal processes. Since the company had grown organically from a start-up, they did not have all their processes documented. One manager said,

> Creative people do not like documenting everything but with increased cross-border linkages between development and implementation, we probably do need some "bureaucracy." What is a good way to formalize processes? Clients are skeptical about solutions that are not properly documented.

Pihl summarized the difference between innovation and growth:

> Technology alone is not innovation. In order to succeed at foreign markets you have to get your processes in place. You have to compete for customers but also to attract talented employees in order to serve different markets.

Where should Pihl and his team focus? What would each focus area provide to the company? How could they grow to a multimillion-dollar enterprise?

Exhibits

Exhibit 1: glossary of terms

CMTS: Cable Mobile Termination System – A cable modem termination system or CMTS is a piece of equipment typically located in a cable company's headend or hub site, and used to provide high-speed data services, such as cable Internet or Voice over Internet Protocol (VoIP) to cable subscribers.

Ethernet – A local area network first defined by Metcalfe & Boggs of Xerox PARC in 1976. Specified by DEC, Intel and XEROX (DIX) as IEEE 802.3 and now recognized as the industry standard.

FPGA – Field-programmable gate array (FPGA) is an integrated circuit, a microcontroller designed to be configured by the customer or designer of a mobile backhaul after manufacturing.

Long Haul Trunk – Communications pertaining to circuits that span large distances, such as the circuits in interstate and international communications.

Mobile backhaul – Intermediate links between the core mobile communication network, or backbone, of the network and the small sub-networks at the "edge" of the entire hierarchical network.

Mobile Satellite Services – Mobile satellite services (MSS) refers to networks of communications satellites intended for use with mobile and portable wireless telephones.

PilotSync™ synchronization technology – PilotSync™ is patented technology owned by Modesat that enables working with near-zero roll-off at any bandwidth and modulation scheme in mobile communication networks.

This technology enables significantly higher data throughput and communication link reliability at lower hardware cost in microwave radio, satellite and cable modem applications than earlier Technologies.

Point-to-point Mobile Wireless Router – A wireless router is a device in a wireless local area network (WLAN) that determines the next network point to which a packet should be forwarded toward its destination.

Point-to-Point Radio – In telecommunications a point-to-point radio means radio connection between two nodes or endpoints.

SDH/SONET – Synchronous Digital Hierarchy and Synchronous Optical Networking. Standardized multiplexing protocols that transfer multiple digital bitstreams over optical fiber using lasers or highly coherent light from light-emitting diodes.

TDM – Time division multiplexing in which two or more bitstreams or signals are transferred from the receiver point of view simultaneously as subchannels in one communication channel, but are physically taking turns on the channel.

WiMAX (Worldwide Interoperability for Microwave Access) – A communication technology for wirelessly delivering high-speed Internet service to large geographical areas. It is a part of a "fourth generation," or 4G, of wireless-communication technology.

Wireless radio link -- Permanent wireless connection in a two-way radio communication system (usually based on microwave), part of a more extensive telecommunication network.

Source: All definitions from Wikipedia and Network Dictionary.com (http://www.networkdictionary.com/telecom/l.php)

Exhibit 2: diagram of mobile backhaul

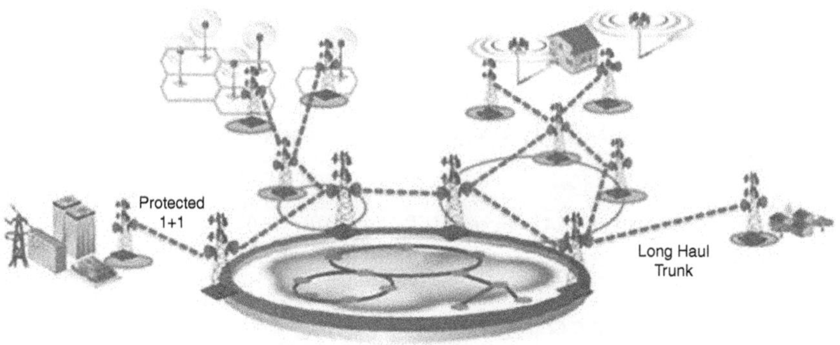

Figure II.10.2 Modesat: diagram of Mobile Backhaul

Note: All dotted lines represent the mobile backhaul.

Source: Company files and authors' own creation/adaptation.

Exhibit 3: background of Modesat's original engineers

Dr. Leonid Letunov

Dr. Letunov was the author of the patent behind PilotSync™ technology. Dr. Letunov worked from 1973–1994 at various defense enterprises of the former USSR. Since 1995, he has been Chief Designer at design bureau MODEC, Gomel, Republic of Belarus. He carried out work under contract to Andrew Corporation, Setur and Tenatronics Ltd. Dr. Letunov has authored 41 printed works and holds more than 98 patents in the fields of electro-compatibility applications, phase noise measurement applications and data transmission applications.

Dr. Leonid Letunov received his PhD from the Moscow Research Institute of Radio Physics in 1985.

Aleksandr Grigoriev

Together with Leonid Letunov, Aleksandr Grigoriev was the author of the patent behind the PilotSync™ synchronization technology. Previously, Grigorjev worked at various defense enterprises of the former USSR. From 1995, he has been the head of digital engineering at design bureau MODEC, Gomel, Republic of Belarus. He carried out work under the contract with Andrew Corporation, Setur and Tenatronics Ltd. He has five publications to his name. His research interests include the theory of communication, digital technologies, modem technologies and mathematical simulations.

Aleksandr Grigoriev graduated from Saint Petersburg Electrical University as a specialist in Radio Technology in 1982.

Source: Modesat Website (2008) Accessed February 11, 2012: http://web.archive.org/web/20090208060956/http://www.modesat.com/about/people/

Exhibit 4: Modesat core product: Modem IP (Intellectual Property Cores)

When discussing the business model, Modesat IP Core-based solution has both advantages and disadvantages when compared with the more traditional chipset solution.

IP Core-based modem (FPGA + licensed IP Core firmware)

Advantages:

- Flexible, easy to make changes
- Allows tailor-made solutions
- Some new functionality (SDR)
- Short development period of 6–9 months
- Cost-efficient development

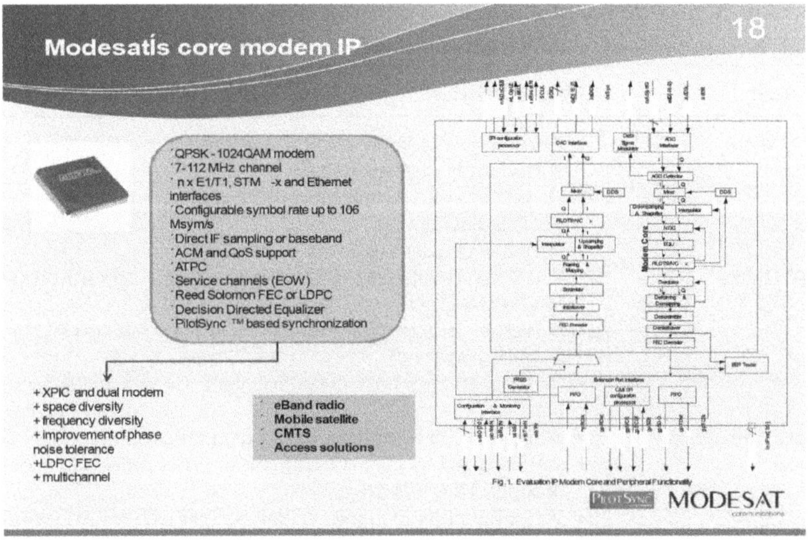

Figure II.10.3 Modesat: core product – modem IP (Intellectual Property Cores)

Disadvantages:

- FPGA still expensive, but price dropping
- IPR and fraud risk by clients
- Relatively high power/resource consumption

More traditional chipset-based business model (ASIC or SoC – System-on-Chip)

Advantages:

- Long tradition, simple to sell
- No fraud by clients
- Less IPR risks (e.g., reverse engineering)
- Low power/resource consumption
- Cheaper

Disadvantages:

- Limited flexibility, need addition of controllers
- Large minimum quantities
- Very long development period (2–3 years)
- Very expensive development

Source: Company files and authors' own creation/adaptation.

Exhibit 5: mobile backhaul market information

Table II.10.2 Modesat: mobile backhaul market information

Market	Characteristics
PTP MWR	• Fairly large market of US$150 million for modem chips with double-digit growth rates • Driven by overall migration to 3.5 and 4G networks (mobile backhaul) • Very few chipset providers (Provigent)
PTP CIDER	• Small market of US$1 million for modem chips, however 50–100%+ growth rates p.a. • Driven by overall migration to 3.5 and 4G networks (mobile backhaul) • No modem chip providers (Provigent to enter 2011 second half)
Fixed SatCOM	• Market of US$10 million for modem chips • Standardized by DVB-S2, difficult to enter unless cheaper product, HDTV is driver • Very oligopolistic market (Hughes, Comtech leading with >60%), mostly in-house development of modems
Mobile SatCOM	• Market potential of US$10 million for modem chips annually 2013 • Not standardized yet, available solutions are of low capacity • No specialized modem chip vendor
CMTS	• Market of US$500 million • Cable modem market saturated, low Broth rate <5% p.a. with high competition from semiconductor companies
PMR	• TETRA & TETRAPOL • Dominated by NSN and EADS internal developments, specialized market
PLMR/NodeB	• Large market of US$250 million 2014, CAAG 7% • High competition from Oualcomm, Freescale, Broadcom, etc.
PLMR/Pico-macrocells	• Highly growing market due to deployment of LTE • High competition from semiconductor companies like Broadcom, Marvell

Source: Company files and authors' own creation/adaptation.

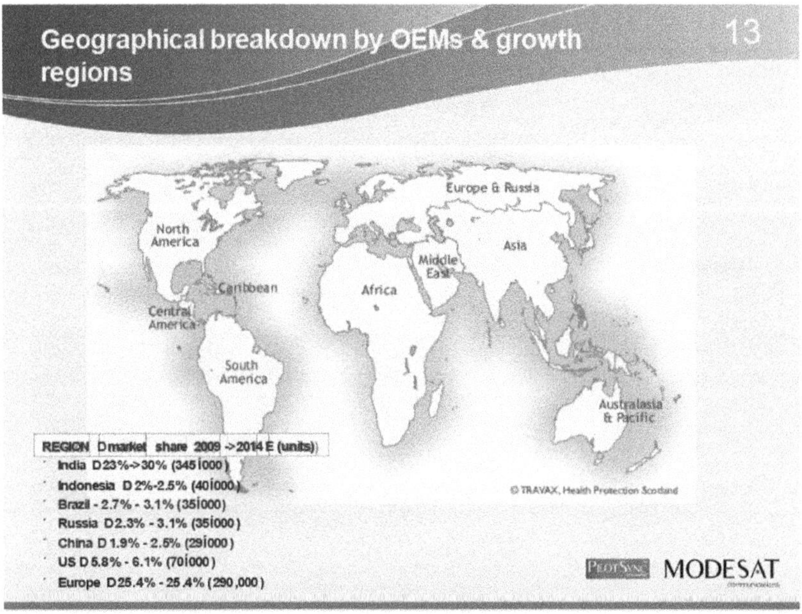

Figure II.10.4 Modesat: geographical breakdown by OEMs and growth regions

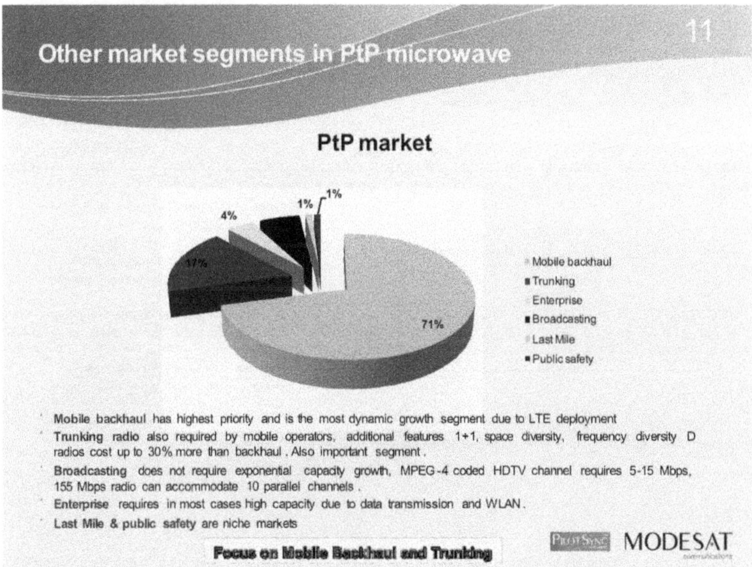

Figure II.10.5 Modesat: other market segments in PTP Microwave

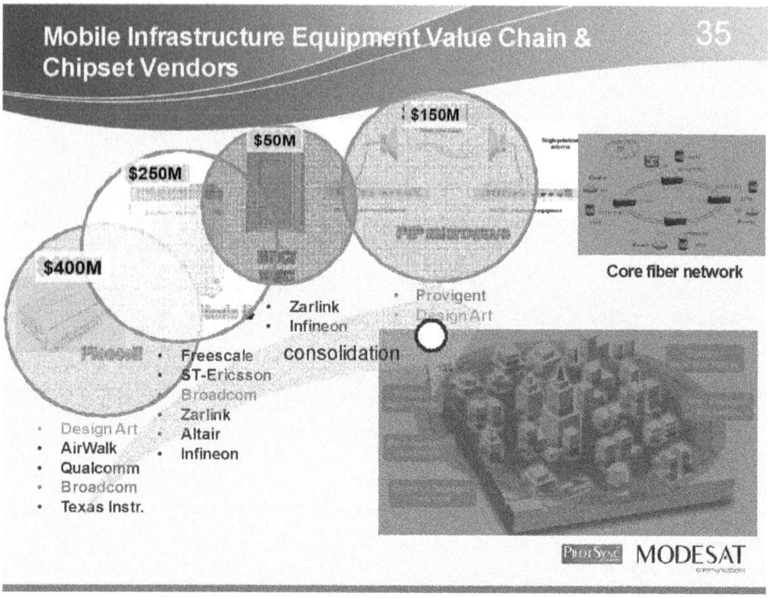

Figure II.10.6 Modesat: mobile infrastructure equipment value chain and chipset vendors

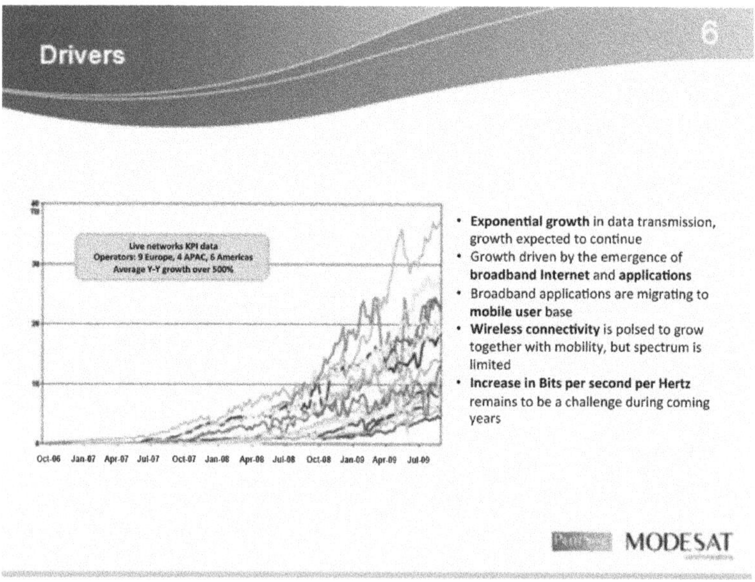

Figure II.10.7 Modesat: drivers

Source: Company files and authors' own creation/adaptation.

Exhibit 6: Modesat's Core Competencies and Market Opportunities

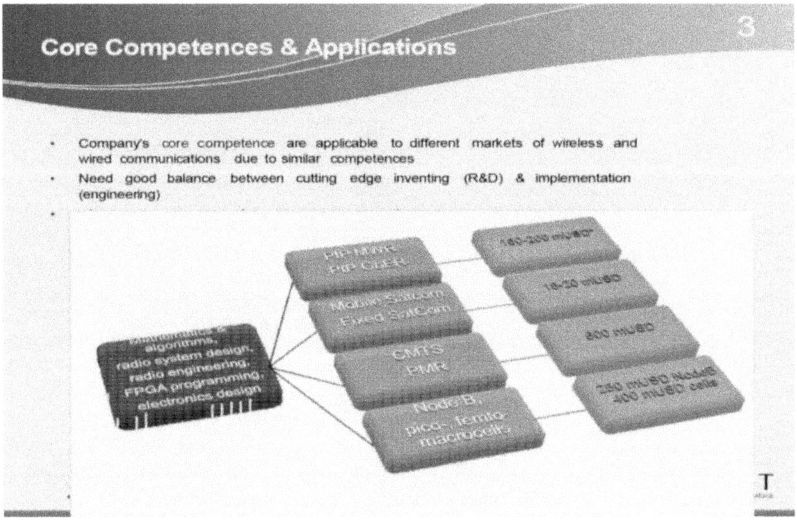

Figure II.10.8 Modesat: core competences and applications

Source: Company files and authors' own creation/adaptation.

Exhibit 7: Modesat office in Tallinn, Estonia

Figure II.10.9 Modesat: office in Tallinn, Estonia

Source: Company files and authors' own creation/adaptation.

Exhibit 8: Tarmo Pihl

Figure II.10.10 Modesat: Tarmo Pihl

Source: Company files and authors' own creation/adaptation.

Notes

1. OÜ is an Estonian abbreviation for a private limited company.
2. Modems are a device that helps to transfer signals and information between analog and digital.
3. Modesat Website. 2006; available from: http://web.archive.org/web/20060810144727/http://www.modesat.com/?nodeid=57&lang=en.
4. Ambient Sound Investments. May 23, 2006, January 31, 2012; available from: http:/asi.ee/news/asI_buys_stake_in_modesat_communications.
5. Ibid.
6. Veteran executive takes helm of Modesat. July 22, 2008, February 11, 2012; available from: http://asi.ee/news/veteran_Executive_takes_helm_of_modesat.
7. Ibid.
8. "Modesat Communications raised €1,85 million in series A funding," (October 27, 2010). Accessed February 11, 2012: http://www.asi.ee/news/modesat-communications-raised-eur-1–85m-in-series-a-funding.
9. "Former Executive VP of Samsung Electronics joins Modesat Communications," (November 25, 2010) Accessed February 11, 2012: http://www.modesat.com/former-executive-vp-of-samsung-electronics-joins-modesat-communications/.
10. The three types of technologies mentioned are different protocols of parcelling information to send information through mobile networks.

11. "Mobile Backhaul Equipment and Services Market Highlights" (April 12, 2011). Accessed February 12, 2012: http://www.infonetics.com/pr/2011/2H10-Mobile-Backhaul-Equipment-and-Services-Market-Highlights.asp.
12. "Mobile Backhaul Equipment and Services Market Highlights" (April 12, 2011). Accessed February 12, 2012: http://www.infonetics.com/pr/2011/2H10-Mobile-Backhaul-Equipment-and-Services-Market-Highlights.asp.
13. "Infonetics" (April 12, 2010), accessed February 12, 2012: http://www.infonetics.com/pr/2010/Mobile-Backhaul-and-Microwave-Market-Highlights.asp.
14. Ibid.
15. Ibid.
16. "Mobile Backhaul Costs to Quadruple in Five Years" (September 15, 2011). Accessed February 12, 2012: http://www.marketingcharts.com/direct/mobile-backhaul-costs-to-quadruple-in-5-yrs-19283.
17. "Broadcom buys Provigent for US$340 million" (March 21, 2011). Accessed February 12, 2012: http://www.broadcom.com/press/release.php?id=s558912.
18. "Broadcom Gains Microwave Transmission Technology with Acquisition of Provigent Company; Expands Portfolio for Mobile Backhaul" (March 21, 2011); accessed February 12, 2012: http://www.broadcom.com/press/release.php? id=s558912.
19. Ibid.

CASE 11: Pipistrel: The Freedom of Flight

Frank la Pira

Slovenia. Inspirational, captivating, interesting.... All of these adjectives define the founder of this venture: a small start-up in the industry of ultra-light aircraft construction. The firm went on to break many aviation records and won three international NASA competitions.

The discussion centers on an important strategic decision: Should the company remain in its current segment or take a large financial risk to build a completely new and innovative airplane model, which would allow the firm to enter a new market segment?

The wheels of the aircraft of Ivo Boscarol, CEO of Pipistrel, touched down on the grass strip at Ajdovščina Airport, 70 kilometers west-southwest of Ljubljana in Slovenia. The vast expanse of grass looked sparse and uninhabited, as usual. Aircraft rarely parked outside because of the Burja, a cold north-northeast katabatic downslope wind in the Adriatic that blew in gusts.

Boscarol had just landed his company's Sinus aircraft after demonstrating its performance characteristics and handling to a new buyer from Russia. The new buyer had been waiting for several days to fly the aircraft because the Burja wind had been blowing down the Vipava valley in the past few days, gusting up to 100 kilometers per hour, prohibiting flight.

Sinus was the first of Pipistrel's line of composite construction aircraft; its fuselage was decorated with decals celebrating the many honors the company had earned over the past 25 years. Pipistrel had come a long way since 1989, when it was manufacturing motorized hang gliders. The company had started in the ultralight aircraft (ULA) category and had modified its aircraft to fit into the light-sport aircraft (LSA) category.

Now the company was at a crossroads. It could expand their line of aircraft within the LSA category, where it had built its reputation, or it could transition into the general aviation (GA) category. There were many factors to consider.

The legacy GA builders, such as Cessna and Piper, had been building aircraft the same way for the past 50 years. It seemed to be high time for the industry to undergo a shake-up, but was it the right move for Pipistrel with the global financial crisis and the euro crisis in full swing? Even Germany's growth had decreased by 0.6%. Would the current distribution channel be appropriate if Boscarol decided to build a US$300,000 aircraft to compete with Cessna and Piper? After all, it was a different target market; the market for four-seat aircraft was the United States because of fuel costs and the ease of traveling across the country. More than 70% of Pipistrel's aircraft had been sold outside the European Union with little support from the U.S. market. Could the company afford the estimated €50 million investment and three years of certification before it could deliver the first aircraft? Boscarol knew the Slovenian government would support him, but he'd still have to dig deep.

Nevertheless, as he turned off the engine, he felt pleased with his achievements thus far.

History of Pipistrel

Designing and manufacturing aircraft wasn't Boscarol's first business. Printing (e.g., advertising buttons, among many other products) was his first business. He also had a passion for photography and, as a keen fan of rock music, spent many late hours taking pictures of rock musicians; he even managed some rock bands. "The photography helped me pay my way through college. However, I got so busy with my businesses that I never finished my economics degree."

At that time he also developed an interest in flying. "I worked long hours and didn't have the time to go flying during the day, which was restricted in Yugoslavia then. During the late 1980s it was difficult to fly an aircraft freely under Yugoslavia's totalitarian regime; the military controlled all aircraft movements," Boscarol said. He wanted to fly whenever and however he pleased. On a visit to Italy he saw a motorized hang glider. He decided then and there that he was going to own and fly his own aircraft, so he bought it to take back home to Yugoslavia.

"I knew it was going to be difficult, if not impossible, to bring the glider into the country in one piece, since it was not legal to own a private ULA at the time, but I purchased it anyway." So he imported it into Yugoslavia in bits and pieces, disguised as parts for something other than an aircraft.

When he finally got all the bits and pieces and put them back together, he wasn't satisfied with the construction. "It not only looked dangerous, it was dangerous. I'm a bit taller than most people so I began to modify the craft to make it safer and tailor it to suit me," he said. In the early days of ultralight aircraft, the early Rogallo hang gliders were the inspiration. They looked very disconcerting: made of aluminum and wire, with the wing made of fabric and a small engine attached to the rear.

Normally, modifications to an aircraft were not permitted without approvals and drawings that had been overseen by federal aviation bodies, which also required extensive design drawings, etc., all of which had be carried out by a licensed aircraft maintenance engineer (LAME). However, as the ULA category for aircraft did not require certifications, the aircraft (and the pilot) didn't need a license in those days; anybody could build one and make any modifications they saw fit, as long as they didn't exceed the required weight limitation. "So as I made many modifications to suit my needs, other ultralight pilots started to ask me to make similar modifications to their aircraft. Eventually the Italian company I purchased the hang glider from contacted me and wanted me to make the same modifications to its aircraft."

As he spent more and more time modifying hang gliders, he recognized an opportunity and decided to build his own hang glider. "When I realized that there was a market for these aircraft I approached the Yugoslav aviation authority to get the required permits and approvals to build and sell ultralight aircraft, since they were technically not permitted in Yugoslavia." He was received with a great deal of jocularity and laughter at the idea that a private individual would try to build an aircraft in the Socialist Federal Republic of Yugoslavia. "Ivo is very stubborn; he would not take no for an answer, and so he managed to convince the aviation department that he was serious," said the public relations manager. Furthermore, what kept the aviation department bewildered was that he wanted to build an ultralight. "Ultralight? What is that?" they said! The aviation department knew nothing about ultralights, since the country's aviation department was managed mostly by the military. The aviation department then contacted another state-owned aircraft manufacturer in Slovenia. The department asked if there was anyone who could help it, someone who was known as an expert in the field. The name it was given was Ivo Boscarol.

After many meetings, the department gave him its approval. The problem, however, was that there were no systems, exams or regulations for people who wanted to manufacture their own ultralight aircraft. Boscarol took this opportunity to write the legislation and the exams, which he himself was then required to pass to get approval to manufacture his aircraft. He subsequently wrote many of the regulations and requirements for manufacturing ultralight aircraft in the industry. He became the first totally private aircraft manufacturer in the former Yugoslavia.

This was one of the many firsts that Pipistrel achieved through Boscarol's management. Boscarol described his motivation: "When I was younger I used to love 007 movies. I loved them because the innovative cars and planes impressed me – particularly because it seemed to me that the designs were not too far from reality. I think we've lost that; most of what we see in theaters today is so far from reality because all we see are computer-generated graphics. So, I saw my role in making it happen: something new and different – and truly innovative. After all, isn't that what life is about, doing new and fun things?"

Market Leaders in General Aviation

The aviation industry was made up of three internationally recognized categories: commercial aircraft (airlines), aerial work and general aviation. In the field of general aviation, Piper and Cessna were the market leaders.

Even today, Piper and Cessna aircraft are the most common aircraft to be seen on the tarmac and parking areas of general aviation airports. During their heyday, these aircraft sold in the hundreds of thousands. The center of aviation at most airports was the flying school, where not only instructional flight took place but where most recreational pilots gathered to share their experiences, or where they went to rent an aircraft for a weekend retreat, or to spend a day out flying.

Through the end of 2009, Piper had produced 144,000 aircraft in 160 models, 90,000 of which are still flying. Today in the single-engine class, Piper produces five aircraft: three of the high-performance models' prices start from US$900,000 to US$2.13 million. They are typically all-metal construction and vary little from their original 1960s designs. The new Piper Archer is priced at US$320,000 with a cruise speed of 128 knots (257 kilometers per hour) and a range of 522 nautical miles (822 kilometers), whereas the Piper Arrow is a retractable undercarriage version of the Archer with a cruise speed of 137 knots (254 kilometers per hour) and a range of 880 nautical miles (1,640 kilometers). This was the market Pipistrel's Panthera Prototype would compete in.

Cessna, like Piper, began producing aircraft in 1927. In 1975 the company celebrated the 100,000th sale of a Cessna aircraft. Of all the Cessnas, the 172 Skyhawk was the most popular aircraft it built. Up until 2010, 43,000 Skyhawks had been sold. The Skyhawk is still in production today, with two models: the Skyhawk and the Skyhawk SP. Cessna produced many different types of single-engine aircraft for various purposes. Cessna has always differentiated itself from the Piper by its high-mounted wing.

Cessna still produces eight single-engine piston aircraft, including the Skycatcher, which is the only two-seat LSA aircraft it produces and sells. The rest are in the normal category with prices starting at US$274,900 for the Skyhawk four-seater up to US$734,000 for the luxurious four-seat Corvalis that cruises at 235 knots (435 kilometers per hour) for 1,250 nautical miles (2,135 kilometers). Cessna also produces two models of its workhorse, the Stationair single-engine six-seat aircraft.

Both Cessna and Piper released an LSA category aircraft in the past few years. Cessna has the 162 Skycatcher, which it currently sells for US$149,900. It has a maximum cruise speed of 118 knots. Like all Cessna single-engine aircraft, it is an all-metal fabrication (aluminum) aircraft. While Cessna has 700 preorders at the original price of US$111,000, it has had problems getting the aircraft to market at this price. Furthermore, it has been estimated that the 700th person who ordered the aircraft will not receive it until the end of

2017. Problems with Chinese production have limited aircraft deliveries to 30 per year, considerably less than the estimated 300 per year. Piper took a different road and, rather than creating a new aircraft, it purchased an existing light-sport aircraft from Czech Sport Aircraft and labeled it a Piper SportCruiser, which sells for an average price of US$129,000.

The Rise of Light-Sport Aircraft

The light-sport aircraft category had become extremely popular over the past 10 years, with 2,600 manufacturers in the ultralight light-sport category worldwide. While the traditional general aviation aircraft industry was in decline, the light-sport category grew significantly during the same period. In the United States, which is the largest market for aviation, between 2005 and 2011 the number of aircrew licenses granted in the light-sport category grew 3,250% while in the private pilot's license category the number of licenses granted decreased by 14.5%. A similar perspective can be extrapolated from Europe, as more than 90% of aircraft sales were in five countries: Spain, France, Italy, Germany and the United Kingdom. The United Kingdom was problematic for light-sport aircraft in that the country did not recognize the LSA or ultralight category and therefore U.K. residents who wanted to own an ultralight aircraft could purchase it but it had to be registered in an approved country.

The rapid increase in the popularity of light-sport aircraft was the result of several important factors. First, the aircraft in this category were cheaper to build and therefore cheaper to service and operate. Second, the barriers to obtaining a license to fly such an aircraft were lower than for a standard private pilot's license, since the aircraft are smaller, less complex and much easier to fly. For those who wanted to fulfill their aspirations of flying, doing so was much easier and cheaper in the light-sport category. What's more, many of the aircraft were designed so that the wings could be removed, enabling owners to store the aircraft at home, providing they had somewhere to park a seven-meter-long vehicle. That represented a significant amount of savings, since the owner/pilot didn't have to store the aircraft at an airport hangar, where space was at a premium and therefore rentals could be very high, considerably adding to the cost of aircraft ownership.

The cost of purchasing and operating a new light-sport aircraft was substantially less than purchasing a new Cessna or Piper single-engine aircraft. Piper had all but abandoned that market segment; it manufactured only two light aircraft, plus one light-sport aircraft it had purchased and rebranded as the Piper SportCruiser. Cessna had eight aircraft in the single-engine four-seat category and one light-sport aircraft known as the 162 Skycatcher. In their heyday Cessna and Piper produced numerous models in the four-seat category. For instance, Piper had 160 different aircraft in that category and Cessna had about the same number.

Another major hindrance was the cost of maintenance of a Cessna or Piper GA aircraft. All maintenance had to be carried out by a licensed aircraft maintenance engineer (LAME), and the cost of fuel was significantly higher because they had higher fuel consumption and used a unique blend of fuel designed for their engines: avgas (aviation gasoline). A new Pipistrel aircraft could start from US$60,000, depending on the optional equipment added. The aircraft used fuel that was identical to the fuel used in everyday vehicles. While the average fuel consumption for the smallest Cessna 152 (two-seater) was about 25 liters per hour, a Pipistrel aircraft such as the Sinus used less than 10 liters per hour. And yet the speed and fuel range of the aircraft were comparable. Many of the LSA manufacturers today use the latest technology and are therefore able to produce an aircraft that is far superior to the traditional Cessna or Piper, whose technology is still based on their original 1960s designs.

Another limiting factor to a would-be pilot was the cost and time involved in earning a private pilot's license and keeping it up to date. A normal pilot's license for a Cessna or Piper aircraft required a minimum of 45 hours of flight training (depending on the country) and theory training, which required passing nine theoretical exams (depending on the country) within 18 months. The medical examination, which is of a high standard, had to be renewed every three to five years (depending on the country and age of the applicant) and regular flying was required to keep the license current. Furthermore, the medical examination for a private pilot's license was quite expensive since it could be carried out only by an approved medical examiner (AME) who had been trained by the federal aviation department.

Light-sport aircraft were usually smaller and lighter, with a maximum takeoff mass of no more than 600 kilograms, a maximum stalling speed in the landing configuration of not more than 45 knots[1], a maximum seating capacity of no more than two people, a single, non-turbine engine fitted with a propeller and a non-pressurized cabin. A sport pilot could carry only one passenger and still had to learn meteorology, technology and navigation theory. License rules varied by country; you could earn a pilot's license with as little as 30 hours (EASA Europe) of flight training provided you had passed your medical, theoretical and practical training. A light-sport pilot in Europe could expect to pay €5,000 or more to get a pilot's license, whereas the cost of a private pilot's license was a minimum of €7,000 plus all the other added expenses, such as the considerably higher running cost of the aircraft.

According to Craig Fuller, president of the Aircraft Owners and Pilots Association (AOPA) in the United States: "The cost of an aircraft and flying is a serious concern," he said, "but there aren't a lot of ways we can control that." He was more worried that product liability insurance costs were once again contributing appreciably to the overall cost of flying. A recent study in the United States found that almost 80% of private pilots who started out never earned their licenses because of the cost it involved.

Pipistrel – Alternative Aviation in Slovenia

When Pipistrel started its company, it was unimaginable for a private person to own their own aircraft, let alone their own aircraft manufacturing facility in Yugoslavia. If ultralight pilots wanted to fly, they had to do it covertly. They had to wait until the regular sports and army pilots had finished flying for the day and then they would sneak in an hour or two of flying before darkness fell. Since the ultralight pilots flew late in the evening in aircraft with triangular-shaped hang-glider wings on which lights were installed, the local people jokingly referred to them as "bats." "Pipistrellus" is the Latin name of a genus of bat, which is where the name Pipistrel originated.

The existence of a private aircraft manufacturer that offered an alternative to military-sponsored flying at army-regulated sports airfields was what really made flying available to the general public in Yugoslavia.

Pipistrel's first manufactured aircraft was a powered hang glider (see **Exhibit 1**). From 1987 as an individual and from 1989 as an official company, Boscarol and Pipistrel had produced more than 500 powered hang gliders through 1995 – their first big sales success. Boscarol, the CEO of Pipistrel d.o.o. Ajdovščina, said, "For about eight years we made only hang gliders; that couldn't go on forever. The market always grows and develops, and to remain successful one needs to keep innovating and offering something new. Back then ultralight aircraft were, like hang gliders, made of tubes and fabric."

Not satisfied with the ultralight designs of the day, they decided to build the first fully composite carbon fiber ultralight aircraft and to make it faster, smoother and cheaper using all the latest technology. "Our main idea was to offer something different, more sophisticated – an aircraft that would offer pilots the freedom to go gliding on their own, without an aerotow and without a helper at the wing tips." This line of thinking resulted in an entirely new aircraft in the ultralight category, unknown in Europe at the time. At the Friedrichshafen Aviation Expo in Germany, Pipistrel released the prototype for the Sinus aircraft. It immediately received worldwide media attention and 30 orders. It was the world's first-ever two-seat motor glider in the ultralight class. It was a revolution: the first ultralight made of composite material. This gave the company the international recognition it needed.

In the very first year of production, more than 100 orders were received for the Sinus. According to the company's marketing brochure, the Sinus was: "Fast, quiet, economical and very versatile – it provides the pilot with an easy and quick takeoff and then offers a wide range of uses, from cross-country flying to gliding, training new pilots, aerial photography or just recreational flying."

Today it produces eight aircraft designs. Seven are in the ultralight or the light-sport aviation category (depending on which country you are in, since different countries have different rules). Two aircraft provide an electric or a piston engine option, one of which is a single-seater. While most of the aircraft have good glide ratios for gliding, only three are specifically designed solely for gliding: the Taurus (two-seater) and its electric version (Taurus Electro), and the Apis (single-seater), whereas the Sinus, Virus, Virus SW and its versions can be used as touring motor gliders.[2] Since 1995, when the company started building composite aircraft, it has sold more than 1,200 aircraft (see **Exhibit 4**).

The shock of the financial crisis was felt all over the world, including at Pipistrel in Slovenia. At Pipistrel's 2010 New Year get-together the employees were being seated to receive an update on Pipistrel's future. The mood was somber, given that there were many rumors and concerns flying around about the future of the company. Boscarol approached the session with excitement and announced that Pipistrel was going to enter and win the next NASA Google Green Flight Challenge. Tine Tomažič, R&D engineer and test pilot, added that the competition was to be held at the end of 2011 at NASA's Moffett Field in California. "After my speech my employees looked at me and at each other and started to laugh as they were applauding my speech. They thought I was joking or that I was crazy," said Boscarol. "With Ivo's inspiration, commitment and determination to win we built the G4, an electric-powered twin-hull aircraft that took first place in NASA's Google Green Flight challenge," said Tomažič.

Design and Manufacturing

The aircraft designs were usually the result of Boscarol's inspiration and vision, along with input from employees and customers. "Twenty-five years in aviation has given me a good understanding of the industry." Boscarol described his creativity process: "I get my best ideas walking, during a massage or having a shower; then my job is to convince my engineers, by working with them, since they only see the technical side of things. Together we work to achieve my vision of the aircraft. The process usually starts with a presentation of my concepts to my engineers. And they normally tell me that they're impossible."

One example was the Taurus self-launching glider: "I wanted an aircraft that would break with tradition. I saw that it was important to have side-by-side seating, instead of isolating the passenger by seating him or her in the back, and I wanted to have traditional landing gear so that the gliders didn't need assistance to land or maneuver on the ground. [Traditionally gliders were designed with fore and aft seating and wing-tip wheels that required external assistance for maneuvering on the ground.] I also wanted a glider that didn't need a tow aircraft to get airborne. That's why the Taurus has a retractable motor. The engine provides the power to get to the gliding altitude; then it's retracted and the aircraft behaves like a normal glider."

Pipistrel considered the design and development of new aircraft as a key element of their success, investing 20%-25% of their annual revenue in design, development and prototyping. Their research & development center included numerous laboratories for researching aerodynamics, composite materials and new and more efficient sources of energy. The building also housed a department for prototyping and testing with a rapid prototype-milling machine that was linked to a CAD computer that could create a prototype of a whole airframe in less than a day.

Employees had ample opportunities to contribute to the design development and improvement of the aircraft. Each Pipistrel employee received €10 for contributing an idea, regardless of whether or not the idea improved some part of the product or process. At the end of each month, the best idea received €500 and the best idea at the end of each year received €5,000. This approach resulted in an average of three or so good ideas a month from the 85 employees.

After a new model was created, 70% of the manufacture of the aircraft was outsourced to manufacturers that were better equipped to make the parts cheaper and more efficiently. Pipistrel then assembled the aircraft in its facilities, which gave them ample opportunity to control the quality of the finished aircraft. The time from conception to a flying prototype usually took somewhere between six months and two years.

For their production system they purchased the 20 Kan-Ban, or "20 keys" system. It was the same method Toyota used in their production and quality manufacturing system. In line with their environmental policy, they had very little scrap left over and what was left over was recycled. Employees cleaned their own workspaces so that they had total control of their work area. Each aircraft contained over 5,000 parts, and all these bits and pieces were controlled using an inventory management software system where each item was barcoded when it entered into and out of their inventory system. If they had any problem with a part, they could trace the part back to its original manufacturer, the batch number and all the employees who handled the part including, the installer and the time it was installed. If an owner reported a faulty part, they could trace that part back to the order and to all the other aircraft that had the same part installed from that same batch so they could replace that part with a new part.

Distribution

Pipistrel sold its aircraft through a worldwide distribution network. Usually each distributor was entitled to the whole country, or if it was a very large country like the United States or Canada then there were usually several distributors or a distributor and a promoter operating in the area. Distributorships were not easily available; the barriers to entry were high, requiring substantial aviation experience with a flight instructor's license. Furthermore, the distributor was required to own at least one Pipistrel aircraft and be committed to working with the company to make Pipistrel aircraft certified for flight in that country. Certification required a considerable amount of time and effort, particularly for a new model entering a country. Taking on a Pipistrel distributorship required a full-time commitment. (See **Exhibit 5** for further information.)

Company Philosophy: Ecolution

Knowing the general aviation industry was in decline because of increasing cost and very little concern for an aircraft's environmental impact, Boscarol decided that the future of aviation lay with a philosophy he called Ecolution: evolution and a concern for ecology.

> "The philosophy of Ecolution is applied to everything we do: how we make the aircraft design eco-friendly. To produce airplanes that fly better, we must try to design their shapes in an aerodynamic way, with clean lines and smooth surfaces. This enables the maximum possible lift and as little drag [air resistance] as possible. ... The results of this kind of aircraft design are: better flight characteristics (for example, glide ratio), less power to keep the aircraft in the air, which means lower fuel consumption and lower CO_2 emissions and less noise."

To maintain consistency with this philosophy throughout the company, the company built a state-of-the-art manufacturing facility. Boscarol said, "The building has been such a success and its savings so significant that we sell power back to the grid and the difference in savings means that we pay for our cost of production, plus we recoup an average yearly return of 20% on the cost of operating the building."

Achievements

"Pipistrel has won numerous awards," the engineering manager commented. "Ivo is a celebrity here in Slovenia. In 2011 he won the Slovenian Person of the Year award. So it is very difficult for him to travel anywhere without people following him around and wanting to talk with him. In 2010 he won the European Business Award. In 2003 he won the Slovenian Entrepreneur of the Year award and among these prizes, there are many awards for his personal flying achievements." The innovative aircraft designs had won Pipistrel many awards, but one of Ivo's most treasured awards was the Paul Tissandier FAI Award. The diploma, established by the FAI in 1952, was named after Paul Tissandier, Secretary General of the FAI from 1919 to 1945. It was awarded to those who had served the cause of aviation and sporting aviation in particular, by their work, initiative and devotion or in other ways. Examples of other awards included the Readers' Digest "Most Trusted Businessman" award and the Golden Order for services to the country, which could only be awarded by the president of the Republic of Slovenia.

The Sinus held a multitude of world records and aviation milestones including a FAI 500 kilometer triangle in gliding. Sinus was the winner of the World Championship WAG 2001 in Spain and runner-up in 2005. The Virus SW was the result of Pipistrel winning the NASA centennial challenges in 2007 and 2008. *Popular Science* magazine chose the Taurus Electro as one of the top innovations of 2008. In 2011 the Taurus Electro also won the Lindbergh best electric aircraft prize established by Erik Lindbergh, the grandson of the legendary aviation pioneer Charles Lindbergh, who was the first person to fly across the Atlantic. The Gold Medal was given to Pipistrel for best industrial design for the Taurus Electro.

For the third time Pipistrel won a NASA competition, the NASA Google Green Flight Challenge. After Pipistrel won Boscarol announced:

> "We are happy to have had the opportunity to raise the limitations of electric flight one step higher. What was science fiction three years ago is reality today! The Pipistrel aircraft have overtaken the automotive industry – as no car in the world is capable of driving 250 miles with the average speed higher than 100 miles per hour and the fuel consumption of less than one gallon per passenger – what is more, we did this regardless of the weight limitations in aviation."

Team Pipistrel's winning four-seat, electric-powered aircraft, the Taurus G4, flew nearly 200 miles nonstop, while achieving more than 403.5 miles per gallon, an equivalent of 1.94 gallons (7.34 ltrs) for the 403.5 miles (650 km) at an average speed of 172 kilometers per hour, which was almost double the efficiency of the piston-powered aircraft in the competition. Boscarol believed that there was much that electric aviation could achieve. At the end of the acceptance speech, Boscarol issued a challenge to NASA that in two years it would hold a challenge for the electric aircraft that came closest to the speed of sound.

Among the many awards and competitions, Pipistrel aircraft achieved several remarkable aviation feats: in 2004 Sinus was the first light aircraft to fly around the world, including a nonstop long-range flight from Pisa to Lisbon and Athens to Nordkapp. The Virus SW repeated the flight around the world in 2012, flew over the top of Mount Everest and landed in the Antarctic. The third flight around the world with Pipistrel aircraft was accomplished by a team of French scientists, "Wings for Science," in 2013, while a Sinus was the first light sport aircraft to cross the Tasman Sea from Australia to New Zealand!

The Next-Generation Aircraft

Pipistrel had already begun investigating the general aircraft market.

The specifications and performance the engineers had achieved through the computer simulations were impressive. The four-seat, 200-knot (370 km/h), 40 ltrs per hour composite aircraft, code-named 007 at the very beginning (after Ivo's favorite movie franchise) and later Panthera, was far and away the best performer in its class in terms of speed, fuel consumption and range. "It is our most ambitious project yet," he said.

Unfortunately the engineers didn't share the same level of enthusiasm. Previous experience had shown that financial estimates could be off by as much as 50%. And while the aircraft design had achieved Ivo's specifications and performance on paper and in simulations, they were concerned that delays and production problems, particularly since there was a lot of new technology in this new aircraft, could easily result in a blowout of the predicted cost. His chief engineer was strongly against it. "I'm not sure we have the resources to do this successfully," he said. If the cost did double it would make Panthera even more expensive than the competitors' aircraft. If that were so, would the final resulting aircraft be sufficiently attractive to the market against competitors' offerings to justify purchasing from a small Slovenian company such as Pipistrel?

This question, when raised by his Sales and Marketing manager, didn't concern Ivo. He responded: "We have a history and a brand that is well known and we are able to produce highly innovative and superior aircraft." He added, "People who are willing to pay US$300,000 to US$500,000 for an aircraft – particularly high-net-worth individuals – want something different, something superior."

Boscarol had strong feelings on the subject:

> "Years ago, people said it was impossible to produce an aircraft light and streamlined enough to be safe and efficient. We did it. People said it was impossible to fly around the world in a small (ultralight) aeroplane without assistance. We did it. People also said it was impossible to produce an aircraft fast enough and efficient enough to be successful at the NASA Challenges. We went ahead and did what nobody did before – we won three NASA Challenges. Now they say it is impossible to make a practical electric-powered aircraft. We did it back in 2007 with the first electric two-seater in the world. Clearly we see and do things differently and have a pioneering vision. We do not imitate, we innovate!"

The Future

He'd originally hoped that they could keep the price of the Panthera Prototype to US$300,000 but after calculating the costs it appeared that his chief engineer may have been right: he was not going to be able to keep the price of the prototype at US$300,000.

He stood at the hangar door looking out onto the airfield at an approaching aircraft – a new customer being trained in his new Virus. He wondered with the economy dragging its feet to recover in the United States and the growing unemployment problem in the EU what the next year would bring and whether he should stay in the industry he knew. As he stood in the corridor of the hallway to his office he couldn't help but notice the trophy cabinet was full of trophies with every Pipestrel model represented. Was the full trophy cabinet an omen for the Panthera? "I need to have the trophy cabinet rearranged," he thought.

Was this a smart investment? Should they pursue the declining market segment in an attractive, but foreign market or focus on light aircraft locally?

Exhibits

Exhibit 1: powered hang glider (trikes)

Figure II.11.1 Pipistrel: powered glider (trikes)

Source: Company files and authors' own creation/adaptation.

Exhibit 2: understanding the Pipistrel aviation categories and licensing

Table II.11.1 Pipistrel: Understanding the Pipistrel Aviation Categories and Licensing

Aircraft	Category	License required	Cruise speed	Fuel burn	Endurance
Sinus	TMG	UL/LSA/TMG/LAPL (depends on the country) (S)	200 km/h	9.2 LPH	5.8hrs
Virus	TMG	UL/LSA/TMG/LAPL (depends on the country) (S)	225 km/h	9.5 LPH	5.7hrs
Virus (SW)*	Ultralight or LSA	UL/LSA/TMG/LAPL (depends on the country) (S)	246 km/h	13.6 LPH	6.9hrs
Taurus Glider[a]	Ultralight or LSA	UL/LSA/TMG/LAPL (depends on the country) (S)	120 km/h		N/A
Apis – Glider[a]	Ultralight	LAPL (S)	144 km/h		N/A
Panthera prototype	PtF GA CS-23	PPL	374 km/h	<40 LPH	5.0hrs

Note: [a]The purpose of the engine on a glider is to get the aircraft to the gliding altitude and to provide assistance for landing.

*There are a number of variations to this Aircraft as there are many engine configurations; this assumes a standard configuration SW80.

Source: Company files and authors' own creation/adaptation.

Exhibit 3: light sport aircraft EU

Under the EASA, Certification Specifications for Light-Sport Airplanes Annex
Initial date issued 27 June 2011

Light-sport airplanes are approved to fly during daylight hours only in visual flight conditions:

(a) A maximum takeoff mass of not more than 600 kg for airplanes not intended to be operated on water or 650 kg for airplanes intended to be operated on water.
(b) A maximum stalling speed in the landing configuration (VSO) of not more than 83 km/h (45 knots) CAS at the aircraft's maximum certified takeoff mass and most critical center of gravity.
(c) A maximum seating capacity of no more than two persons, including the pilot.
(d) A single, non-turbine engine fitted with a propeller.
(e) A non-pressurized cabin.

What is a Light-Sport Aircraft?

The FAA has defined light-sport aircraft as simple-to-operate, easy-to-fly aircraft that, since initial certification, has continued to meet the following performance definition:

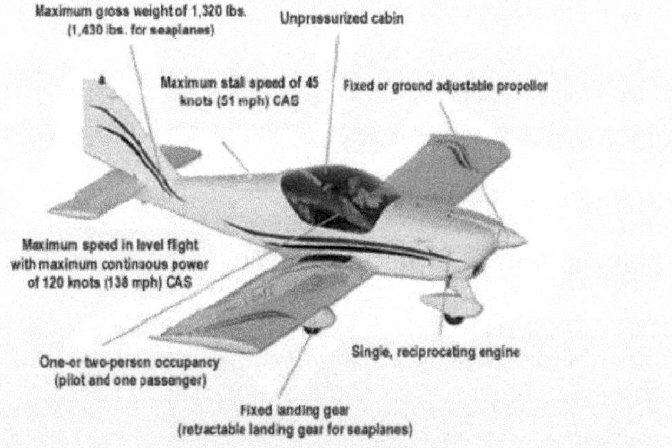

In addition to fixed-wing airplanes, the definition of a light-sport aircraft also includes powered parachutes, weight-shift control aircraft (i.e., Trikes), balloons, airships, gliders and gyroplanes. For more information on the definition of a light-sport aircraft, click here.

Any aircraft that meets the definition of a light-sport aircraft as called out in FAR Part 1.1 is eligible to be operated by a sport pilot. These aircraft can be certificated in any category, such as standard, experimental amateur-built, experimental exhibition, experimental light-sport aircraft (E-LSA), or special light-sport aircraft (S-LSA).

Figure II.11.2 Pipistrel: what is a light-sport aircraft?

Source: Company files and authors' own creation/adaptation.

Exhibit 4: Pipistrel aircraft and configurations

Table II.11.2 Pipistrel: aircraft and configurations

Aircraft type	Engine configurations			Purpose
Sinus (2 seat)	ROTAX 912 UL – 80 hp			Glider, Cruiser, Trainer
Virus (2 seat)	ROTAX 912 UL – 80 hp			Glider, Cruiser, Trainer
Virus SW (2 seat)	ROTAX 912 UL – 80 hp	ROTAX 912 UL – 100 hp at MTOW,[a] 475 kg or ROTAX 912 100 hpiS	ROTAX 912 UL – 100 hp MTOW,[a] 600 kg	High-speed Cruiser, Trainer
Taurus Electro (2 seat)	40 kw synchronous 3-phase electric motor			Gliding
Taurus (2 seat)	50 hp 2 stroke			Gliding
Apis (1 seat)	Hirth 27 hp	2 stroke engine		Gliding

Note: [a] Maximum Takeoff Weight (MTOW) can be increased on the 100 hp Virus SW.

Source: Company files and authors' own creation/adaptation.

Exhibit 5: Pipistrel dealerships

There are two possibilities of representing us. You can either apply as a distributor or as a promoter. As a promoter we ask you to buy at least one aircraft; as distributor we ask you to buy the number of aircraft we consider suitable for the size of your country. We are very selective with our dealer appointments as we wish to develop a strong, successful and supporting team from day one.

Distributor

For a distributor there is a list of requirements. Some of these include (ideally):

- Sell all Pipistrel's products (trikes, 3-axis UL aircraft, propellers, etc.)
- Have a broad range of flying experience
- Be an experienced pilot to be able to safely demonstrate the aircraft
- Be a current flight instructor (trikes and 3-axis aircraft) to train new owners on our aircraft
- Have a service center, access to a maintenance facility or a trained mechanic to assemble, maintain and repair our range of aircraft
- Live on or close to an airfield (or have a direct right to its use) suitable for demonstration throughout the year

- Have access to a clean, uncluttered hangar suitable for customer visitations
- Work side-by-side with local authorities to obtain all required permits to fly for all Pipistrel aircraft and to support the costs of the homologation procedures
- Prepare advertising materials in native language of the areas you will cover
- Be regularly present at air shows, fly-ins, local magazines and so on
- Be able to hold sufficient stock of spare parts to provide after-sale support
- Translate all necessary documentation to your local (native) language
- Provide the customers and authorities with the relevant service and technical documentation
- Be available for contact at all times, have a mobile phone, daily Internet access, as well as a PC (min. req. Windows 98, Word 2000, Excel 2000, AutoCAD 14, Adobe Acrobat Reader)
- Enjoy flying and meeting people
- Be loyal, honest, trustworthy and forthright with customers
- Maintain at least one demonstration aircraft at all times
- Have composite construction experience as we plan to offer the aircraft as a kit in the future; distributors will need to be familiar with construction techniques to answer customers' inquiries
- Distributors are allowed to use the Pipistrel logo for official releases,
- documents, publications and so on
- Distributors are allowed to make their own selling and pricing policies, however the price list must be presented to Pipistrel
- Distributors are allowed to design, build and/or sell other aircraft
- Distributors are allowed to sell products competitive to Pipistrel
- Upon first order, the newly appointed distributor will receive a written certificate, which will entitle him/her to officially represent Pipistrel
- This certificate is subject to rechecking and renewal every (1) year

Once a fixed agreement between the distributor and Pipistrel d.o.o. Ajdovščina is reached, Pipistrel will stop working with individual customers from the country discussed, and all inquiries will be forwarded and handled directly and exclusively by the appointed distributor.

We are also keen to hear your view on how you can contribute to this dynamic team.

We understand that some of you may not meet all the above criteria, but we urge you to proceed with your application anyway.

In addition to addressing the above criteria, please try to answer the following questions as well when you send us mail:

- Are you in a position to purchase a demonstration aircraft?
- How many aircraft do you expect to sell per year?

- What are your marketing and sales plans and experience in these areas?
- In what area of geographical operations do you see for you to be successful?
- What is your capacity for the storage and supply of basic spare parts and accessories?

Promoter

Promoters are allowed to promote only one model of our aircraft in their region, both locally and as broadly as possible. Promoters must work side-by-side with local authorities to obtain all required permits to fly all Pipistrel aircraft. Promoters are to be regularly present at air shows, fly-ins, local magazines and so on. Promoters have no direct authority over the sales of aircraft; Pipistrel will be free to sell directly to the country in question, especially to the customers who will contact Pipistrel directly.

If you are interested in becoming our distributor or promoter and if you believe you can satisfy most of our requests, write us an email with your comments and eventual proposals. We are definitely open to discussion on all questions and requests you may not be able to satisfy fully.

Source: Company files and authors' own creation/adaptation.

Exhibit 6: regulation in the aviation industry

The aviation industry is a highly regulated industry. All aviation categories are affected by the rules and regulations that originate from ICAO, the International Civil Aviation Organization. ICAO's mandate is to standardize rules for air travel worldwide, and it does so through the issue of Standards and Recommended Practices (SARPS), which it encourages countries to adopt. While it has no authority, its recommendations are introduced into most Western countries, particularly when the issues refer to the use of airways and air traffic control.

Europe also has the European Aviation Safety Agency (EASA). Its role is to promote the highest common standards of safety and environmental protection in civil aviation in Europe and worldwide. It is the centerpiece of a new regulatory system, which provides for a single European market in the aviation industry. Furthermore, each country has its own federal aviation body which interprets the ICAO and the EASA rules and construes their own versions. On the opposing side are the industry bodies that see their role as advocates for their constituents from over-regulation from ICAO and EASA and zealous federal aviation bodies. The largest of these in the general aviation industry is the Aircraft Owners and Pilots Association (AOPA). Each country has its own chapter and there's an international chapter known as IAOPA.

General aviation is further categorized into at least seven sub-categories. The categories relevant to Pipistrel are: private personal travel, air tourism (personal), recreational flying and air sports.

Until recently, the European Aviation Safety Agency (EASA)[3] didn't have a category for ultralight aircraft. All ultralight aircraft, under 475 kilograms in weight, were included in a category that was for aircraft that didn't fit any of the existing categories. At the end of 2011 EASA introduced a special category for these aircraft and named it the CS – LSA Light Sport Aviation.[4] This category is for single-engine, two-seat aircraft weighing less than 600 kilograms (U.S. and European LSA aircraft requirements, **Exhibit 3**).

With the introduction of the LSA category EASA also introduced the Light Aircraft Pilot license (aeroplane) (LAPL)(A). Countries who adhere to the EASA standards require their pilots to complete 30 hours of flight training and the same theory training required for a private pilot's license before their LAPL flight test. LAPL licensed pilots are permitted to fly aircraft with a takeoff mass of 2,000 kilograms or less, carrying a maximum of three passengers, such that there are never more than four persons on board the aircraft.

Applicants for a LAPL must also pass a medical examination. The medical examiner will review the applicant's complete medical history if available. The initial assessment and all subsequent reassessments after age 50 and assessments in cases where the medical history of the applicant is not available to the examiner shall include at least the following: (1) clinical examination; (2) blood pressure; (3) urine test; (4) vision; (5) hearing ability.[5]

For an LAPL to keep his license current he/she is only required to have completed, in the last 24 months, as pilots of aeroplanes: (1) at least 12 hours of flight time as PIC, including 12 takeoffs and landings; and (2) refresher training of at least one hour of total flight time with an instructor. Otherwise he must complete a flight test with an instructor.

"Private pilot"(PPL) means a pilot who holds a license which prohibits the piloting of aircraft as pilot in command in operations for which ANY remuneration is given. It enables the pilot to fly the aircraft privately. This license is designed for pilots' personal enjoyment, travel and air sport; this does not include sailplanes, balloons or helicopters, all of which are in a separate category altogether. However, a PPL enables the holder to fly any aircraft in a lower (LAPL or TMG) category as long as he or she has received adequate training on the aircraft.[6] There is no limit on the number of seats or people he or she can carry.

Applicants for a PPL must pass nine theory exams[7]; they must also complete a minimum of 45 hours of flight instruction plus have a class-two medical certificate.[8] A PPL medical differs in that the private pilot can only receive his medical clearance from an Approved Medical Examiner (AME), whereas a GMP (general medical practitioner) may approve an LAPL medical certificate. A class-two medical examination is much more stringent and is carried out more often than that of an LAPL.[9]

In order for private pilots to keep their licenses current, they are required to fly as pilot in command and include three takeoffs, approaches and landings every 90 days. All of the above-mentioned conditions vary according to a country's federal aviation department regulations.

Source: Company files and authors' own creation/adaptation.

Exhibit 7: safety

According to Bob Miller, publisher of the monthly *Over the Airwaves*, safety problems are a significant factor in the decline of general aviation. "To put it in perspective," he said, "learning to fly isn't like driving a car. In the United States we suffer about 300 fatal accidents a year, 80% of which are attributable to pilot error, because the teacher failed to teach. Well over 75% [of those pilot error accidents] can be traced back to faulty instruction."

Source: Company files and authors' own creation/adaptation.

Exhibit 8: airport locations and city expansions

Citizens in most countries adopt the NIMBY approach (*not in my backyard*). Most airports situated outside of built-up areas, because of population expansion soon find themselves in the center of new communities. People move into these areas because of the cheaper value of land, unfortunately in close proximity to an airport, and then realize that living next to an airport with its noise pollution and potential hazard is not so pleasant after all and try to have the airport closed or limit the number of operations at that airport. Evidence shows that most accidents do indeed happen in the vicinity of an airport, either during the takeoff or landing.

Source: Company files and authors' own creation/adaptation.

Exhibit 9: government regulations

Other contributing factors to the slow demise of the general aviation industry are the increasing regulatory requirements. One of the most recent problems is the recreational pilots' fuel tax. The owner or renter of an aircraft in Europe who wants to fly his aircraft purely for recreational purposes will find the fuel cost is higher for him/her than other pilots. Also, Italy is currently discussing the introduction of a wealth tax on the purchase of light aircraft. Ongoing issues like these are what discourage potential pilots from pursuing their aviation dreams.

Source: Company files and authors' own creation/adaptation.

Exhibit 10: perception of the LSA industry by general aviation

The LSA has its own problems as well. While this sector has been expanding very rapidly, the number of manufacturers and the highly fractured nature of the industry have attracted many dissenters. Some influential aviation journalists regard the LSA category aircraft as too fragile to replace the older, more robust aircraft, such as the Cessna and Pipers of the last 50 years.

Ed Downs, a renowned author/aviator with considerable aviation experience, recently wrote: "Many, if not most, S-LSA offerings now on the market come from a European Advanced Ultralight design heritage. The European Advanced Ultralight is not related to the term 'ultralight' as it is used in the United States; it is a light, almost fragile, airplane intended for private ownership or club use. After several iterations and adaptations, these European based offerings meet American Society for Testing and Materials (ASTM) design standards but, in the view of this writer, retain elements of delicacy. In other words, many are terrifically fun to fly and meet required design and ultimate load limits, but may not be well suited to the rough and tumble world of the American Fixed Based Operator (FBO)."[10] Downs is arguing that SLA aircraft are not suited for flying schools or for heavy use organizations as the construction is not designed to sustain the rigors of regular rental to inexperienced pilots for recreation or flight training.

Downs argues that, "The European Advanced Ultra Light is not related to the American term 'ultralight.'" This may have been true before EASA issued the LSA, late in 2012, but the LSA category in Europe is identical to the LSA category in the United States except that the United States places more restrictions on their aircraft than does the EASA in Europe, which has a detrimental effect on performance; however, manufacturers in Europe strive to build types that can be flown on both sides of the Atlantic in the respective LSA class with only small modifications.[11]

Source: Company files and authors' own creation/adaptation.

Exhibit 11: Ecolution

Ivo Boscarol had always seen himself as pushing the boundaries, to do things better, cheaper, faster than anybody else. And with this idea in mind and an understanding that the aviation industry as a whole was in decline because of increasing costs and very little concern for an aircraft's environmental impact, he decided that the future of aviation was with a philosophy he called Ecolution – combining evolution and the concern for ecology.

Figure II.11.3 Pipistrel: Ecolution

The following is an extract from Pipistrel's marketing material:

> The philosophy of Ecolution is applied to everything we do: how we make the aircraft design eco-friendly. To produce aeroplanes that fly better, we must try to design their shape in an aerodynamic way, with clean lines and smooth surfaces. This enables the maximum possible lift and as little drag (air resistance) as possible. Because of better flight characteristics, it is possible to make aircraft which can glide very well and therefore fly without the engine (or with the engine turned off). The result of such aircraft design is: better flight characteristics (for example, glide ratio), less power to keep the aircraft in the air, which means lower fuel consumption and lower CO2 emissions, and less noise.

Figure II.11.4 Pipistrel: Energetically self-sufficient building

He further explained: "To make environmentally-friendly aeroplanes, the production must begin with an environmentally-friendly building. That's why we decided to build a modern, state-of-the-art facility which would use all the available knowledge on rational use of renewable energy sources. Our target was to build an energetically completely self-sufficient building with no emissions and no pollution, so before we even began building, we had to plan everything with this goal in mind. Our aim was that the building would have to fulfill its ecological function regardless of whether it was economically justified or not and therefore it should incorporate all of the latest technology available." And despite the negativity and difficulty of convincing the engineers and contractors who didn't share his dream of zero emissions, two years later the building was finished. "The building has been such a success and its savings so significant that we sell power back to the grid and the difference in savings means that we pay for our cost of production plus we recoup an average yearly return of 20% on the cost of operating the building."

Source: Company files and authors' own creation/adaptation.

Notes

1. It is the slowest speed at which an aircraft can fly. If the aircraft slows further, it will enter an uncontrollable descent.
2. Touring Motor Glider means a specific class of powered sailplane having an integrally mounted, non-retractable engine and a non-retractable propeller. It shall be capable of taking off and climbing under its own power.
3. EASA is the aviation body that provides the rules and regulations of aviation in the European Union. Countries must be signatory to this organization. In the ultralight aircraft category, many countries still have their own requirements regarding size, weight and performance of ultralight aircraft.
4. LSA (Light Sport Aviation) Category is to be found in **Exhibit 3**. All of Pipistrel's aircraft fit in this category.
5. EASA COMMISSION REGULATION (EU) No 1178/2011 of November 3, 2011, page L311/177.
6. Conditions apply and depend on the country.
7. EASA COMMISSION REGULATION (EU) No 1178/2011 of November 3, 2011, page L311/22.
8. It is rare for student pilots to achieve their license in 45 hours; usually, it takes 60 or more hours.
9. EASA COMMISSION REGULATION (EU) No 1178/2011 of November 3, 2011, page L311/179.
10. Cessna Skycatcher – Featured – In Flight USA. Accessed on February 28, 2012: http://inflight.squarespace.com/featured/2010/10/12/cessna-skycatcher.html.
11. Aeromarket. Accessed on February 29, 2012: http://www.aeromarkt.net/index.php?&lng=1&cll=editorial&ID=2942.

CASE 12: PKF Betar Company: "Meters" Away from Further Growth

Anna Svirina

Russia. Inside a difficult institutional context, a medium-sized and mature family-run gas/water meter producer tries to determine the best strategic choices for the company; however, other macro-political forces affect their decision-journey.

Introduction

In early 2007, Renat Fardeev, CEO of Russian-based PKF Betar, had received very disappointing news: the Russian Federal Anti-Monopoly Service had started an official investigation into Betar's practice of selling water meters. The basis for the investigation was the government's belief that Betar had reached 49% market share. Betar refuted such a high market share number since the figure included all of the fake Chinese-manufactured meters that illegally used the "Betar" brand name. It calculated its own market share to be 31%.

Nonetheless, Fardeev and the company's top executives, Vladimir Zaitsev and Vladislav Tsivilin, now had to decide on a course of action. The anti-monopoly investigation would surely divert time and resources away from another vital issue: the question of future product development. The largest shift underway within the utility meter industry was the development of "smart meters" (devices that permitted two-way real-time monitoring and control). Betar executives knew that they would need to make a major investment between €300,000 and €400,000 in order to develop their own "smart meter" and secure the appropriate certificates and approvals.

Having started ten years earlier in 1996, the company had grown to €16 million in revenues, €1.6 million in profits and 300 employees (see Exhibit 1 for Betar's financial history). Over the last seven years, the company had grown at an average rate of 34% and had successfully expanded into Belarus and Kazakhstan. Potential partners from Azerbaijan, Kyrgyzstan and

Mongolia had approached Betar to sell water meters in their respective countries. Fardeev and his executives wondered which opportunity would be the most appropriate for the future.

The water meter industry

As of 2007, the installed base of water meters was approximately 700 million units globally.[1] By comparison, the installed base of electric meters was approximately 1.3 billion units and gas meters, 300 million units.[2] The new and replacement market for commercial and residential properties accounted for approximately 10% of the installed base (70 million units per year).[3] Growth was expected to exceed 100 million units per year within five years driven by strong demand in China. Some industry observers believed that further growth existed since about 30% of water points were not metered.[4] The size of the water meter market in Russia was approximately 8.5 million units and €59.5 million as of 2006.

Many countries were increasingly pushing for greater energy and resource efficiency and were enacting laws and guidelines to reduce electricity, gas and water consumption. Several governments had started programs to improve the efficiency of commercial and residential properties, which often involved providing monetary incentives for the installation of updated equipment. Pushed by the drive for greater energy efficiency, the main trends within the water meter industry were sub-metering, AMR (Automatic Meter Reading), AMI (Advanced Metering Infrastructure) and smart meters.

Sub-metering involved the measuring of consumption of different parts of the same building. The most common applications were in office buildings or multi-residential dwellings where new meters were installed to measure individual consumption (instead of consumption for the building as a whole). AMR permitted information about consumption to be sent automatically to the utility to be used for billing and analysis. Whereas AMR provided the possibility of one-way communication, AMI enabled real-time two-way communication between the meter and a central system. As part of AMI solutions, "smart meters" were deployed on site to read, transmit and receive information about consumption. Smart meters allowed utilities and customers to remotely control and monitor energy use and were deployed for electricity, gas and water applications. Currently, smart meters made up about 5% of global demand and were concentrated in Europe and North America. Industry observers had predicted massive growth of smart meters over the next ten years.

Betar's principal Russian competitors were "APZ" (Arzamas Instrument Plant) and Itelma. APZ held 10% and Itelma held 9% of the Russian water meter market.[5] APZ and Betar were the only two Russian companies producing water meters in the country; all of the other national competitors, including Itelma, offered sold and distributed re-branded Chinese-made products.

At a global level, the main competitors in the global water meter market were Sensus (US), Neptune (US), Badger (US), Hydrometer/Sappel (Germany), Arad (Israel), Landis+Gyr (Switzerland) and Actaris (Luxembourg). There was some consolidation expected within the market; in early 2007, the US company Itron had announced that it would be acquiring Actaris to boost its presence in Europe (see Exhibit 2 for more information about the industry).[6]

Company evolution

Renat Fardeev, Vladimir Zaitsev and Vladislav Tsivilin came together in Chistopol,[7] Russia to produce water meters in 1996. The three men had met at Chistopol Vostok Watch Makers Inc. The founders saw high potential in metering devices due to the rising prices of water and gas, which meant that local utilities would be interested in modernizing their metering equipment and setting up energy-saving initiatives. They designed and manufactured their first two water meters – SHV-15 and SGV-15 – in the Chistopol Vostok Watch Makers facility. By spring 1997, they had acquired licenses to sell the two products in Russia. Betar emphasized product quality and employee safety, eventually gaining quality certificates ISO 9001, ISO 14001 and OHSAS 18001 from European Bureau Veritas.

Russia The company made its first sales in the Chistopol region and began to quickly grow within Tatarstan.[8] In 2000, the Russian government initiated energy efficiency and saving programs due to a rapid rise in the price of energy and water; the price of water was increasing by 8% per year. Furthermore, water suppliers increased the minimum chargeable quantity of water in the residential sector. The price increase and the new minimums provided the necessary impetus for households to install water meters to help control water consumption.

Betar began setting up distribution centers in different regions such as Stavropol (in the southwest of the country), Yekaterinburg (in the Urals) and eventually in larger cities such as Moscow and Saint Petersburg. The company aimed to sell to diverse customer groups: individual households, construction companies, industrial companies, public utilities and governments.

In setting up the distribution network, Betar opted to find partners who would take care of end-to-end sales. The partner would be responsible for the day-to-day operation of their distribution point including local advertising, logistics and warehousing. Betar maintained all production rights (including the production of spare parts), guarantee services and trade-in services. Betar became the only company within Russia to develop a robust guarantee – if water meters ceased to function, Betar agreed to take back the old water meter and replace it with a new one. In finding suitable partners, Fardeev commented:

> From the beginning, we wanted to bring on partners to sell. Sales take a lot of resources and are highly regional. We were looking for partners with the ability to develop strong relationships with the diverse set of customers.

By 2007, Betar had set up 35 distribution centers throughout Russia.

Belarus The company's first internationalization experience into neighboring Belarus quickly followed the release of its first two products. Betar's co-founder, Zaitsev, was Belarusian and believed that a strong opportunity existed to sell Russian-made water meters in his home country. First, Russian equipment-building products were seen to be of high quality in Belarus, which allowed the company to obtain the appropriate certificates with ease. The country's authorities additionally authorized Betar to provide trade-in and guarantee services, giving the company greater cash flow stability for the long term. Second, Zaitsev was able to find a highly qualified distribution team to sell water meters through distributors to local clients. Third, Belarus had shown strong support of energy- and resource-saving initiatives and was passing regulations insisting on equipping new buildings with metering devices. The government was providing subsidies for production units and households to install water meters. Controlling authorities were reasonable and in some cases quite helpful since Betar was participating in a national priority program on energy and resource saving; for example, Belarus had easy taxation procedures and did not insist on total control over producers. Exporting to Belarus was free of value-added taxes (VAT) and the government gave a tax break (half of the standard 24% corporate tax rate) to all profits generated by the Belarussian sales office. Finally, unlike other countries where fake water meters were common, the Belarussian market had very little competition.

Ukraine Inspired by a successful expansion into Belarus, Betar looked to Ukraine as a third potential market for its water meters. Like Belarus, Ukraine also had high demand for resource- and energy-saving equipment, offered government programs for water meter equipment installation and also considered Russian equipment to be of high quality. Despite the positive indicators, the expansion turned out to be a failure. Ukrainian authorities had refused to grant Betar a compatibility certificate. What was frustrating to Betar was that the Ukrainian authorities had imposed rules with retroactive force after Betar's initial application. Betar also found the Ukrainian taxation system to be more hostile than the Belarussian system. Betar was supposed to pay 20% VAT, 25% corporate income tax, public utility tax and 36% social tax (based on salary payments). While there were government programs for installation of resource- and energy-saving equipment, the stimulus was not provided directly to homeowners and commercial building owners. Additionally, all of the Ukrainian distribution companies insisted on exclusive distribution rights. On top of everything, the Ukrainian market was infiltrated with fake water meters from China, making it hard to convince customers to opt for higher quality meters. A Betar executive commented:

> We were quite disappointed with the experience in Ukraine. We couldn't get the compatibility certification since they kept coming up with new rules after our application. When we asked ourselves why the experience

> in Belarus was so different, we realized that our Belarussian team was very adept at communicating with the government and other businesses. We took that for granted.

Kazakhstan The opportunity to sell meters in Kazakhstan came to Betar after a distributor contacted Betar to sell its meters. Like Belarus, Kazakhstan had also initiated government energy- and resource-saving programs, which included the installation of water and gas meters in households and production premises. The country taxation rules were seen by Betar's management to be reasonable as companies were obliged to pay only three taxes: 30% corporate income tax, 11% social tax and 14% VAT. And, while it was necessary to secure appropriate licenses and a compatibility certificate, Kazakhstan government authorities were not obtrusive in monitoring Betar's operations.

Between 2003 and 2005, Betar's Kazakhstan partners had secured the compatibility certificate and built up a distribution system (which allowed them to become exclusive distributors for the country). At one point, Betar started producing small quantities of water meters in Kazakhstan but decided to pull back on the initiative due to concerns over costs and quality. Fardeev commented on the experience of entering Kazakhstan:

> Even if a country has energy- and resource-saving initiatives, it is necessary to have strong partners that can build a good distribution network in the country. It doesn't make sense for a distributor to demand exclusive rights for the whole country unless they prove themselves to know how to run a strong network while understanding government policy. At one point, we thought we could produce there but wanted to gain the cost efficiencies and quality assurance of producing in our main facility in Russia.

One of the more challenging moments in the development of the Kazak market occurred when Betar had been accused of damage caused by one of its water meters. Upon investigating the water meter in question, Betar quickly realized that it had not produced the water meter but that it was a fake product illegally using the "Betar" brand name. Betar and its Kazakhstan partners found that the problem was widespread; approximately 10% of the water meters installed in the country had the fake "Betar" trademark. Furthermore, some of the water meters were being sold back into Russia through Kazak distributors. The Kazakhstan partners located the company importing the fake meters from China and involved the Kazak police to close down the operation.

Company situation as of 2007

By 2007, Betar had grown its profitability by a 82.7% compound annual growth rate from €0.5 million in 2002 to €1.6 million in 2006. Its portion of sales from Belarus and Kazakhstan had grown from 2.84% to 9.4%.

Table II.12.1 PKF Betar: company economic situation

Year	Total profits, Euro	% of revenues from foreign markets
2002	489,577	2.84
2003	689,545	4.00
2004	971,190	5.63
2005	1,312,419	7.61
2006	1,620,270	9.40

Source: Company files and authors' own creation/adaptation.

Despite the successful growth, Betar had to confront a number of obstacles. First, under Russian tax rules, the company exceeded the official limits of a "small business" and thus was subject to corporate taxation taking its tax rate from 15% to 24%. The rules stipulated that corporations were required to pay fixed amounts every month regardless of cash flow or sales. In addition, the company had to pay 26% social tax (based on the total gross salary paid by the company) instead of 14% previously and 18% value-added tax (VAT). Second, because of its size, Betar was obligated to abide by strict regulatory and reporting requirements for the government, which added additional cost and complexity. Finally, the company was constantly under scrutiny. Inspections typically had resulted in confirming Betar's adherence to laws and regulatory requirements, but the effect on time and resources for the company was enormous. The most recent investigation was perhaps the most worrisome – Betar had been informed that it was being investigated for monopolistic practices.

Anti-monopoly investigation

Betar was the largest producer of water and gas meters with 31% market share in Russia. Other Russian producers of water and gas meters had a maximum market share of 8.8% and henceforth did not interest authorities too much. Strangely enough, one of the reasons that Betar was under investigation was because Russian authorities had counted Betar's market share to be much higher, at 49%. The difference between the two figures was that the authorities were counting all of the fake Chinese products that had illegally used the "Betar" brand name. Betar had reported the problem to the Russian authorities, arguing that the fake Chinese meters were being illegally smuggled into Russia and were therefore a matter to be dealt with by the government. Russian authorities responded that as a private company, Betar was responsible for solving the problem of fake products by itself. Furthermore, Betar felt that the Russian government put domestic companies at a disadvantage by requiring two additional certification tests over and above the tests required by US and European competitors.

In the circumstance that Betar was found to be "too big," the government would force them to take action such as selling off a part of their company. With a ruling against the company, Betar would have the opportunity to appeal the decision; however, appeals usually took up to two years. To prepare for whatever outcome, Fardeev was eager to make the company's next steps count.

Next steps

There were two major considerations that would help the company prepare itself for the future:

1. Develop new products, namely AMI solutions and "smart meters"
2. Expand internationally

Product development of smart meters

Company executives knew that the future of the water- and gas-meter market would be in AMI and "smart meters," meters that provided utility companies with real-time information and control over energy and resource use through a combination of hardware and software. In order to offer smart meters as part of its product portfolio, Betar would have to invest in developing new meters and the corresponding software. Already, many European companies had begun to offer smart meters and several countries around the world had initiated programs to encourage the rollout of smart meters to better manage energy and water.

Although it was unclear how much money it would cost to develop smart meter technology, company executives estimated that it would cost between €1 and €2 million. There were potential licensing agreements with foreign firms but Betar executives wanted to be able to offer their own solution. Fardeev commented:

> It costs a tremendous amount for us to develop sophisticated smart meters. We know the market is going in that direction. We made the first steps in developing smart meters in 1997 when we produced heated water meter equipment with remote data output for the Moscow company "Eneleko." Even though the project was eventually stopped, we're confident the market will come back. It just may not be immediate.

In 2006, Betar's research and development department started working on an integrated metering system with remote data control under the working name "Observer." The idea was to create a complex of metering equipment for each apartment unit of an apartment building (including water meters for heated water and cold water, electric power supply meter, heat meter and gas meter) that would transfer data via wireless connection to a remote data control device. The data control device would be located outside of each apartment unit allowing energy supply and service companies to access the data from each apartment by communicating with the device directly or via the Internet, where the data would be duplicated for authorized access.

Fardeev insisted that all new products be developed in-house only. Investments to date in the "Observer" product were estimated at approximately €300,000 including a test device in a real house in Chistopol as a working sample.

International expansion

It was quite obvious to Betar company management that increasing revenues from the domestic market would be challenging, especially considering the anti-monopoly investigation underway. At the same time, Fardeev and Betar's executives felt that they could increase market share within Russia by continuing to open distribution points. Currently they had 35 distribution points throughout the country and almost all of them were very profitable, providing 12% EBITDA on average. Betar had plans to open another 20 distribution points over the next five years (mostly in eastern Russia) including 11 in 2007. Betar executives believed that the Russian market could produce revenue growth of 25% annually. However, taking into consideration the problem with the potential anti-monopoly regulation, Betar executives were keen to diversify revenues and ensure that revenue growth could also come from outside of Russia.

And, while the Russian government wanted to encourage European and Chinese companies to enter the market, European and Chinese markets were closed to Betar because they were not able to gain compatibility certificates. So most of the immediate potential for international growth was limited to smaller countries in the region. Fardeev commented:

> The Belarus and Kazakhstan experiences were very positive and both add value to Betar. However, there is not a lot of room for further expansion in those countries. Now we have to decide where to move next. The three main countries that seem to have strong opportunities are Azerbaijan, Kyrgyzstan and Mongolia. All have two things in common: we've been contacted by distributors asking to carry our products and the governments are launching energy- and resource-saving programs shortly. The rest is quite different.

Azerbaijan A distributor from Azerbaijan had contacted Betar proposing that they would help secure the compatibility certificate for Betar's products and gain entry into a government support program resulting in the installation of Betar's meters in half of the country's newly constructed buildings. The Azerbaijani market was estimated at about 100,000 units annually (approximately €550,000) with projected growth of approximately 5% to 15% for the next few years. The potential partners insisted that they had an informal agreement with the government to be the main partner for water meters. The Azerbaijani taxation system over the last few years had become more transparent. Even though Betar would be exporting products to its local partner, in order to participate in government programs Betar would have to register its own company in the country through which it would sell to the partner. Betar would thus be subject to the following taxes: 22% corporate income tax, 24% VAT and 1% property tax.

On the negative side, Betar executives predicted that the Azerbaijani market would not provide a lot of growth after five years. The potential partners were insisting on keeping and co-financing a distribution center for at least ten years and were willing to put the commitment into the legal agreement. Second, although Azerbaijani partners were promising special conditions with government relationships, they were not able to provide any evidence. Third, Betar executives were uncertain that Azerbaijani partners would be able to solve the problem of fake products from China. Fourth, although Azerbaijan's taxation system was improving, there were some additional administrative regulations on small business that led to extra costs which could be a maximum of 15% of annual profits. Finally, Azerbaijani partners were demanding exclusive rights to start working, and refused to sign an agreement without exclusivity.

Under the proposed scenario, Azerbaijani partners were willing to pay transportation costs while paying Betar its listed wholesale price of approximately €5.50 to €6.00 resulting in a slightly higher EBITDA for Betar of 14.5% EBITDA. The partners wanted payment terms of 30 days. Fardeev commented:

> It looks like there's a good opportunity in Azerbaijan to diversify our sales even further. However, the Azerbaijani partners are insisting on exclusive distribution rights in order to start acting, which has created an atmosphere of uneasiness in our negotiations.

Kyrgyzstan Distributors from Kyrgyzstan contacted Betar with an offer of an easy certification procedure and immediate payment terms. The Kyrgyzstan market had an estimated market size of over 200,000 units (€1.2 million) including both households and industrial users of water meters. The municipal government of Kyrgyzstan's capital city, Bishkek, was aiming to outfit all of the government's water intakes with industrial water-metering devices and later upgrade them to more automated solutions. The Kyrgyz partners believed that they could become the leading supplier of choice to the government and were willing to invest in a production facility and guarantee that they would purchase future automated solutions from Betar. Furthermore, it did not appear that fake water meters had infiltrated the country. Finally, the country's taxation system was quite stable since 1995 and there were only two taxes: 30% corporate income tax and 20% VAT.

The major downside to the Kyrgyz proposal was the political situation. The country's president, Kurmanbek Bakiyev, had come to office shortly after the "Tulip Revolution" in early 2005 where the outgoing president had fled the country. Throughout 2006, public protests had called on Bakiyev to reduce presidential powers, reform the constitution and eradicate corruption.[9] And, although the government had proposed energy- and resource-saving programs, it was unclear as to whether the current government would last.

Betar expected to make about 9% to 10% in EBITDA. Fardeev commented on the Kyrgyz opportunity:

> It seems like there could be strong profit opportunity if we were to enter Kyrgyzstan. The country doesn't have a problem with fake products and the partners seem to be willing to grow the market on a long-term basis. The main cause for concern is the stability of the country's political situation. If the new government is also ousted from power, many of the energy- and resource-saving initiatives may not come to fruition. Furthermore, I'm a bit concerned about the reliability of the partners. There have been a few instances where we negotiate with them and then they disappear for a few months.

Mongolia The potential Mongolian partners had approached Betar with an immediate opportunity to become one of two preferred suppliers to the government. Much like other countries in the region, the government was planning to finance energy- and resource-saving programs throughout the country and wanted to secure 20-to-25-year supply arrangements with companies who had long-term prospects of developing more automated solutions for the future. The government was planning to allow only two companies – one Russian and one German – into the market with sales split 50–50 between them. The market size was estimated at about 500,000 units (approximately €3.0 million). The Mongolian partners assured Betar that the regulatory requirements and compatibility certificates would be easy to secure. The company also believed that it would be able to regulate the smuggling of fake Chinese meters into the country. The partners were willing to negotiate payment terms (likely between 15 and 40 days).

There were some downsides to entering Mongolia. First, the partners had requested that Betar cover the transportation and security costs, which would reduce Betar's EBITDA from about 5% to 7%. Furthermore, Betar would be subject to 10% corporate income tax, 20% social tax, 10.75% customs payments and 10% VAT. Second, as part of the contract, Betar would be obligated to open up a factory to produce meters in Mongolia after four years if the growth rate of sales hit a minimum threshold of 10% per year. Finally, the Mongolian partners wanted complete control over all pricing and operational decisions; Betar would have less control over their product than in other countries.

Fardeev commented:

> The Mongolian partners have shown us great perspectives, but we understand that if we enter this market, we would have almost no control over our partner's actions. The profitability is lower than the other prospects but the sales guarantees feel a little stronger. The challenge for us is that then we would be contractually obligated to open up a production facility, where it would be hard to reach economies of scale and manufacture at the same cost as we do in Chistopol.

"Meters" away from further growth

Fardeev and Betar executives were aware that the anti-monopoly investigation could become a tremendous distraction for dealing with the development of "smart meters." In the case they were forced to reduce domestic market share, how would they stabilize their cash flow? Would it make sense to try to expand into all three countries at once? Could that mean too much distraction and time taken away from product development? Would it be better to pursue only one international expansion at a time? If so, which country?

Exhibits

Exhibit 1: Betar's financial history

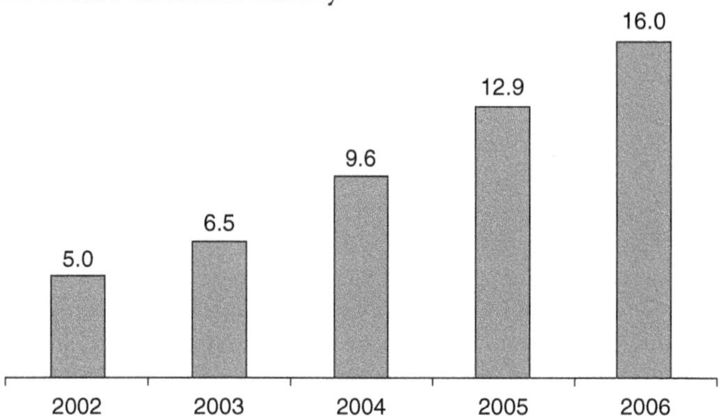

Figure II.12.1 PKF Betar: historical revenues (€ millions)

Source: Company files and authors' own creation/adaptation.

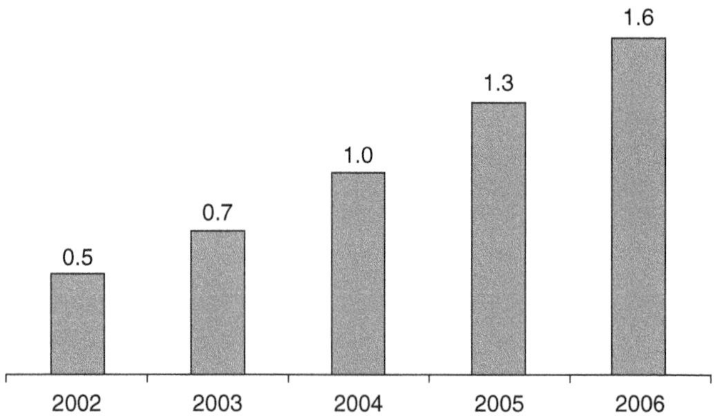

Figure II.12.2 PKF Betar: historical profits (€ millions)

Source: Company files and authors' own creation/adaptation.

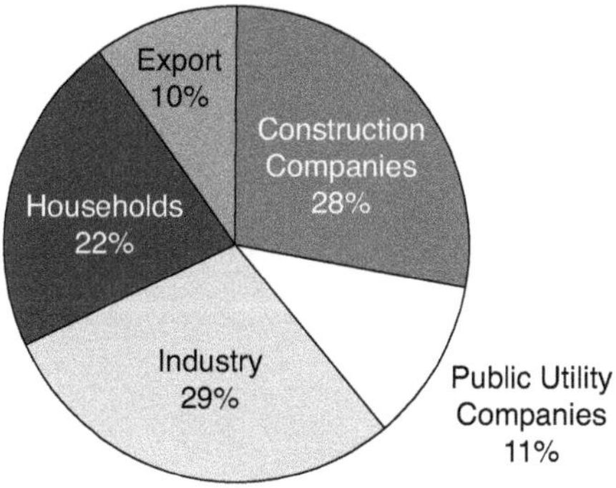

Figure II.12.3 PKF Betar: breakdown of sales in 2006
Source: Company files and authors' own creation/adaptation.

Exhibit 2: market information[10]

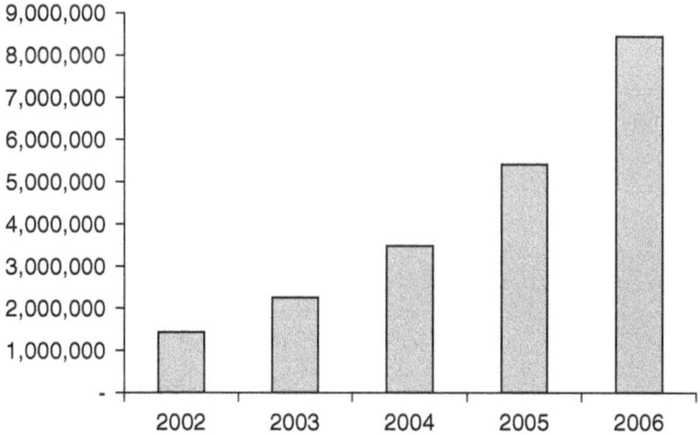

Figure II.12.4 PKF Betar: market size (number of units of water meters in Russia)
Source: Company files and authors' own creation/adaptation.

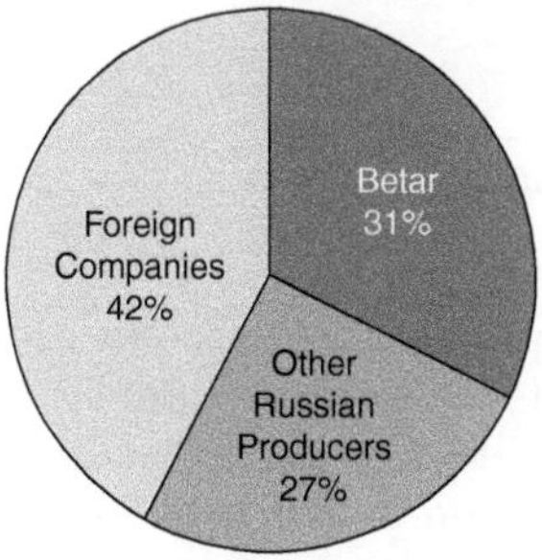

Figure II.12.5 PKF Betar: market share (water meters in Russia)
Source: Company files and authors' own creation/adaptation.

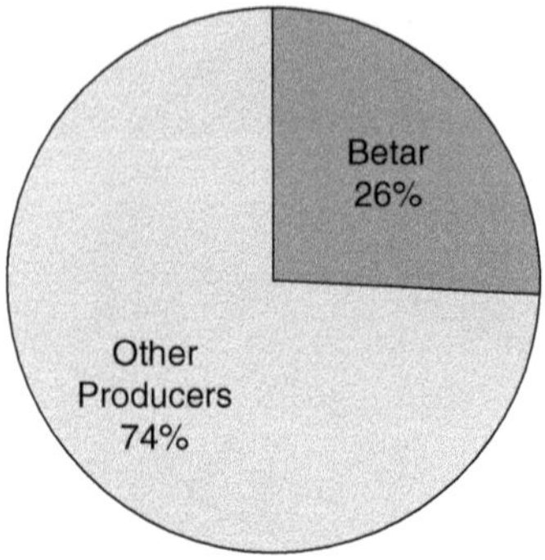

Figure II.12.6 PKF Betar:: market share (water meters in Belarus)

Source: Company files and authors' own creation/adaptation.

Exhibit 3: photos of products

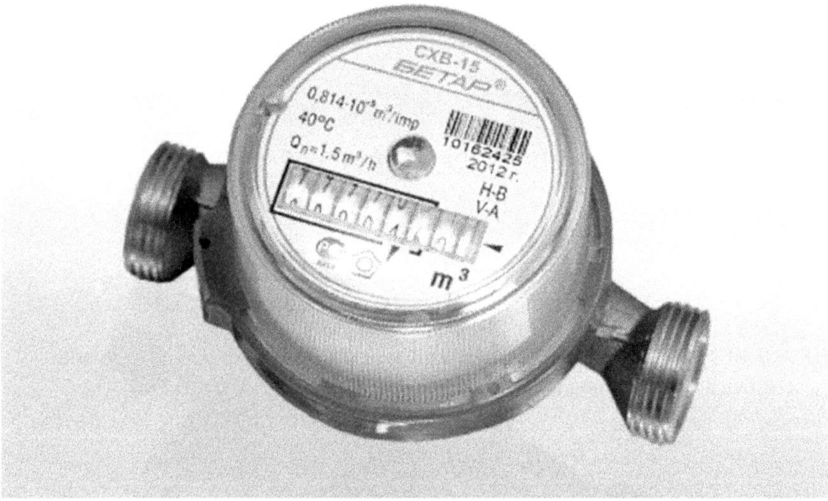

Figure II.12.7 PKF Betar: water meter SHV-1.5

SHV-15 is Betar's first product. It came out on the market in 1997 and is used by households for measuring cold-water consumption between 5–40° C. The pressure in the pipe has to be under 1.0 MPa to provide an accurate measurement. The product is Betar's best seller and is registered in the National Register of Measuring Equipment under #16078–05. Guarantee period is 42 months.

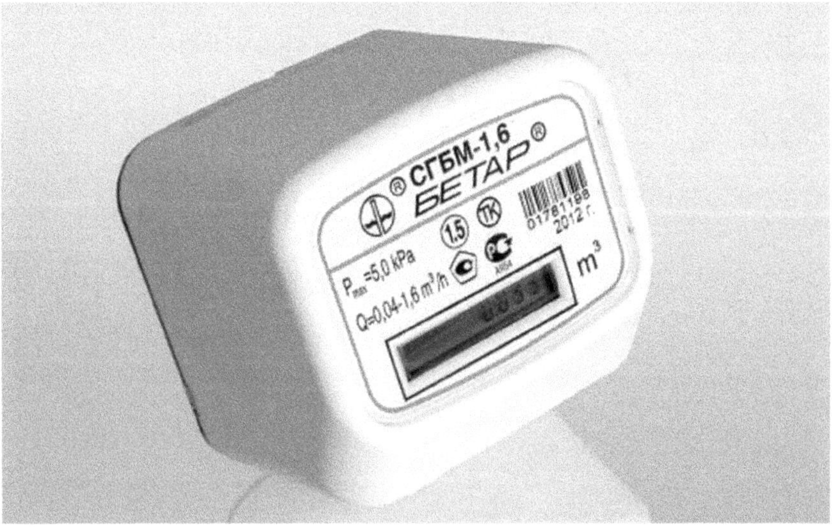

Figure II.12.8 PKF Betar: gas meter SGBM-1.6

The SGBM-1.6 is designed for household use and measures gas consumption of individual users. This meter is providing measuring accuracy when outside temperature is in the range of –10 to +50ºC, with humidity up to 95%. The gas meter can be used for both horizontal and vertical gas pipes. This meter allows performing pressure test of gas pipes without removing the equipment, and using gas during meter calibration.

Gas meter SGBM-1.6 has four modifications: a simple one (without temperature correction); without temperature correction with impulse output; with temperature correction; with temperature correction and impulse output.

The meter is equipped with "Calendar" function, which tracks shut-off periods. The meter is registered in the National Register of Measuring Equipment under #27702–11. Guarantee period is 12 years.

This meter is designed for households and is equipped with non-volatile memory, internal rater with up to four rate types, electronic seal and infrared port. The meter is registered in the National Register of Measuring Equipment under #46956–11. Guarantee period is 72 months.

The SVMT-50D is used to measure the amount of water flowing in the pipe of industrial consumers when the temperature of the water is within the range of 5 to 90ºC. The pressure in the pipe has to be under 1.0 MPa to provide accuracy of the measurement. The meter is insensitive to magnetic fields and has to be installed horizontally. The product is registered in the National Register of Measuring Equipment under #28747–05. Guarantee period is 18 months.

Figure II.12.9 PKF Betar: electricity meter ESO-211

Figure II.12.10 PKF Betar: industrial water meter SVMT-50D

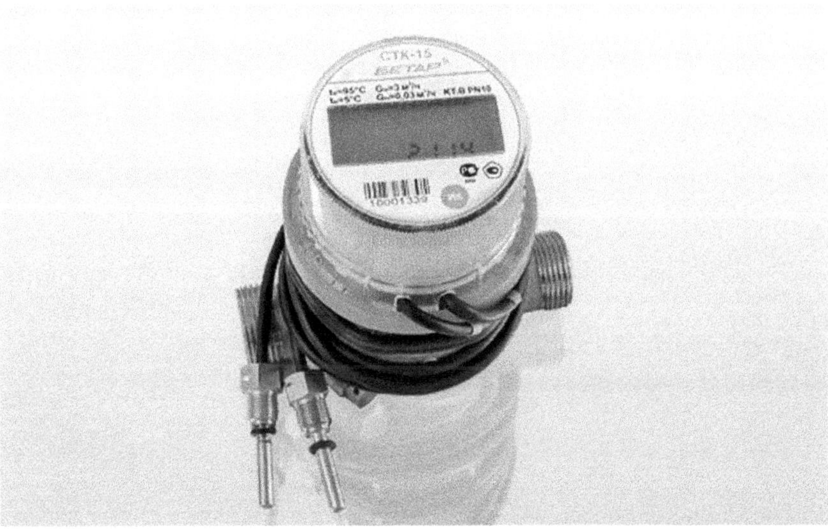

Figure II.12.11 PKF Betar: heat meter STK-15

The STK-15 is a heat meter designed for household use only. The range of temperatures within which the meter provides necessary accuracy is between 5 to 150°C. The meter is equipped with impulse output. Working temperature is 90°C. Guarantee period is 24 months.

Source: Company files and authors' own creation/adaptation.

Notes

1. "View Detailed Surveys of the 15 Largest Water Meter Markets, 87% of the World Market Volume inside the 2006 Edition of *The World Water Meter Report*," *M2 Presswire*, January 29, 2007.
2. Itron Annual Report 2007, December 31, 2007, sec.gov, p. 2.
3. "View Detailed Surveys of the 15 Largest Water Meter Markets, 87% of the World Market Volume inside the 2006 Edition of *The World Water Meter Report*," *M2 Presswire*, January 29, 2007.
4. Itron Annual Report 2007, December 31, 2007, sec.gov, p. 2.
5. "Energy Saving Measuring Equipment," *Ros Business Consulting Report*, Moscow, 2010.
6. "View Detailed Surveys of the 15 Largest Water Meter Markets, 87% of the World Market Volume inside the 2006 Edition of The World Water Meter Report," *M2 Presswire*, January 29, 2007.
7. Chistopol is a town with a population of about 65,000 people located approximately 1,000 kilometers east of Moscow.
8. Chistopol is located within Tatarstan. Tatarstan is an official Republic within Russia. Tatarstan's capital is Kazan.

9. "Kyrgyz protesters call for change," *BBC News*, accessed September 10, 2013: http://news.bbc.co.uk/2/hi/asia-pacific/6105610.stm
10. "Energy Saving. Measuring Equipment," *Ros Business Consulting Report*, Moscow, 2010.

CASE 13: Russian Cosmetics:* "Healing" Skin Care Products in Russia

Anna Svirina

Russia. A strategic challenge regarding the marketing, sales and distribution strategies for their products is the focus of this case about a Russian family business that produces and sells cosmetics.

"Working in Russia is always a force majeure. The only difference is that it can be a total force majeure or a light force majeure." – Valentin Dmitriev,* CEO of Russian Cosmetics

**The name of the company and its founder-CEO are disguised.*

Introduction

In late 2007, founder and CEO of Russian Cosmetics, Valentin Dmitriev, was thinking through a major change to his company's channel and product strategy. Should he focus on selling his "healing" skin care brands through retail channels or cater solely to the professional sector such as cosmetologists, beauty salons and spas?

Dmitriev's concept of a Russian skin care company had been through several stages of evolution. In 1998 he had co-founded the cosmetics brand RusCosmo. Two years later, the company split into two, and by 2002 he had re-formed the company as Russian Cosmetics. Having built the company largely on a direct sales model (similar to many international competitors like Avon and Oriflame), he disbanded the direct sales model in favor of selling to both retail and the professional sector in 2003.

Dmitriev knew that he had to battle both channels' negative perceptions of the quality of a domestic brand. To gain credibility, he had acquired two foreign cosmetics laboratories in France and Switzerland, which culminated in the placing of a three-city label, "Paris–Geneva–Moscow," on Russian

Cosmetics products. Dmitriev believed that the association with the well-known "capital of beauty" – Paris – was essential in battling the negative stigma toward Russian-made cosmetics.

If he were to choose the retail path, he believed he would have to spend considerable marketing funds to compete head-to-head with the big budgets of well-known international brands such as Unilever and L'Oréal. This would be a challenge considering Russian Cosmetics' revenue was estimated at just over €5,000,000 in 2007. Dmitriev commented:

"Of course, great marketing campaigns would start to change the brand perception. I believe it is possible to prove we are producing high-quality cosmetics in Russia. We just don't have 5 to 15 years to prove it!"

In choosing the professional segment, he would need to convince cosmetologists and beauty salon owners to adopt a domestic brand. It was common to hear salon owners say:

"We're not sure that a Russian company will be able to provide high-quality products for a very long time. Furthermore, our clients would not understand if we were using Russian cosmetics instead of well-known French brands."

Dmitriev thought about the best course of action. With limited resources, should he divert his focus to one channel only? If so, which channel?

Russian personal care market

The total personal care market in Russia was estimated to be between US$6.5 and US$7.5 billion as of 2007.[1] The market had experienced rapid growth throughout the past five years, advancing by about 12 to 13% compound annual growth rate (CAGR).[2] Per capita spending was estimated to be about US$88 per person (in contrast, France ranked number one in per capita spending, at US$245 per person).[3] Despite the low per capita spending, some observers suggested that Russian women spent about twice as much of their disposable income on cosmetics as US and European women.[4] Beauty was seen to be an important aspect of Russian culture. As such, many observers believed that the entire market would undergo dynamic growth during the next decade.

The entire market was broken down into six main categories: fragrances (approximately 10% of the market), hair care (20%), makeup (20%), oral care (17%), skin care (13%) and toiletries (20%). Skin care comprised a smaller portion of the total personal care market than that of the rest of the world, which accounted for about 28% of the overall market. The skin care segment was further broken down into facial treatments (50% of skin care), hand/body lotions (25%), baby care (20%) and sun and men's care (the remaining 5%).

Skin care segment

Skin care represented about US$900 million of annual sales in Russia. Russian Cosmetics competed in the skin care segment and primarily focused on skin regeneration products. Industry observers typically talked about two main segments for skin care treatments: an older generation that sought natural ingredients and skewed toward local brands, and the younger generation that were more interested in foreign brands and often relied upon the advice of retail sales staff.[5]

The top five companies in skin care accounted for nearly 40% of the market. The top brands were not nearly as concentrated:

Table II.13.1 Russian Cosmetics: companies and top brands market share: skin care

Companies' market share: skin care		**Top brands' market share: skin care**	
L'Oréal	10.8%	Dermo-Expertise by L'Oréal	3.4%
Avon	8.7%	Chistaya Liniya by Kalina	3.3%
Oriflame	7.5%	Vichy by L'Oréal	2.4%
Kalina	6.7%	Faberlic by Faberlic	2.3%
Beiersdorf	4.4%	Cherny Zhemchug by Kalina	2.3%

Source: Company files and authors' own creation/adaptation.

Sales channels

There were three primary sales channels for skin care products:

1. Retailers (approximately 70% of the market)
2. Direct Sales (20%)
3. Professional Market (10%)

Retailers Retail channels for skin care products included pharmacy and drugstores, department stores and independents. Whereas about 70% of cosmetics overall were sold through department and specialty stores,[6] the majority of skin care products were sold through pharmacy and drugstores. Industry observers suggested that the difference was how women differentiated personal care products – fragrances often aligned more to fashion and were therefore alongside clothing at department stores whereas skin products were more often associated with health and wellness and were thus more commonplace at pharmacy and drugstores.

There were approximately 30,000 to 60,000 pharmacy and drugstores throughout the country.[7] The top five chains represented about 10% of the overall market share.[8] As of 2006, the top pharmacy chains were: Apteki 36,6 (1,000 stores), Rigla (490 stores), Pharmacor (approximately 400 stores), Implozia (372 stores) and O3 (146 stores).[9] L'Oréal, Kalina and Beiersdorf primarily sold their skin care products through pharmacy and drugstores. The pharmacy and drugstore channel was outpacing the growth of other cosmetics channels; experts estimated that in 2007, retail sales of cosmetics at pharmacy and drugstores grew by over 20%.[10]

Direct Sales The direct sales model was based on individuals as independent sales representatives (typically, they paid a small fee for this status). Representatives sold products through their personal networks of friends and family. For each sale, the representative would receive a commission. Avon, Oriflame and Faberlic all pursued the direct sales model. Direct sales had been extremely popular in Russia throughout the 1990s as there was a large pool of willing individuals to sell the products and the retail landscape was relatively underdeveloped. However, as the free market economy grew into the 2000s, many new retail formats emerged and competition from all channels strengthened. As a rough estimate, there were between 75,000 and 125,000 representatives engaged in the direct sales of cosmetics.

Professional Market The professional market was made up of two primary channels: beauty salons/spas and independent cosmetologists. Most of the beauty salons/spas were independently owned and most were single locations, although some small chains existed in different regions. There were approximately 1,000 beauty salons in Moscow and Saint Petersburg and between 300 to 500 salons in the cities with over one million inhabitants (Russia had 15 cities with populations over one million people – see Exhibit 1 for a map). There were approximately 950 smaller cities and towns and each town had between five and ten beauty salons.

Independent cosmetologists were typically women aged 25 to 60 years old who marketed their services through word-of-mouth and performed treatments in their own homes or at the customer's home. In the country there were between 20,000 and 25,000 cosmetologists with the 15 largest cities having between 1,000 and 2,500 serving their market. In general, cosmetologists were much more affordable than spas and beauty salons, offering similar treatments for about a quarter to half the price.

The top brands in the professional market were L'Oreal (France), Algologie (France), Janssen by Johnson & Johnson (US), Payot (France) and Lacote Guam (Italy).

Valentin Dmitriev

Born in 1962 in Moscow, Dmitriev graduated from the Military Academy of Space Engineering with a specialty in the field of adaptive managing systems. He became an officer in the Soviet army under the Space Forces branch. During his time as an officer, he developed 30 patents in adaptive managing systems. With the dissolution of the Soviet Union, like many civil servants, Dmitriev did not receive wages for a number of months. This led him to start working as a salesperson for the cosmetics company Oriflame. He commented:

> I needed to find a way to support my family as I had not been paid in three or four months. There wasn't really a retail industry to speak of but

> there were a number of vacancies in direct sales. Cosmetics interested me because of the high value to weight ratio. Cosmetics are easier to move around and distribute than bulkier items.

In 1997, Dmitriev left Oriflame since he felt that opportunities for further professional growth were limited. He moved to the Russian cosmetic company, Chistaya Liniya (meaning "Russian Line," later renamed to "Faberlic" in 2001), where he secured a position as a manager and business trainer for direct sales personnel. At the time, Chistaya Liniya had produced Russia's first oxygen cosmetic. With solid experience in two strong direct sales cosmetics companies, Dmitriev was ready to start his own business where he could create his own set of values and a unique offering to the Russian market.

Company evolution

Dmitriev joined forces with two other former managers from Oriflame and Faberlic to establish RusCosmo on June 1, 1998. Each of them had invested approximately US$20,000 in the new business. The initial investment allowed the company to set up a 400-square-meter laboratory in the small city of Zhukovsky (40 kilometers southeast of Moscow), with initial production runs of 200,000 units per month.

On August 17, 1998, the Russian government defaulted on its debt, which led to the devaluation of the ruble (the value of the ruble dropped from 6.3 rubles per US dollar at the beginning of August 1998 to 31 rubles per dollar by December 1998). Despite the financial chaos, the default provided extra opportunities for domestic production companies since Russian consumers were forced to pay five times more for imported products in a matter of months. With 95% of the cosmetics market made up of imported products, RusCosmo had a rare opportunity to capitalize on the situation.

First products

Launched under the brand name RusCosmo, the company's first line of products were healing skin creams and moisturizers. The products did not contain artificial preservatives or dyes and boasted properties that helped with healthy skin maintenance and anti-aging. The products were considered to be relatively inexpensive; they were approximately half the price of well-known European brands: before the devaluation of the ruble, RusCosmo cosmetics were on par with other Russian brands priced between 40 and 60 rubles whereas well-known French cosmetics were over 100 rubles. Dmitriev commented:

> Russian women want to love and be loved. And they believe they need to be extra beautiful to attract men, so they tend to use a lot of skin care products. When Russian women started to earn more money, they started

> to spend more on their beauty – specifically on French cosmetics. But we can offer them better quality for much better prices, and make something really Russian and really special.

The direct sales model

RusCosmo promoted their Russian-made cosmetics products through direct sales channels, namely via women who sold cosmetics directly to customers without intermediaries or retail shops. The sales model was similar to other direct sales cosmetics companies like Oriflame and Avon that recruited women, supplied them with samples and catalogs to sell the cosmetics to their friends and family and paid out a commission of 10% to 30% for each sale. Dmitriev's prior experience as a salesperson and business trainer helped to establish a similar system for RusCosmo. The company sought women who were passionate about the idea of providing Russian women with a local alternative. Unlike Western European markets where direct sales accounted for about 15% of overall cosmetics sales, in Russia direct sales represented over 70% of the market in the 1990s (by 2007, direct sales dropped to 20% of the cosmetics market). The reason for the high proportion of direct cosmetics sales was due to the lack of retailers and the availability of the female workforce, many of whom had been left without jobs in the transition to the market economy in the 1990s. Direct sales offered an opportunity for women: the flexibility to work when they wanted and start a job without a traditionally long interview process. By the end of 1999, the company had grown to approximately €100,000 in revenues and 35 commissioned sales representatives.

Splitting the company and a fresh start

In 2000, Dmitriev and his partners realized that he and the other co-founders had differing visions for future growth and they decided to split the company. Dmitriev was keen to acquire a cosmetics company in Western Europe in order to combine the strength of Western European cosmetic technologies with Russian production capabilities. At the time, RusCosmo's partners wanted to continue growing nationally before exploring international opportunities. The company was split; the partners got the intellectual property rights on the technologies behind the products. Dmitriev retained the right to use the brand name RusCosmo as well as the direct sales force of 60 women. Dmitriev was permitted to continue producing at the facility in Zhukovsky. Dmitriev talked about his vision going forward:

> Now that I was truly on my own, I really wanted to make sure that I could achieve my vision of a vertically integrated company where we would do everything from development and production through to marketing and sales. I first needed to find the ability to produce a differentiated product – my idea was to integrate military technologies for healing wounds into beauty products!

Within the first few months of starting the new company, he launched a new brand called "Charovnitsa" (meaning "Charmer" in Russian). The Charovnitsa brand was created to highlight the national character of Russian women – strength and beauty.

New production capabilities

Even though Dmitriev could continue producing at the original facility in Zhukovsky, he started searching for alternative manufacturing sites. Dmitriev found Tulskaya Kompaniya based on the outskirts of Moscow. The company was specialized in the production of hyaluronic acid[11] and associated products that helped heal wounds and damaged skin. Since the end of the Soviet Union, the manufacturing unit had attempted to diversify its activity by producing and selling bandaging materials, shoe covers and biologically active substances. While the company had maintained its team of researchers and engineers, it had not been able to become profitable. Dmitriev approached the management of the company (whose ownership was split among six people) and explained his vision for his new company and how the expertise of Tulskaya Kompaniya could be integrated into the company. Dmitriev knew that securing a hyaluronic acid producer would allow him to cut the costs of his cosmetics by 10% to 15%. The managers, led by Yuri Nikolaenko, the head researcher and general manager, were excited at the prospect of joining forces. Dmitriev acquired the majority of shares through a friendly takeover.

Under the new structure, Nikolaenko became the general manager of the plant. The facility began producing anti-aging skin creams using hyaluronic acid. Dmitriev commented on how quickly the new production facility came online:

> It was a big win to find such a talented team at Tulskaya Kompaniya. Prior to acquiring the company, they already had higher than average labor productivity, but they were trying to do everything at once. However, after acquiring and focusing them on the production of hyaluronic acid and cosmetics, the productivity became three times higher than the industry average. I attribute the big jump in productivity to the shared values and vision of creating a strong Russian cosmetics company, using military technologies those people had dedicated their lives to.

Research and development lab at Moscow State University

In an effort to build a completely vertically integrated cosmetics company with a complete lineup of products, Dmitriev approached Maria Kolesnikova, a chemistry professor at Moscow State University to establish a cosmetology laboratory in the chemistry faculty of the university in 2001. Dmitriev commented:

> It was important for me to become the owner of all of the company units and not to just "rent" out expertise. I believe this is the only sustainable

> model. Luckily, Maria and I both coincided on the vision of having a strong cosmetics laboratory in Russia to build the idea of a truly vertically integrated company. It was also important to both of us that all of the cosmetics from the company were put under rigorous tests for health and safety. We were fortunate that Maria had her own devoted team who were dedicated to the idea of building a Russian cosmetics brand. Much like the Tulskaya plant, productivity in the lab was about three times higher than a regular research lab.

The partnership with the laboratory allowed the company to develop a new product, B-Studio, which was positioned as a successor to the Charovnitsa brand.

Establishing Russian cosmetics

Upon integrating the Tulskaya plant and the Moscow State University laboratory, Dmitriev created a holding group called Russian Cosmetics. He was interested in further expanding the production capabilities as he thought that he might find additional opportunities like the Tulskaya plant. He explained:

> I was looking for another production unit from the former Soviet military-industrial complex which I could merge with Russian Cosmetics, but was not able to find one. I thought, "Maybe, it's time to look at setting up a facility in France," which would allow me to leverage the famous "Paris" label.

Foray into France

In 2002, Dmitriev acquired a small French cosmetics laboratory called Fitcosma International in the outskirts of Paris for €250,000. Dmitriev discovered the French laboratory through his contacts at a company that organized cosmetics exhibitions. The company was not highly profitable and the owners were interested in selling the facility. Dmitriev believed that the facility was attractive for a number of reasons. First, it had specific machinery to produce ampoule cosmetics – there were only a handful of production units in France with similar capabilities. Second, the company had several original cosmetics formulas which could be included in different product lines. The company had 20 employees. Within the first few months, Dmitriev was disappointed by the lack of productivity with the French laboratory. He commented:

> I was surprised by how low the productivity was – much lower than our facilities in Russia. Employer regulations in France are strict, and it's almost impossible to fire inefficient workers. They have a lot of breaks. They also demand air conditioning in the laboratory, which should not be used for technology reasons when making cosmetics. If you take the air

> conditioning away, they'll go on strike. So in order to work around that, one has to put preservatives in beauty products.

Dmitriev talked about the experience overall:

> I became the first Russian cosmetics company to acquire a French lab. I had no idea of what I would find. I needed to make some adjustments to the management team but kept the knowledge of the workers. In general, I find it difficult to communicate with French colleagues and not only because of the language. We could talk for hours and hours and not get to the point.

With capabilities in the research lab and Russian and French production facilities, Russian Cosmetics was able to put the "Paris-Moscow" label on its anchor brand, "Cosmo Professional." It also launched an all-natural skin cleanser called FitFlora, which it positioned like a French brand.

Changing the sales strategy

By the middle of 2003, Dmitriev started having trouble with the direct sales force since many of the best salespeople starting leaving Russian Cosmetics to secure permanent jobs in other companies. Dmitriev recalled:

> When Russia first transitioned to a market economy, one of the quickest ways to find a job was to do direct sales. That's how I got my start. But, by the late 1990s, the economy was growing rapidly and was providing a wide variety of job opportunities. By 2003, it was very hard to find salespeople willing to work on commission only through the direct model. So we had to start transforming.

The transformation called for the establishment of a smaller permanent sales force dedicated to serve beauty salons, spas and independent cosmetologists as well as retail drugstores.

Growth at home and abroad

Under the new strategy of selling to retailers and cosmetologists, Russian Cosmetics started investing time in getting customers through trade shows. Exposure at major international cosmetics trade shows such as InterCHARM hosted annually in Moscow allowed the company to expand its presence within Russia as well as CIS (Commonwealth of Independent States) and Eastern European countries. Its core markets of Russia, Belarus, Kazakhstan, Armenia and Azerbaijan provided the majority of the company's revenues.

In 2003, Russian Cosmetics made its second international acquisition when it purchased Phytoscience S.A., a laboratory in Geneva, for €300,000. The laboratory had strong capabilities in producing hyaluronic acid and glycolic acid. Its main product, Hyalial, was a type of implant containing hyaluronic acid that helped increase the volume of lips and cheek bones.

A family business

Dmitriev's wife Inna had become involved in the business early on and provided the essential "women's insight" into solving problems. When the company split in two in 2000, she provided the necessary support and Dmitriev believed that she was a major part of the reason that the first line of products had been successful. Dmitriev commented, "When my wife started working with me, we started finding solutions to quite a few problems: both in business and in the family. Working together provided better understanding for both of us."

Over time, Dmitriev's children became involved. Dmitriev's son Alexey had started working at the age of 18 managing the real estate of Russian Cosmetics' different facilities. His daughter Nadezhda, proficient in English and French, was able to create strong connections with the employees in France. He commented:

> I'm not very strong with other languages but the people in France were a lot more receptive to my daughter. When she visited the French laboratory, she made a number of business process improvements. After that, we went to the Swiss lab and she quickly recognized that some of their processes could be integrated back into our facilities in Russia. Even though she is a university student, a lot of this seemed to come to her naturally.

Dmitriev commented on the involvement of his children:

> For me, this company is something I have created in my second, post-Soviet, post-military life. But I don't know what feeling my children have toward Russian Cosmetics. I hope they will inherit the company and be more creative than my wife and I are, and get better results, and leave this business to their children ... but what will happen when they start to have their own families?

As of 2007, his wife Inna and son Alexey held vice president posts. Nadezhda was still in university.

Russian cosmetics in 2007

Russian Cosmetics was a radically different company in 2007 than its beginnings nearly ten years earlier. The company was projecting sales over €5,000,000 for the year with four production facilities (two in Russia, one in France and one in Switzerland) and 172 employees. Other than the on-site managers of the production facilities, all other management functions were performed from the head office in Moscow. (See Exhibit 2 for key financial figures.)

Products The company had eight different product lines that covered different aspects of "healing" skin care products for aesthetic medicine such as chemical peels, mesotherapy,[12] biorevitalization and fillers. Cosmo

Professional accounted for about 40% of overall revenues and was positioned as an all-natural bio skin cream with no preservatives, no artificial dyes and no synthetic components. Its other primary products in order of sales were: FitFlora Paris (20% of sales), B-Studio (10% of sales), Hyalial (10% of sales) and Giabeauty+ (10% of sales). (See Exhibit 3 for a list and description of the company's product lines.)

Marketing Overall, Russian Cosmetics wanted to position itself as a high-tech beauty company. Cosmo and FitFlora brands stood for natural ingredients, no preservatives and high efficacy in improving skin. The pricing strategy was to be comparable to Russian competition. Having control over the production facilities and the ability to produce key ingredients was expected to give Russian Cosmetics a margin advantage over competitors that relied on other companies to manufacture their product.

To date, Russian Cosmetics' promotional efforts have largely been around trying to educate its channel partners – drugstores, salons and independent cosmetologists – on the benefits of its products. The company's promotional budget of €105,000 was split between:

- In-store point-of-sale signage and contests for the drugstore market (15%)
- Print advertisements in popular Russian beauty magazines (25%)
- Educational seminars and master classes for cosmetologists (50%)
- Website and other printed materials (10%)

The cost of trade shows was included under selling costs and was estimated at about €100,000.

Channel strategy

Dmitriev was wondering whether Russian Cosmetics would be better served if he were to maintain the diverse set of channels or focus on growing one particular channel. Having previously moved away from the direct sales channel – where commissioned representatives sold directly to end-consumers – Dmitriev wanted to differentiate the brand on its technical features and high efficacy. As of 2007, Russian Cosmetics' breakdown for sales came from:

- Independent cosmetologists (70%)
- Beauty Salons and spas (15%)
- Pharmacy and Drug stores (10%)
- Other Retailers (5%)

Independent Cosmetologists In the last few years, the company has placed more emphasis on selling to independent cosmetologists who would in turn use Russian Cosmetics' products for treatments. Dmitriev saw the main advantage of selling through this channel as not having to develop elaborate advertising and purchase expensive space and time through mass media. Russian

Cosmetics' domestic and international competition invested heavily in advertising through in-store displays, billboards, magazines and TV. Instead, the emphasis in marketing could be placed on educating the cosmetologists and ensuring that the cosmetologists saw the value in using Russian Cosmetics products over other brands. Finally, cosmetologists did not ask for long payment terms, which helped Russian Cosmetics' cash flow immensely.

The main disadvantage of the independent cosmetologist channel was the rate of growth. The cosmetologists were spread throughout the country and it was time- and resource-intensive to convince them to use Russian Cosmetics' products. Furthermore, the cosmetologists were brand-sensitive and many tended to favor foreign brands. Many were not easy to convince on the quality of products. The main vehicle for meeting and selling to cosmetologists was through the annual trade show InterCHARM. Additionally, Russian Cosmetics offered free educational seminars in major centers to display the benefits of their product. For a first-time purchase, a cosmetologist would only purchase between 1,000 rubles (€28) and 5,000 rubles (€140) of product. Cosmetologists who used Russian Cosmetics' products extensively would purchase between 5,000 rubles' (€140) and 20,000 rubles' (€560) worth of product per year. Russian Cosmetics' unit wholesale price was 225 rubles (€6.30) and Russian Cosmetics' cost was 75 rubles (€2.10). Since cosmetologists used the product in their treatments, it was difficult to predict the price at which the product was offered to the end customer. A best estimate was a final price of 400 rubles (€11.20) per unit.

Beauty Salons Selling to beauty salons had one similarity to selling to cosmetologists in that many of the beauty salon owners attended trade shows such as InterCHARM and were interested in attending free educational seminars. Russian Cosmetics' wholesale price was 225 rubles (€6.30) with a cost of 75 rubles (€2.10). Like cosmetologists, beauty salons used their products in their treatments so the price to the final customer was not always clear; an estimate was a final price of 450 rubles (€12.60). However, in general beauty salons were seen to be more brand-sensitive than cosmetologists. Some salons wanted to create a "premium" experience for their customers and insisted on using only well-known French products. Dmitriev recalls that an owner of a beauty salon had said to him: "We're not sure that a Russian company will be able to provide high-quality products for a very long time. Furthermore, our clients would not understand if we were using Russian cosmetics instead of well-known French brands."

Pharmacy and Drugstores Pharmacy and drugstores offered a wide variety of pharmaceutical and cosmetic products. One of the main benefits of this channel was making products available to more end-consumers by selling to a few big customers. In addition, the presence of being in well-known pharmacy and drug chains added to the legitimacy of the brand. However, the channel came with several challenges. First, the stores were brand-sensitive and favored larger, well-known brands that were recognized by customers. Second, they required suppliers to provide the product at lower prices in addition to giving marketing support for point-of-sale advertising and promotional markdowns. Third, the major chains often purchased products through distributors; distributors usually required between 10% and 30% margin for distributing products. Finally, major chains demanded payment terms ranging from 30 to 180 days.

On average, the retail price was 350 rubles (€9.80) per unit; the distributor sold to the retailer for 250 rubles (€7.00) and Russian Cosmetics' price to the distributor was 140 rubles (€3.92). Russian Cosmetics' cost was 75 rubles (€2.10). Pharmacy and drugstores often demanded in-store marketing support that worked out to be between 5% and 10%. Furthermore, the larger chains requested volume discounts of an additional 2% to 5% for orders over one million rubles (€28,000). As of 2007, Russian Cosmetics was selling to Apteki 36,6 and Pharmacor.

Other Retailers The remaining retailers were a mix of independents selling general merchandise. Generally, Russian Cosmetics' products were sold to this channel through trade shows. Russian Cosmetics did not actively pursue other retailers and did not offer payment terms or marketing support.

Thoughts on Russian cosmetics' sales channels

Dmitriev shared his thoughts on Russian Cosmetics' diverse mix of sales channels:

> I started this company using a direct sales force as the retail environment was quite nascent in the late 1990s. However, as retailers started to grow and drugstores saw the value in offering skin care cosmetics as additional ways to boost revenues, I thought that it would be appropriate to offer our products at these venues.
>
> I was a bit surprised since I initially thought that consumers would be going to drugstores to buy healing products and would take the advice of the pharmacist. It turned out to not be so true: drugstore consumers were very influenced by advertising and price promotions. Quality was not the main concern. The competition also became quite fierce in drugstores especially when L'Oreal started to actively promote the Vichy brand. Unilever also started to expand their presence.
>
> I felt that integrating the positive image of French cosmetics and pursuing quality would allow us to create a competitive edge against the big players. When we switched our focus from the direct sales model to independent cosmetologists, I was certain that we would be set up for success. The problem is scalability. It's hard to grow quickly with the independent cosmetologist channel. We can only reach so many through the trade shows and our educational seminars.
>
> Should we continue to pursue a mixed sales strategy? Should we try to build one at the expense of the other? How can we continue to carve out a niche in this incredibly competitive market?

Exhibits

Exhibit 1: map of Russia[13]

Figure II.13.1 Russian Cosmetics: map of Russia

Source: Free World Maps. Accessed: http://www.freeworldmaps.net.

Cities with more than one million people:

1. Moscow 11.6 million
2. Saint Petersburg 5.0 million
3. Novosibirsk 1.5 million
4. Yekaterinburg 1.4 million
5. Nizhny Novgorod 1.3 million
6. Samara 1.2 million
7. Kazan 1.2 million
8. Omsk 1.1 million
9. Chelyabinsk 1.1 million
10. Rostov-on-Don 1.1 million
11. Ufa 1.1 million
12. Volgograd 1.0 million
13. Perm 1.0 million
14. Krasnoyarsk 1.0 million
15. Voronezh 1.0 million

Table II.13.2 Russian Cosmetics: GDP per person

	1999	2000	2001	2002	2003	2004	2005	2006
US$	4,200	7,700	Not avail	9,300	8,900	9,800	1,000	12,200
€	3,942	8,350		9,864	7,877	7,887	8,847	9,721

Note: Exchange rates were an annual average from Oanda.com.

Source: Accessed March 17, 2013: http://www.indexmundi.com/g/g.aspx?c=rs&v=67.

Exhibit 2: Russian Cosmetics profit and loss statement

Table II.13.3 Russian Cosmetics: revenues, expenses and profits (euro)

	2003	2004	2005	2006	2007
Revenues	98,600	128,180	205,088	328,140	525,025
R&D costs	4,930	15,381	24,610	39,376	84,004
Selling costs	59,160	76908	123,052	196,884	315,015
Advertisement/ promotion	19,720	25,636	41,017	65,628	105,005
Profits	**14,790**	**10,254**	**16,407**	**26,251**	**21,001**
Profitability ratio	***15.0%***	***8.0%***	***8.0%***	***8.0%***	***4.0%***

Source: Company files and authors' own creation/adaptation.

Table II.13.4 Russian Cosmetics: number of Russian cosmetics' employees

	2003	2004	2005	2006	2007
Number of employees	116	131	139	151	162

Source: Company files and authors' own creation/adaptation.

Exhibit 3: Russian Cosmetics products

Cosmo Professional

- Cosmo Professional (Paris) is Russian Cosmetics' line of wellness products including facial cream, hand cream, vitamin complex, masque, mousse, milk and tonic
- Use: wellness cosmetics for home use
- Benefits: no preservatives, artificial dryer, synthetic components
- Specific features: natural cosmetics, sea products ingredients and hypoallergenic odorants
- Produced in: France
- Price: cream from 925 rubles (€25.12), masque from 625 rubles (€17.00), milk from 639 rubles (€17.35), tonic from 642 rubles (€17.45)

FitFlora

- FitFlora (Paris) is a natural line of professional phytocosmetics with a unique patented technology, CERACTIV. This line includes facial and hand creams, masques, ampoule cosmetics and massage treatment
- Use: professional cosmetics
- Benefits: no preservatives or synthetic components
- Specific features: addresses skin healing, possibility to provide individual therapy
- Produced in: France
- Price: cream from 2,826 rubles (€76.74), masque from 190 rubles (€5.16), milk from 1,560 rubles (€42.30), ampoule cosmetics from 1,010 rubles (€27.45)

B-studio

- B-studio (Paris – Moscow) is a line of nano cosmetics, based upon "Nano Shuttle" technology. This line includes facial and hand creams, serosities and hair care treatment, and is a successor of the Charovnitsa line.
- Use: professional cosmetics
- Benefits: no preservatives or synthetic components
- Specific features: skin care of deep levels of skin
- Produced in: France and Russia
- Price: cream from 2,826 rubles (€76.74), masque from 190 rubles (€5.16), milk from 1,560 rubles (€42.30), ampoule cosmetics from 1,010 rubles (€27.45)

- Based on the highly insinuative diatomaceous algae, this technology creates unique nano structures which allow active components to penetrate deeply into the skin

Giabeauty

- Giabeauty (Moscow) is a mesotherapy treatment ampoule cosmetics produced by the Russian laboratory Fitocosmos
- Use: by cosmetologists and salons only
- Benefits: based on pure 2% hyaluronic acid
- Specific features: provision of active components to problem parts of the skin and moistens the skin
- Produced in: Russia
- Price: 2,900 rubles (€79.00)

Avualon

- Avualon (Moscow) is a line of injection compositions produced by Fitocosmos laboratory for biorevitalization
- Use: by cosmetologists and salons only
- Benefits: stimulates elaboration of natural hyaluronic acid
- Specific features: provokes intensive blood circulation and metabolic processes
- Produced in: Russia
- Price: 2,100 rubles (€55.80)

Hialyal

- Hialyal (Geneve) is a line of implants used for face skin outline correction
- Use: by cosmetologists and salons only
- Benefits: based on synthesized hyaluronic acid (considered to be the purest)
- Specific features: lips and cheekbones volumes increase; effect is seen for 8–9 months
- Produced in: Switzerland
- Price: 5,500 rubles (€149.00)

Hya+

- Hya+ (Moscow) is a series of sterile wound anaplerotic tissues produced by Fitocosmos laboratory.
- Use: by cosmetologists and salons only
- Benefits: contain hyaluronic acid, anesthetic agent, antioxidant and anti-infective agent of vegetative origin raising one another's efficiency
- Produced in: Russia
- Price: from 65 rubles (€1.75)

Hyaheal

- Hyaheal (Moscow) is an artificial synovial liquid for intra-articular injection produced by Fitocosmos laboratory
- Use: regenerative therapy in case of arthrosis
- Benefits: based upon 1% hydrogel of hyaluronic acid
- Produced in: Russia
- Price: from 2,350 rubles (€63.80)

BeautyVita

- Beauty Vita a line of nutrient cosmetics designed to solve a number of nutrition problems in beauty therapy
- Use: home use on cosmetologist's recommendation
- Benefits: provides nutrition balance
- Produced in: France and Russia
- Price: from 169 rubles (€4.60)

Source: Company files and authors' own creation/adaptation.

Notes

1. "Russia: The Jewel of the European Personal Care Market," *Kline Group* (September 17, 2009), accessed February 13, 2013: http://www.klinegroup.com/news/speeches/HBA_Russia%20Presentation.pdf, p. 17.
2. Ibid.
3. Ibid.
4. "Professional view on salon market" (March 3, 2013), accessed March 10, 2013: http://cosmeticsrussia.livejournal.com/.
5. "Russia: The Jewel of the European Personal Care Market," *Kline Group* (September 17, 2009), accessed February 13, 2013: http://www.klinegroup.com/news/speeches/HBA_Russia%20Presentation.pdf, p. 16.
6. Parfenenkova, M. (2008). "Косметика заполняет аптечные полки" (March 24, 2008), accessed March 22, 2013: http://www.rbcdaily.ru/market/562949979040941.
7. Hautaniemi, E. (2012). "Oriola-KD Corporation," *Nomura Healthcare Conference*, London, June 28, 2012, p. 17.
8. Ibid.
9. Karhu, A. (2008). "Pharmacy Industry in Russia and in the Baltic States," *Lappeenranta University of Technology*, p. 69.
10. Parfenenkova M. (2008). "Косметика заполняет аптечные полки" (March 24, 2008), accessed March 22, 2013: http://www.rbcdaily.ru/market/562949979040941.
11. Hyaluronic acid is a protein that is found in skin tissue. It is often used in cosmetics for anti-wrinkle cream.
12. Mesotheraphy was viewed as a non-medical procedure, which involved injecting vitamins into the skin to reduce cellulite or excess weight.
13. Free World Maps. Accessed: http://www.freeworldmaps.net.

CASE 14: Selena Group: Internationalizing through Multilocality

Sylwia Sysko-Romańczuk

Poland. This case is about an entrepreneur who has built his company in a very different way and with a unique organizational setup and mindset.

After nearly two decades, the founder moved to the Board and hired a new CEO. Fundamental questions need to be answered to keep the company on its successful course: Is the current company structure still viable to grow effectively in the future? How should the founder and the new CEO collaborate, considering the different markets and growth contexts they encounter? What could such a change at the top – with two very different personalities – mean for the company?

On October 6, 2011, Krzysztof Domarecki, former CEO and now 77% majority shareholder and Supervisory Board Chairman of Selena Group, met the new CEO, Jarosław Michniuk, for his official handover. Selena Group was a Polish holding which offered, among other products, polyurethane assembly foam, silicone sealants and building adhesives in the Polish and foreign markets. A few months earlier, Domarecki had tendered his resignation from the post of CEO and begun his transfer to the Supervisory Board. As founder and CEO, he had achieved much over the past 19 years: 880 million PLN (€220 million) in annual revenues, the average operating profits (EBIT) and the average rate of revenue growth in the last six years stood at around 6% and 22.6% respectively despite the global economic slowdown. The company had gone from start-up to international business, thanks largely to Domarecki's leadership and philosophy of "multi-local" internationalism. Now, Michniuk would take the reigns, marking the end of an era for the company, and the beginning of a new one.

Competition had heated up in recent years and the market was evolving. Growth in the PU foam, adhesives and sealants markets was driven by penetration in new application markets, differentiation and innovations. Soudal, Selena's main competitor, was growing rapidly. They had recently announced a joint venture in the Indian market and a takeover of the Shijia company, which had a sizable share of the Chinese market. Soudal had also recently announced its plans to open a new Research Center for innovations. Michniuk would need to take the company in a new direction to position Selena Group for long-term financial sustainability.

Selena Group

The Group consisted of 30 companies in Poland operating in 18 countries, with manufacturing plants in Poland, Brasil, Korea, China, the United States, Turkey and Spain. Selena ran orders in more than 70 markets across four continents. In 2010, revenue from foreign markets constituted 67% of total revenue of the Group. Thanks to its foreign presence, Selena Group had grown into one of the three largest manufacturers of polyurethane foam in the world.

Krzysztof Domarecki as an entrepreneur

During the latter half of the 1980s, Poland experienced what many called the political thaw, followed by a number of economic reforms that made it easier to do business. As a result, the first limited liability companies were formed, and many young people made extra money trading goods with foreign countries.

Domarecki began his entrepreneurial career in India and Singapore. He did not make a lot of money, but he gained an excellent knowledge of the people, culture and customs. He said, "I find sheer pleasure in building relationships with others. I step into their lives every day. I'm not just a tourist, watching them go by as they live." Domarecki became particularly interested in India, and in order to gain a better insight into the local lifestyle, he spent some time living in a Hindu temple. Though he didn't start a lasting business from these travels, they had a profound impact on him.

In 1986, on one of his trips to Singapore, Domarecki bought a PC, which he brought home. It was the third PC in Wrocław. A year later, he sold it for a significant profit. In 1987, together with his friends and colleagues from the Wrocław Technical University, he founded Technimex, the first company trading in computer equipment and software in Poland. Unfortunately, from the end of the 1980s, computer margins began to drop in Poland, so the company started to look to the Soviet Republics for development opportunities. The Russians had nothing to pay with, so Domarecki agreed to a barter. The Ministry of Provisions of one of the Republics suggested that instead of computers, Technimex should pick some goods from their storehouses for the barter. Domarecki chose construction materials, as he knew there was significant demand for them in Poland. Radiators and bathtubs sold best; polyurethane foam, just like in the USSR, was not of great interest to construction companies. The barter helped Domarecki learn more about construction materials and their market demand. The business thrived to the extent that one day, at a Board meeting, the company's key accountant said that the income gained by Domarecki's department was higher than the revenues of all the other departments combined.

Founding Selena Ltd.

At the end of the 1980s, the profitability of the computer business was dropping, and greater opportunities began to arise in the construction materials market. Domarecki took advantage of that opportunity. When the shareholders decided to split the company, Domarecki invested his own part of the capital in the formation of Selena Ltd., a private enterprise trading in construction materials.

Selena Ltd. was set up on July 4, 1992, having only three regular employees. In 1994 it was already number one in the Polish market in sales of polyurethane foam, and number two in the field of silicone sealants. It had a network of sales offices (16 local offices throughout Poland), its own brand and 23 suppliers from Western Europe working for its labels. Such a model was common in the trade: 80% of all construction materials were manufactured for private label.

Of the then top seven players in the foam and silicone market, Selena Ltd. was the only company without its own manufacturing capabilities. In 1994, Selena's board decided to integrate the value chain and launched their own manufacturing process of silicone sealants, Carina Ltd., located in Siechnice (13 km from the heart of Wrocław). Production started in 1997. It was a separate company from the one that had already been involved in the sale of goods in the Polish market. Three years later, in 1999, they started polyurethane foam production. Domarecki set up another company, also located outside of Wrocław, in a different location than the silicone production plant (Orion Ltd. in Dzierżoniów). As a result of that investment, the total capacity of both companies was bigger than the whole demand in the Polish market.

In the 1990s, international competitors like Henkel, Bostik or middle-sized companies from Western Europe (Illbruck, Soudal, Den Braven), known as producers of high-quality products, were operating in Poland through their export sales departments or their own sales branches. The manufacturing process took place in the West. These companies also produced foam or sealants, but they were only supplements to the products offered. However, they could ensure the company's profitability, relying on sales of insulation systems and/or mineral wool.

Domarecki's personal and business philosophy

In 1996 Domarecki began to fly to the United States to represent Selena at business fairs, where the topic of globalization was popular. Rather than seeing globalization as the exportation of goods across borders, he had a different view based on his earlier experiences with foreign markets and his active role in a number of trade negotiations with suppliers from Western Europe. In his opinion, global meant multi-local: it was the possibility to operate at the same time in many foreign markets, not only to export products to neighboring countries. Competitive advantages of a multi-local approach combined economies of scale, competence in brand management, and good knowledge of local markets and local and regional competitors. He claimed that:

> Multi-locality means understanding the distinctness of the local market, and drawing conclusions in business terms stemming from this distinctness. In China, the United States, Spain or Russia, a receptacle for drinking tea looks different. Why is the glass different? Because the culture of the country is different. The same happens with foam, silicone or adhesive. Each culture created a distinct construction technology, for example in the United States, users require a long, "open time of adhesive," as they have a technological process which makes it necessary for the adhesive to stay wet for 20 minutes, whereas a Chinese starts working immediately, and needs the adhesive to hold within 20 seconds; the task is the same: slat gluing. Therefore, we should offer a different product to everybody: the basic parameters should be the same, but their modifications should take into consideration regional building tradition, acceptable level of performance and climate conditions. Distinct culture refers also to distinct marketing communication addressed at the mentality of different nations. As a result, foreign companies have to learn that each market is governed by different requirements in terms of the product's parameters, technology, packaging, language, or size of the can. The world, even within industry, consists of many different markets, which are connected but are governed by different rules of the market game.

Such an approach required creating revenue synergy from different markets and cost discipline across operations.

In his visits to the United States, Domarecki came across the notion of core competence, which greatly impacted him. He said, "Management and marketing are applied sciences. I took a book, pored over it page by page and applied the knowledge."

Based on the experience of the Polish market of Selena Ltd., the core competencies were marketing, sales, collecting receivables, organizing traders' work, routing in the market, and motivating salesmen. He realized that none of these functions resembled the functions of a production plant. He noted:

> Neither managing traders, nor marketing, nor promotion is suitable for production. Therefore, I established another separate company in another

> town, aimed solely at silicone production. From the very beginning, we called it differently: Carina Silicones. The goal of its Management Board was only to learn silicone production on the global level of knowledge achievements. Their scope of duties involved machines, technology, raw materials, production errors, lean management, motivating production staff. Such a solution facilitated the act of drawing conclusions and taking appropriate steps down to the bottom. If we combine core competence with the application of the principles of logic, we arrive at the conclusion that it is necessary to allot the two completely.

The same approach was applied to the production of foam, sealants and adhesives. He realized that they involved completely different processes. Domarecki explained his understanding of the notion of core competence in the Selena business:

> In order to compete on the worldwide scale, you have to be the best at something. If a given managerial team is focused on creating a given value or on developing a given technology, and shall compete in this field with the best, it shall experience a process of intensified learning: first, in terms of catching up with the competition; next, in terms of racing against it. The process of intensified learning starts with being focused not distracted. The information flow between colleagues from rival foam and silicone companies is of secondary importance, as they can offer quite a limited value which is less important than the fact that those who deal with foams shall be the best in the world in their field. Let's keep in mind what the purpose is: it is world mastery in a given category. They have to be good at what they do, not at relations.

Entrepreneur's dilemmas: whether, when and how to go international

In 1996 the company had amassed significant financial surpluses. Part of those surpluses was invested in the new plant, Carina Ltd. However, Domarecki doubted that the Polish domestic market was absorptive enough. He was thinking about the private consumption of a part of the surpluses gained by Selena. This option was clearly against his understanding of the affirmation of life, which was heavily impacted by his philosophical interests. He considered the possibility of diversifying the product portfolio of the company. This second alternative was more interesting, realistic and potentially profitable, because he had already received a concrete offer from the food industry. However, Domarecki still had fresh memories of business model erosion from his experiences with the computer company back in the 1980s and with construction materials trading. Diversification allowed for limiting business risk; however, it made it difficult to build up a coherent business. Building developers also made an offer, but Domarecki rejected it immediately.

He could also sell the company, but he had already experienced that with Technimex and did not consider it the best option for the moment. He was not ready to develop his business from scratch, especially because the one he was running was thriving. In 1999 it was clear that the only option left was to reach out to foreign markets.

International expansion

From the very beginning, international expansion did not mean "simply export," but, rather, to be seen in a given country as an international company with local products. In each country a local marketing and trade office and a local warehouse were established, which allowed the company to sell directly to the local client. They also used the already existing distribution net, employed local traders, and provided marketing communication in the local language. In other words, they placed local marketing and trade companies in local states. While international competitors were operating in foreign markets through export departments, Domarecki decided to set up the company Selena Co. in Wrocław, with the objective of sales development in markets outside of Poland. By definition, it was not supposed to deal with the domestic market, like Selena Ltd., but rather create international markets' competences. For Domarecki it was purely an intellectual job. This was what he was most good at. He resigned from the post of CEO of Selena Ltd., and took the position of CEO at the newly set up company.

It was opportunism that defined the choice of countries prioritized for expansion (see Exhibit 1). At the beginning of Selena's international expansion, Domarecki assumed that it was more important to have some local market position and develop over time than to have nothing. He started to conquer Europe, especially Poland's neighbors. Simultaneously, Selena started to capture the markets of Western Europe. In that part of Europe, results were weak in comparison with their Central and Eastern counterparts. The former market was saturated and the power structure among the main competitors was fixed. The results of the first phase of the international conquest were seen in the structure of sales revenue in 2004: Poland diminished to 47% and increased EU to 26%, CIS (former Soviet countries) to 21%, Asia to 4% and North and South America to 2%.

In 2005 Domarecki changed his priorities in international expansion (see Exhibit 2). He closed the company in Italy and began to deliver products into the Italian market from Wrocław. At the core of his international strategy were emerging markets all over the world. In the structure of sales revenue in 2007 Poland had 38%, EU 14%, CIS 36%, Asia 5% and North and

South America 7%. To accelerate that expansion, Selena needed more funds, which he obtained from the capital markets. In 2008 Selena appeared on the Warsaw Stock Exchange (see Exhibit 3).

Domarecki was often the first to conquer international markets. His approach to discovering new markets could be explained with the Turkish case. When he decided to enter the Turkish market, he did not go to Istanbul, as commercial expeditions of multinationals usually did, but to a small town in the north of the country. What he found there was pure Islam with no trace of Western Europeans. He spent a few days with the local inhabitants in order to understand them, and not only for the purpose of doing business. On a Sunday afternoon, he went to a mosque and spent four hours watching how Turkish Muslim families behaved. After a couple of days, a few men approached him and started a conversation about business. They pointed out that they did not run a registered business activity, and they did not function as a legal entity. At that time, it was speculated that in Turkey there were from about 80 to 150,000 unregistered companies which did not pay taxes but functioned successfully nonetheless. They were not referred to as a gray area or a stop leading to crime. They did not legally employ any workers, but a number of people actually worked for many of them. Domarecki was told that their tribe had been there for more than 1,000 years; some of them still bred rams, an activity they had been doing for ages; others locally built houses. For all these years, they had not been registered as companies. One of the Turks explained, "Officials from Ankara launched such an obligation only 80 years ago, so they should wait twice as long."

According to Domarecki, entering foreign markets required not only openness to other people, but first and foremost, their affirmation. The Western impartial approach was ineffective in establishing interpersonal and future business relations. In business one had to be able to like and trust his or her customers and treat them as one's friends. As a result of the visit, Domarecki found a legal solution to provide products locally.

From the beginning of international expansion, it was clear that the quality of Selena's products was the key element of the company's strategy, as reflected in its mission: "Advantage through product." It meant that the company was focused on achieving the highest quality in each of its product groups and solutions. This approach helped Selena to locate its products on premium and upper-premium shelves ensuring a high unit margin by local market standards. One of the clients explained what, in his opinion, the high quality of Selena's offer meant. He said, "Selena's products always provided what they promised." The development of production technology offered the modification of products' formulas in order to adjust them to customers' needs in respective foreign local markets. It also allowed for the creation of formulas enabling the use of raw materials accessible to foreign markets. Selena was proving the quality of its products not only by fulfilling international standards, for example ISO 9001, but also by obtaining attestation certificates and product quality certificates issued by respective authorities in a given country. This approach resulted in the elaboration of a unique formula and the launching in 2000 of TYTAN 65, the world's first high-yield PU gun foam. Domarecki was able to make TYTAN a very well-known brand all over the world.

Until 2010, Selena's international expansion consisted in pursuing domination in technological specializations on the international scale, in order to be among the three biggest polyurethane foam manufacturers, one of the top ten global sealant suppliers, and enter the group of 30 biggest world producers and suppliers of building and industrial adhesives (see Exhibits 4 and 5). Thanks to local market penetration, Selena was the leader in the Russian market; it had a 30% share in the Romanian market and 20% in Kazakhstan, considering the sales of the polyurethane assembly gun foam. To achieve that, the company focused on geographical market diversification, as well as on expanding the number of key product groups. Geographical expansion was preceded by an analysis of the attractiveness of respective markets, especially in terms of their size, specific local conditions of running a business activity, growth potential and competitiveness. International expansion developed through three kinds of companies: trade-marketing, production and a mix of the two. In the countries characterized by a high growth potential, companies were created, and in the stabilized markets capital-based connections were made, or alliances with local companies were contracted. Such an attitude was to provide the durability of margins thanks to a proper combination of countries.

The strategy of entering new markets involved expanding the product offering, strengthening and developing distribution networks, and, due to logistical reasons, building new production powers. Expanding the product offering began with the Polish market (the testing market for the whole group). Next, depending on foreign market absorption, new products were added to the offer in a given market. After some time, customer expectations started to shift from buying only products to buying system construction solutions.

International organization

From year to year, international expansion resulted in an increase of companies within the group. Their distinctness led to natural integration in the group. Such a role was granted to Selena FM, the parent company in the Selena Group. It integrated functions on a very general level, creating corporate standards, leaving the issues stemming from the markets' distinctiveness to daughter companies. In Selena FM, there were no common functions. There were integrating functions (see Exhibit 6) performed by each department. For example, the accounting department set the standards for the accounting, trained subordinate accounting divisions, and set uniform standards in the scope of IT; the controlling department set the standards of reporting; the HR department built the employer brand and supported the companies in the processes of soft HR. The Business Unit function was to integrate product managers and the sales of the respective companies together with R&D, technology, production and production logistics into one business team. The aim was to move the business unit in the same direction.

The geographical region integrated trade companies of a given area, for example Central and Eastern Europe. There were a total of eight regions. The type and structure of distribution channels also differed from market to market, and was based on the local determinants, which Selena respected. For example, the US market was dominated by superstores for construction products and independent trade representatives (brokers working for different companies). In Europe, that type of sales channel was of marginal importance. As a general rule, in most countries distribution was organized through hundreds or thousands of local building warehouses. As far as Selena was concerned, 90% of total sales came from retail (hundreds or thousands of local building warehouses, small bazaar shops like in Kazakhstan, building platforms or DIY networks), where professionals (small- and mid-sized companies) used to buy products based on their brand. They expected to provide simple system solutions (complex offer for special purpose, like heating systems) with high-quality products and fast, competent, technical advisory services. However, for an individual customer buying mainly at the DIY chain, serviceability, the expected effect guaranteed, trust of the brand and an effective www communication channel were of primary importance. By contrast, for B2B clients, the brand was not of primary importance. The priorities were product quality proven by certificates and technical advisory services.

Integration functions of Selena FM were constructed in such a way as not to disturb the core competences of respective business entities. In Domarecki's point of view, the core competence of the trade-marketing companies was to sell as well as possible in the domestic market: the competitive level was set by domestic market competitors. They did not have to compete with the whole world. They did not even have to know the other's foreign markets. At the same time, the role of production companies was to be the world master in a given production; for them, the level of their competition was determined by world competitors, not those from the domestic market.

Everybody had to focus on the field at which they could be best. Domarecki explained:

> We have a matrix structure. Within one business unit we have, for example, three manufacturing plants. One of them is in China, the second is in Poland, and the third in Spain. The world is so extensive that it is difficult to provide worldwide production through just one company, taking into consideration limitations resulting, for example, from logistics, or customer service. Therefore, a given business unit integrates given plants referring to the product, for example silicone plants. Each produces silicones but does for a specific geographical region. It occurs, though, that silicones from one geographical region might be shifted to another region due to the allocation of production capacity, or cheaper raw materials. This is called using the globalization effect. The core competence is within the business unit. Such BU has its central R&D, which cooperates with all plants.

In order to produce high-quality products tailor-made to local markets (physical and chemical parameters), Domarecki decided to set up production plants in different parts of the world. Some chemical products would not survive transportation through the ocean without detriment to their quality. Selena had 15 production plants all over the world. None of its competitors had so many plants in such different regions. The localization of production plants implied the necessity to stock with different suppliers. The local suppliers very often could not guarantee the same quality of raw materials. It was not the case in Europe, as it was in Turkey and China. This resulted in the implementation of an audit system, which helped to select suppliers from different countries and a quality control system of raw materials incoming to a plant. That was why Selena focused on building solid relations with many partners from different countries. There was no central purchasing department, but that was seen as a future challenge.

In Selena FM, there was the position of a Global Production Manager (Business Unit Manager), who performed integrating functions for various manufacturing plants according to types of products. The integrating function consisted of setting production criteria for all companies, implementing uniform management standards and measuring standards, developing new products and preparing market forecasts for trade-selling companies in each market, as well as marketing communication of new products. In trade-marketing companies, sales targets for a given market were specified at the level of the management board of a given company, based on negotiations with its proper Business Unit Manager. In Domarecki's opinion, consensus was the best way to achieve effective managerial decisions. In case of conflict, he was the last resort to decide.

Global sales and production were finally integrated in Selena FM, but each company had to fulfils its own P&L requirements, not the Business Unit as a whole (see Exhibit 7). New companies were expected to deliver profits within three years.

Selena FM was the knowledge center for all companies within the holding. New ideas came into Selena FM, and then were transferred into new products for all markets. It also provided marketing support for all trade-marketing companies (design of labels and packages, marketing communication of all products), respecting their cultural preferences.

International organizational culture

Domarecki was a very strong leader, personally involved in developing his multi-local company globally. He had an open approach to understanding human thinking, which helped create a culture of listening to the customers. It was common practice that product managers and sales representatives did not only analyze numbers from reports, but also went to construction sites to talk to the workers. There they learned a lot about local construction technology and traditions.

In 2010 Selena employed about 1,600 workers, most of whom were from local markets. In Domarecki's point of view, each market was governed by different requirements not only in terms of the product's parameters, technology, packaging, language, or size of the can; the same rule was applied to business processes. For example, the methods of motivating the Chinese were different from the methods of motivating Americans. To ensure an understanding of this approach to business, Domarecki paid careful attention to the selection of staff for the management boards of the companies. He recruited most of them in person. The recruitment criteria were both strong managerial competence and a cultural coherence with the manager's new environment; the latter included knowledge about the new market and the local culture. As a rule, local managers were employed in local companies, especially as far as trade-marketing companies were concerned. It was the fastest way of acquiring the knowledge about local market circumstances. When the construction tradition and the ethos of work differed a lot, mixed teams of Polish and local managers were established. The transfer of human resources at the international level was seen to be a challenge for future development.

Appointment of a new CEO: 2011

In June 2011 the Supervisory Board of the Selena Group made the decision to appoint Jarosław Michniuk as President of the Management Board of Selena FM SA (see Exhibit 8). Since 2008 he had held the position of Senior Vice President for styrenics in Europe, Africa and the Middle East.

One of Michniuk's greatest successes thus far had been the development of a commodity-based business model for BASF. Based on styrenic plastics, the model was described by Michniuk himself in the following way:

> Lean production streamlined the product portfolio and simplified logistics. This resulted in lowering the operational costs, but fulfilling at the same time most significant customer requirements. "Simply successful" was the motto – the entire package is great in its simplicity, as it responds to all the possible questions which you can ask in the realm of business. I am truly proud of the project and of the people who took part in it.

He always believed that one of the major problems of business, as part of a company's development, was its complexity. He had experienced it while working for 17 years in sales and marketing in the B2B market for BASF. At that time, clients could order hundreds of colors of products in the styrenic plastic group – ABS. To produce this variety, BASF would manufacture ten tons in one color, then convert the machines and appliances to manufacture the remaining products in a different color. Such a production model generated immense costs. Michniuk and his team suggested a new conception of the product: the client gets one basic natural color, and BASF will teach him or her how to create the desired color. Having in mind the new product, the company constructed a production plant in Antwerp. The plant's capacity was 200,000 tons per annum, one big reactor, three production trains for just three ABS grades, all in one natural color. One line could produce one grade on a 24-hour, seven days a week basis. The product was not dyed; it kept its natural white shade, and it preserved its quality parameters, because there were no production changeovers. It was extremely important for the client to know that the product always behaved in the same way, and that its proper color was always the same. Product dyeing was done by the client's processing equipment by dint of the so-called master batches or pigments, which BASF also offered through its project partners. The client would then add the pigment to get the desired color. Thanks to this approach, the product was available at the storehouse within ten working days, because BASF did not produce on the made-to-order basis, but rather on the made-to-stock basis. Before that, the average period of waiting for the right color was six weeks. The client had to buy in advance and create huge inventory costs. It was typical, for instance, that manufacturers of vacuum cleaners had up to one thousand tons of colored ABS in stock. With the new concept, they needed just 30 to 50 tons of natural ABS plus tiny volumes of pigment concentrates. Over the year, most clients converted from the dyed ABS to natural ones. Michniuk stated:

> I come from a company where we had more than 1,000 SKUs, and after the launch of the commodity-based business model, we limited them to

> roughly 200. I know exactly what it means, how it is done and what the curse of complexity on business is. I come from a simpler business model, from a B2B market. Selena is focused on retail, which means a small shop and a small distributor, a small construction platform and a bazaar in Kazakhstan. If we want to be multi-local, we have to use appropriate distribution channels in every market. It needs to be done, however, in the simplest possible way as far as business operations are concerned. The ideal case would be to have simple, low cost back-end processes, being able to offer a wide range of customized products. Here, you need to have an idea and act in an intelligent way.

Michniuk was not adamant about the fact that Selena was to launch a commodity-based business model. Yet he claimed that the company had to give its client what they really needed, and to think twice about what their true needs really were. In its strategy, Selena focused on constant enlargement of its product base, which was supposed to ensure further growth in the market niche which it served. Michniuk further explained:

> We aim to turn Selena into a big company.... It's not about repeating the things everyone does. Domarecki says you have to get satisfaction from what you do – after all, you do it not because you want to earn another million. This business is a life path for him. Just like for me.

Having said that, he had doubts about both the changes in the industry and the sustainability of the current Selena business model. The main competitor in retail, Soudal from Belgium, was focused on its product portfolio without multiplying the SKUs, and its distribution development was based on local partners, joint ventures or acquisitions (China, Turkey, India). In contrast, Dow Corning from the United States was focused on sealant products offered to different industries. The global competitors, Henkel or Sika, had capital resources for technologically advanced products proven by certificates, sales supported by professional, technical advisory services and a strong position in B2B. Moreover, the growing competition from China, with its high-quality products at lower prices, was a near-future challenge.

Exhibits

Exhibit 1: key facts in the history of Selena's international expansion

2011

- Selena becomes the sole shareholder in Quilosa by acquiring the remaining 49% stake in the Spanish company Industrias Quimicas Löwenberg (Quilosa) – manufacturer and distributor of construction chemistry products in **Spain**
- Production starts in Nontong facility in **China**

2010

- Launch of the innovative 360 degree applicator for Tytan Professional sealants; Selena is the first manufacturer to implement the solution on a large scale
- Acquisition of 100% shares in waterproofing materials manufacturer Matizol SA – producer of roofing felt and shingles from Gorlice; thanks to the acquisition, Selena can develop a complementary product offer for roof work contractors
- Establishment of Selena **Slovakia** s.r.o. – distributor of Tytan and Artelit brands for the Slovakian market
- Launch of Tytan Styro 753 – technologically innovative adhesive for foamed polystyrene that is seven times easier to apply, five times faster to cure and three times stronger to bond than traditional adhesive mortars

2009

- Launch of construction works in the Nantong Economic and Technological Development Zone in **China** – production plant for mounting foams, sealants and adhesives; on schedule, production in the Chinese plant shall start toward the end of 2010; Selena is the first Polish investor in the Nantong Zone
- Acquisition of 51% of shares in the Spanish company Industrias Quimicas Löwenberg (Quilosa) – manufacturer and distributor of construction chemistry products in **Spain**; thanks to the acquisition both Selena and Quilosa can strengthen their competitive stance in Europe
- Acquisition of 100% of shares in the Russian company OOO Kvadro – distributor of PU foams and sealants for the Russian market; thanks to the acquisition Selena can strengthen its position and increase its market share in **Russia**

2008

- Launch of an innovative Tytan Professional O2 PU foam line on the CEE market
- Acquisition of 85% of shares in Polyfoam Yalitim Sanayi ve Tic Ltd., a **Turkish** company specializing in the production and distribution of PU foam for door and window installation
- Establishment of Selena Nantong Building Materials Co. Ltd. in **China** and start of an investment in Nantong economic zone near Shanghai to construct a production facility
- Establishment of Tytan EOS Sp. z o.o. and acquisition of two production facilities in Krzeszowice and Lubin manufacturing products for thermal insulation systems, fixing ceramic tiles, as well as plasters and adhesive mortars

- April 18, 2008 – Initial Public Offering of Selena FM SA shares on the main quotation market of Warsaw Stock Exchange

2007

- Start of operations in **China**: establishment of Selena Shanghai Trading Co., specializing in distribution of foams and sealants, and launch of silicone production by Foshan Chinuri Selena Chemical Co. joint venture
- Commencement of operations in **Russia** through Selena Sever and Selena Vostok, distributors of foams, sealants and adhesives under the Group's own brands

2006

- Establishment of Selena **Bulgaria** Ltd. – distributor of foams, sealants and adhesives under the Group's own brands as well as products manufactured outside of the Group

2005

- Award of ISO 9001:2000 quality assurance to Libra – manufacturer of adhesives and sealants

2004

- Establishment of Selena **Ukraine** Ltd. – distributor of foams, sealants and adhesives under the Group's own brands as well as products manufactured outside of the Group
- Establishment of Selena Sulamericana Ltda in **Brazil**, manufacturer of polyurethane foams and distributor of foams, sealants and adhesives, both under the Group's own brands and as private label, in Brazil and other countries in South America

2003

- Development of a unique formula and launch of production of TYTAN Lexy – the world's first high-yield PU straw foam
- Establishment of Finselena Oy in **Finland** – distributor of foams, sealants and adhesives under the Group's own brands
- Establishment of Selena **Italia** – distributor of foams, sealants and adhesives under the Group's own brands and as private label in Italy and other countries in the Mediterranean Basin and in the CEE

2002

- Establishment of Selena CA Ltd. in **Kazakhstan** – distributor of foams, sealants and adhesives under the Group's own brands as well as products manufactured outside of the Group

- Establishment of Selena Deutschland GmbH in **Germany** – distributor of foams, sealants and adhesives under the Group's own brands and as private label in Germany, Austria, Luxembourg and Switzerland

2001

- Award of ISO 9001:2000 quality assurance to Orion – producer of polyurethane foams
- Establishment of Selena USA Inc. – distributor of foams, sealants and adhesives under the Group's own brands and as private label in the **United States** and Canada
- Establishment of Selena Hungaria Kft in **Hungary** – distributor of foams, sealants and adhesives under the Group's own brands and as private label
- Establishment of Selena Bohemia s.r.o. in the **Czech Republic** – distributor of foams, sealants and adhesives under the Group's own brands as well as products manufactured outside of the Group
- Establishment of Hamil Selena Co., joint venture company in **South Korea** – manufacturer of polyurethane foams and their distributor in the South Korea and other Asian countries

2000

- Elaboration of a unique formula and launch of production of TYTAN 65 – the world's first high-yield PU gun foam
- Establishment of Selena Romania s.r.l. in **Romania** – distributor of foams, sealants and adhesives under the Group's own brands as well as products manufactured outside of the Group in Romania and Moldavia
- Establishment of Libra, manufacturer of adhesives located in Dzierżoniów

1996

- Establishment of Orion, manufacturer of polyurethane foams located in Dzierżoniów
- Establishment of Carina, sealants production plant located in Siechnice

1992

- Set up of the first Selena Group companies: Selena S.A. and Selena FM S.A. (at that time trading as PBM)

Source: Company files and authors' own creation/adaptation.

Exhibit 2: Selena's characteristics of strategic segments for investments in 2008

Table II.14.1 Selena Group: characteristics of strategic segments for investments in 2008

North America	South & East Asia
OECD Countries **High rate of population increase** **Big Land Area** **GDP 2.5%** **Size of building materials market: 1 x GDP** **Growth driver: MEX**	Countries with large population High rate of population increase High GDP growth rate GDP 7.5% Size of building materials market: 1.4 x GDP Growth driver: CHN, IND
South America	**Central Europe**
Developing countries **High rate of population increase** **Poor housing conditions** **GDP 4.2%** **Size of building materials market: 1.1 x GDP** **Growth driver: AR, CL**	UE countries High GDP growth rate Housing deficit GDP 4.5% Size of building materials market 1.4 x GDP Growth driver: RO, BG, SK
Near East	**CIS (the Commonwealth of Independent States)**
Petro countries and tourist countries **High rate of population increase** **High GDP growth rate** **GDP 5.6%** **Size of building materials market: 1.5 x PKB** **Growth driver: UAE, SA, EG**	Extensive countries High rate of population increase Poor housing condition GDP 6% Size of building materials market: 1.7 x GDP Growth driver: RU, KZ

Source: Company files and authors' own creation/adaptation.

Exhibit 3: Selena's exchange quotation

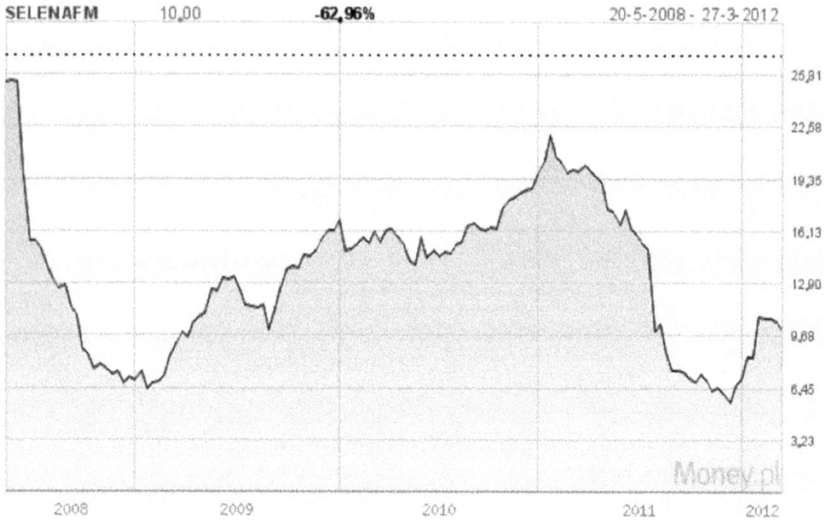

Figure II.14.1 Selena Group: exchange quotation
Source: Company files and authors' own creation/adaptation.

Exhibit 4: Selena's products and their market features

Selena offered a broad range of products for professional contractors as well as DIY users. The Group's strategy involved primarily selling goods under its own brands, however, Selena was also open to cooperation with private label customers.

Selena's key offer included:

1. **Polyurethane foams**[1] are the most versatile polymers in existence today. PU (polyurethane) occurred in mainly two forms; PU foams and PU non-foams. Rigid PU foams were used primarily as an insulation material in construction and refrigeration applications whereas Flexible PU foams were used mainly as a cushioning material in transportation, furniture, bedding, carpet underlay and packaging. Growth of end-use industries such as construction and electronics was expected to drive polyurethane demand in the next years.

PU foam market

The global market for polyurethanes was estimated at 13,650.00 kilotons in 2010 and was expected to reach 17,946.20 kilotons by 2016, growing at a CAGR of 4.7% from 2011 to 2016. In terms of revenue, the market was estimated to be worth US$33,033 million in 2010 and was expected to reach US$55,479.68 million by 2016, growing at a CAGR of 6.8% from 2011 to 2016. North America, Asia-Pacific and Europe dominated the polyurethane market and together accounted for 95% of the global polyurethane demand in 2010. North America and Western Europe were mature markets and were expected to grow at a sluggish rate. However, Asia-Pacific, Eastern Europe and South America were expected to drive the demand for polyurethanes in the coming decade. The furniture and interior industry dominated the polyurethane market, accounting for 28.01% of the total demand in 2010. The second largest end use of polyurethanes was in the construction industry, which accounted for 24.98% of the overall market in 2010. Electronic appliances, however, were the fastest growing market for polyurethanes. Polyurethane demand for electronic appliances grew at a CAGR of 7.3% to 2011. Both flexible and rigid PU foams registered decline during 2008 and 2009, with the demand for flexible PU foams registering steeper decline in the United States and Western Europe.

2. **Sealants**[2] (silicones, acrylics, siliconized acrylics, rubber and other sealants) **and adhesives** (mounting, wood, parquet, floor covering, upholstery) – two chemically similar but functionally different groups of formulated products. Sealants are used to create an impenetrable barrier to gas or moisture. Adhesive products are used to create a bond between two materials. Adhesives and sealants are made from precise blends of petroleum-derived plastic resins, synthetic rubber elastomers, and agents or additives used to enhance certain characteristics. The final formulation ultimately depends on the end use. Industries that typically use adhesives and sealants include construction, consumer products, assembly, packaging, labeling and transportation.

Adhesives and sealants market

The global market for adhesives was estimated to reach US$38 billion and sealants to reach US$6.5 billion by 2017. For adhesives alone, the estimated 2010 market stood at US$10.9 billion with 8.1 billion pounds. For sealants the estimated 2010 market stood at a value of US$1.5 billion and demand of 825 million pounds. Growth in the adhesives and sealants market over the past few years was driven by growing product penetration in new application markets, product differentiation and innovation and it was expected to continue in the next years. Robust demand from developing markets, particularly Asia-Pacific, also bode well for the market. Adhesives and sealants were of great use across innumerable industrial and commercial applications.

> However, given its use by many end-use industries such as packaging, automotive, electronics, footwear, construction repair and remodeling, textiles, consumer goods and shipbuilding, all of which succumbed to the recent economic recession-led slowdown, the global market for adhesives and sealants also suffered significant declines in volume and value sales during the period 2008–2009. Decrease in consumer spending, declined manufacturing output and volatility in raw material costs witnessed during this period especially affected demand for adhesives and sealants. Construction, automotive, electronics and woodworking adhesive end use witnessed the steepest declines, while packaging and disposable adhesives fared better.
>
> Innovation and product differentiation based on next-generation technology, which assumed critical importance during difficult economic conditions, will continue to drive growth in the market over the next few years. Next-generation technologies such as new VOC-compliant adhesives and green adhesives and sealants, which made remarkable market entry in recent years, will continue to garner attention and demand from key end-use sectors, given the need for these industries to comply with industrial emissions, water and wastewater concentration and other environmental regulations. The market will also be driven by the growing penetration of adhesives and sealants in new application areas.

Selena's additional offers, mainly produced by others but sold with Selena's brands, included: wood preservatives, wall preservatives, products for roof renovation, building tapes, products for exterior insulation of buildings, screeds and self-leveling compounds, parquet varnishes, primers, PU foam cleaners and foils.

Source: Company files and authors' own creation/adaptation.

Exhibit 5: sales revenue of geographical segments of Selena Group in 2006–2010 (in thousands PLN)

Table II.14.2 Selena Group: revenue by geographical segments in 2006–2010 (in thousand PLN)

Segment	2006	2007	2008	2009	2010
EU	235,318	270,722	288,252	362,769	506,743
East Europe & Asia	183,684	212,664	211,953	247,346	337,650
North & South America	12,589	34,575	29,425	30,501	34,283

Source: Company files and authors' own creation/adaptation.

Table II.14.3 Selena Group: segment net profit 2010 (in thousands PLN)

Segment	2010
EU	88,584
East Europe & Asia	23,221
North & South America	2,123

Note: Profit generated by each segment without costs of administration, overheads, other operating revenue and costs, other financial revenue and costs, income tax.

Source: Company files and authors' own creation/adaptation.

Exhibit 6: Selena Group matrix structure

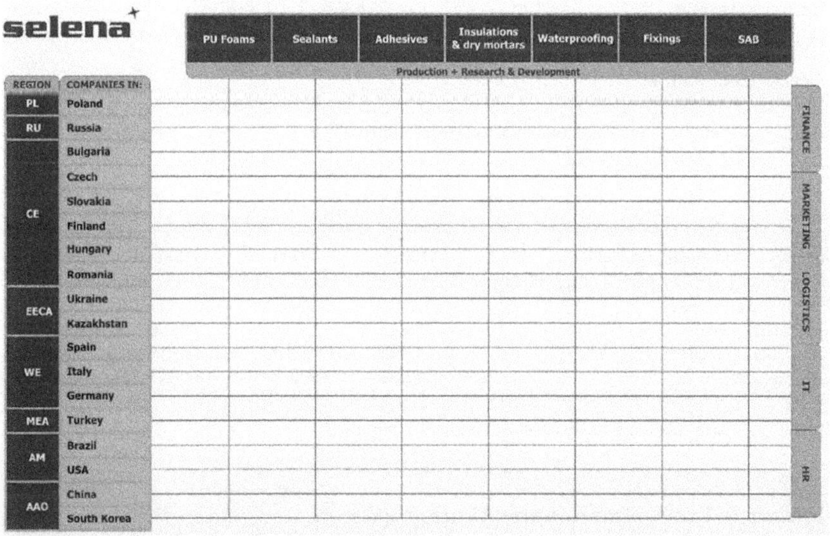

Figure II.14.2 Selena Group: matrix structure

Source: Company files and authors' own creation/adaptation.

Exhibit 7: Selena Group performance in 2005–2010

Table II.14.4 Selena Group: performance in 2005–2010

Key financial figures (PLN thousand)	2005	2006	2007	2008	2009	2010
Revenue from sales	322,009	431,391	517,961	529,630	640,616	878,676
Operating profit (Loss) (EBIT)	22,609	39,805	52,001	7,704	28,734	31,390
Profit (Loss) before tax	18,635	29,908	36,907	15,496	21,480	27,752
Net profit (Loss)	13,319	30,156	34,868	14,257	16,456	24,122
Total assets	180,987	234,587	310,471	432,002	539,328	603,354
Current assets	127,544	158,903	218,471	302,007	311,182	333,719
Total liabilities and provisions	115,801	135,752	161,694	108,390	203,130	244,714
Non-current liabilities	12,166	18,962	26,480	21,198	90,597	61,779
Current liabilities	103,635	116,790	135,213	87,192	112,533	182,935
Total equity	65,186	98,835	148,778	323,612	336,198	358,640
Registered capital	454	454	886	1,136	1,136	1,136
Number of shares **	9,080,000	9,080,000	17,724,000	22,724,000	22,724,000	22,724,000
Dividend per share (declared or paid)	0	0	0	0	0	0.32

Source: Company files and authors' own creation/adaptation.

Table II.14.5 Selena Group: Soudal's key performance in 2007–2010

Key financial figures (€ 000)	2007	2008	2009	2010
Revenue from sales	301,096	320,015	306,329	355,140
Operating profit (Loss) (EBIT)	12,815	14,347	23,230	23,237
Net profit (Loss)	5,357	3,106	15,919	18,886
Total assets	134,051	152,939	144,057	172,387

Source: Company files and authors' own creation/adaptation.

Exhibit 8: Krzysztof Domarecki biography

Krzysztof Domarecki, born on 16 November 1959 in Kłodzko, founder and main shareholder of the Selena Group, a holding of companies which produce and distribute construction chemicals worldwide. Graduated from the Law Faculty at the Wrocław University; also studied philosophy. In 1983–1991 worked at the National Law Department of Wrocław University, doing research on, for example, constitutional court system and presidential system.

In 1992, he founded and led, until 1999, Selena S.A., the first company in the Selena Group specializing in the sale of construction chemicals in Poland. Selena S.A. was among the pioneering companies which in the early

Figure II.14.3 Selena Group: Krzysztof Domarecki

1990s brought modern construction chemicals into the market, including silicone sealants and polyurethane foams for installation of windows and doors.

In 1999–2007, Krzysztof Domarecki was Management Board President of Selena Co. S.A. – the company which manages the international operations of Selena. At that time Selena was rapidly expanding into foreign markets, with a focus on building a strong distribution network and promoting its own brands: Tytan and Artelit. Currently the Selena Group sells its products in 50 countries, also through its own trading companies located in 16 countries. The Group comprises 29 companies, including 11 modern production plants.

In 2007, Krzysztof Domarecki became Management Board President of Selena F.M., the Group's holding company which sets the Group strategy, coordinates and supervises the operations of individual subsidiaries. Since April 2008, the shares of Selena FM SA have been quoted on the Warsaw Stock Exchange.

For his activities Krzysztof Domarecki received an award in the "Entrepreneur of the Year" competition organized by Ernst & Young in the "Corporate Social Responsibility" category; he also received the title "He Who Changes the Polish Industry" from the *New Industry* economic monthly magazine (*Nowy Przemysł*). From 2008 till 2011, he has been a member of the Scientific Council of the Polish Building Research Institute.

Krzysztof Domarecki's non-business interests include travel, philosophy and religion studies. He likes to spend his leisure time with his family, cycling or skiing.

Source: Company files and authors' own creation/adaptation.

Exhibit 9: Jarosław Michniuk's biography

Jaroslaw is a graduate of Mechanical Engineering at Technical University of Warsaw with a degree in Plastics Processing.

Between 1982 and 1985, as process engineer with Polskie Nagrania, he devised a new method for eliminating internal stress in vinyl records and drew full technical documentation for their production.

Between 1985 and 1988, with the R&D Institute of Electron Technology, he researched properties of epoxy resins for application in microelectronics and worked on semiconductor encapsulation in the production of integrated circuits LSI and VLSI. During that time, he authored numerous papers on IC's encapsulation and assembly and three patent applications concerning the area.

In 1989, with ZEUS – one of the first private-owned modern-technology companies in Poland – he worked as Chief Process Engineer.

Figure II.14.4 Selena Group: Jaroslaw Michniuk

Source: Company files and authors' own creation/adaptation.

In 1990, he became sales carrier with Steo, where he worked as sales rep for the Rohm and Haas group. His main responsibility was sales of epoxy resins for the semiconductor industry in Central Europe.

In 1991, he joined BASF, where he found his place for the next 20 years. During that time, he advanced his career from Sales Representative and Product Manager through Director and Member of the Board with BASF Polska responsible for the sales of BASF and Basell plastics in Poland. In 2001 he became Regional Sales Manager for Styrenics in Central Eastern Europe.

In 2004, upon moving to Germany, he became Marketing Director for Europe, next to become acting Group Vice President for North America, headquartered in Mexico and Florham Park, United States, responsible for sales and marketing, logistics, manufacturing and technical support in styrenic polymers.

Since 2008 he was BASF's Senior Vice President for Styrenics in EMEA. Lately he has co-managed the project of carving out styrenics business from the BASF group, as Styrolution, and he prepared the company for independent joint venture operations with Ineos.

He has been active in the plastics industry, contributing to the development of industry associations both in Poland and in Europe, for example the Polish Association of EPS Producers and Converters, PlasticsEurope, and the Polish Association for Plastics Industry. He has received numerous awards for his personal achievements and BASF's contribution to industry events across Poland and Europe.

Notes

1. "Global Polyurethane market to reach 9.6 million tons by 2015," *Plastemart*, accessed: http://www.plastemart.com/Plastic-Technical-Article.asp?LiteratureID=1674&Paper=global-polyurethane-market-PU-foams-thermoplastic-elastomers.
2. "Global growth of adhesives and sealants to be driven new applications, product differentiation, innovations," *Plastemart*, accessed: http://www.plastemart.com/Plastic-Technical-Article.asp?LiteratureID=1729&Paper=global-growth-adhesives-sealants-driven-new-applications-product-differentiation-innovations.

CASE 15: SOLARIS Bus and Coach: A Bus Tour to Global Markets

Jolanta Mazur

Poland. This case is about a bus manufacturer founded in Poland in 1996 that, by 2009, had achieved national and international success, with more than US$400 million in revenues and 1,500 employees. However, the company's future strategy and next moves needed to be decided. Which role would "buses for the desert" play in those considerations?

The case illustrates and poses questions for decisions on numerous challenging issues, such as market-entry strategy, market segment choices, country selection for further expansion, as well as branding.

"A" Case internationalization

As the ten-year association period came to an end in the beginning of a new century, Polish entrepreneurs were getting ready for Poland's full membership in the EU. Many of them considered making their first steps on the foreign markets. Others planned to strengthen their international presence.

In 2002 Polish entrepreneur Krzysztof Olszewski, founder of Solaris, a Polish bus company, turned his full attention expanding his business beyond Poland. He had known from the start that the Polish bus market was too small to satisfy his ambitious growth plans. Now he needed to consider whether the timing was right, which foreign markets to attack, and how to approach it. It was not easy to answer these questions. The newly announced brand name, Solaris, was completely unknown to potential buyers, unlike the brand names of the big competitors – MAN, Mercedes, Scania, Volvo. It took a lot of time to position a new brand on the B2B markets. Should Krzysztof look for some market niches to avoid a direct competition with the global players, or should he challenge them on their major markets? What value proposition could he offer to attract customers?

The beginning

In the late 1960s, when Krzysztof Olszewski moved from Wrocław, Poland to study mechanical engineering in the capital city, Warsaw was an important location for the automotive sector. Poland was then still within the Eastern Bloc, and although governed by Poles, clearly in the Russian orbit (it remained so until the fall of the Berlin wall in late 1989). In 1951, just after the Second World War, a new automotive factory (FSO) was built in Warsaw, though the city was still almost completely devastated by the war. The first model produced there was Warszawa, which was based on a license from the Soviet Union. Years later, the FSO factory started manufacturing licensed Polish Fiats.

However, not many people could afford the luxury of a new car. To fill the demand, some Poles imported secondhand vehicles from the West, usually ten or more years old. These used cars eventually needed service, but the spare parts were not available in Poland. The few local private garages tried to meet the demand, supplying car owners with the necessary new and used spare parts for imported cars of all brands. To be allowed to run a car repair shop one had to obtain a craftsman (master) certificate.

After his second year of studies at Warsaw Polytechnics Krzysztof Olszewski, seeing a gap in the market, took a break from school to join a craftsmanship program. After the third year, he took another break to go to Sweden with his new wife, Solange, to work there and earn some money. They saved the money to use as their seed capital for a future repair business. By 1976 Krzysztof was the proud holder of both a Mechanical Engineering Department diploma and a craftsman certificate in car repairing. Meanwhile, Solange graduated from the Medical University and began to practice as a dentist in a state-owned clinic. It was time for Krzysztof to find a job and put his training to use. Most of his friends had already started working in state-owned companies and other public institutions. Krzysztof could not imagine himself joining them. With the craftsman certificate he started working in a car repair garage. Soon, with the money they brought from Sweden, Krzysztof and his wife bought half of the garage.

Being an entrepreneur was not a politically accepted career and certain limitations made it more difficult. Private businesses were hardly tolerated by the authorities. They could not grow beyond the limit of 10. One of the other challenges was running the business with no local suppliers. Krzysztof started traveling to West Germany to buy spare parts. The Polish currency was not convertible into Western ones and purchasing the necessary amounts of German marks for shopping was not easy. In spite of the difficulties, he was happy to be his own boss. The car repair shop attracted a number of loyal customers who felt they could rely on the owner's engineering expertise, small but professional team and the flow of necessary spare parts (which were imported in suitcases and rucksacks by the entrepreneur himself).

As he had done many times before, in December 1981 Krzysztof Olszewski scheduled a shopping trip to West Berlin. He intended to come back to Warsaw just after mid-December, early enough to join the family for Christmas. At that time Krzysztof and Solange had two children, three-year-old Małgorzata (Margaret) and newly born Jan. As planned, Krzysztof embarked on his trip. The trip did not go as planned, however.

On the cold Sunday morning of December 13, 1981, recent strikes and protests in Poland that had been organized by Solidarity, the independent trade union in the Eastern Bloc (*Solidarność*), were put to a sudden end. Martial law was imposed by the Military Council for National Salvation to, "save socialism" in Poland. The borders were sealed, airports were closed, road access to main cities was restricted and telephones were disconnected. Soon, mail was censored and trade unions were declared illegal. All major institutions and factories were placed under military management and control. Solidarity activists were imprisoned.

Krzysztof was still in Berlin. In the papers, he read about tanks in the streets of the Polish cities and he was terrified. His first thought was of his family, but he could not contact them by phone. The news from Poland made him lose expectations for better times politically and economically in his country. He was convinced that his dreams of growing a business in a free, market economy country would never come true. "*What should I do? Would it be wiser to stay in Berlin and give up hopelessly challenging the system?*" It was not an easy decision, but he decided not to return to Poland, but to stay in Berlin, expecting his family would join him soon. The authorities wanted to punish those who had chosen not to return from the West and repeatedly refused passports for his family. After two years, finally the whole family was together in Berlin.

Olszewski at Neoplan Bus GmbH, Germany

In January 1982 Krzysztof Olszewski joined Neoplan Bus GmbH, an automotive manufacturer of city buses, coaches and trolley buses established in 1935 by Gottlob Auwärter in Stuttgart. In 1985 Krzysztof Olszewski, the engineer from Poland, was promoted a director of the Neoplan factory in Berlin (the fourth one, the fifth factory was later established in the United States). Thanks to his technical and organizational abilities, the Berlin factory was after some years considered the best in the family of the five. He could have been proud of himself, but Krzysztof was not fully satisfied performing the role of a hired manager. His entrepreneurial instinct told him to look for more.

Solange and her husband were drinking coffee after an early Sunday dinner at their home in Berlin when Krzysztof said, "I proved my loyalty and managerial skills to Neoplan. I think I deserve a promotion to the corporation's board of directors. I would like to co-create this company, not just manage it. I am going to ask for this promotion tomorrow." On Monday he reached home later than usual. "I had to go for a walk and think things over," he said before Solange managed to ask what kept him so long. "Did you talk to Neoplan's president today? What did he say?" He turned to her and answered, "You would not believe what he said! In his opinion the positions on the board can be offered exclusively to the members of Auwärter's family. And I do not belong to this family!" Krzysztof realized he could not expect anything more than he had already managed to achieve within Neoplan group.

While Krzysztof had been working his way up at Neoplan in Germany, however, Poland had undergone major political and economic reforms. The first non-communist government after the Second World War began, in 1989, to visibly turn the country toward democracy and a market economy. In December of 1991 an agreement on Poland's association with the European Union was signed which indicated a perspective of full membership in ten years. The barriers restricting the trade between Poland and EU countries were to be removed in March 1992 and Poland promised to allow European investors to establish their companies in its territory.

Krzysztof Olszewski spotted the opportunity to be an entrepreneur again in his country. He did not hesitate to face a new challenge, even though the family enjoyed living in Berlin. Krzysztof was appreciated for his work at Neoplan, Solange was a lecturer in a medical school of Freie Universität Berlin, Małgorzata[1] and Jan were studying. Krzysztof did not intend to break all the ties with Berlin straight away. For some time he continued his work for Neoplan five days a week, and during weekends he traveled to Poland in order to establish and develop a trading company: Neoplan Polska Sp. z o.o. (Ltd.). On August 2, 1994 it began to operate as a commercial representative of Gottlieb Auwärter GmbH in Warsaw.

Just selling buses was not what he hoped for. He began to consider manufacturing buses in Poland. Many people advised not to do it. They warned him, "The big players divided the global market among themselves. You cannot do anything about it! It is too late to start now from scratch!" It took him only one year to establish the bus manufacturing company. At that time it employed 36 people. It was fully owned by Olszewski who still hoped to cooperate with Neoplan. The buses were to be offered under the Neoplan brand, and produced based on Neoplan's technology. In 1999, Neoplan needed more capital to face the growing competition and falling prices. Neoplan GmbH bought 30% of the shares in Neoplan, Polska with Olszewski owning the remaining 70%.

His strong educational base and almost 15 years of experience in the bus industry, his German business partner and the entrepreneur's wife's support were the most valuable assets Krzysztof had for building his new business. These resources were highly important. The factory needed contracts and a source of financing for the manufacturing process if it were to grow. The first contract was won in a competition for 72 modern low-floor buses for the city of Poznań. Finding a bank willing to finance the vehicles' production in a Polish factory with no earlier manufacturing history was a challenge. Some Polish banks refused just as all the German ones he approached had. So many times he asked himself, "How should I convince the bankers that my calculations are reliable, that I shall be able to pay the money back in time? Why do they need a long sales history record instead of looking into the future? There must be a way to get the first deal financed!" Planning the consecutive visits in different banks, Krzysztof became aware that he was running out of time. He would have already had to start purchasing supplies if the conditions of the contract were to be met. With the same materials he had presented before, he went to Bank Handlowy S.A. in Warsaw. This time the visit was well worth the effort. The bankers trusted him and promised financing. "One should never give up! Only the ones who do not give up have a chance of being successful!" he thought to himself.

The next smaller orders came also from Poznań and some other local clients. Between 1996 and 1999 the factory manufactured a bus adapted for blood donation services for Katowice Voivodship blood unit, a bus serving Oriflame Co. as a showroom on wheels, and a VIP bus for the Warsaw Airport. The company proved its technical abilities, but Krzysztof Olszewski knew that in order to grow it needed bigger contracts for regular buses.

The manufacturing process initially took place in rented factory buildings. Buses were produced under Neoplan's license and brand name. Neoplan Polska's market was restricted to Central and Eastern Europe in order to avoid competition between the Polish company and Neoplan Bus GmbH in the Western markets. A new factory in Bolechowo near Poznań was under construction. It was ready to operate in March 1996. Surprisingly quickly the company gained a visible position on the Polish bus market. The Neoplan partnership was an advantage. The well-recognized Neoplan brand was considered a marketing strength and the German partner supplied the bus designs. At a certain point Krzysztof's partner's (Solange's) money was also a support. However, soon Krzysztof Olszewski discovered the disadvantages of the relations with Neoplan, Germany. He said, "I am like McDonald's licensee, functioning by Neoplan's rules, building a brand name of Neoplan! I would like to implement my own creative ideas!"

Founding Solaris

At the end of 2000, due to the major foreign investments in the bus and truck industries in Poland (Volvo, MAN, Scania) Poland started to turn into the major bus production center in Europe. Olszewski feared that the growing position of his company on the home market might be challenged by the global players who located their factories next door. With this perspective in mind he knew he had to find customers abroad. With Neoplan Bus GmbH as shareholder, he could only look east to find the new markets.

In 2000 it was obvious that MAN SE was interested in purchasing Gottlob Auwärter GmbH& Co KG. Krzysztof Olszewski understood it was the moment to buy out Neoplan, Polska's 30% shares before the acquisition took place. It was not easy to put together the required sum. Part of it was financed by a loan from Kredyt Bank S.A. In the fall of 2000 Krzysztof Olszewski managed to buy out the Neoplan Polska shares. That way he avoided having MAN as a new partner-competitor. He also broke free from the market restrictions imposed by Neoplan Germany. In 2001, Gottlob Auwärter GmbH& Co KG, including Neoplan Bus GmbH, was acquired by MAN SE.

In 2001, the whole bus manufacturing company was again fully under Krzysztof Olszewski's control. Solange Olszewski easily adapted to the new situation. She joined the company to support her husband, supervising sales, marketing and customer service as Vice President. They renamed the company Solaris Bus & Coach Sp. z o.o. (Ltd.) and started manufacturing buses according to Solaris designs under the Solaris brand name (see Exhibit 1). Later the company's mascot and a symbol of low-floor city buses – a green dachshund – was designed. It symbolized the major features of the city buses, such as a low-floor and eco-friendliness. Each city bus produced in Bolechowo factory began using the new mascot (see Exhibits 1 and 2). In addition to city buses and intercity ones, designed for short journeys, Solaris introduced coaches, adjusted for long-distance passenger transport.

The bus markets

Buses were assembled from many parts manufactured in various factories worldwide. The big corporations assembled buses using engines and many other parts manufactured within the groups. For example, engines manufactured by MAN SE were installed in MAN and Neoplan buses. In the case of smaller producers, like Solaris, usually only the bus bodies were produced internally, while other parts were outsourced.

Buses are used as city buses, intercity buses and coaches. General statistical data considers all three categories buses. Usually buses are replaced after 10 to 15 years, but sometimes it takes longer.

City buses were as a rule acquired by comparatively big municipal transport institutions and the city's budget determined its demand. If a city's budget was tight, the buses would have to serve more years. Replacement of the city bus fleet was also a PR instrument used by the mayoral candidates before elections. Municipal transport institutions invited suppliers to competitive bidding procedures. The price was an important purchasing factor, though not the only one. Low-floor or at least low-floor entrance buses became a standard on the international city bus market. Customers also expected a modern design and interior. Due to the short distances between the stops and street traffic, city buses, unlike intercity ones, were responsible for much of the noise and pollution in towns.

As pollution was one of the major problems in big cities, pollution-reducing technologies were appreciated. However, new technologies were expensive, which reduced demand for innovative products in less affluent markets. New technologies in bus manufacturing include hybrid engines, which reduced gasoline consumption and pollution in comparison to diesel engines. The choice of a hybrid engine brand depended on local environmental conditions. CNG buses powered by gas were the cheaper alternative of hybrid buses. They required a network of gas stations in the region in which they operated. The innovations were recently concentrated on bus weight reductions, which helped save petroleum. The most popular solution was applying aluminum to produce bus frames. Aluminum producers supported it.

Private rather than public institutions ran intercity transport in many cases. Some intercity transport companies were not very big and did not own many buses. The services were offered first to commuters. There were many cities that attracted a high number of commuters on a daily basis. School buses were included to this category. Intercity buses were not heavy-duty vehicles like the city ones; moreover they did not have to be as well equipped as long-distance coaches, therefore they were relatively cheaper. Price was an important buying decision factor, especially for the small private buyers and when public funds were to be spent.

The demand for coaches came from private tourist operators. Their purchases depended on the competitive situation in the markets they served. The contracts for coaches were usually smaller than the ones for city buses. The coaches used for long distance, also international travel, were well equipped (comfortable seats, toilets, luggage compartments, television screens), which affected prices. The respected manufacturers' brand names were well perceived by tourists, and therefore also preferred by the operators. Immediate availability was also an important factor, but probably not as crucial as in the case of city buses.

All kinds of buses had to be adjusted to the climate and other local geographic conditions. Buses ordered by Norwegian customers differed a lot from buses which were to be driven in African countries. But it was not only the climate that counted. The landscape characteristics were also important. For example, suitable models of buses have to be offered for the winding roads of mountain region cities. To meet diversified requirements, large-scale manufacturers offered a range of standard models adjusted to several model conditions. Smaller producers were more flexible and willing to build the vehicles which individually met the needs of each customer. Such special needs may be a consequence of a certain road surface. In the case of gravel roads, windscreens get hit and broken comparatively frequently. This is why the Danish customers preferred windscreens divided into two parts and favor such customized vehicles. This way they save in case they have to replace the broken part. Solaris, unlike the big manufacturers, offered such adjustments. Designing the vehicle according to individual needs was an example of customer co-creation, based on a series of consultations between the buyer and manufacturer.

The buyers of any kind of bus expected complete service availability, with a guarantee that the vehicles would be ready to use at any time. An out-of-order situation caused problems for passengers. Easier bus servicing was also a concern for bus designers. Buyers looked for a respected manufacturer with brand-name components (primarily engines) to satisfy their expectations of quality and reliability.

Transportation industries were considered the world's highest growth sectors, playing a major role in trade, integrating countries and regions and societies' development. But in times of economic slowdown, they suffered demand decreases, like the majority of other industries. The major world players had a tough year in 2001. The recession which started earlier in North America caused reductions in demand. The situation was repeated soon in Western Europe. The global economic downturn hit MAN SE, Daimler AG, Volvo and others and was expected to intensify the competition among them.

The Polish bus market in 1997–2001

In the 1990s Poland started to restructure its economy from a centrally planned into a market economy. Many new institutions were introduced in a short period of time. The general tendency was to decentralize decision-making and foster entrepreneurship. As Poland lacked local capital, foreign investors were interested. The big European truck and bus manufacturers began establishing factories in the western and southern parts of the country, attracted by a skilled workforce and a comparatively large local and big pan-European market potential.

The local demand for buses between 1997 and 2001 was comparatively high, but there were ups and downs in the numbers of buses sold. The most buses were sold in 1997 (see Exhibit 3). The Polish market was divided between Polish and international manufacturers.

Autosan S.A. – a Polish company situated in Sanok, started its history in 1832. It began to produce buses in 1926. For many years, Autosan kept its leading position in Poland. It was focused on manufacturing school and intercity buses.[2]

Jelcz S.A. – a Polish factory established in 1952 producing trucks and buses (school and city buses in particular). Once the second biggest supplier, they gradually started to lose market share.[3]

MAN Truck & Bus – Monachium, the biggest company of the MAN group. A global player present on the majority of world markets having invested heavily in locations outside Germany, including Poland. MAN Truck and Bus started to focus on the BRIC countries and some other markets of South America and South Africa, while Poland was considered the company's important manufacturing center for European clients.[4]

Irisbus – a bus manufacturer established through the merger of the bus and coach divisions of several European companies including Iveco, Renault, Heuliez, Ikarus, Karosa and Orlandi Iveco with factories situated in Europe (France, Italy, Spain, Czech Republic, Hungary and beyond).[5]

Kapena S.A. – a Polish manufacturer of small buses established in the 1980s. An Italian company, Cacciamali, was its major shareholder[6].

AB Volvo – a global manufacturer of heavy-duty trucks, buses, construction machinery, aircraft engines and engine parts. In 1999 Volvo sold its automobile business to Ford Motor Company, concentrating on commercial vehicle manufacturing. It tried to take over Scania in 2000, but the European Commission blocked the deal. In 1995 Volvo started investing in Poland, relocating its bus manufacturing potential from some Western European countries (Germany, Denmark, Finland). The bus production in Poland was initiated in 1996 and in 2000 the biggest bus manufacturing factory in Europe started to operate in Wrocław, Poland.[7]

Scania AB – a company established in 1900 as Maskinfabriks in Sweden. Scania AB started its history as a bus and truck producer in 1995. It became a global player, a manufacturer of trucks, buses and coaches, and industrial and marine engines with production facilities situated in Europe and South America. In Słupsk, Poland Scania established an assembly of bus bodies.[8]

Daimler AG – an owner of Mercedes-Benz brand name – one of the biggest world players in the automotive industry. It ranked first as the manufacturer of commercial vehicles. Its corporate headquarters were located in Stuttgart, Germany, and its European bus manufacturing factory was situated in Mannheim, Germany. In 1995 Daimler AG acquired Stera, which became a part of EvoBus GmbH, a member of Daimler Group.[9]

Between 1997 and 2001 two leading traditional local suppliers, Autosan and Jelcz, ranked first on the Polish market, but their shares were not stable. There was a trend toward decline, especially in the case of Jelcz. Surprisingly the market shares of the biggest global players at that time, however growing, were not very high in comparison to Polish manufacturers' (including Neoplan Poland) shares. During that period, Neoplan's share in buses sales in Poland amounted to approximately 13% (see Exhibit 4). The last year Neoplan Poland's market share was registered was 2000. In 2001 Solaris replaced Neoplan (see Exhibits 5 and 6).

Going international. First steps

Bus producers had to constantly look for new customers and new foreign markets to be successful in sales. To avoid the high import custom duties, big corporations invested abroad. Big emerging markets and free-trade zones were attractive FDI locations.

Krzysztof Olszewski understood the need for internationalization right from the start. "We cannot rely only on the Polish market demand," he said to his wife when they were discussing the consequences of FDI in the big bus and truck corporations in Poland. "Right now they are concentrated on exports, but it may change in the future. Our market is too small for so many players."

The first export deliveries were executed in 2000, the initial year of Solaris Bus & Coach history. City buses were exported to Czech Republic for Ostrava Municipal Transport Company under the Solaris Urbino brand name. This contract was the consequence of the division of markets between Neoplan Poland, and Neoplan Bus GmbH. In 2001 there were no market restrictions, but the bigger orders still came from the Central and Eastern Europe region (Lithuania). The same year ABUS, an independent transport operator in Berlin, placed an order for two Solaris Urbino 12s. They were the first city buses designed and manufactured in Poland purchased by a Western European customer. The business performance in 2001 was not bad; the company's net income reached 16,883,229 Polish zlotys, leaving room to invest in the new markets. Such investments were necessary as the share of exports in the total revenues was still not high, and accounted for only 17% (see Exhibit 7).

The major product in Solaris's portfolio was city low-floor buses, so big, densely populated cities should have been targeted. Big cities invested in public transportation systems in order to prevent too many cars entering downtown areas. It was natural for a newly established company to first look for the customers in neighboring countries, especially when the first orders came from them.

Czech Republic. Its population was about ten million people. The majority of them (75%) lived in urban areas. The country area was 78,866 square kilometers. Only Prague was a city with a population exceeding one million inhabitants (1.2 million). The next biggest towns were Brno (almost 0.4 million) and Ostrava (0.3 million). Czech Republic, like others in the region of Central and Eastern Europe (Poland, Slovakia, Baltic states, Bulgaria, Romania) was struggling with problems of political and economic transformation. City budgets were not big, but fleet replacement and modernization was badly needed.[10]

Slovakia. The country population was only about 5.4 million people, living in an area of 49,000 square kilometers. Slovakia was much less urbanized than the Czech Republic (over 50% lived in towns). In 2001, the capital Bratislava had 0.43 million inhabitants.[11]

Lithuania was one of the Baltic states with a population of 3.5 million, including over 0.5 million living in the capital (Vilnius). The area was 65,200 square kilometers.[12]

Latvia. Another Baltic state of 64,589 square kilometers populated by slightly above two million people, Latvia's population was therefore far below the EU average. The capital, Riga, was the biggest city, with over 0.7 million inhabitants.[13]

Estonia. Only 1.4 million inhabitants populated the third Baltic state in 2000 (about 0.4 million in the country capital, Tallinn). The urban population was about 69% of the total number of residents in 2001. The area of Estonia was 45,228 square kilometers, including 1,520 islands in the Baltic Sea.[14]

Russian Federation. The population of Russia exceeded 144 million people living in the biggest country in the world with a total area 17,075,400 square kilometers. The size of the country resulted in big differences in population density and urbanization. Russia's capital, Moscow, the biggest European city, had about ten million inhabitants. There were some local manufacturers of buses in Russia. In Saint Petersburg, Scania initiated the production of buses. It was never easy to do business in Russia, as clear market rules did not regulate the majority of business relations, however MAN was successful in penetrating the market of this giant country.[15]

Ukraine. However relatively big, both as far as area (603,700 sq.km) and population (47 million residents), the country did not seem to be a promising partner for the time being due to political and economic problems.[16]

Germany. Germany had a population of about 82 million people. The urban population was about 80%. The biggest cities by number of inhabitants were: Berlin – 3.3 million; Hamburg – 1.7; Munich – 1.2; Koln-Ruhr area – 1.0; Frankfurt – 0.6; Essen – 0.6; Dortmund 0.6; Stuttgart 0.6; and Dusseldorf 0.6. Many more people lived in the urban areas around the cities. The area of the country was 357,093 square kilometers, so the country was densely populated. Germany was a market economy and an affluent country. Big global suppliers were already well established there, including the German supplier and market leader MAN.[17]

Krzysztof also considered some other European countries which had fewer residents but were more affluent and therefore interested in high standards of city public transport and environmental standards. The more affluent the country, the bigger the purchases, he expected. GNI per capita in 2001 of selected countries is presented in Exhibit 8.

Switzerland. A country of 41,290 square kilometers, was populated by over seven million people. The Alps Mountains accounted for 60% of the country's total area. There were no very big cities in the country. The largest one, Zurich, had about 0.36 million inhabitants.[18]

Sweden. Sweden had an area of about 450 square kilometers and a population of over nine million people; almost 0.9 million of them lived in the capital, Stockholm (Stockholm's greater urban area was almost two million people). The next biggest cities were Götteborg (0.5 million) and Malmö (about 0.3 million).[19]

Norway. The country had a population of over four million people. The majority of them (over 70%) resided in urban areas. Major centers of population included the capital, Oslo (0.5 million), and Bergen (0.2 million). Norway's area was 323,802 square kilometers.[20]

What other foreign markets should have been considered in Europe and beyond? How about FDI? Where?

Krzysztof Olszewski was aware that to successfully enter overseas markets, he needed direct investments. The two countries with the biggest population numbers, China and India, were the first choices to consider. China, which was in the process of building a modern bus industry, invited partners from Japan and Western Europe (Germany) to support local companies in implementing the newest technologies. Golden Dragon Bus Co. Ltd., a joint venture established in 1992-was a good example of this policy.[21] Krzysztof Olszewski decided to start the investigation from India, planning to evaluate the country's demand potential and investment environment. After a number of trips to India and numerous analyses, he was convinced it was not the right place to establish a foreign subsidiary. In that huge country, with over a billion inhabitants, city buses were not a popular means of passengers' transportation in the majority of towns. Therefore a substantial demand for this vehicle category could not be expected. Besides, the entrepreneur's assessment of the technical skills of the local workforce was far from positive. "I cannot let the quality of buses go below the standards I can assure in Poland." Having said that, he decided to continue investing in Poland for the time being and to concentrate on the European market, expecting that Poland would soon join the EU.

But competing on the demanding European markets with the global players was not easy. "What to do to win the international customers' recognition and trust for the brand name? How to convince the German customers to buy more Solaris vehicles?" Germany was the world leader in modern technologies, the fatherland of MAN, Mercedes and other recognized automotive brands. At the same time, the image of technological products designed and manufactured in Poland was far from positive, so Solaris could not count on a favorable country-of-origin effect. Luckily the buses with German and Scandinavian logos were also produced in Poland in large quantities, which helped to improve Poland's perception in the eyes of potential buyers.

After these early export experiences, Krzysztof Olszewski felt the need to develop a clear international strategy for the future. At the top of his mind were the following questions: which foreign markets to concentrate on; what role should international business play overall; and how should he organize for this? The task of winning trust for Polish-made buses was ever present especially if the company wished to compete on criteria other than price.

Exhibits

Exhibit 1: Solaris logo and mascot – a green dachshund

Figure II.15.1 Solaris: logo

Figure II.15.2 Solaris: mascot (a green dachshund)

Source: Company files and authors' own creation/adaptation.

Exhibit 2: a green dachshund on the bus front

Figure II.15.3 Solaris: a green dachshund on the bus front

Source: Company files and authors' own creation/adaptation.

Exhibit 3: buses sales in Poland in 1997–2001

Table II.15.1 Solaris: bus sales in Poland in 1997–2001

Year	1997	1998	1999	2000	2001
Numbers of buses sold	1,714	1,520	1,314	1,646	1,402
Yearly sales dynamics in %	n.a.	–11.3	–13.6	+25.3	–14.8

Note: Number of buses.

Source: Solaris bus & coach. Accessed February 26, 2012: http://infobus.pl/text.php?id=150; http://infobus.pl/text.php?id=151; http://infobus.pl/text.php?id=152; http://infobus.pl/text.php?id=153; http://infobus.pl/text.php?id=154.

Exhibit 4: major suppliers' shares in the total sales on the Polish bus market in 1997–2001 (in %)

Table II.15.2 Solaris: major suppliers' sales market share on the Polish bus market in 1997–2001 (in %)

Suppliers' brand/year	1997	1998	1999	2000	2001
Autosan	36.1	34.2	44.4	43.3	34.6
Jelcz	27.8	25.0	25.6	23.7	17.8
Neoplan	13.0	15.3	13.0	13.2	–
Solaris	–	–	–	–	15.3
MAN	0.8	3.6	4.4	5.9	9.5
Kapena/Irisbus	0.4	2.3	2.0	4.1	6.7
Volvo	2.6	8.6	4.3	3.7	7.3
Scania	2.0	2.6	1.9	2.3	2.9
Mercedes	1.8	1.0	n.a.	2.0	3.1

Source: Solaris Bus & Coach. Accessed February 26, 2012: http://infobus.pl/text.php?id=150; http://infobus.pl/text.php?id=151; http://infobus.pl/text.php?id=152; http://infobus.pl/text.php?id=153; http://infobus.pl/text.php?id=154; JMK Analizy Rynku Transportowego. Accessed February 26, 2012: http://infobus.pl/text.php?id=153.

Exhibit 5: major suppliers' shares in the Polish bus market in 2000

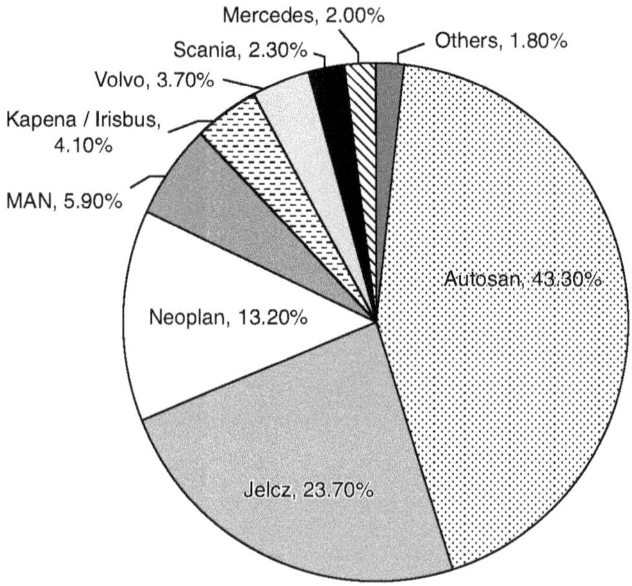

Figure II.15.4 Solaris: major suppliers' share in the Polish bus market in 2000

Source: Company files and authors' own creation/adaptation.

Exhibit 6: major suppliers' shares in the Polish bus market in 2001

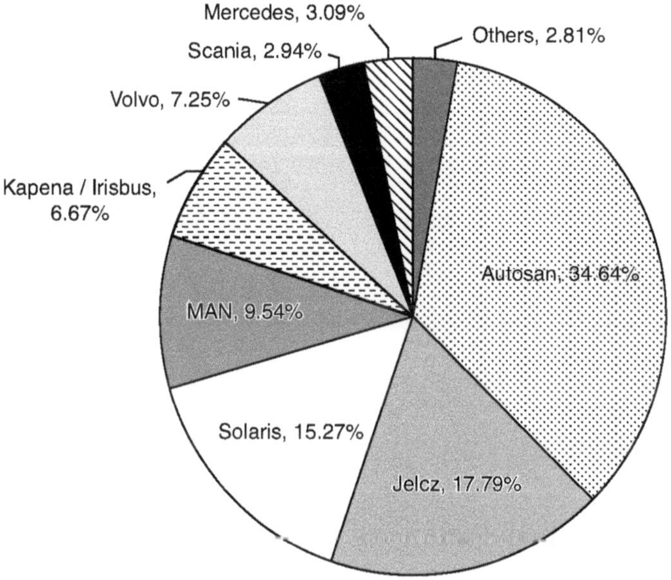

Figure II.15.5 Solaris: major suppliers' share in the Polish bus market in 2001
Source: Company files and authors' own creation/adaptation.

Exhibit 7: Solaris bus & coach S.A. revenues structure in Polish Zlotys, and export sales share in total revenues in 2001

Table II.15.3 Solaris: revenues and export sales in 2001 (in Polish zlotys)

Total revenues	Domestic	Exports	Export shares in %
269,091,227	223,132,082	45,959,145	17

Source: Company files and authors' own creation/adaptation.

Exhibit 8: GNI per Capita (formerly GNP per capita) the gross national income, converted to US dollars using the World Bank Atlas method, divided by the midyear population in 2008

Table II.15.4 Solaris: GNI per capita (formerly GNP per capita) the gross national income

Bulgaria	1,730	**Greece**	12,320	**Poland**	4,670
Czech Rep.	5,750	**Hungary**	4,720	**Russian Fed.**	1,780
Denmark	30,610	**Latvia**	3560	**Slovak Rep.**	5,640
Finland	24,810	**Lithuania**	3,420	**Sweden**	27,670
France	23,180	**Netherlands**	25,560	**Switzerland**	37,790
Germany	23,870	**Norway**	37,530	**UK**	26,020

Note: Converted to US dollars Using the World Bank Atlas Method, Divided by the Midyear Population in 2008.

Source: Data: GNI per capita, Atlas method, The World Bank. Accessed June 7, 2012: http://data.worldbank.org/indicator/NY.GNP.PCAP.CD?page=2.

"B" case: the Dubai invitation

The last day of September 2006 president Krzysztof Olszewski and his team were back from the Hannover Fair where they had demonstrated the range of Solaris buses. Participating in the major fairs was an important element of Solaris's internationalization strategy. As always there were many problems worth discussing after the fair experience, but this time one of them dominated. It seemed Solaris had a chance to sell a substantial number of city buses to Dubai. The invitation to negotiate the contract came from the representatives of Dubai Roads and Transport Agency, who visited the Hannover Fair. Olszewski had mixed feelings about the deal. On one hand, he knew that there would be fewer buses sold in 2006 than the year before, so the big order for the year to come was welcome. But on the other hand, entering the exotic, unknown market seemed challenging and risky.

Evolution of domestic business (2002–2005)

The Polish bus market was worse in 2002 than in 2001. There were only 1,221 buses sold (including 601 city buses). Sales went down by 13% in comparison to the previous year. There was less demand to share among the suppliers. After 2002, the local demand never reached the levels registered in the late nineties (see Exhibit 1). Local budgets became tighter, limiting the demand from municipal buyers in all regions. Moreover the central government cut financing for school bus purchases. During this difficult period, Solaris strengthened its position as a supplier of buses in its home market at the expense of the traditional local producers, dominating the market in the old days (see Exhibit 2). It was the result of a proactive innovation strategy. The young company not only invested in manufacturing facilities but also in its R&D potential. The R&D department grew bigger and each year the new models of vehicles were added to the portfolio. In 2002 a new generation of Solaris Urbino city buses was introduced, the next year the trolleybus Trollino 15 (the longest trolleybus in the world) and the coach Solaris Vacanza 13 were offered. In 2004, city bus Solaris Urbino CNG (gas-powered) and Solaris Urbino III were introduced. Gradually the efforts to supply modern tailor-made vehicles gained buyer appreciation, positively influencing sales (see Exhibit 3). The Solaris team managed to penetrate the new regions of Poland (Silesian district and northern region) but Krzysztof Olszewski understood that only exports could let revenues grow at a required rate.

Evolution of international business (2002–2005)

Between 2002–2005 bus exports from Poland kept increasing (see Exhibit 4) and Solaris played a growing role. Since 2002, Solaris worked hard to gain international acceptance. It seemed that the strategy adopted by the company was effective as the share of international business was growing and exports began to exceed sales at home (see Exhibits 5 and 7). That year, Berlin Transport Company (BVG), a major bus customer in Europe, ordered one Solaris Urbino. This deal was considered a trial purchase. It was not substantial in value terms, but it might have meant an occasion to enter the important and competitive German market. In 2002 most of the vehicles exported by Solaris went to the customers from the Eastern and Central European countries. The buses were sold again to the Czech Republic, to Estonia and Hungary, but also to Switzerland, Malta and other countries. All together that year, 126 buses were exported. Later, they began exporting buses and trolleybuses to Sweden, Italy and to new customers in Germany.

In 2003 the situation began to change. That year Germany for the first time was Solaris's major export market (55 buses sold). In 2004 Solaris managed to sell 110 buses to a new German client. In the early years Switzerland and Italy were also important export markets. The majority of other orders were not large (see Exhibit 6), which did not let the producer save on economies of scale. Solaris engineers had to prepare the full documentation for each of these small deals, which cost time and money, but it was the only way to let the customers know the product.

In 2004 Berlin Transport Company (BVG) ordered 260 Solaris Urbino 18 to be supplied in the consecutive years. Solaris's flexible attitude toward customers' needs helped in winning that contract. Krzysztof Olszewski noticed that BVG was struggling with overemployment. He proposed to deliver the vehicles requiring the final assembling, so that 35 BVG employees could be engaged in finishing the job. MAN's managers must have been very upset with Solaris's success on their home market and reacted very brutally trying to put an end to the newcomer's German market penetration. The contract specification required the installation of MAN engines in the buses ordered by BVG. MAN SE refused to sell the engines to Solaris, expecting that the contract would be broken, as all the buses in the BVG fleet were until then equipped exclusively with engines by MAN. BVG was surprised with the situation and their representatives contacted MAN SE to solve it, but were not offered a positive answer. Then Solaris proposed a new solution, which was accepted by BVG. MAN's engines were to be substituted by DAF engines. This way a Dutch company gained a new client. After this incident, MAN SE changed its restrictive policy toward Solaris and the Polish manufacturer never again had problems with supplies from the group.

Since 2002 financial performance indicators (revenues and net income) grew substantially every year (see Exhibits 7 and 8). Krzysztof Olszewski started to think about an IPO. To get ready for it in July 2005 he changed the legal status of Solaris into a joint stock company (Solaris Bus & Coach S.A.). He soon abandoned the idea of going public fearing a hostile takeover.

Hannover Fair

In 2006 Krzysztof Olszewski decided to show the new Urbino city bus hybrid at the Hannover Fair organized by IAA – Internationale Automobil Ausstellung, which took place as usual in September. Besides the hybrid one, the whole range of bus models was presented. The entrepreneur knew that they deserved international visibility and did not hesitate to locate his products next to the buses offered by such giants as MAN SE and Daimler AG. It was the morning of September 23 when four gentlemen dressed in traditional Arab clothes entered the Solaris stand. The visitors from Dubai Roads and Transport Authority inquired about the buses produced by Solaris. While leaving they asked where was the closest city with a large fleet of Solaris buses. That city was Berlin, where 260 vehicles were delivered for BVG. Saying goodbye to the guests, the Solaris team did not expect to see them again at the fair. But two days later, the visitors from Dubai came back to inform Solaris about their intention to invite the company to competitive bidding for 620 city buses.

"Later we found out that during the day between the two visits to Solaris, the four gentlemen managed to go to Berlin and consult BVG on the quality of our buses. The opinion of the actual owner of the bus fleet must have been good, as they came back with an offer," said Mateusz Figaszewski, Deputy Director of Solaris Marketing Department.

The same invitations were addressed to the two big automobile corporations, MAN SE and Daimler AG.

Solaris soon received the invitation. "It is great to be invited to the game with two of the biggest bus world brands, but at the same time very challenging," said President Olszewski. "Should we go ahead? What are the risks of the eventual contract? What kind of problems may be faced in this completely unknown market?"

The Risk Committee was to answer these questions. The group, headed by the president, consisted of board members and the managers of several departments, including sales, finance, operations and aftersales services. The salespeople could not wait to show their enthusiasm about the contract. "It is a great opportunity to sell so many buses, to enter a new market, to make our brand known better internationally! We cannot lose this chance of extending our exports." The president turned to the rest of the group members, noticing some concern on their faces. "And what is your opinion, gentlemen? What are the risks of accepting the invitation?"

"The invitation is written in such bad English that we do not even completely understand the buyers' requirements! And this is only the beginning!" said Zbigniew Włodarczak, Finance Director. Legal advisors confirmed his comment.

"Let us discuss the problems we may face in Dubai," proposed president Olszewski.

"May I?" asked one of Solaris's legal advisors. "I have to warn you that I see severe legal problems. First, according to the proposition, Dubai jurisdiction is to rule the contract; second, you should understand that Solaris is not allowed to act alone in the market. It has to deal with the local company, which will be an intermediary between the producer and the Dubai Roads & Transport Authority. This company will be suggested by the buyer and we shall have to accept this suggestion!"

"Why is that?" asked Paweł Kaczalski, Operations Manager.

"We shall have to deal with the company owned by the royal family member if we want to get the contract!" answered the legal advisor.

"As far as I know," said Mr. Włodarczak, "due to the natural environment in Dubai (heat up to 60 degrees Celsius, dust, salty climate), poor quality gasoline used and cultural regimes (front family compartment for women with children and the rear one for the men is a must), buses are required to be designed and equipped differently from the ones for European markets. We should take costs and prices into consideration. Additionally, we should be ready to deliver two prototypes to be used in Dubai within two months, during which the seller has the right to suggest changes before large-scale production will be initiated."

He also mentioned cultural differences as potential obstacles in the contract negotiations. "Dubai is distant not only geographically, but also psychically. Our company does not have any experience in dealing with such a partner."

Mr. Włodarczak added after a while: "The conditions offered by the Dubai partner are very strict. Technical requirements are high (stronger engines, air conditioning appliances and filters, individual interior design, special materials used to adapt to the weather conditions) and meeting them will be expensive. At the same time, the buyer offered only 10% down payment. The full price is to be paid within 60 days after delivery."

He looked around as if he was expecting support from the others gathered. "The next challenge is the currency risk. We should consider the possible euro–US dollar foreign exchange relations as the local dirhama is pegged to the US dollar," he added, stressing the word "risk."

"What do you think about it?" asked Krzysztof, directing this question to his wife, who was responsible for aftersales services.

"Well, the requirement of assuring a full bus servicing within five years aftersales is very hard to meet," she said. This was one of the hardest conditions of the proposal, as establishing the local servicing agency seemed difficult and risky. The buyer did not want to be bothered with servicing the buses and importing spare parts. RTA wanted vehicles ready to be used at any time. The seller was expected to organize effective servicing locally in the country where finding the skilled workforce was a problem. Even training the bus drivers was supposed to be a challenge as some candidates were illiterate and did not know any European languages.

"In other words, many of you suggest that we can win the contract, but lose money and spoil our reputation. What should we do then? Are benefits not worth facing the risks?" asked Krzysztof Olszewski, directing these questions to all staff members gathered. There was no clear view of what should be done. Finally they all agreed that some investigation was required to support the decision process. "OK then. We'll go to Dubai, look around and find out whether we are able to meet the buyer's expectations at a reasonable cost. We have to get acquainted with the market. Our present information is too scarce to decide now," said Olszewski.

Dubai's bus-purchasing plans were the consequence of introducing "a comprehensive plan to develop a mass transit system linking the Emirate's communities via metro, trams, buses, water taxis, ferries, new roads and bridges." In 2006 the representatives of the Roads and Transport Agency started to consider suppliers. The following year it officially announced it would purchase 1,616 buses. There were major European bus manufacturers engaged in the negotiations, but some resigned from signing contracts. Daimler AG signed a small contract for 80 buses. Solaris needed to thoroughly consider their decision.

Exhibits

Exhibit 1: bus sales in Poland in 2002–2005

Table II.15.5 Solaris: bus sales in Poland in 2002–2005

Year	2002	2003	2004	2005
Number of buses	1,221	1,028	1,083	1,059
Yearly dynamics in %	–12.9	–15.8	+5.4	–2.2

Source: Accessed February 26, 2012: http://infobus.pl?text.php?id+37734; http://infobus.pl/text.php?id=22417; http://www.bankier.pl/wiadomosc/Polski-rynek-autobusow-w-2004-r-1245993.htmlfrom=nxt.

Exhibit 2: major suppliers' shares in the total bus' sales in Poland in 2002–2005 (in %)

Table II.15.6 Solaris: major suppliers' shares in the total bus sales in Poland in 2002–2005 (in %)

Suppliers brand/year	2002	2003	2004	2005
Autosan	36.20	41.54	30.01	21.25
Jelcz	12.69	12.55	11.08	12.46
Solaris	9.26	10.31	11.36	11.24
MAN	11.38	n.a.	n.a.	6.42
Kapena/Irisbus	4.67	6.13	11.54	10.95
Volvo	6.31	n.a.	n.a.	2.74
Scania	2.38	n.a.	n.a.	4.15
Mercedes	3.36	n.a.	n.a.	4.82

Note: In the beginning of this century, another Polish company, AMZ Kutno, managed to rank high on the list of bus suppliers (8.76% in 2002), but it lost its good position in the next years.

Source: Info Bus. Accessed March 01, 2012: http://infobus.pl/text.php?id=22417&from=nxt; CMS Auto. Accessed March 26, 2012: http://cms-auto.com.pl/

Exhibit 3: Solaris total sales of buses in 2002–2005 (numbers of vehicles)

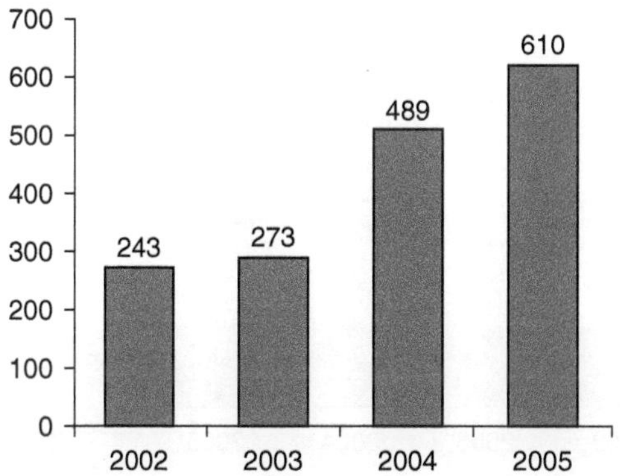

Figure II.15.6 Solaris: total sales of buses in 2002–2005 (numbers of vehicles)

Note: Includes Trolleybuses and Coaches.

Source: Company files and authors' own creation/adaptation.

Exhibit 4: exports of buses from Poland in 2002–2005

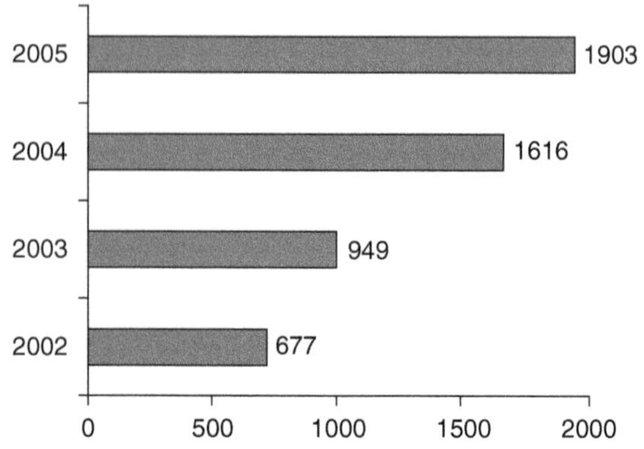

Figure II.15.7 Solaris: exports and buses from Poland in 2002–2005

Source: "JMK Analizy Rynku Transportowego presented by Gazeta Wyborcza." Accessed December 11, 2012: http://bi.gazeta.pl/im/2/9015/m9015982.jpg

Exhibit 5: Solaris total sales versus total exports of buses in 2002–2005 (numbers of vehicles)

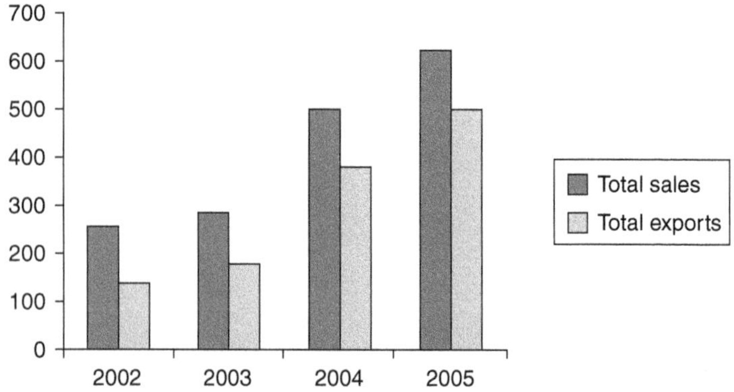

Figure II.15.8 Solaris: total sales versus total exports of buses in 2002–2005 (number of vehicles)

Note: Includes Trolleybuses and Coaches.

Source: Company files and authors' own creation/adaptation.

Exhibit 6: the Solaris major export markets in 2002–2005 (numbers of vehicles exported)

Table II.15.7 Solaris: major export markets in 2002–2005 (number of vehicles exported)

	2002	2003	2004	2005
Leading export markets/ numbers of buses exported	Latvia (61) Czech Rep. (15) Slovakia (10) Switzerland (10) Estonia (10) Germany (8) Hungary (8)	Germany (55) Latvia (31) Italy (26) Czech Rep. (17) France (11) Slovakia (8) Estonia (5) Switzerland (5) Sweden (3)	Germany (110) Switzerland (42) Czech Rep. (30) Lithuania (30) Italy (26)	Germany (229) Lithuania (70) Italy (41) Switzerland (37) Latvia (32) Czech Rep. (31) Hungary (26) France (11)

Source: Company files and authors' own creation/adaptation.

Exhibit 7: Solaris bus & coach S.A. revenues in 2002–2005

Table II.15.8 Solaris: revenues and export sales' share in 2002–2005 (in Polish zlotys)

Year	Total revenues	Domestic	Exports	Export share in %
2002	212,129,369	103,738,695	108,390,674	51
2003	263,360,158	94,221,623	169,138,535	64
2004	462,767,367	155,649,537	306,117,830	66
2005	659,217,225	171,984,175	487,233,050	74

Source: Company files and authors' own creation/adaptation.

Exhibit 8: Solaris bus & coach S.A. net income in 2001–2005 (Polish zlotys)

Table II.15.9 Solaris: net income in 2001–2005 (in Polish zlotys)

Year	Net Income
2001	16,883,229
2002	3,197,243
2003	4,160,147
2004	15,182,318
2005	29,479,053

Source: Solarisbus. Accessed March 11, 2012: http://www.solarisbus.pl/busmania,aktualnosci,news_list,727,0.html

Notes

1. She was studying three majors, journalism among them, at the same time she was managing two gas stations.
2. Autosan. Accessed March 01, 2012: http://www.autosan.eu/pl/str/17/historia.
3. Jelcz. Accessed March 01, 2012: http://www.jelcz.com.pl/historia.html.
4. Mantruckandbus. Accessed February 26, 2012: www.mantruckandbus.pl/mn-prod-neu/man2/master/datapool/mediapool/200/man_geschaeftsbericht_2011_en.pdf. Man. Accessed March 11, 2012: www.man.eu/MAN-Downloadgalleries/EN/Investors_Relation/Quarterly_Reports/March_6_2002_MAN_Group.pdf.
5. Infobus. Accessed February 26, 2012: http://infobus.com.pl/text,php?id=94.
6. Skyscrapercity. Accessed March 01, 2012: http://www.skyscrapercity.com/showthread.php?t=1422882.
7. Volvo Group. Funding Universe. Accessed March 01, 2012: http://www.volvogroup.com/group/poland/pl-pl/Pages/Volvo_Group_Poland.aspx, http://www.volvobuses.com/bus/poland/pl-pl/aboutus/historia/wazne_daty/Pages/dates.aspx http://www.fundinguniverse.com/company-histories/AB-Volvo-Company-History.html.
8. Scania. Accessed March 1, 2012: http://www.scania.com/scania-group/scania-around-the-world/.
9. Daimler. Accessed March 1, 2012: http://www.daimler.com/company. Accessed March01,2012:http://www.daimler.com/Projects/c2c/channel/documents/94632_ir_20220_fy_E.pdf.
10. Nations Encyclopedia. Atlas agp. Accessed June 07, 2012: http://www.nationsencyclopedia.com/Czech-Republic-POPULATION.html. Accessed June 13, 2012: http://atlas.agp.pl/index.php?wyswietl=czechy.
11. Indexmundi. Accessed June 07, 2012: http://www.indexmundi.com/slovakia/population/html.
12. Unstats. Atlas agp. Accessed June 06, 2012: http://unstats.un.org/unsd/demographic/meetings/egm/symposium2001/docs/symposium_46.htm#_Toc8190640. Accessed June 10, 2012: http://atlas.agp.pl/index.php?wyswietl=litwa.
13. Worldwide Tax. Accessed June 07, 2012: http://www.worldwide-tax.com/latvia/latpopulation.asp.
14. Nation Encyclopedia. Accessed June 10, 2012: http://www.nationsencyclopedia.com/Europe/Estonia-POPULATION.html Accessed June 06, 2012: http://www.indexmundi.com/estonia/area.html.
15. Women Russia, True Knowledge. Accessed June 06, 2012: http://www.women-russia.com/basics.htm Accessed June 06, 2012: http://www.trueknowledge.com/q/population_of_moscow_2001.
16. Atlas agp. Accessed June 10, 2012: http://atlas.agp.pl/index.php?wyswietl=ukraina.
17. Mongabay. Answers. Trading Economics. Accessed June 07, 2012: http://www.mongabay.com/igapo/Germany.htm Accessed June 07, 2012: http://www.answers.com/search?q=Germany+Area. Accessed June 07, 2012: http://www.tradingeconomics.com/germany/population. Accessed June 06, 2012: http://www.tradingeconomics.com/germany/urban-population-percent-of-total-wb-data.html.
18. Atlas agp. Stadt Zuerich. Accessed June 07, 2012: http://atlas.agp.pl/index.php?wyswietl=szwajcaria Accessed June 07, 2012: http://www.stadt-zuerich.ch/content/portal/en/index/portraet_der_stadt_zuerich/zahlen_u_fakten.html.

19. FCO. Accessed June 07, 2012: http://www.fco.gov.uk/en/travel-and-living-abroad/travel-advice-by-country/country-profile/europe/sweden/.
20. Index Mundi. Accessed June 07, 2012: http://www.indexmundi.com/norway/area.html.
21. Golden Dragon Bus. Accessed June 10, 2012: http://www.goldendragonbus.com/Press-more.aspx?Classid=27&Unid=163.

References

Aiello, G., R. Donvito, et al. (2008). "An International Perspective on Luxury Brand and Country-of-Origin Effect." *Brand Management* 16(5–6): 323–337.

Aldrich, H. E. (1999). *Organizations Evolving*, New York: SAGE Publications.

Bartlett, C. A., and S. Ghoshal (1990). "Managing Innovation in the Transnational Corporation." In C. A. Bartlett, Y. Doz and G. Hedlund, *Managing the Global Firm*. London: Routledge, 215–255.

Beise, M. (2004). "Lead Markets: Country-Specific Success Factors of the Global Diffusion of Innovations." *Research Policy* 33(6–7): 997–1018.

—— (2005). "Lead Markets, Innovation Differentials and Growth." *International Economics & Economic Policy* 1(4): 305–328.

Chu, P.-Y., C.-C. Chang, et al. (2010). "Countering Negative Country-of-Origin Effects: The Role of Evaluation Mode." *European Journal of Marketing* 44(7/8): 1055–1076.

Deephouse, D., and S. Carter (2005). "An Examination of Differences between Organizational Legitimacy and Organizational Reputation." *Journal of Management Studies* 42(2): 329–360.

Duckworth, A. L. (2007). "Grit: Perseverance and Passion for Long-Term Goals." *Journal of Personality and Social Psychology* 92(6): 1087.

EBRD (1996). "Infrastructure and Savings." *Transition Reports*. EBRD. London: European Bank for Reconstruction and Development, 24.

—— (1997). "Business Performance." *Transition Reports*. EBRD. London: European Bank for Reconstruction and Development.

—— (1999). "Ten Years of Transition." *Transition Reports*. EBRD. London: European Bank for Reconstruction and Development, 24, 142.

Ellet, W. (2007). *The Case Study Handbook: How to Read, Discuss, and Write Persuasively About Cases*, Boston MA: Harvard Business Review Press.

Gaedeke, R. (1973). "Consumer Attitudes Toward Products 'Made In' Developing Countries." *Journal of Retailing* 49(2): 13.

Graf, B. (2004). "CGW – Computer Graphics World." *The Balkanization of Animation* 27(8).

Jain, S. C. (2012). *Handbook of Research in International Marketing*. Cheltenham: Edward Elgar Publishing.

Johnson, S., J. McMillan, et al. (2002a). "Courts and Relational Contracts." *Journal of Law, Economics, and Organization* 18(1): 221–277.

—— (2002b). "Property Rights and Finance." *American Economic Review* 92(5): 1335–1356.

Levitt, B., and J. G. March (1988). "Organizational Learning." *Annual Review of Sociology* 14: 319–340.

McMillan, J., and C. Woodruff (2002). "The Central Role of Entrepreneurs in Transition Economies." *Journal of Economic Perspectives* 16(3): 153–170.

Peng, M. W. (2001). "How Entrepreneurs Create Wealth in Transition Economies." *Academy of Management Executive* 15(1): 96–110.

Reuber, R., and E. Fisher (2011). "When Nobody Knows Your Name: Country-of-Origin as a Reputational Signal for Online Business." *Corporate Reputation Review* 14: 37–51.

Reynolds, P. S., S. M. Camp, et al. (2002). "Global Entrepreneurship Monitor 2001 Executive Report." *Global Entrepreneurship Monitor.* Babson Park/London: Babson College and London Business School.

Rindova, V., I. Williamson, et al. (2005). "Being Good or Being Known: An Empirical Examination of the Dimensions, Antecedents, and Consequences of Organizational Reputation." *Academy Of Management Journal* 48(6): 1033–1049.

Sarasvathy, S. (2001). "Causation and Effectuation: Toward a Theoretical Shift From Economic Inevitability to Entrepreneurial Contingency." *Academy of Management Review* 26(2): 243–263.

Schumpeter, J. (1934). *The Theory of Economic Development.* Boston: President and Fellows of Harvard College.

Segarra, J. A. (2009). A Starting Point: Reflections on Education. Barcelona: *IESE Manuscript.*

Stinchcombe, A. (1965). "Social Structure and Organizations." In James M. March, *Handbook of Organizations*. London: Routledge, 142–193.

Index

GPSR Compliance
The European Union's (EU) General Product Safety Regulation (GPSR) is a set of rules that requires consumer products to be safe and our obligations to ensure this.

If you have any concerns about our products, you can contact us on

ProductSafety@springernature.com

In case Publisher is established outside the EU, the EU authorized representative is:

Springer Nature Customer Service Center GmbH
Europaplatz 3
69115 Heidelberg, Germany

www.ingramcontent.com/pod-product-compliance
Ingram Content Group UK Ltd.
Pitfield, Milton Keynes, MK11 3LW, UK
UKHW041912040925
462611UK00003B/227
* 9 7 8 1 3 4 9 4 9 5 9 7 9 *